Jon E. Lewis was a boy once and is the father of a boy (and a girl) now. His previous books include *Fatherhood: An Anthology*, *The Mammoth Book of Pirates*, *The Mammoth Book of True War Stories*, *The Mammoth Book of the West*, *The New Rights of Man*, *The Mammoth Book of the Edge*, and *The Mammoth Book of How It Happened*.

The Mammoth Book of

BOY'S OWN STUFF

JON E. LEWIS

RUNNING PRESS
PHILADELPHIA · LONDON

Constable & Robinson Ltd
3 The Lanchesters
162 Fulham Palace Road
London W6 9ER
www.constablerobinson.com

First published in the UK by Robinson,
an imprint of Constable & Robinson, 2008

A copy of the British Library Cataloguing in Publication
Data is available from the British Library

UK ISBN 978-1-84529-709-1

1 3 5 7 9 10 8 6 4 2

First published in the United States in 2008 by
Running Press Book Publishers

9 8 7 6 5 4 3 2 1
Digit on the right indicates the number of this printing

US Library of Congress number: 2008923887
US ISBN 978-0-7624-3380-3

Running Press Book Publishers
2300 Chestnut Street
Philadelphia, PA 19103-4371
www.runningpress.com

Visit us on the web!

www.runningpress.com

Printed and bound in the EU

This one's for my son and my father, Tristram and Eric.

IF
by Rudyard Kipling

If you can keep your head when all about you
   Are losing theirs and blaming it on you,
If you can trust yourself when all men doubt you,
   But make allowance for their doubting too;
If you can wait and not be tired by waiting,
   Or being lied about, don't deal in lies,
Or being hated, don't give way to hating,
   And yet don't look too good, nor walk too wise:

If you can dream – and not make dreams your master;
   If you can think – and not make thoughts your aim;
If you can meet with Triumph and Disaster
   And treat those two impostors just the same;
If you can bear to hear the truth you've spoken
   Twisted by knaves to make a trap for fools,
Or watch the things you gave your life to, broken,
   And stoop and build 'em up with worn-out tools:

If you can make one heap of all your winnings
   And risk it on one turn of pitch-and-toss,
And lose, and start again at your beginnings
   And never breathe a word about your loss;
If you can force your heart and nerve and sinew
   To serve your turn long after they are gone,
And so hold on when there is nothing in you
   Except the Will which says to them: "Hold on!"

If you can talk with crowds and keep your virtue,
   Or walk with Kings – nor lose the common touch,
If neither foes nor loving friends can hurt you,
   If all men count with you, but none too much;
If you can fill the unforgiving minute
   With sixty seconds' worth of distance run,
Yours is the Earth and everything that's in it,
   And – which is more – you'll be a Man, my son!

CONTENTS

FOREWORD

In this bright new world of screen amusement at the tap of a key or the flick of a switch it's easy to forget that boyhood should be about making bows and arrows, creating volcanoes from cupboard goods, learning up more facts than your friends about cars, and even building something BIG like your own canoe. But it's safe to say that a boyhood without such things is not a boyhood that a man will look back on and remember with pleasure. No man is going to regret not having spent more time in front of a screen as a boy.

The Mammoth Book of Boys' Own Stuff is a bogglingly large guide to getting a life as a boy, from learning how to trap game to making secret ink, from learning the basics of carpentry to performing magic tricks.

And here's the small print. Boyhood is about having fun. But it's also about learning. Boyhood is when you need to begin to explore the world and your place in it. There is no avoiding that; however the payoff is a) you'll be topps at skool b) the more you learn as a boy the better informed you will be as a man. So *The Mammoth Book of Boys' Own Stuff* provides some of the basics all boys need to know, in geography, grammar, science, maths, history and literature. Boyhood is also the right time to train your character. You'll find valuable instructions inside, as well as examples to hold before you of courage and endurance, such as Scott at the South Pole and Jack Travers Cornwell, the boy sailor who won the Victoria Cross at the battle of Jutland in 1916. Boys need such heroes.

A guide to life, the universe and pretty much everything *The Mammoth Book of Boys' Own Stuff* is full of entertainment as well as important facts on how to be an all-round great person. There are short stories by such ace writers as Rider Haggard and H.G. Wells. And included for no extra cost – the world's official funniest joke.

When I was a boy I had a book in my bookcase titled *Every Boy's Book of Hobbies*. It was written in 1911 by Cecil H. Bullivant. My father had inherited a copy and had passed it down to me. (In turn I've passed it down to my son.) Bullivant thought that hobbies–doing constructive things–resulted in a boy being "well balanced" and a stranger to "narrow mindedness". Many of Bullivant's suggested hobbies are outdated now (for instance collecting wild bird's eggs, which is against the law in most Western countries) but some have proved timeless, and one or two are reproduced on the following pages. Boys, after all, will always like nailing together bits of wood and keeping pets. Boys *will* be boys. In *The Mammoth Book of Boys' Own Stuff* I have tried to blend the best of boyhood from the past with modern information. The book is, if you like, Bullivant's *Hobbies* rewritten for the 21st century. His hope was that his book would be the *vade-mecum* (a teacher-impressing Latin phrase meaning 'come with me!') for a boyhood well done. It's my hope for *The Mammoth Book of Boys' Own Stuff* too.

Jon E. Lewis 2008

Acknowledgements

All books are collaborations, this one more than most. My son Tristram checked out many of the instructions (the DIY volcano was his favourite exercise – and his mother's least favourite), and my father provided me with the Holy Grail, Cecil Bullivant's *Every Boy's Book of Hobbies*. Freda, my daughter, served as a temporary tomboy in the experiments department. My wife Penny was, as always, my best advisor. At Constable and Robinson, thanks go to my editor Pete Duncan. Thanks too to Hugh Lamb for proof-reading and to Jaqueline Jackson for managing the difficult end stages of production.

Permissions Acknowledgements

The author has made every effort to contact the owners of copyrighted material in this book and to secure the necessary permission to reproduce such copyrighted material. Regrettably in some instances it has not proved possible to locate and secure the necessary permissions. Any queries regarding copyrighted material should be addressed to the author c/o the publishers.

HOW TO MAKE A WATER BOMB

Origami is the Japanese art of paper-folding. This design for a paper box also makes a useful water bomb. You need a piece of paper six inches (150mm) square; the paper can be pretty much any sort – high-quality note or exercise paper works well – but it must be square. Here's what to do;

1 Fold the paper in half in both directions and crease well.

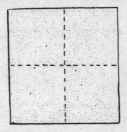

2 Turn the paper over and fold diagonally in both directions.

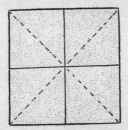

3 Fold the folded corners between the fingers and thumbs and push inwards towards the point. This will give you the familiar dart flight.

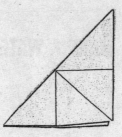

4 Then press flat.

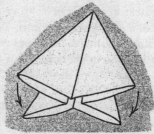

5 Press down firmly and then fold the corners up to the centre point.

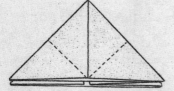 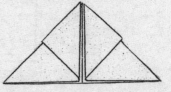

6 Turn over and repeat with the other two corners.

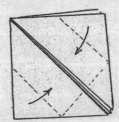

7 Fold the outer corners to the centre and then fold the top points down, as indicated by the dotted lines. Turn over and repeat on the other side.

8 Fold the two small upper corners down into the little pockets just below them. Turn over and do the same on the reverse side. Press all the folds down firmly and then, holding lightly, inflate by blowing into the small hole at the base as indicated by the arrow. Your water bomb is now ready to be filled with water. Bombs away!

Instructions © 1979 Eric Franklin and The Scout Association

Reprinted from The Cub Scout Annual 1980 with the permission of the Scout Association.

NUMBERS

The History of Numbers

Ever wondered why we count in tens? Because we have ten fingers or digits. Children begin counting on their fingers, just as our ancestors did. We use the ten basic symbols or digits – 0, 1, 2, 3, 4, 5, 6, 7, 8, 9 – to write all our numbers, although their value changes depending upon their place in a figure. For example the figure 7 means seven ones (7 × 1) but in the figure 70 means seven tens (7 × 10). The ten counting system is also known as the decimal system, from the Latin *decem*, meaning ten. The decimal system is not quite universal. Among those who use another counting system are the Bakairi of Brazil who have just two number words. In the language of the Bakairi one is *tokale* and two *ahage*. Three is *ahage tokale* (2 + 1), four is *ahage ahage* (2 + 2) and so on. The ancient Babylonians counted in tens up to sixty, which they regarded as a new unit. Among the first civilized people, the Babylonians – who lived in what is now Iraq – were responsible for dividing an hour into sixty minutes and a circle into 360 degrees (6 × 60). Another ancient civilization, Rome, used letters for numerals. Here are the main Roman numerals:

Roman		Roman		Roman	
I	1	XIX	19	CM	900
II	2	XX	20	M	1,000
III	3	XXX	30	V̄	5,000
IV	4	XL	40		

V	5	L	50	$\overline{\text{X}}$	10,000
VI	6	LX	60	$\overline{\text{L}}$	50,000
VII	7	XC	90		
VIII	8	C	100	$\overline{\text{C}}$	100,000
IX	9	CC	200	$\overline{\text{D}}$	500,000
X	10	CD	400		
XI	11	D	500	$\overline{\text{M}}$	1,000,000

Roman numerals don't just belong to ancient history – they're still used today. The Queen of England, for instance, is always referred to as Elizabeth II, not Elizabeth 2. Dates are sometimes written in Roman numerals: 2008, for instance is MMVIII.

The main problem with Roman numerals is that they are difficult to do sums with, which is why we use the numerals 0, 1, 2, 3, 4, 5, 6, 7, 8, + 9. We call these Arabic numerals, although they were really invented by the Hindus in India around 200 BC. Arabic numerals are a lot easier to use than Roman ones. In Arabic numerals nine is 9, whereas in Roman numerals it is IX.

Multiplication Table

The best way to learn your multiplication tables is by endless rote. "One times one is one, two times one is two . . ." Know your tables up to 12 ×. You may sound like a parrot while you're learning them but you'll end up knowing something that will be useful all your life. Here's a handy table to get you started.

1	2	3	4	5	6	7	8	9	10	11	12
2	4	6	8	10	12	14	16	18	20	22	24
3	6	9	12	15	18	21	24	27	30	33	36
4	8	12	16	20	24	28	32	36	40	44	48
5	10	15	20	25	30	35	40	45	50	55	60
6	12	18	24	30	36	42	48	54	60	66	72
7	14	21	28	35	42	49	56	63	70	77	84
8	16	24	32	40	48	56	64	72	80	88	96
9	18	27	36	45	54	63	72	81	90	99	108
10	20	30	40	50	60	70	80	90	100	110	120
11	22	33	44	55	66	77	88	99	110	121	132
12	24	36	48	60	72	84	96	108	120	132	144

Prime Numbers

A prime number is only divisible by itself and 1. The prime numbers between 1 and 1,000 are:

2	97	227	367	509	661	829
3	101	229	373	521	673	839
5	103	233	379	523	677	853
7	107	239	383	541	683	857
11	109	241	389	547	691	859
13	113	251	397	557	701	863
17	127	257	401	563	709	877
19	131	263	409	569	719	881
23	137	269	419	571	727	883
29	139	271	421	577	733	887
31	149	277	431	587	739	907
37	151	281	433	593	743	911
41	157	283	439	599	751	919
43	163	293	443	601	757	929
47	167	307	449	607	761	937
53	173	311	457	613	769	941
59	179	313	461	617	773	947
61	181	317	463	619	787	953
67	191	331	467	631	797	967
71	193	337	479	641	809	971
73	197	347	487	643	811	977
79	199	349	491	647	821	983
83	211	353	499	653	823	991
89	223	359	503	659	827	997

SCOTT OF THE ANTARCTIC: HIS DIARY OF THE EXPEDITION'S HEROIC END

A torpedo officer in the Royal Navy, Robert Falcon Scott was chosen to lead Britain's attempt to be the first to 90 degrees South – the South Pole. On 18 January 1912 Scott and his four companions – Captain Lawrence "Titus" Oates, Edgar Evans, Edward Wilson and H. "Birdie" Bowers – reached the Pole . . . but only to find that they had been beaten to it by a rival Norwegian team led by Roald Amundsen. On the return to base camp Scott's team, running low on supplies and exhausted by man-hauling their sledges (Amundsen had used dogs for pulling), encountered freakishly cold conditions. Scott recorded the expedition's doomed but heroically brave final days in his diary:

Monday 5 March

Lunch. Regret to say going from bad to worse. We got a slant of wind yesterday afternoon, and going on 5 hours we converted our wretched morning run of 3½ miles into something over 9. We went to bed on a cup of cocoa and pemmican solid with the chill off. (R. 47.) The result is telling on all, but mainly on Oates, whose feet are in a wretched condition. One swelled up tremendously last night and he is very lame this morning. We started march on tea and pemmican as last night – we pretend to prefer the pemmican this way. Marched for 5 hours this morning over a slightly better surface covered with high moundy sastrugi.

Sledge capsized twice; we pulled on foot, covering about $5\frac{1}{2}$ miles. We are two pony marches and 4 miles about from our depôt. Our fuel dreadfully low and the poor Soldier nearly done. It is pathetic enough because we can do nothing for him; more hot food might do a little, but only a little, I fear. We none of us expected these terribly low temperatures, and of the rest of us Wilson is feeling them most; mainly, I fear, from his self-sacrificing devotion in doctoring Oates' feet. We cannot help each other, each has enough to do to take care of himself. We get cold on the march when the trudging is heavy, and the wind pierces our worn garments. The others, all of them, are unendingly cheerful when in the tent. We mean to see the game through with a proper spirit, but it's tough work to be pulling harder than we ever pulled in our lives for long hours, and to feel that the progress is so slow. One can only say "God help us!" and plod on our weary way, cold and very miserable, though outwardly cheerful. We talk of all sorts of subjects in the tent, not much of food now, since we decided to take the risk of running a full ration. We simply couldn't go hungry at this time.

Saturday 10 March

Things steadily downhill. Oates' foot worse. He has rare pluck and must know that he can never get through. He asked Wilson if he had a chance this morning, and of course Bill had to say he didn't know. In point of fact he has none. Apart from him, if he went under now, I doubt whether we could get through. With great care we might have a dog's chance, but no more. The weather conditions are awful, and our gear gets steadily more icy and difficult to manage. At the same time, of course, poor Titus is the greatest handicap. He keeps us waiting in the morning until we have partly lost the warming effect of our good breakfast, when the only wise policy is to be up and away at once; again at lunch. Poor chap! it is too pathetic to watch him; one cannot but try to cheer him up.

Yesterday we marched up the depôt, Mt Hooper. Cold comfort. Shortage on our allowance all round . . .

Sunday 11 March

Titus Oates is very near the end, one feels. What we or he will do, God only knows. We discussed the matter after breakfast; he is a brave fine fellow and understands the situation, but he practically asked for advice. Nothing could be said but to urge him to march as long as he could. One satisfactory result to the discussion; I practically ordered Wilson to hand over the means of ending our troubles to us, so that any one of us may know how to do so. Wilson had no choice between doing so and our ransacking the medicine case. We have 30 opium tabloids apiece and he is left with a tube of morphine. So far the tragical side of our story.

The sky was completely overcast when we started this morning. We could see nothing, lost the tracks, and doubtless have been swaying a good deal since – 3.1 miles for the forenoon – terribly heavy dragging – expected it. Know that 6 miles is about the limit of our endurance now, if we get no help from wind or surfaces. We have 7 days' food and should be about 55 miles from One Ton Camp to-night, $6 \times 7 = 42$, leaving us 13 miles short of our distance, even if things get no worse. Meanwhile the season rapidly advances . . .

Wednesday 14 March

No doubt about the going downhill, but everything going wrong for us. Yesterday we woke to a strong northerly wind with temp. −37°. Couldn't face it, so remained in camp till 2, then did 5¼ miles. Wanted to march later, but party feeling the cold badly as the breeze (N.) never took off entirely, and as the sun sank the temp. fell. Long time getting supper in dark.

This morning started with southerly breeze, set sail and passed another cairn at good speed; halfway, however, the wind shifted to W. by S. or W.S.W., blew through our wind clothes and into our mits. Poor Wilson horribly cold, could [not] get off ski for some time. Bowers and I practically made camp, and when we got into the tent at last we were all deadly cold. Then temp. now midday down −13° and the wind strong. We *must* go on, but now the making of every camp must be more difficult and dangerous. It must be near the end, but a pretty merciful end. Poor Oates got it again in the foot. I shudder to think what it will be like tomorrow. It is only with greatest pains rest of us keep off frostbites. No idea there could be temperatures like this at this time of year with such winds. Truly awful outside the tent. Must fight it out to the last biscuit, but can't reduce rations.

Friday 16 March or Saturday 17

Lost track of dates, but think the last correct. Tragedy all along the line. At lunch, the day before yesterday, poor Titus Oates said he couldn't go on; he proposed we should leave him in his sleeping-bag. That we could not do, and we induced him to come on, on the afternoon march. In spite of its awful nature for him he struggled on and we made a few miles. At night he was worse and we knew the end had come.

Should this be found I want these facts recorded. Oates' last thoughts were of his mother, but immediately before he took pride in thinking that his regiment would be pleased with the bold way in which he met his death. We can testify to his bravery. He has borne intense suffering for weeks without complaint, and to the very last was able and willing to discuss outside subjects. He did not – would not – give up hope till the very end. He was a brave soul. This was the end. He slept through the night before last, hoping not to wake; but he woke in the morning – yesterday. It was blowing a blizzard. He said, "I am just going outside and may be some time." He went out into the blizzard and we have not seen him since.

I take this opportunity of saying that we have stuck to our sick companions to the last. In case of Edgar Evans, when absolutely out of food and he lay insensible, the safety of the remainder seemed to demand his abandonment, but Providence mercifully removed him at this critical moment. He died a natural death, and we did not leave him till two hours after his death. We knew that poor Oates was walking to his death, but though we tried to dissuade him, we knew it was the act of a brave man and an English gentleman. We all hope to meet the end with a similar spirit, and assuredly the end is not far.

I can only write at lunch and then only occasionally. The cold is intense, −40° at midday. My companions are un-endingly cheerful, but we are all on the verge of serious frostbites, and though we constantly talk of fetching through, I don't think any one of us believes it in his heart.

We are cold on the march now, and at all times except meals. Yesterday we had to lie up for a blizzard and today we move dreadfully slowly. We are at No. 14 pony camp, only two pony marches from One Ton Depôt. We leave here our theodolite, a camera, and Oates' sleeping-bags. Diaries, etc., and geological specimens carried at Wilson's special request, will be found with us or on our sledge.

Sunday 18 March

Today, lunch, we are 21 miles from the depôt. Ill fortune presses, but better may come. We have had more wind and drift from ahead yesterday; had to stop marching; wind N.W., force 4, temp. −35°. No human being could face it, and we are worn out *nearly*.

My right foot has gone, nearly all the toes – two days ago I was proud possessor of best feet. These are the steps of my downfall. Like an ass I mixed a small spoonful of curry powder with my melted pemmican – it gave me violent indigestion. I lay awake and in pain all night; woke and felt done on the march; foot went and I didn't know it. A very small measure of neglect and I have a foot which is not pleasant to contemplate. Bowers takes first place in condi-tion, but there is not much to choose after all. The others are still confident of getting through – or pretend to be – I don't know! We have the last *half* fill of oil in our primus and a very small quantity of spirit – this alone between us and thirst. The wind is fair for the moment, and that is perhaps a fact to help. The mileage would have seemed ridiculously small on our outward journey.

Monday 19 March

Lunch. We camped with difficulty last night and were dreadfully cold till after our supper of cold pemmican and biscuit and a half a pannikin of cocoa cooked over the spirit. Then, contrary to expectation, we got warm and all slept well. Today we started in the usual dragging manner. Sledge dreadfully heavy. We are 15½ miles from the depôt and ought to get there in three days. What progress! We have two days' food, but barely a day's fuel. All our feet are getting bad – Wilson's best, my right foot worse, left all right. There is no chance to nurse one's feet till we can get hot food into us. Amputation is the least I can hope for now, but will the trouble spread? That is the serious question. The weather doesn't give us a chance – the wind from N. to N.W. and –40° temp to-day.

Wednesday 21 March

Got within 11 miles of depôt Monday night; had to lie up all yesterday in severe blizzard. Today forlorn hope, Wilson and Bowers going to depôt for fuel.

22 and 23 Blizzard bad as ever – Wilson and Bowers unable to start – tomorrow last chance – no fuel and only one or two [rations] of food left – must be near the end. Have decided it shall be natural – we shall march for the depôt with or without our effects and die in our tracks.

Thursday 29 March

Since the 21st we have had a continuous gale from W.S.W. and S.W. We had fuel to make two cups of tea apiece and bare food for two days on the 20th. Every day we have been ready to start for our depôt 11 *miles* away, but outside the door of the tent it remains a scene of whirling drift. I do not think we can hope for any better things now. We shall stick it out to the end, but we are getting weaker, of course, and the end cannot be far.

  It seems a pity, but I do not think I can write more.

R. Scott.

Last entry.
For God's sake look after our people.

The bodies of Scott, Wilson and Bowers – together with Scott's diary – were found six months later by the part of the expedition which had remained at base camp. A cairn was built over the resting place of Scott, Wilson and Bowers, and a plaque erected 20 miles further south, as close to where Oates had died as could be determined. The plaque read:

Hereabout died a very gallant gentlemen, Captain LEG Oates of the Inniskilling Dragoons. In March 1912, returning from the Pole, he walked willingly to his death in a blizzard, to try and save his comrades, beset by hardships. This note is left by the Relief Expedition of 1912.

It might be added that they were gallant gentlemen all.

THE GREAT SPEECHES I

"The Gettysburg Address"
by President Abraham Lincoln

President Lincoln of the United States delivered this speech on 19 November 1863 at the Union cemetery at Gettysburg, Philadelphia. It was the first time the world heard the words "government of the people, by the people, for the people".

Four score and seven years ago our fathers brought forth on this continent, a new nation, conceived in Liberty, and dedicated to the proposition that all men are created equal.

Now we are engaged in a great civil war, testing whether that nation, or any nation so conceived and so dedicated, can long endure. We are met on a great battle-field of that war. We have come to dedicate a portion of that field, as a final resting place for those who here gave their lives that the nation might live. It is altogether fitting and proper that we should do this.

But, in a larger sense, we cannot dedicate – we cannot consecrate – we cannot hallow – this ground. The brave men, living and dead, who struggled here, have consecrated it, far above our poor power to add or detract. The world will little note, nor long remember what we say here, but it can never forget what they did here. It is for us the living, rather, to be dedicated here to the unfinished work which they who fought here have thus far so nobly advanced. It is rather for us to be here dedicated to the great task remaining before us – that from these honoured dead we take increased devotion to that cause for which they gave the last full measure of devotion – that we here highly resolve that these dead shall not have died in vain – that this nation, under God, shall have a new birth of freedom – and that government of the people, by the people, for the people, shall not perish from the earth.

THE PRESIDENTS OF AMERICA

President	Party	Served
1) George Washington	Federalist	1789–97
2) John Adams	Federalist	1797–1801
3) Thomas Jefferson	Republican	1801–09
4) James Madison	Republican	1809–17
5) James Monroe	Republican	1817–25
6) John Quincy Adams	Republican	1825–9
7) Andrew Jackson	Democrat	1829–37
8) Martin Van Buren	Democrat	1837–41
9) William Henry Harrison	Whig	1841
10) John Tyler	Whig	1841–5
11) James K. Polk	Whig	1845–9
12) Zachary Taylor	Whig	1849–50
13) Millard Fillmore	Whig	1850–3
14) Franklin Pierce	Democrat	1853–7
15) James Buchanan	Democrat	1857–61
16) Abraham Lincoln	Republican	1861–5
17) Andrew Johnson	Democrat	1865–9
18) Ulysses S. Grant	Republican	1869–77
19) Rutherford B. Hayes	Republican	1877–81
20) James A. Garfield	Republican	1881
21) Chester A. Arthur	Republican	1881–5
22) Grover Cleveland	Democrat	1885–9
23) Benjamin Harrison	Republican	1889–93
24) Grover Cleveland	Democrat	1893–7
25) William McKinley	Republican	1897–1901
26) Theodore Roosevelt	Republican	1901–9

27) William Howard Taft	Republican	1909–13
28) Woodrow Wilson	Democrat	1913–21
29) Warren G. Harding	Republican	1921–3
20) Calvin Coolidge	Republican	1923–9
31) Herbert C. Hoover	Republican	1929–33
32) Franklin D. Roosevelt	Democrat	1933–45
33) Harry S. Truman	Democrat	1945–9
34) Dwight Eisenhower	Republican	1953–61
35) John F. Kennedy	Democrat	1961–3
36) Lyndon B. Johnson	Democrat	1963–9
37) Richard Nixon	Republican	1969–74
38) Gerald Ford	Republican	1974–7
39) Jimmy Carter	Democrat	1977–81
40) Ronald Reagan	Republican	1981–9
41) George H.W. Bush	Republican	1989–93
42) William ("Bill") Clinton	Democrat	1993–2001
43) George W. Bush	Republican	2001–8

A SIMPLE BOW AND ARROW

A bow is a lethal weapon and should never be aimed at anyone or any living thing.

Those words of warning out of the way, shooting arrows at a target is a sport which calls for concentration, strength and perseverance.

It's good fun too. Here's how to make a longbow – the sort of bow that Robin Hood used.

The king of bow woods is yew, but it is relatively uncommon and highly poisonous, so you are much better off searching for a suitable length of rowan (mountain ash), hazel, oak, elm, ash, birch, osage orange, lemonwood, juniper or ironwood.

Ideally, you should take the wood from a small sapling growing in a dense wood, where trees have to "shoot for the sun" so grow straight and slim. Cut a straight length of wood approximately 3 feet long from your chosen tree. (If you are tall, say over 5 feet, cut a piece 4 foot long). Using a knife, gently taper the ends, remembering to cut away from you.

Then find the centre of your bow, mark it, and wind string or wool below it to make a handle.

Now you need to carve a notch about two inches in from each end; this is where you will tie the string for the bow. Putting the string on a bow is known as bracing. Use a timber hitch knot (also known as a round turn and two half hitches) as in Figure 1 to permanently tie your string to the bottom notch. Then with the bottom end of the bow on the floor bend the bow slightly and, pulling the string tight, tie it to the top notch with a simple loop. Having a simple loop at the top means that you can easily re-brace your bow if you need to.

Figure 1

The English archers that won the battle of Crécy and Agincourt used bow strings made from the stalks of the common nettle. These strings could take a weight of 140 lb and a boy would be unable to pull them. In fact, few modern men could do. So you'll want something easier and less stingy. Nylon string is ideal.

Arrows need to be straight, or they will wobble in flight. Bamboo makes for good straight arrows. Other acceptable woods for arrows are birch, hazel, alder, willow and pine. Cut lengths of 18–24 inches, and sharpen one end with your knife, so that it will stick in the target.

To make the arrow stable in flight you will need to fix flights to the non-business end. Bird feathers or pieces of plastic cut with scissors make the best flights. Cut three grooves in the arrow and fix the flights as in Figure 2. At the flight end cut a groove or nock to fit the bow string

Before you start firing your arrows you may want to make yourself a "bracer" from a stout piece of cloth, and tie this to the inside of your bow arm. This is to stop your arm becoming sore from the bow string slapping against it when you release your arrows. You'll also find that when the arrow goes over your bow hand it can take the skin off, so wear a glove.

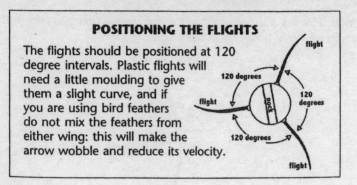

POSITIONING THE FLIGHTS

The flights should be positioned at 120 degree intervals. Plastic flights will need a little moulding to give them a slight curve, and if you are using bird feathers do not mix the feathers from either wing: this will make the arrow wobble and reduce its velocity.

Figure 2

To fire an arrow: stand sideways to the target with the bow held up by your non-dominant hand (for most people their left hand) and with the arrow resting on this hand as in Figure 3. Pull the arrow back with two or three fingers of the other hand. Close your left eye, sight the target – and loose off the arrow.

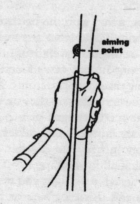

Figure 3

I said at the outset that a bow and arrow should never be aimed at a living thing. There is one exception: a survival situation. If you are stranded far from civilization a bow and arrow makes for a good hunting weapon. At a pinch you can make bowstring from cloth. Bits of metal, flint and glass make for deadly arrowheads.

It would have to be a survival sitation, though. Hunting game with a bow and arrow is illegal in most Western countries.

PIRATOLOGY

Pirates and Privateers

There have been pirates for almost as long as mankind has had boats. There were "searobbers" in Ancient Greece and Ancient Rome, while the Vikings were nothing but boat-borne plunderers. But the "Golden Age" of piracy was the seventeenth and eighteenth centuries, and was brought about by Spain's conquest of South America. The plundered treasures of the Aztecs and Incas needed to be shipped back to Madrid – and every sailor with a criminal gleam in his eye made his way to the Caribbean with a view to robbing the Spanish treasure ships en route. Some of these plunderers were issued with licences to rob by their governments, especially if the government happened to be at war with Spain; these licensed sea-robbers, of whom England's Sir Francis Drake was one, are more accurately called "privateers". "Buccaneers", meanwhile, were semi-official robbers, men whose government turned a blind eye to their larcenies against Spain. But most sea-robbers were pirates pure and proper, men – and sometimes women – out for their own personal gain.

And sometimes the gain was vast. In 1695 the famous pirate captain Henry Avery captured a treasure ship and netted himself £325,000.

The Pirate's Code

Some pirates, especially the infamous Blackbeard (aka Captain Edward Teach), were bloodthirsty criminals of whom nothing good could be said. But generally the sea thieves abided by a code of honour, as to how their ship was run and what share of loot each should have. Here is the code of piratical conduct from Captain Batholomew Roberts' ship, from around 1722:

i. Every man has a vote in affairs of moment: has equal title to the fresh provisions or strong liquors at any time seized, and [may] use them at pleasure unless a scarcity make it necessary for the good of all to vote a retrenchment.

ii. If they defrauded the Company to the value of a dollar, in plate, jewels or money, marooning was the punishment. If robbery was only between one another they contented themselves with slitting the ears and nose of him that was guilty, and set him on shore, not in an inhabited place but somewhere where he was sure to encounter hardships.

iii. No person to game at cards or dice for money.

iv. The lights and candles to be put out at eight o'clock at night. If any of the crew after that hour still remained inclined to drinking, they were to do it on open deck.

v. To keep their piece, pistols and cutlass clean and fit for service.

vi. No boy or woman to be allowed among them. If any man were found seducing any of the latter sex, and carried her to sea disguised, he was to suffer Death.

vii. To desert the ship or their quarters in battle was punished by Death or Marooning.

viii. No striking another on board, but every man's quarrels to be ended on shore, at sword and pistol.

ix. No man to talk of breaking up their way of living till each had a share of £1,000. If, in order to do this, any man should lose a limb or become a cripple in their service, he was to have 800 dollars out of the public stock, and for lesser hurts proportionately.

xi. The musicians to have rest on the sabbath day, but the other six days and nights none, without special favour.

Reprinted from Captain Johnson's *A General History of the Robberies and Murders of the Most Notorious Pirates*, 1724.

The Pirate's Flag

The pirate flag was an important part of the pirate's arsenal. It was a means of intimidating their victims. At first pirate flags had a red background, since red was the traditional colour of a banner flown in a battle in which no quarter would be given. Such a flag was known to the French humorously as *jolie rouge*, meaning "pretty red". *Jolie rouge* was the origin of "Jolly Roger", the name by which the pirate flag is generally known. By the late 1600s, however, most pirates flew a black flag – black being the colour of Mystery and Death – and were beginning to adorn their Jolly Rogers with symbols. The most popular symbols were the skull, the crossbones, the skeletons, the swords – all standing for Death – and the hour glass, signifying that time was running out for the victim. Jolly Rogers were rough affairs, run up by the pirate ship's sailmaker or any sailor who was handy with a needle. Here are some of the most notorious pirates and their Jolly Rogers:

Captain John "Calico Jack" Rackham

Captain Rackham was nicknamed 'Calico Jack' for his habit of wearing white Indian cloth. He was a pirate of the Caribbean sea, and was the lover of the female pirate, Anne Bonny. According to legend, when Rackham's ship was apprehended by the authorities only Bonny and another female pirate, Mary Read, fought back, at which Bonny condemned Rackham as a coward. He was hanged in 1720.

Captain Blackbeard

Blackbeard, whose real name was Edward Teach, only enjoyed a fifteen-month career as pirate – but it was enough to make him the most infamous of the pirates who sailed the seven seas. According to an account of Blackbeard from the seventeenth century, his appearance alone was enough to frighten victims into surrender;

"[His] beard was black, which he suffered to grow of an extra-vagrant length; as to breadth, it came up to his eyes. He was accustomed to twist it with ribbons, in small tails, after the manner of our Ramillies wigs, and turn them about his ears. In time of action he wore a sling over his shoulders, with three brace of pistols, hanging in holsters, like bandoliers; and stuck lighted matches under his hat, which, appearing on each side of his face, his eyes naturally looking fierce and wild, made him altogether such a figure that imagination cannot form an idea of a Fury from Hell more frightful."

Blackbeard is said to have married fourteen times. Most of his piracy was committed in the Caribbean and along the Atlantic coast of America, using a captured merchantman he renamed the *Queen Anne's Revenge* and on which he installed a mighty forty cannons. The British authorities which then controlled America decided to put an end of Blackbeard's depredations and the pirate was intercepted by a Royal Navy patrol commanded by Lieutenant Maynard at Ocracoke Inlet on 2 December 1718. Blackbeard and Maynard met in combat, and

Blackbeard was about to deal the naval officer a mortal blow with his cutlass when a British seaman attacked him from behind. With blood pumping from his neck, Blackbeard continued to swing his cutlass at his attackers and it took five shots and twenty severe sword wounds to fell him.

Blackbeard's Jolly Roger depicts a horned skeleton holding a spear next to a bleeding heart; in its other hand the skeleton holds an hourglass.

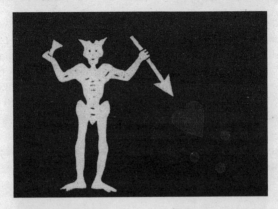

Captain Edward Condent

Condent was one of the more successful pirates. A Briton, he was elected pirate captain around 1718 and successfully marauded along the Brazilian coast, before taking prizes from the west coast of Africa. He then cruised the Red Sea and Indian Ocean for a year. Near Bombay in October 1720 Condent

captured an Arab ship containing a precious cargo valued at more than £150,000. The riches were shared out among Condent and his men, after which the wily pirate captain decided to abandon his life of crime. Upon negotiating a pardon from the French, he married the daughter of a prominent French official and settled down in Brittany as a merchant.

Captain Edward England

England, whose real name was Seegar, was a pirate active in the Caribbean, Atlantic and Indian Oceans from 1717 to 1720. Unusually for a pirate he was troubled by his conscience and disliked prisoners being treated cruelly. His crew had no such scruples and eventually mutinied against England, marooning him in Mauritius. England eventually made his way to Madagascar, where he lived on the charity of other pirates before dying a pauper.

England was the only pirate captain to fly the 'skull and crossbones' Jolly Roger in the pure form.

Captain Henry Avery

Captain Henry Avery's capture of the Moghul of India's treasure ship, *Gang-I-Sawai*, after a two-hour battle in June 1695 ranks as one of the most successful piratical exploits. Although many of Avery's crew were hunted down and hanged, Avery fled to Ireland where he vanished into thin air.

Avery flew both a red and a black Jolly Roger.

Captain Edward Low

The English pirate Edward Low was almost as sadistic as Captain Blackbeard. When his cook failed to please him, Low had the man burned alive. Off the coast of Massachusetts, Low captured several whalers and cut off the ears of two of the captains, and cut out the heart of another. Eventually, Low's own crew turned against him and marooned him in the West Indies in 1724, where he is thought to have died.

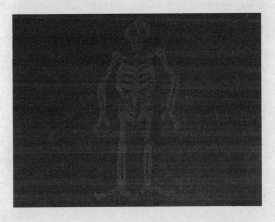

The Pirate's Song

To the mast nail our flag it is dark as the grave,
Or the death which it bears while it sweeps o'er the wave;
Let our deck clear for action, our guns be prepared;
Be the boarding-axe sharpened, the scimitar bared:
Set the canisters ready, and then bring to me,
For the last of my duties, the powder-room key.
It shall never be lowered, the black flag we bear;
If the sea be denied us, we sweep through the air.
Unshared have we left our last victory's prey;
It is mine to divide it, and yours to obey:
There are shawls that might suit a sultana's white neck,
And pearls that are fair as the arms they will deck;
There are flasks which, unseal them, the air will disclose
Diametta's fair summers, the home of the rose.
I claim not a portion: I ask but as mine –
'Tis to drink to our victory – one cup of red wine.
Some fight, 'tis for riches – some fight, 'tis for fame:
The first I despise, and the last is a name.
I fight, 'tis for vengeance! I love to see flow,
At the stroke of my sabre, the life of my foe.
I strike for the memory of long-vanished years;
I only shed blood where another shed tears.
I come, as the lightning comes red from above,
O'er the race that I loathe, to the battle I love.

SAS SURVIVAL SKILLS I: MAKING FIRE

Fuel, Heat and Oxygen

You have to bring three things together to make fire – fuel, heat and oxygen. Take away any one of these, and the fire goes out. About a fifth of all the air around us is oxygen. All you have to do is make sure that there is free passage of air around – and especially up through – the fire.

Heat – the heat to start the fire – you have to provide. Friction in one form or another is the usual way, but you can use the rays of the sun, and perhaps even electricity, in its place.

Different Forms of Fuel

You have to provide fuel in three quite different forms – tinder, to catch the spark; kindling, to set the flame; and the fuel itself, to keep the fire going.

Most fuel will not burn when it's wet. The water surrounds it and cuts off the air supply. Non-porous fuels like coal will burn when they are wet, however, and liquid fuels like oil, kerosene and petrol are completely unaffected by water.

But in most parts of the world it's wood and vegetable matter that you'll be burning, and this you must keep dry. Gathering and storing fuel for the fire is a very good example of how forward thinking pays dividends. But there is always something you can do to make a fire, even if you're shivering to death in a freezing rainstorm and the matches are soaked through.

Look for:
 1 A sheltered place to build a fire
 2 Old, dead wood
 3 Kindling
 4 Tinder

Take these tasks one at a time. Look for a rock overhang on the lee side of a hill or outcrop; or a low fallen branch, or a fallen tree. At this stage you're looking for protection for the fire, not shelter for yourself.

Gathering fuel

Dead wood, as long as it's not actually lying in water, will usually have some dry material in it somewhere, but the best sources are dead timber that's still standing, and dead branches that are still attached to the tree. Look for the bark peeling off.

The main difference between kindling and proper fuel is its size. Remember, the kindling takes up the sparks and glowing embers from the tinder and turns it into flames that will ignite the fuel.

Small, bone-dry twigs are the best, but if necessary you can make "fire-sticks" by shaving larger pieces of shallow cuts to feather them. This is a job much better done in advance.

Tinder must be dry. Absolutely, perfectly dry. You should have some already, packed up securely in a water-tight box next to your skin. If not, you'll have to find some.

Don't look too far to start with: you won't need very much. Try the lining of your pockets and the seams of your clothes. The lint that collects there makes good tinder, except for wool. Dry bark, shredded into tiny pieces; dread grass, fern and moss; dead pine needles; downy seedheads from thistles and smaller plants: all these make good tinder, as long as the material is dry.

The common factor is the size of the individual pieces or fibres. They must be tiny, so that as much of their substance as possible is exposed to the air and to the spark or flame.

The vital spark

If you don't have matches or a lighter that works, there are several alternative ways to start a fire. If you have direct sunlight and a magnifying lens, you can use the glass to focus the sun rays on to the tinder and start it burning that way. But this won't work at night in a rainstorm!

Alternatively, you could use the "flint and steel" method.

If you have a so-called "metal match" (a metal strip with tiny flint chips embedded in it), then use that, scraping your knife blade along it to produce a shower of sparks.

Or look for a piece of flint or other very hard stone. Then you can use your knife to strike sparks off it; use the back of the blade. If you have a piece of hacksaw blade, you should use that to save damaging your knife.

Alternative technology

There are two other ways of making fire. The bow and drill, and the fire saw both rely on friction between two pieces of wood. You have to make a small part of one of those pieces hot enough to set the tinder going. It is possible – but you'll only need to try it once to become fanatical about carrying matches with you everywhere you go!

Fire Bow

Making a fire from the friction of wood upon wood really is a last-ditch alternative. The few aboriginal tribes that still make fire this way spend a very long time selecting exactly the right materials. Nevertheless, in the desert, where it's perfectly dry, it is possible to start a fire in this way.

You'll need:
1 A piece of green hardwood, about a metre (3 ft) long and 2½ cm (1 in) in diameter.
2 A piece of dry hardwood, 30 cm long and 1 cm in diameter.
3 A 5 cm hardwood cube, or a shell or a suitable stone.
4 A piece of dry softwood, 2½ cm thick.
5 A cord for the bow-string.

To make the fire bow:
1 Make the bow loosely using the cord and the long piece of hardwood.

2 Round off one end of the short piece of hardwood, and taper the other slightly.

3 Carve out the centre of the hardwood cube to fit the taper, or find a stone or shell of the right shape.

4 Make a depression in the softwood, close to one edge, and make a groove from it that leads to the edge.

5 Put some tinder next to the end of the groove.

6 Loop the bow-string round the drill, maintain pressure on the top with the cap, and work the bow backwards and forwards to create friction between the hardwood drill and the softwood

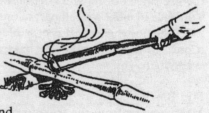

baseboard. Wood dust will build up in the groove, and the end of the drill will become red-hot and ignite it.

Fire Saw
You'll need:

1 A piece of bamboo, 5–8 cm in diameter and 1/2 metre long.

2 A forked stick, to anchor it into the ground.

To make the fire saw:

1 Split the bamboo length ways.

2 Cut two notches in a straight line across the two exposed edges near to one end.

3 Brace the notched bamboo with the forked stick.

4 Fill the space between the notches with a handful of tinder.

5 Saw in the notches until the tinder ignites.

Fire Tongs

1 Make a thong (a strip or string of tough material) using rattan (a sort of tropical vine), leather or very tough cord.

2 Split a dry stick and hold the split open with a small wedge.

3 Run the thong through the split.

4 Place a small wad of tinder in the split.

5 Secure the stick with your foot and run the thong back and forth to create frictional heat. The tinder will eventually ignite.

Hints for the Firemaker

When you're making a fire under difficult conditions, you must start small and add to it very carefully. If you've been unable to find a site sheltered from the wind, then you must make a windbreak, although it may be simpler to dig a sloping trench and light the fire inside that.

If the ground is very wet, use stones as a base, but make sure that they're not porous. Wet, porous stones can explode: that will not only injure you, but also blow the fire all over the place.

Don't worry about making an elaborate fireplace at this stage. Get the fire alight first.

THE LOG CABIN PILE

This is a very good way of laying a fire. Plenty of air can circulate and it will not collapse until it's well away.

Make a nest of dry grass and the smallest twigs. If you can find a dry bird's or mouse's nest, so much the better. It will have down and fur mixed in with the grass, and probably some dry droppings too – all of them excellent tinder.

Put your tinder inside. Arrange dry kindling over it in the shape of a cone, or make a lean-to by pushing a green stick into the ground at an angle of about 30 degrees and build up the kindling along it to make a sort of tent.

Make sure that you've got all the materials you need to hand before attempting to light the fire – you may only get one chance, and at the beginning you'll have to work quickly, adding small amounts of kindling as the fire grows.

Keep the fire going

If you have a choice of different types of wood to use as fuel, use softwood – pine and spruce, for example – as the first load of fuel, but be careful of sparks. These woods contain resin and burn quickly. To keep the fire going, use hardwood such as oak or beech. They're much longer lasting.

You can use a mixture of green and dry wood to keep the fire going through the night, but don't just dump wood on it without thinking. Make sure that you keep a good stock of fuel close at hand, and arrange it so that the heat from the fire will help to dry the fuel out. Keep kindling at hand, too, so that you can revive the fire quickly if it looks like dying out.

Improving the fire

How you improve the fire site depends on what you're going to use it for. A fire that you use for smoking food, for instance, isn't much use for anything else. Its purpose is to produce lots of smoke inside an enclosure. You won't be able to cook on it, and it won't give out much warmth.

The hobo stove

You can cook on an open fire, but it's not very efficient; it's better to construct a stove of some sort. The simplest stove needs something like a 5-gallon oil drum. Punch poles in one end and in a ring all around the side at the same end. Cut out a panel about two inches above that ring of holes. Punch a large hole in one side of the drum near the other end, to let the smoke out. Place the stove on a ring of stones to allow the air to circulate from underneath.

Now you can transfer some of your fire into the stove, stoke it through the cut-out panel and cook on top. It'll give off enough heat to keep you warm, too, and has the very positive benefit of not showing sparks and flames like an open fire does.

The Fire Pit

A fire pit

You can achieve much the same effect by digging a circular pit, and then another smaller one, slantwise, that meets it at the bottom. The slanting hole is for the air to circulate up through the fire, so dig it on the side of the prevailing wind.

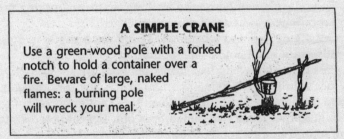

A SIMPLE CRANE

Use a green-wood pole with a forked notch to hold a container over a fire. Beware of large, naked flames: a burning pole will wreck your meal.

Adapted from *The Mammoth Book of The Secrets of the SAS and Elite Forces*, edited by Jon E. Lewis, 2002. Copyright © 2002 Constable & Robinson/Jon E. Lewis

TIN CAN TELEPHONE

Take two 14-oz (420-g) tin cans – bean cans are ideal – and open with the sort of tin opener which makes a vertical cut into the top; tin openers which horizontally slice off the top of the tin can are going to leave a sharp edge and you'll end up looking like the painter van Gogh.

Eat the contents (if you're hungry; if not place in a china bowl and put in the refrigerator. Don't give beans to the dog, especially a Labrador!)

Carefully clean out can with washing-up brush, making sure to keep fingers away from any sharp edges.

Get a long nail and a hammer. Using the hammer and nail gently tap a small hole in the bottom of each can.

Pass the end of a length of string (between 5yd/m and 10yd/m is ideal) through the hole in bottom of the first can, threading from the outside to the inside. Then *tie* a knot in the end of the string, so that it can't be pulled back out. Repeat process with the second can.

The tin can telephone is now ready for use. Find a friend or sibling or, failing those, a parent. Pull the cans apart so that the string is taut. By arrangement, one of you speaks into his can while the other one has the can to his ear. You'll hear them loud and clear.

POET'S CORNER

Let's face it, poetry does not have a good reputation with most boys. But sometimes poetry can express moments in life and in history better than anything else. So here are some of the world's greatest poems. At the very least they'll make you wonder, at the very most they'll help you understand.

"The Tyger" by William Blake

William Blake (1757–1827) lived for most of his life in London, earning a humble living from writing, illustrating and printing his poetry.

Tyger! Tyger! burning bright
In the forests of the night,
What immortal hand or eye
Could frame thy fearful symmetry?

In what distant deeps or skies
Burnt the fire of thine eyes?
On what wings dare he aspire?
What the hand dare seize the fire?

And what shoulder, and what art,
Could twist the sinews of thy heart?
And when thy heart began to beat,
What dread hand? And what dread feet?

What the hammer? What the chain?
In what furnace was thy brain?
What the anvil? What dread grasp
Dare its deadly terrors clasp?

When the stars threw down their spears,
And water'd heaven with their tears,
Did He smile His work to see?
Did He who made the Lamb make thee?

Tyger! Tyger! burning bright
In the forests of the night,
What immortal hand or eye,
Dare frame thy fearful symmetry?

"Ozymandias" by Percy Bysshe Shelley

Shelley was the original teenage rebel and was expelled from Oxford University for criticizing religion, which was taboo in Georgian England. He died in 1822 aged thirty in a boating accident in Italy.

I met a traveller from an antique land
Who said: Two vast and trunkless legs of stone
Stand in the desert. Near them, on the sand,
Half sunk, a shattered visage lies, whose frown,
And wrinkled lip, and sneer of cold command,
Tell that its sculptor well those passions read
Which yet survive (stamped on these lifeless things),
The hand that mocked them and the heart that fed:
And on the pedestal these words appear:
"My name is Ozymandias, king of kings;
Look on my works, ye Mighty, and despair!"
Nothing beside remains. Round the decay
Of that colossal wreck, boundless and bare,
The lone and level sands stretch far away.

"Jabberwocky" by Lewis Carroll

The real name of Lewis Carroll (1832–1898) was Charles Dodgson. He was the son of a vicar and spent most of his adult life at Oxford University, where he lectured in mathematics and wrote the children's books which made him famous. The lines below come from Alice's Adventures in Wonderland.

'Twas brillig, and the slithy toves
    Did gyre and gimble in the wabe:
All mimsy were the borogoves,
        And the mome raths outgrabe.

"Beware the Jabberwock, my son!
    The jaws that bite, the claws that catch!
Beware the Jubjub bird, and shun
        The frumious Bandersnatch!"

He took his vorpal sword in hand:
    Long time the manxome foe he sought—
So rested he by the Tumtum tree,
        And stood awhile in thought.

And, as in uffish thought he stood,
    The Jabberwock, with eyes of flame,
Came whiffling through the tulgey wood,
        And burbled as it came!

One, two! One, two! And through and through
    The vorpal blade went snicker-snack!
He left it dead, and with its head
        He went galumphing back.

"And hast thou slain the Jabberwock?
    Come to my arms, my beamish boy!
O frabjous day! Callooh! Callay!"
        He chortled in his joy.

'Twas brillig, and the slithy toves
    Did gyre and gimble in the wabe:
All mimsy were the borogoves,
        And the mome raths outgrabe.

"The Charge of the Light Brigade"
by Alfred Lord Tennyson

On the morning of 25 October 1854, during the Battle of Balaklava, the Light Brigade of the British Army made a head-on charge into the Russian artillery at the end of the valley. The incident is famously regarded as a blunder, because the Light Brigade had probably been meant to attack a Russian position at the side of the valley. There is another way of looking at the Charge of the Light Brigade: as one of the greatest examples of bravery on the battlefield. As the 666 troopers lined up on their horses to attack the Russian cannon they knew that many of them would die in the doing. And they did. Of those who charged 156 were afterwards reported killed or missing. The Victorian poet Alfred Tennyson wrote a stirring celebration of the Charge. Here it is:

Half a league, half a league,
　Half a league onward,
All in the valley of Death
　Rode the six hundred.

"Forward, the Light Brigade!
Charge for the guns!" he said:
Into the valley of Death
　Rode the six hundred.

"Forward, the Light Brigade!"
Was there a man dismay'd?
Not tho' the soldier knew
　Someone had blunder'd:
Theirs not to make reply,
Theirs not to reason why,
Theirs but to do and die:
Into the valley of Death
　Rode the six hundred.

Cannon to right of them,
Cannon to left of them,
Cannon in front of them
　Volley'd and thunder'd;

Storm'd at with shot and shell,
Boldly they rode and well,
Into the jaws of Death,
Into the mouth of Hell
  Rode the six hundred.

Flash'd all their sabers bare,
Flash'd as they turn'd in air
Sab'ring the gunners there,
Charging an army, while
  All the world wonder'd:
Plunged in the battery smoke
Right thro' the line they broke;
Cossack and Russian
Reel'd from the saber stroke
  Shatter'd and sunder'd.
Then they rode back, but not
  Not the six hundred.

Cannon to right of them,
Cannon to left of them,
Cannon behind them
  Volley'd and thunder'd:
Storm'd at with shot and shell,
While horse and hero fell,
They that had fought so well
Came through the jaws of death
Back from the mouth of hell,
All that was left of them—
  Left of six hundred.

When can their glory fade?
Oh, the wild charge they made!
  All the world wonder'd.
Honor the charge they made!
Honor the Light Brigade—
  Noble six hundred!

"Oh Captain! My Captain!" by Walt Whitman

Whitman wrote this elegy on the occasion of the assassination of President Abraham Lincoln in 1865.

O Captain! my Captain! our fearful trip is done,
The ship has weather'd every rack, the prize we sought is won,
The port is near, the bells I hear, the people all exulting,
While follow eyes the steady keel, the vessel grim and daring;
   But O heart! heart! heart!
      O the bleeding drops of red,
         Where on the deck my Captain lies,
           Fallen cold and dead.

O Captain! my Captain! rise up and hear the bells;
Rise up – for you the flag is flung – for you the bugle trills,
For you bouquets and ribbon'd wreaths – for you the shores a-crowding,
For you they call, the swaying mass, their eager faces turning;
   Here Captain! dear father!
      This arm beneath your head!
         It is some dream that on the deck,
           You've fallen cold and dead.

My Captain does not answer, his lips are pale and still,
My father does not feel my arm, he has no pulse nor will,
The ship is anchor'd safe and sound, its voyage closed and done,
From fearful trip the victor ship comes in with object won;
   Exult O shores, and ring O bells!
      But I with mournful tread,
         Walk the deck my Captain lies,
           Fallen cold and dead.

"The Road Not Taken" by Robert Frost

A native San Franciscan (he was born in 1874), Frost spent most of his life amidst the woods and meadows of New England. His blending of wisdom and observations on nature made him one of the most popular American poets of the twentieth century.

Two roads diverged in a yellow wood,
And sorry I could not travel both
And be one traveler, long I stood
And looked down one as far as I could

To where it bent in the undergrowth;

Then took the other, as just as fair,
And having perhaps the better claim
Because it was grassy and wanted wear;
Though as for that, the passing there

Had worn them really about the same,

And both that morning equally lay
In leaves no step had trodden black.
Oh, I marked the first for another day!
Yet knowing how way leads on to way

I doubted if I should ever come back.

I shall be telling this with a sigh
Somewhere ages and ages hence:
Two roads diverged in a wood, and I,
I took the one less traveled by,

And that has made all the difference.

"Vitai Lampada" by Sir Henry Newbolt

Sir Henry Newbolt (1862–1938) is remembered mainly for his patriotic poems, of which "Vitai Lampada" is the most famous. He was also a lawyer and historian.

There's a breathless hush in the Close to-night –
Ten to make and the match to win –
A bumping pitch and a blinding light,
An hour to play and the last man in.
And it's not for the sake of a ribboned coat,
Or the selfish hope of a season's fame,
But his Captain's hand on his shoulder smote
"Play up! play up! and play the game!"

The sand of the desert is sodden red, –
Red with the wreck of a square that broke; –
The Gatling's jammed and the colonel dead,
And the regiment blind with dust and smoke.
The river of death has brimmed his banks,
And England's far, and Honour a name,
But the voice of schoolboy rallies the ranks,
"Play up! play up! and play the game!"

This is the word that year by year
While in her place the School is set
Every one of her sons must hear,
And none that hears it dare forget.
This they all with a joyful mind
Bear through life like a torch in flame,
And falling fling to the host behind –
"Play up! play up! and play the game!"

"In Flanders Fields" by John McCrae

John McCrae was a field surgeon with the Canadian Army during the First World War. His famous poem "In Flanders Fields" was prompted by the death of a close friend during the Battle of Ypres in 1915. McCrae himself died on active service, in January 1918, from pneumonia and meningitis. He was buried with full military honours.

In Flanders Fields the poppies blow
Between the crosses, row on row,
    That mark our place; and in the sky
    The larks, still bravely singing, fly
Scarce heard amid the guns below.

We are the Dead. Short days ago
We lived, felt dawn, saw sunset glow,
   Loved, and were loved, and now we lie
      In Flanders fields.

Take up our quarrel with the foe:
To you from failing hands we throw
   The torch, be yours to hold it high.
   If ye break faith with us who die
We shall not sleep, though poppies grow
      In Flanders fields.

"Dulce Et Decorum Est" by Wilfred Owen

Owen was a junior officer with a British regiment in the trenches of the First World War. "Dulce Et Decorum Est" is probably the most famous anti-war poem ever written. Owen, who won a Military Cross for valour, was killed in action a week before the Armistice.

Bent double, like old beggars under sacks,
Knock-kneed, coughing like hags, we cursed through sludge,
Till on the haunting flares we turned our backs
And towards our distant rest began to trudge.
Men marched asleep. Many had lost their boots
But limped on, blood-shod. All went lame; all blind;
Drunk with fatigue; deaf even to the hoots
Of gas shells dropping softly behind.

Gas! GAS! Quick, boys! – An ecstasy of fumbling,
Fitting the clumsy helmets just in time;
But someone still was yelling out and stumbling,
And flound'ring like a man in fire or lime . . .
Dim, through the misty panes and thick green light,
As under a green sea, I saw him drowning.
In all my dreams, before my helpless sight,
He plunges at me, guttering, choking, drowning.

If in some smothering dreams you too could pace
Behind the wagon that we flung him in,

And watch the white eyes writhing in his face,
His hanging face, like a devil's sick of sin;
If you could hear, at every jolt, the blood
Come gargling from the froth-corrupted lungs,
Obscene as cancer, bitter as the cud
Of vile, incurable sores on innocent tongues, –
My friend, you would not tell with such high zest
To children ardent for some desperate glory,
The old Lie: Dulce et decorum est
Pro patria mori.

MORSE CODE

Morse Code was invented by surprise, surprise, Mr Morse.

In the 1840s Samuel F.B. Morse, an American, patented an electric telegraph system which sent a pulse of electricity down the line to control an electromagnet in the receiving office. Since the electromagnet had a stylus attached to it, varying the length of pulse meant that the stylus made a short or long indentation on paper. Even more cleverly, Mr Morse ascribed each letter of the alphabet an individual set of short or long marks. A, for instance was.–

Morse's method meant that text messages could be sent quickly and easily over long distances. The world record for "copying" Morse is seventy-five words in a minute.

Although developed for the telegraph, Morse code was just as suited to radio when it came on the scene in the 1890s. On radio, a dash was sent as a long audible pulse, a dot a short one. Not until the development of the commercial computer in the 1960s did Morse lose its crown as the main electronic coding system for high-speed international radio and telegraphic communication.

Morse, however, is still widely used and understood by the world's military and emergency services. Morse is simple to learn and can be transmitted by just about anything you can lay your hands on in an emergency. Morse-coded messages can be sent by:

TORCHLIGHT – long flash for dash, short for dot.

WHISTLE – long blow for dash, short for dot.

FLAG – left for dash, right for dot.

If you don't have a flag, use your shirt. Trapped submariners have even sent Morse messages by banging on the vessel's hull with a spanner.

The one Morse message every boy needs to know is SOS, short for 'Save Our Souls'.

In Morse, SOS is dot dot dot – dash dash dash – dot dot dot.

The Morse Code Alphabet

A .▬	N ▬.	0 ▬▬▬▬▬
B ▬...	O ▬▬▬	1 .▬▬▬▬
C ▬.▬.	P .▬▬.	2 ..▬▬▬
D ▬..	Q ▬▬.▬	3 ...▬▬
E .	R .▬.	4 ....▬
F ..▬.	S ...	5 .....
G ▬▬.	T ▬	6 ▬....
H	U ..▬	7 ▬▬...
I ..	V ...▬	8 ▬▬▬..
J .▬▬▬	W .▬▬	9 ▬▬▬▬.
K ▬.▬	X ▬..▬	**Fullstop** .▬.▬.▬
L .▬..	Y ▬.▬▬	**Comma** ▬▬..▬▬
M ▬▬	Z ▬▬..	

TEN BOOKS TO READ
BEFORE THE AGE OF TEN

R.M. Ballantyne, *The Coral Island*, 1858.
Ralph, Jack and Peterkin are shipwrecked in the South Pacific in the ultimate boys' adventure.

BB, *Down the Bright Stream*, 1944.
The last four gnomes in England go in search of a new home.

Richmal Crompton, *Just William*, 1922.
The comic misadventures of schoolboy William Brown.

Roald Dahl, *The BFG*, 1982.
A small girl is stolen by a giant. Luckily, he's the Big Friendly Giant. Illustrated by Quentin Blake.

Charles Dickens, *A Christmas Carol*, 1843.
How the miser Scrooge learns the meaning of Christmas.

C.S. Lewis, *The Lion, the Witch and the Wardrobe*, 1950.
Christian-influenced tale of four children who enter a wardrobe and end up in an enchanted land.

Jack London, *The Call of the Wild*, 1903.
A pet dog, Buck, has to survive in the frozen Yukon during the gold rush.

A.A. Milne, *Winnie the Pooh* and *the House at Pooh Corner*, 1926–8.
The warm-hearted tales of a toy bear, his owner Christopher Robin, and assorted friends in Hundred Acre Wood.

Robert Louis Stevenson, *Treasure Island*, 1883.
The classic adventure story of pirates and buried gold.

E.B. White, *Charlotte's Web*, 1952.
A barn spider spins a friendship with a pig.

CARPENTRY

There is little exaggeration in saying that a knowledge of carpentry is indispensable to every boy. Putting aside for a moment the fact that the desire to "make something" is inherent in human nature, there is scarcely a hobby under the sun which does not demand a certain amount of practical skill and constructive ability. No matter what his hobby, the ardent devotee likes to do everything for himself, and without a knowledge of the rudiments of carpentry, how can he hope to accomplish this? There is, moreover, a very practical side to the question. The great majority of schoolboys have had to realise the fact that pocket-money is not inexhaustible, and that the purchase of cabinets, bookshelves and so forth makes sad havoc with the weekly or monthly allowance. Now all this can be remedied with a little practical knowledge of sawing and planing. A few pence will purchase the wood, a certain amount of care will ensure its being properly worked, and with an outlay of perhaps two or three shillings, the hobbyist will find himself in possession of a cabinet or similar article for which he would possibly have had to pay perhaps as many pounds.

A great deal of misunderstanding has arisen concerning the terms carpentry and joinery. So general is the confusion between the two words that what is generally termed carpentry is in reality nothing but joinery. It may therefore be explained at once that carpentry, technically known as "Carcase Work", is the art of fixing together large pieces of timber for making roofs, sheds, and similar parts of general building work.

Joinery, as its name implies, refers to the making of joins, and fitting smaller pieces of wood together in the construction of boxes, tables, drawers, shelves, and the interior fittings of houses, etc.

THE OUTFIT

An old proverb says that a bad workman complains of his tools. But there is something more than the proper manipulation of tools required to make a good workman. Care and precision are essential qualities in a carpenter, for without them the best tools in the world are useless.

As the cost of the outfit is no inconsiderable item in the equipment of a carpenter's shop, it must be clearly understood from the beginning that a certain amount of expense will be involved in connection with the hobby.

SAWS

(1) Carpenter's hand-saw, with teeth varying in number from 5 to 6½ to the inch. These saws are generally made from about 20 in. to 28 in. in length, and have wooden handles to suit the conformity of the hand; a medium size, say 26 in., is recommended.

(2) Tenon saw, with a 14-in. blade and a brass or iron back to render the blade stiff. This saw is used for cross-cutting and making neat joints.

(3) Dovetail saw. This is a miniature tenon saw with a blade 7 in. or 8 in. long and an open handle. Price from 2s. 6d.

(4) Pad or keyhole saw. This tool is used for cutting keyholes and making all small turned cuts in woodwork. The handle, which is hollow, has a brass ferule with two screws which hold the taper blade at any length required.

(5) Bow saw or turning web. This is used for cutting curves, round outlines, etc.

PLANES

(1) Jack plane, used for knocking off rough surfaces and preparing coarse work for the trying plane.

(2) Trying plane, for use after the jack plane. It smooths the roughly-worked surface.

(3) Smoothing plane. This is employed for finishing and giving the final touches to all prepared work.

CHISELS

Chisels can be purchased in sizes ranging from $\frac{1}{16}$ in. to $1\frac{1}{2}$ in. The larger sizes should be bevelled if possible, as such work as dove-tailing is greatly facilitated thereby.

FIG. 1.—How to hold a Chisel.

The sash mortice chisel is a strong, handy tool, useful for working the lighter portions of morticing.

An example of how to hold a chisel is shown in Fig. 1.

GOUGES

Gouges, made in similar sizes and at similar prices to chisels, are ground, or, as carpenters say, cannelled, inside and outside.

Scribing gouges are sold in different curves, Fig. 2, and are used for preparing one curved surface to butt against another, Figs. 3 and 4.

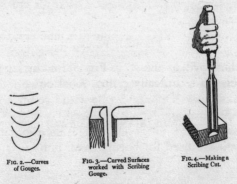

FIG. 2.—Curves of Gouges.

FIG. 3.—Curved Surfaces worked with Scribing Gouge.

FIG. 4.—Making a Scribing Cut.

Firmer gouges are made stiffer than the above, and those with an outside cannel are used for scalloping out depressions beneath the surface of any work.

DRAW-KNIFE

This instrument is used, as shown in Fig. 5, for roughing out curves and rounded surfaces, and also for making chambers.

SPOKESHAVE

The spokeshave is employed for finishing the work after the draw-knife has been used.

METAL RATCHET BRACE

This implement, which is used for boring holes of any size, is especially handy for working in awkward positions.

FIG. 5.—A Draw-knife.   FIG. 6.—Using the Plough Plane.

PLOUGH PLANE

This is employed, as shown in Fig. 6, for cutting grooves or, as this process is technically called, rebating.

GIMLETS AND BRADAWLS

These tools are used for boring small holes.

SCREWDRIVERS

For ordinary use cabinet-makers' screwdrivers are the best to obtain, and are sold in large and small sizes.

HAMMER

A hammer of the London or Exeter pattern can be obtained from any ironmonger.

MALLET

A good beech-wood mallet is the most serviceable.

SET-SQUARES AND BEVELS

Carpenters' squares, with good ebony or rosewood stocks, and bevels similarly made, can be obtained from any toolmaker.

GAUGES

These are sold in two patterns: The simple gauge, for marking a line parallel to a planed surface; the morticing gauge, for marking off tenons and mortices as shown in Fig. 7.

Fig. 7. – Morticing Gauge

SUNDRIES

A two-foot rule, spirit-level, pair of spring-nut American combination compasses, pair of carpenters' pincers, and a gluepot, all of which can be obtained for about 1s. each, will be necessary to complete the outfit of the workshop.

SOME HINTS ON SAWING

When sawing, the utmost care must be exercised to avoid the use of any wilful force in driving the saw. The action should be even and regular, with an easy, steady motion. Any violence or undue exertion will either cause the saw to snap, or will buckle it up and render it useless for further work.

When using the tenon saw mark the wood with a sharp knife, instead of with a pencil. This is known as making a "striking line", and, as it produces a narrower and more exact line than a pencil, a neater cut is ensured.

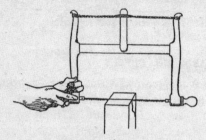

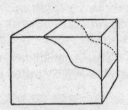

FIG. 8.—Using the Bow Saw.   FIG. 8A.—Marking for Bow Saw.

As a general rule, it may be remarked that in all sawn joints, such as the housing joint, the saw is worked inside the striking line on the one piece of wood, and outside it on the other.

For using the bow saw, Fig. 8, both sides of the wood should be marked with the desired curve, as seen in Fig. 8A, as this prevents any uneven sawing on either side.

PLANES AND PLANNING

There is a certain knack required in holding a plane which has much to do with success in turning out good work. Fig. 9 illustrates the correct method of holding either the jack or trying plane. As the smoothing plane is somewhat differently shaped, a glance at Fig. 10 will demonstrate how it should be held.

FIG. 9.—Correct position in which to hold Jack Plane.   FIG. 10.—Holding the Smoothing Plane.

To ascertain whether the surface of a small piece of wood has been planed evenly, the wood should be held level with the eye, the iron of the set-square placed across it and passed from end to end. If any light appears between the metal and the wood, it proves an uneven surface.

In Fig. 11 is seen the method of ascertaining if an adjacent side is at right angles to a level surface. The stock of the set-square must be placed

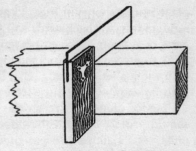

FIG. 11.—Using the Set-square.

against the side already proved level, and the blade or iron pressed closely against the freshly-worked surface from end to end. If it fits tightly against both surfaces of the wood, the angle of the edge is certainly true.

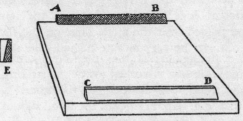

FIG. 12.—The "Trueing Sticks".

To discover if a large surface, such as the top of a table, is evenly planed, two pieces of wood known as "trueing sticks" are placed as shown in Fig. 12, and the eye is run along to notice if the top lines AB and CD exactly coincide. These "trueing sticks" can be made by sawing through the length of a squared-up piece of wood, E, Fig. 12, shown in section.

When planes are purchased new from the tool-maker, the iron, or blade, is ground back at an acute angle to allow of several whettings on the oilstone. The method of sharpening a

FIG. 13.—Sharpening a Plane Iron.

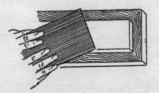

FIG. 14.—Sharpening a Plane Iron.

plane iron is shown in Figs. 13 and 14. The blade must be held
rigid and drawn backwards and forwards with an easy motion,
great care being taken to prevent any "wobbling".

To remove a plane iron, tap the fore part of the plane smartly
with the mallet; the wedge that keeps the blade in position can
then be extracted, and the iron taken out.

Practice alone will teach the exact amount that the blade
should project beneath the under surface of the plane, but it
must not be allowed to protrude too far, as this will ruin the
edge of the iron when any attempt is made to plane.

SHARPENING CHISELS AND GOUGES

Chisels are sharpened with the bevelled side against the
oilstone. When sufficient edge has been obtained, the tool
should be turned and passed over the stone once on the flat
side, this serving to remove the very minute turned edge that
will have been produced by rubbing one side of the metal.

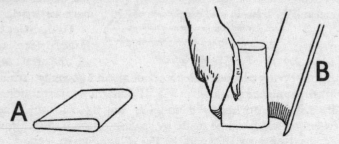

Fig. 15. – Whetting an Inner Cannelled Gouge.

Outer cannelled gouges are sharpened on the oilstone in the
same manner as chisels. Inner cannelled gouges are whetted on
a slip stone A, as shown at B, Fig. 15.

THE OILSTONE

Care should be taken in the selection of an oilstone, and it
must be noticed especially that there are no flaws in the surface,
which should be of a silvery-grey colour.

The whetting capacity may be tested by running the thumbnail from end to end. If it be a good stone it will give the nail a
perceptible edge.

Sweet oil or neat's-foot oil is the best to use with the oilstone, and a few drops only should be applied to the surface.

MATERIAL

Yellow deal should always be employed for outside work, as, the turpentine not having been extracted, this wood is less subject to the effects of weather.

White deal, which contains no turpentine, is suitable for all inside work. The prices of both these woods are very moderate, and spare pieces for small work can always be obtained very cheaply from any carpenter if he is told for what purpose they are required.

NAILS

Carpenters usually employ cut clasp nails. These should be driven into the wood with the grain. French nails, which are round, are also largely used, and may be purchased at the same price.

GLUE

Glue should be used quickly, and applied liberally, but not with undue profusion.

``KNOTTING''

Before painting wood it is essential that the knots be covered with "knotting". If this is neglected, when the paint has dried, the knots in the material will show up aggressively through the colour.

JOINTS
THE GLUE JOINT

When two lengths of wood are to be glued side by side, as, for example, in making the surface of a table, the following method should be employed:

With a jack plane smooth the edges to be glued, finish with the trying plane, and test them with the set-square. When this

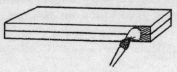

FIG. 16.—The Glue Joint.

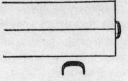

FIG. 17.—Clamp for Glue Joint.

has been done lay the two pieces in the position they will eventually occupy, and hold them against the light to ascertain if any unevenness is apparent. If there should be any, it must be rectified before proceeding further.

Place the boards one upon the other, as in Fig. 16, and sweep the glue-brush over both edges at once.

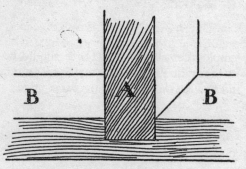

FIG. 18.—The Housing Joint.

Now place the glued edges together, rub the two boards several times against one another, up and down, finishing in position. Lay them on a level surface, and temporarily fasten them together with small clamps, as in Fig. 17.

The glue should be allowed twenty-four hours to harden, and when dry the surface may be cleaned with the plane, and any unevenness removed with sand-paper.

THE HOUSING JOINT

The housing joint depicted in Fig. 18 is made in the following manner: For the sake of example, let it be supposed that the two pieces of wood A and BB measure ¾ in. square, and that A is to be fitted into B.

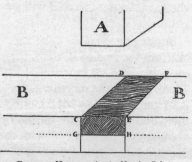

FIG. 19.—How to make the Housing Joint.

Two parallel lines, CD and EF, Fig. 19, must be marked with a striking knife across BB at a distance of ¾ in. from each other. Set the gauge to ¼ in. and mark a line at GH on both sides of the wood, and also mark the perpendicular lines CG and EH with the set-square.

Placing the tenon saw against the inside of the line CD, cut down to G and repeat the process at EF, sawing down to H. Holding a ⅝ in. chisel as in Fig. 1, cut away the portion between the saw-cuts, shaded in Fig. 19.

The end of A can now be inserted in this joint, and secured with a nail from the other side of BB.

THE MORTICE JOINT

This joint is shown complete in Fig. 20. In this case the tenon C, cut in the piece of wood B, exactly fits the mortice or hole in A.

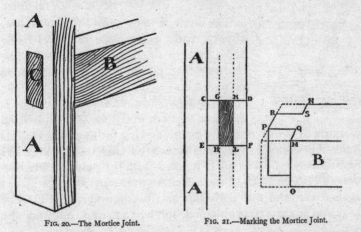

FIG. 20.—The Mortice Joint.   FIG. 21.—Marking the Mortice Joint.

Supposing A and B to be 1 in. quartering, at the distance of 1 in. from the end of B, mark the straight line MN, Fig. 21, and carry it round all four sides of the wood as partly seen at MO. Then, setting the mortice gauge to ⅓ in., mark the lines PQ and RS from the end to MN. Continue these lines down the end of the wood B, and again on the opposite side of the quartering.

Make two parallel cuts with the tenon saw along and through the wood at PQ and RS as far as the line MN. Then, turning the wood on its side, saw down the line MO as far as Q, and similarly from N to S, which will detach the pieces on each side, shown by dotted lines in the figure, and leave the tenon QPRS to fit into the mortice in A.

To cut this mortice, mark off CD and EF at 1 in. from each other in the other piece of quartering A, and continue the lines all round the wood with the morticing gauge still set at ⅓ in.; then mark the lines GH and KL, making similar lines on the opposite sides.

Working each side alternately, chisel out the shaded portion with a mortice chisel as shown in Fig. 22, until the mortice is complete and ready to receive the tenon previously cut in B.

FIG. 22.—Making a Mortice.

MITRE JOINTS

The joint A shown in Fig. 23 is very simply made, each piece of wood being sawn in turn upon the mitre block. The ends are then placed in position and glued or nailed.

When an angle other than a right angle is required, as seen in B, Fig. 23, a full-sized working drawing should be made showing the angle GFH. The lines KE and CL are then drawn parallel to GF and FH respectively, and a line FD marked from the point of intersection to F. The stock of the bevelling iron must then be placed against GF and the blade put into position against FD. The required angle is thus obtained, and when marked out upon the

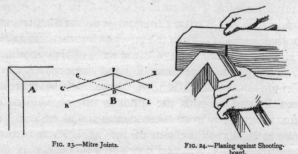

FIG. 23.—Mitre Joints.   FIG. 24.—Planing against Shooting-board.

wood, and sawn, the pieces can be placed against the shooting-board as seen in Fig. 24, and smoothed off with a trying plane.

The object of dovetailing, shown in Fig. 25, is to make a lock joint that shall prevent two pieces of wood, A and B, straining away from each other.

Supposing that A and B are each ½ in. thickness, start work on the piece B by marking a line AC, Fig. 26, with a marking gauge, the point of which is sufficiently sharp to cut the line in

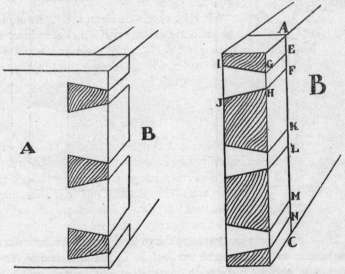

FIG. 25.—The Dovetail Joint.   FIG. 26.—Pins for Dovetail.

the wood. The line AC must be ½ in. from the end of B, and must be carried round on all four sides of the wood.

At a distance of ¼ in. from A mark the point E on the line AC, and from E measure ⅛ in. to F. Mark K ¾ in. from F, and the points L, M, N, at alternate distances of ⅛ in. and ¾ in., as seen in Fig. 26. By means of the set-square carry lines similar to EG and FH from all these points to the edge of the wood.

Fig. 27 shows the same piece of wood viewed from the other side. On the line AC mark E ³⁄₁₆ in. from A, F ¼ in. from E, G ⅜ in. from F, and so with the other points as shown in the diagram. Carry lines from these points to the edge as before, and join them across the end of the wood to those already marked on the other side and illustrated in Fig. 26.

Cut down through the thickness of the wood with the dovetail saw at IG and JH, Fig. 26, as far as the line AC, repeating this with all the other points. When this has been done remove the portions shown in shading, Fig. 26, with a chisel, thus leaving three dovetail pins.

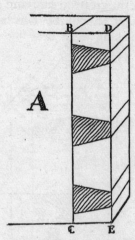

FIG. 27.—Markings for the Pins.   FIG. 28.—Sockets for Dovetail.

Upon the other piece of wood the reverse process is carried out on the side, as may be seen from Fig. 28. The gauge is run down at ½ in. as before, but on the line BC points are marked to correspond with those made in Fig. 27, whilst against DE they are made to correspond with those shown on AC, Fig. 26. The shaded parts in Fig. 28 are sawn and chiselled out, and when completed make three sockets to hold the pins already described.

The two pieces of wood can then be fitted together and glued.

FIG. 29.—The Templet.

THE TEMPLET

By using the templet shown in Fig. 29 this laborious method of marking out the wood is simplified. This templet, which can be purchased from any carpenter for a few pence, is made of some hard wood and has a flange on either side. For marking off the dovetails the templet is placed on its side, the flange against the edge of the wood, as shown in Fig. 30, and the lines struck in against the side.

All complicated work is adapted from one or other of the joints above described. The greatest care and precision should be exercised in making them neat and true, as the whole success of joinery depends upon the accurate construction of the joint employed.

FIG. 30.—Using the Templet.

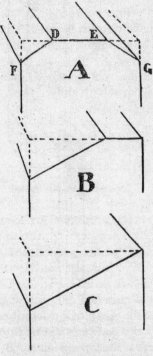

FIG. 31.—Chamfers and Bevel.

CHAMFERS AND BEVELS

The equal chamfer shown at A, Fig. 31, is made by dividing the end of the wood into three equal parts by lines at D and E. On the side of the wood are marked off F and G according to the angle required. The portions included in the dotted lines on either side are then roughed off with the drawknife and finished with the trying plane.

The unequal chamfer seen at B, Fig. 31, is made by dividing the end of the wood into two unequal portions, and then working in the same manner as above described.

To make the bevel C, Fig. 31, draw a line on the side of the wood as in the case of the chamfer, and then pare down until this line is reached and the required angle has been obtained.

HOW TO MAKE A CARPENTER'S BENCH

All joinery and carpenter's work is done upon a proper bench, which can be made according to the following instructions.

A glance at Fig. 32 will show the appearance of the bench when completed.

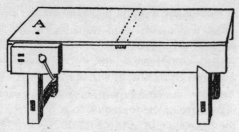

FIG. 32.—The Carpenter's Bench.

Cut three 9 in. boards of 1¼ in. stuff, each 7 ft. in length, and, after planing and smoothing, glue them together with a glue joint, and leave to dry for twenty-four hours.

Now set to work upon the four legs, which must be cut of 3 in. by 3 in. quartering in pieces 2 ft. 6 in. long. Square off both ends of each leg.

For the rails cut four lengths of 3 in. by 2 in. wood, each length measuring 2 ft. Make a dovetail pin at both ends of two of

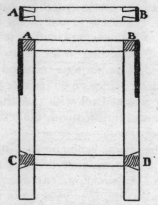

FIG. 33.—Legs and Rails for Bench.

FIG. 34.—Legs prepared for Side-board.

these pieces to fit into sockets in the legs at the top as seen at AB, Fig. 33.

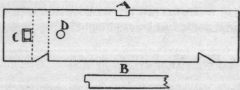

FIG. 35.—Flaps for Front Side of Bench.

The two lower rails must be morticed and wedged into the legs as seen at CD, Fig. 33.

The two flaps shown at the sides

of the bench, Fig. 32, are cut of 1 in. stuff, 7 ft. long and 9 in. wide, and are let into the legs in the following manner: cut portions from the outside of each leg as shown in black, Fig. 34, sufficiently deep to contain the flap seen in Fig. 35, and to allow it to come flush with the outside of each leg.

Before fastening them, however, in each flap cut a notch A in the centre of the top edge, to contain the centre beam B seen in the diagram and in the dotted lines in Fig. 32, which is made of 2½ in. quartering, and will extend from one side to the other beneath the top.

A bench chop and screw, Fig. 36, must now be purchased from any carpenter for about 3s. 6d. Two holes, one square, C, and the other round, D, Fig. 35, should be cut in the left-hand front of one of the flaps to receive the rod and screw of the chop, to come each side of the leg. At the same time a wooden channel or box must be fixed to the inside of the adjacent leg to contain this rod and allow it to slide backwards and forwards with ease.

Fasten the screw nut of the chop to the inside of the round hole D, insert the chop screw, and the whole contrivance will be complete.

The cross beam can now be fastened in the slots already made to receive it, and placed in position as indicated by the dotted lines. The top of the bench may then be screwed in its place.

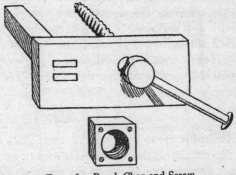

FIG. 36.—Bench Chop and Screw.

At one end of the bench, A, Fig. 32, a stop will have to be made for planing against. A large screw proves the best for this purpose, as it can be adjusted to whatever height is required.

Reprinted from *Every Boy's Book of Hobbies* by Cecil H. Bullivant, 1911.

HOW TO POLISH YOUR SHOES

You are probably wearing trainers as you read this, but there are times when only leather shoes will do – any occasion when a suit or uniform is required, for instance.

Well-polished shoes stand out from the crowd and show an attention to appearance that armed forces officers and head-masters love. The author once watched a TV documentary in which an applicant for a naval cadetship was rejected because he had not bothered to polish the back of his shoes.

Here's how to polish shoes to get a parade-ground shine. It will take time – at least two hours – but it's worth it.

Step I

Assemble the following kit: a tin of black or brown shoe polish – depending on the colour of shoes to be cleaned – of superior quality (the polish inside the tin must be moist; if it's cracked and dry reject it); an atomizer or sprayer filled with water; three soft cotton cloths or dusters; an old but stiff toothbrush.

If the shoes are dusty or dirty wet one of the cloths with water from the tap/faucet and wipe over. Dirt or mud on the heel and sole can be removed with the toothbrush. Leave to dry.

Step II

When the shoes are ready for polishing, take the kit to a comfortable chair, preferably outside or in a warm shed – but definitely away from your parents' best sofa and carpets.

Step III

Open tin and wrap clean cloth around your index finger. Dab this finger into polish and then apply to shoe in a small circular motion of about an inch in diameter. Cover both shoes with polish in this manner.

It is vitally important not to apply too much polish. To get the "mirror shine" you need to build up the polish in thin layers.

Step IV

Place the shoes somewhere warm for around three minutes to let the polish "go off". Set the nozzle of the sprayer/atomiser to a fine mist and very lightly spray the shoes all over. You only want to dampen the polish. Polish dry with the same cloth you applied the polish with.

Step V

Then apply another layer of polish with your finger pad, again let the polish go off, again dampen and again polish the shoe dry.

Step VI

Repeat step V as many times as you need. You'll know when you've finished because you'll be able to see your face in your shoes! For the ultimate effect, buff fast and light with a clean cotton cloth.

Leave the shoes somewhere cool.

That's it.

THE COMPASS

The compass is an instrument that enables the user to determine North and show the direction of any object in sight. As an instrument, the compass is simplicity itself: a freely rotating needle with a magnetized end points naturally towards magnetic north. While magnetic north is not the same as true north, it is close enough for navigational purposes.

The compass is divided into four main (cardinal) points, these being North, East, South and West. The points midway between the cardinal points are the quadrantal points, NE, SE, SW, and NW. Lying midway between the cardinal and the quadrantal points are the three-letter (intermediate) points: NNE, ENE, ESE, SSE, SSW, SSW, WSW, WNW, NNW.

As well as being divided into points, the compass is divided into 360 degrees, and it is by degrees that courses are usually set. On the compass North is marked as 0 degrees and South at 180 degrees; East is 90 degrees and West 270 degrees.

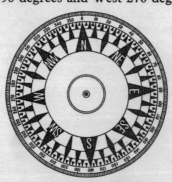

STORY: "THE LAST OF THE LIZARDS" BY EDWARD LESLIE

Professor Ward adjusted his big spectacles and wriggled forward until he was perched insecurely on the extreme edge of his chair.

"I was told to come to you as the one man in Africa likely to be able to help me," he said. "Now what can you tell me of the possibility of giant prehistoric lizards still existing in this country?"

"All things are possible in Africa," replied John Finch, the famous big-game hunter. "Why do you ask that particular question?"

"I have heard queer legends from natives in the interior, and very often there is truth at the bottom of legends."

Outside Finch's bungalow the swift African night had fallen with the suddenness of a curtain. A jackal howled at the rising moon, and from a distant hill came the threatening snarl of a leopard setting out on its night's hunting. Finch tugged at his short grey beard and his keen eyes watched the queer little man opposite. He knew that Professor Ward was one of the leading authorities on extinct fauna.

"I did once meet a man," said Finch, "who said that he had seen animals, or rather reptiles, to be giant lizards."

"Ah! Where is he? I must see him!" the Professor cried excitedly, and he wriggled in his chair like an impatient child.

"You can't; he died of fever two years ago."

"But didn't he tell people of what he had seen?"

"Yes, and they laughed at him."

"But you didn't! I am sure of that, or you would have laughed at me when I asked you. Now why didn't you laugh?"

"Because Africa is the country where impossible things are possible."

Finch rose, and going to a cupboard, took from it what appeared to be a stained piece of old ivory. The Professor snatched at the serrated piece of bone impatiently and turned it over and over in his thin hands. Plainly he did not attach much importance to it. Then something seemed to occur to him for he bent over it eagerly.

"Great fauna and flora!" he ejaculated presently. In times of stress and excitement he was given to uttering extravagant exclamations. Fumbling in his capacious pockets, he brought out a strong magnifying glass and a tape measure. He worked quickly with these for a few moments and then made almost illegible calculations on the back of an envelope. Finally he turned swiftly towards Finch, his eyes glowing with excitement behind their big lenses.

"By the great moa of New Zealand, Finch, if you didn't steal this from a museum, where did you get it?"

"What do you make of it?" countered the hunter.

"Make of it, man? Why, don't you understand that it is part of the lower jaw of no known living beast? Look! Those teeth are the teeth of a grass-chewing animal, not a flesh eater. No canine ever fitted into that empty socket. Man, man, why didn't you send me this before?" The little Professor's voice rose to a plaintive wail.

"You've reached the same conclusion that I have," replied Finch. "I couldn't trace it to any known species."

"But where did you get it?" Ward interrupted.

"From the paw of an old yellow baboon which I shot five years ago in the Chomungwe country. I have always wanted to go back there and follow up that clue," he pointed to the jawbone.

The Professor thumbed the piece of bone and shook his head slowly. Then he glanced again at the calculations on the back of the envelope.

"If it wasn't for the general scientific belief that the race of giant lizards died out several thousand years ago, I should say that this bone came from one which died only recently, because it is not a fossil, it shows very little sign of deterioration, and it would not last long in the tropics."

He pondered a moment and then suddenly made up his mind.

"Will you lead an expedition to the Chomungwe country, and investigate this clue?" he asked Finch.

"I should like nothing better," the hunter replied quickly.

"I wonder," added the Professor thoughtfully, "if we shall be the first men to see what the general public would call a prehistoric animal?"

"Only time will answer that," said Finch.

It was indeed a matter of time. The expedition had to be equipped, and when this was satisfactorily accomplished all the baggage was sent westward by rail for three hundred miles. Thereafter motor-cars and lorries conveyed the explorers a further hundred and fifty odd miles. Then the road ended, and since the country was unsuitable for wheeled traffic, native porters were employed. Tents, bedding, stores, kitchen utensils, ammunition, and much scientific apparatus belonging to the Professor all had to be made up into loads of about fifty pounds weight. These loads were carried on the woolly heads of the porters.

Early one glorious morning, when the first rays of the sun were just creeping above the horizon, the long line of men swung out along the trail. For three weeks they marched, through sand and mud, through heat and rain, until finally one evening they came to the edge of the Chomungwe country. Before them stretched range upon range of huge mountains, their jagged peaks silhouetted against a black and crimson sunset.

Thereafter progress became slow. The atmosphere was hot and moist, and in the valleys the vegetation was so thick that the porters were obliged to cut a path through the tangled growth. This country was seldom visited by white men and even natives were few in number. For several days the expedition wound its laborious way along the stifling valleys and across the low passes that led over the ranges, until at last they reached the spot where Finch had shot the yellow baboon five years previously. Here, when they had ascended a short way up a mountainside, they pitched a permanent camp on a convenient plateau, intending to explore the surrounding country.

Accompanied by two natives, they started before dawn.

And what a country it was! Even the Professor, who was seldom enthusiastic about anything except giant lizards, remarked that the great tangle of peaks and ridges reminded him of a rough sea which had suddenly become frozen. For weeks they probed into hidden and mysterious valleys and ascended to summits that had never before felt the foot of man. Game abounded, and because no man had ever shot there, it was extraordinarily tame. Apes, shy creatures that kept to the forests, they also saw, but none carried a mysterious jaw-bone. The Professor was undaunted by their lack of success.

"We don't expect them to come and meet us," he cried in answer to Finch's remark that the lizards, if any, must be securely hidden. "After all, if they roamed about freely someone else might have discovered them by now. No, we must search very deeply if we are to succeed."

"All right," Finch agreed. "Tomorrow we will climb the Big Twin and get a bird's-eye view, so that we can see if we have missed any valley that looks promising."

The Big Twin was one of a pair of mountain-peaks that stood close together and were so similar in appearance that the explorers had named them the Big and Little Twin.

They started in the grey light that precedes the dawn, accompanied by two natives who carried ropes and the Professor's camera. The climb was not difficult, and presently the trees thinned out, giving place to rocks and slopes of loose scree. The Professor picked up a piece of rock and examined it short-sightedly.

"H'm!" he grunted. "Volcanic origin."

At length they reached the summit, which, although above the treeline, was not sufficiently high to have snow upon it. Nevertheless it was chilly after the heat of the valleys, and both men shivered in the rarefied air. Finch consulted the rough sketch map he had made, and patiently they identified the valleys which they had already explored, making a note of those which they had yet to penetrate. Presently Finch turned to look at the Little Twin which reared its stony head some six miles away. It was connected to the Big Twin by a saddle which they had already noticed from the camp. But the hunter found that it was impossible to see the saddle from above for it was obscured by a low grey cloud.

They decided to descend the Big Twin, cross the saddle, and climb Little Twin from whence they could obtain a better view of the country beyond. After descending a few hundred feet, they entered the grey cloud and for a while groped their way through damp mist. Then they emerged on the saddle itself. For some distance it ran level before it rose in a long slope that led to the top of Little Twin. Yet they had not advanced half a mile before they came to the edge of a steep cliff.

Finch peered over. The cliffs were almost sheer, but he could not see the bottom because of a greyish-white fog that rolled slowly about the rocks. A warm, moist air rose up from the depths, and mingled with it was the smell of decaying vegetation.

The little Professor sniffed.

"H'm!" he grunted. "Volcanic crater. Extinct, of course. Curious, though, this heat rising. Perhaps there are hot springs down there. Let's go and see."

"What! Climb down that?" cried Finch, indicating the precipitous cliffs.

"Why not? We've got ropes. The boys can lower us. If we walk round the edge we might find an easier place to descend."

Not wishing to admit that the little Professor had more courage than he, the hunter agreed. Presently they came to a spot where a recent landslide had made a comparatively easy

The reptile began to move slowly towards them.

slope. Accompanied by the boys they scrambled down, entered the greyish vapour, which was more like steam than fog, and groped their way through it. Presently it cleared and they found themselves at the edge of a steep declivity, gazing at a strange landscape flooded with a curious half-light, due to the sunlight filtering through the fog.

Finch and the Professor stared in amazement. A long way below them was a huge sheet of water, the far side of which was hidden in mist. From the surface rose tiny spirals of white vapour. At their feet was a beach composed of grey sand, while about the foot of the cliff curled and twisted a narrow belt of vegetation.

"Never seen such a place in my life," exclaimed Finch.

"It will look better from close quarters," retorted the Professor. "Come along, we can use the ropes now."

They attached one end to a convenient rock, and went down the steep cliff hand over hand, leaving the two natives to wait for them at the top. Presently, after much scrambling and a considerable amount of puffing on the part of the Professor, they managed to fight their way through the tangled undergrowth and stepped out on to the grey sand.

A strange, forbidding silence hung over the lake. Their voices echoed curiously from the towering cliffs, and unconsciously they spoke in whispers. The heat was intense. Not the burning heat of the upper world, but a stuffy, moist heat which seemed to make breathing difficult. In a few minutes both of them were soaked in perspiration.

The lake was as smooth as a piece of glass. At the foot of the cliffs the rope-like stems of strange plants were twisted about each other in inextricable confusion. Giant ferns, twelve and fifteen feet high, pushed their green shoots through a mass of luxuriant undergrowth.

Suddenly the Professor raised a lean forefinger.

"Look, Finch, just to the right of that big grey boulder. Do you see where the undergrowth has been crushed flat?"

"Yes."

"Well, what has crushed it flat? That means there are animals in the crater, surely?"

"You're right," replied the hunter, and promptly slipped a clip of cartridges into the magazine of his rifle. "By Jove, we might be in another world down here."

"I believe we are in another world," the Professor replied seriously. "Much of this vegetation is strange to me, and I've seen some queer plants in my travels."

They turned and walked towards the edge of the lake. It was impossible to see very far across it because of the spirals of vapour that circled slowly upwards towards the ceiling of mist. The whole place looked ghostly and mysterious. Quite suddenly a long whistling sigh reached their ears. It was a curious noise that seemed to come from every quarter of the compass.

"What on earth was that?" gasped the Professor.

Finch, peering this way and that, shook his head.

"Give it up," he answered. "You know, this place isn't good for any one with nerves."

"Well, I haven't got any," snapped the Professor. "Have you?"

"No."

"Then let's go nearer the lake."

At the edge the hunter stooped and tasted the water. It was slightly brackish and warm. A few yards from the shore they could see masses of yellow weed floating. Suddenly the eerie whistle sounded again, and the Professor jumped.

"Thought you had no nerves," remarked Finch.

"Fool!" The little man flung out an arm. "Look! That's what made me jump. What is it?"

The hunter followed the outstretched finger and saw, lying on the surface of the water, a flat black object that looked rather like a crocodile. Before he had time to examine it through glasses the impetuous Professor had picked up a stone and hurled it in the direction of the object.

At the sound of the splash the dark thing rose out of the water and looked inquiringly in their direction. The flat black object proved to be a long narrow head supported on a swan-like neck. The Professor gasped.

"We've found them! We've found the giant lizards!"

"Unless it's a big snake," suggested Finch cautiously.

But the Professor did not hear. He wanted to see more of this strange creature, and to arouse its curiosity he flung another stone.

The reptile began to move slowly towards them. The water at the edge of the lake was shallow and presently the whole of the strange animal was visible. Its narrow flat head, something like a python's in shape, was small and out of all proportion to its body. This was almost bloated in comparison, greyish in colour and mottled with lighter patches. The legs were short with webbed feet, but it moved on land with surprising ease. It had a thick tail rather like that of a crocodile.

It came so close to the two men that they could see the short bristling whiskers about the large mouth and the tiny pig-eyes with which it regarded them.

"Great fauna and flora!" the Professor cried, hopping on one foot in his excitement, "it's the ninth wonder of the world! D'you realise, Finch, we're the only human beings who have ever set eyes on a creature like this?"

As if in reply, the monster lowered its head and emitted that ghostly whistling sigh which they had previously heard. The silence which followed was eerie.

The lizard came closer. When its neck was vertical its small head was fully fifteen feet from the ground. The water ran in streams off its rounded body.

Frantically the Professor had unslung his camera and was now manœuvring for a good position. The lizard quietly watched him, but when with a crow of delight the little man announced that he had obtained a photograph, it turned swiftly about and rushed into the water in a flurry of foam, quickly disappearing beneath the surface.

"Probably thought you were trying to sing," remarked Finch, as the Professor "Tchk, tchked" with annoyance.

"Fool!" retorted the little man witheringly.

They walked farther along the narrow beach, avoiding the great masses of vegetation at the foot of the cliffs, and they had not gone far before they came upon another of the monsters. This one was lighter in colour and not quite so large. It was feeding peacefully upon the weeds which floated in tangled masses on the surface of the lake. It stared at the intruders for a moment, water dripping from its muzzle, then quietly continued its feeding. Even when the Professor waded waist-deep into the water and took another photograph, it only paused to watch him.

The Professor trotted out of the lake looking like a pleased spaniel.

"Got him!" he cried. "With weed hanging from his mouth. Snakes and scorpions, Finch, this will make 'em sit up at home!"

They now proceeded along the beach to a point where the undergrowth reached the edge of the lake. Here another surprise awaited them, for, as they approached, a long snake-like head and neck rose from the ground to be followed by a huge, rotund body until the whole of the lizard stood facing them. They halted, and suddenly Finch's keen eyes detected something moving in the undergrowth by the lizard's side. Four smaller heads were thrust inquiringly upward.

"My hat, Professor, this one's got young!" cried the hunter.

The little man quivered with excitement as he adjusted his camera.

The Professor, still clutching his camera, felt himself borne aloft.

"Must photograph 'em, must photograph 'em," he cried. "Make a perfectly priceless picture. What fortunate mortals we are!"

He ran forward, peering with his short-sighted eyes into the view-finder. The giant lizard lowered its flat head threateningly and gave a warning snort.

"Look out!" Finch cried. "She thinks you are going to attack her young."

But the Professor was too engrossed to take heed of warnings, for he was anxious to take a close-up photograph of mother and young. The lizard, however, had other ideas. With incredible swiftness for such an ungainly brute, it lurched forward and shot out its long neck. Quite suddenly the Professor found that the image in the view-finder was obscured. He looked up with a frown of annoyance to see the head of the lizard a few feet above him.

Twenty yards away Finch slipped back the safety-catch of his rifle, but he dared not fire lest he should hit the Professor. For an instant man and monster stared at each other. Then the lizard's head swooped down, and, catching the little Professor in its jaws, it wheeled round and made for the lake.

The Professor, still clutching his camera, felt himself borne aloft. He had a momentary glimpse of Finch's amazed face below him. The lizard held the little man across the body in a grip that was firm but not painful. Looking down, Ward saw the water beneath him and the young lizards following their mother like puppies out for a walk.

"If Finch doesn't do something soon," he thought, "this brute will drown me."

And Finch did do something. He raised his rifle, and taking careful aim at the lizard's eye, fired.

The Professor dimly heard the shot, and the next instant he felt the monster check its course. Then its jaws opened and he fell twelve feet into the brackish water with a resounding splash. Finch, lowering his rifle, gave a sigh of relief, for it had been a tricky shot and he might easily have hit the Professor, who was now swimming sturdily for the shore, one hand holding aloft the precious camera.

But the effects of that shot were manifold. While the lizard thrashed its tail in agony, staining the water with its blood, and the echoes of the shot reverberated from the cliffs, a low, muffled roar began, which gradually increased in volume until it filled the crater with a vibrating ear-splitting torrent of sound. The ground on which the two men stood trembled.

"What is it?" shouted the Professor, water running off him in streams.

"Feels like an earthquake," replied Finch. "Keep clear of the cliffs."

They stood by the side of the lake, peering this way and that through the mist. Occasionally they saw a dim, monstrous shape hurrying past. The roaring noise grew louder until the hunter had to put his mouth to the Professor's ear in order to make himself heard.

Finch and the Professor swarmed up the rope.

"Look!" he bellowed, and pointed to the lake.

The water was rapidly sinking. Even as they looked the edge of it vanished into the mists, leaving behind wet grey mud and heaps of yellowish green weeds. At the same instant the roaring redoubled in volume. The mist turned to steam almost too hot to bear, and showers of sand and small stones fell round the two men. They stood side by side, dazed, bewildered, unable to see ten yards in any direction and not knowing where to move for safety.

Gradually the roaring died away until an eerie silence had taken its place. The two men looked at each other questioningly.

"Come on," said Finch. "Let's beat it. This place is unhealthy."

They retraced their steps, and, by means of shouting, eventually discovered the terrified natives. They swarmed up the rope and made their way back to the saddle. Over the Twins hung a thick mantle of mist through which they had to grope their way to camp.

An hour later the Professor came out of his tent almost in tears. In his right hand he held a blotched and stained strip of photographic film.

"Not a picture," he moaned. "Not one. All ruined by water."

It was a fortnight before the fog vanished from the Twins and they were able to get a clear view into the crater. No trace of the lake remained, only a sheet of baked mud interlaced by cracks and grey rocks. Of the lizards there was not a sign.

"That's where they went," Finch said to the despondent Professor, pointing to a gaping hole in the middle of the crater. "The lake drained out through that – went underground and took the lizards with it."

The Professor nodded gloomily.

"Not a single thing to show as evidence of what we have seen," he said. "We'd have been famous and science would have benefited if you hadn't fired that shot."

"This time it's you who are the fool," Finch retorted. "If I hadn't fired I should have had to have furnished the newspapers with a graphic account of your death. Don't be ungrateful."

"Tchk, tchk," replied the little man. "I'm not. You know that." He indicated the crater. "But what are we going to say about this adventure?"

"If you'll take my advice you'll say nothing, unless you want to be branded as the biggest liar that ever came out of Africa."

"I suppose you're right," the Professor agreed.

Which is why the story has never been told until to-day.

First published in *Modern Wonders for Boys*, circa 1938.

FIGHTER ACES OF THE WORLD

An "ace" is generally taken to be a fighter pilot who has shot down five or more enemy aircraft. The greatest fighter aces in history, together with their number of "kills", are:

First World War

Germany/Austria-Hungary

Manfred von Richthofen (Germany) 80
Ernst Udet (Germany) 62
Erich Loewenhardt (Germany) 53
Werner Voss (Germany) 48
Fritz Rumey (Germany) 45
A selection of others:
Oswald Boelcke (Germany) 40
Lothar von Richthofen (Germany) 40
Godwin Brumowski (Aus) 35
Herman Goering (Ger) 22

Allies – France/Belgium, Great Britain, Italy, Russia, Canada, Australia, USA

René Fonck (Fra). 75
William A. Bishop (Can) 72
Raymond Collishaw (Can) 62 (possibly 60)
Edward Mannock (GB) 61 (possibly 73)
James McCudden (GB) 57

Others:
Georges Guynemer (Fr) 54 (possibly 53)
A. Beauchamp-Proctor (SA) 54
Albert Ball (GB) 47 (possibly 44)
Francesco Baracca (Ita) 34
Willy Coppens (Bel) 37
Edward Rickenbacker (US) 26
S.C. Rosevear (US) 23
Alexander Kazakov (Russia) 17

Spanish Civil War

Joaquin Morato Y Castano (Spa) 40
Others:
Stephan Suprun (USSR) 15
Werner Moelders (Ger) 15 [plus 101 WWII]
Frank Tinker (US) 7 (possibly 8)

Second World War

*Axis Powers – Germany, Austria, Hungary,
Rumania, Italy, Japan*

Erich Hartman (Ger) 352
Gerhard Barkhorn (Ger) 301
Gunther Rall (Ger) 275
Otto Kittel (Ger) 267
Walter Nowotny (Ger) 258
Others:
Johannes Steinhoff (Ger) 176
Hans-Joachim Marseille (Ger) 158
Hiroyshi Nishizawa (Jap) c.110
Adolf Galland (Ger) 104
Tetsuzo Iwamoto (Jap) 80
Constantine Cantacuzine (Rum) 60
Adriano Visconti (Ita) 26

Allies – France, Great Britain & Empire, USA, USSR

Ivan Kozuhedub (USSR) 62
Aleksandr I. Pokryshkin (USSR) 59

Richard Bong (US) 40
Mato Dubovak (Yugoslavia) 40
Thomas McGuire (US) 38
Others:
James E. Johnson (GB) 38 (possibly 36)
Pierre Clostermann (Fr) 36
Adolf "Sailor" Malan (South Africa) 35
Brendan E. Finucane (GB) 32
Clive Caldwell (Aus) 28
Douglas Bader (GB) 23

Korea

United Nations

Joseph McConnell (US) 16
James Jabara (US) 16
Manuel J. Fernandez (US) 14
George Davies (US) 14
Royal N. Baker (US) 13.5

North Korea & Allies

Nicolai V. Sutyagin (USSR) 22
Yevgeny G. Pepelyaev (USSR) 19
Alexandr Smortzkow (USSR) 15
L.K. Schukin (USSR) 15 (possibly 14)
Others:
Chszao Bao-tun (China) 9
Kam Den Dek (North Korea) 8

Vietnam

United Nations

Randy Cunningham (US) 5
Robin Olds (US) 5 (plus 12 WWII)

North Vietnam & Allies

Nguyen Toon (North Vietnam) 13
Nguyen Van Coc (North Vietnam) 9

MAKE A FOLDING-WING DELTA GLIDER

From earliest times Man has longed to fly. Many are the legends and stories of attempts to emulate bird flight with the aid of home-made wings. Birdmen actually have achieved some sort of flight with wings strapped to their back, but they have had to rely on a parachute to ensure that the last part of their journey to earth was a reasonably safe one. This model does rather better than that, for it will make smooth, gliding descents as well as other types of model aircraft.

The "birdman" is a Folding-Wing Delta Glider, with the fuselage or body shaped like a human body rather than an aeroplane fuselage. Construction is not difficult and performance is remarkably consistent, provided you ensure that the wing hinges work freely.

Using the full-size plan on page 88 cut out the wing panel pattern from *heavyweight* model aeroplane tissue (the plan shows only *half* the complete panel, so use the pattern on a *folded* piece of tissue to cut the complete panel in one go). Cut the fin from ⅟₁₆-in. sheet balsa. Also cut the ¾-in. length of ⅜-in. square hardwood for the hinge block and drill two holes as shown about ⅟₁₆-in. diameter. The hinge pieces are cut from any thin metal, such as tin, or thin aluminium sheet (*note:* many modern "tins" are now made from aluminium sheet instead of tin-plate).

The wing panels are shown in the second diagram on page 89. Mark out on ⅟₁₆-in. sheet balsa and cut two identical pieces. Score down the line shown, without cutting right through the wood, and round off the tips slightly with sandpaper. The balsa wing panels are then cemented to the tissue centre panel, as

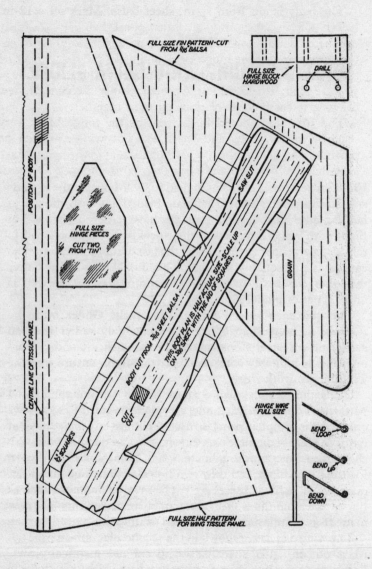

FULL SIZE FIN PATTERN–CUT FROM 1/16 BALSA

FULL SIZE HINGE BLOCK HARDWOOD

DRILL

POSITION OF BODY

FULL SIZE HINGE PIECES CUT TWO FROM 'TIN'

SAW SLIT

GRAIN

BODY CUT FROM 3/16 SHEET BALSA

THIS BODY PLAN IS HALF ACTUAL SIZE. SCALE UP ON 3/16 SHEET WITH THE AID OF SQUARES.

CENTRE LINE OF TISSUE PANEL

CUT OUT

1/2 SQUARES

HINGE WIRE FULL SIZE

BEND LOOP

BEND UP

BEND DOWN

FULL SIZE HALF PATTERN FOR WING TISSUE PANEL

shown in the smaller sketch, so that the pointed ends are ¼-in. apart.

The body is cut from ³⁄₁₆-in. sheet balsa. Mark off a 12-in. length of ³⁄₁₆-in. sheet in ½-in. squares and then copy the body outline on. Cut out with a fretsaw or modelling knife. Also cut out the square for the hinge block and make the slit with a fine saw. After bending two wire hinge pieces to the shape shown, you are ready to assemble the model. Study the general view drawing to see how the various parts fit together.

The first step should be to cement the hinge block very securely in the body, and let it set. The wing can then be positioned by sliding the tissue along the slot in the body. Make sure that you have got the wing even both sides and the front

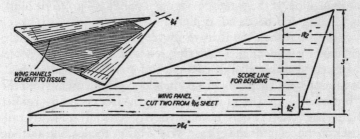

"points" lining up with the hinge block and then lightly cement the edges of the slot top and bottom.

Slip the hinge wires in the hinge block and check that they lie snugly against the front edge of each wing. Then secure by wrapping the metal hinge pieces around the wire. Dimple the metal lightly with pliers to grip the wing panels and check that the wire is still free enough to allow the wing to be twisted about the hinge.

Crack the wing panels along the score lines and bend each tip up ¼ in. Cement coat these cracks for strength. Finally, cement the fin to the right-hand side of the body. The wings should fold neatly flat against the body if they are folded back and also twisted so that the *top* surface of each balsa panel comes against the body. The tissue panel should be folded up neatly *between* the balsa wing panel and body on each side.

A rubber band fastened to the "loop" end of each hinge wire, and, passing around the front of the body, normally holds the wings in the open position. A 5-in. long thread band is about right for this, or two 2½- or 3-in. thread bands tied together.

The band should be strong enough to "snap" the wings open from the folded position but not so strong as to strain the tissue.

Now check the flying trim of your model. Hand launch like any other glider and see if any adjustment is required. If the "birdman" dives, bend the tips of each wing up a little more. If it stalls, bend the tips down slightly, or add a little weight to the nose. A sharp turn in one direction can be cured by warping the fin in the opposite direction.

You can then give the wing-folding mechanism a check. Fold the wings back and hold the model by the wing tips, grasped between thumb and forefinger, and hand launch in a normal manner. The wings should snap open *together* long before the model reaches the ground, so that the "birdman" goes into a normal glide. If the wings do not open *simultaneously*, one hinge is binding and needs adjusting.

Your "birdman" is then ready for flying outdoors, using a catapult for launching. This is simply a 6-in. length of stout dowel with a strong rubber band tied to one end. Instead of a band a 16-in. length of ¼-in. strip rubber tied in a loop can be used. Hold the "birdman" with wings folded and loop the free end of the rubber under the "chin". Point the model nearly vertically upwards, pull back on the catapult and release. With a little practice, and a strong catapult, you should be able to launch your "birdman" to well over 100 feet and at the top of the climb the wings will snap open for the model to descend in gliding flight.

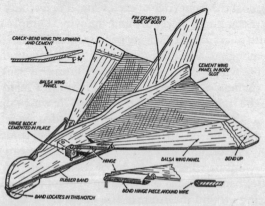

Designed by R.H. Warring. Originally published in *Boy's Own Companion No. 2*, edited by Jack Cox, 1960

FLAGS

The Union Flag

The Union Flag is the flag of Great Britain, and combines the three crosses, of St George, St Andrew and St Patrick. It should always be flown as seen below, with the broad white band on the diagonal arms in the left-hand corner uppermost. The flag, which was adopted in 1606 and took its present form in 1801, should only be called the "Union Jack" when it is flown from the jackstaff of one of her Her Majesty's ships.

The Flag of the USA

The Flag of the United States of America consists of thirteen equal-sized red and white stripes, with a blue rectangle in the canton (the upper hoist quarter) bearing fifty small white stars. The thirteen stripes represent the original thirteen colonies which rebelled against British rule and the stars stand for the fifty US states. The flag is popularly known as the "stars and stripes" or "Old Glory".

The Flag of Canada

The Canadian flag is a vertical triband of red-white-red. In the central pale band is set a red maple leaf – hence the flag's popular name of "The Maple Leaf". The flag was adopted in 1965.

The Flag of Australia

The Australian National Flag is an adapted blue ensign with the Union Jack in the canton. In the quarter below the canton is a large white star representing the British Commonwealth of which Australia is a member. The right-hand half of the flag consists of stars representing the Southern Cross constellation. The flag was adopted in 1954.

The Flag of the Republic of South Africa

The current flag of the Republic of South Africa was intended only as an interim flag to be flown during the country's first non-racial elections in 1994; however, the flag was so popular that it was formally adopted as the permanent national flag in the South African Constitution.

The South Africa flag has horizontal bands of red (on top)

and blue (on the bottom), separated by a central green band which splits into a horizontal "Y" shape, the arms of which end at the corners of the staff side of the flag. The Y embraces a gold V which in turn embraces a black triangle. The red and blue bands are separated from the outside of the Y by thin white bands. The South African flag is the only national flag in the world with six colours. These colours are deeply symbolic: the red stands for the history of blood spilled in South Africa in the years of apartheid, the racial system by which a white minority denied democracy to the country's mainly black population; the green, black and gold are colours from the flag of the African National Congress, the main opposition to apartheid; the blue and white come from the old South African flag, the "Prinsevlag". The new South African flag is therefore a unity of the two South African traditions.

The Flag of New Zealand

Like the flag of Australia, the flag of New Zealand is an adapted blue ensign with the Union Jack in the upper hoist quarter; against the blue background the New Zeland flag contains four red stars with white borders to the right. The stars represent the Southern Cross constellation, as seen from New Zealand.

The Flag of China

Adopted by the communist People's Republic of China in 1949, the Chinese national flag consists of a large yellow star to the left of an arc of four smaller yellow stars in the canton of a red flag. The flag is flown in mainland China, Hong Kong and Macau.

Red is the colour historically associated with communism, but also here symbolizes the blood shed by the Chinese communists during the revolution of the 1940s. The large yellow star signifies the leadership of the Communist Party.

The Flag of Russia

The flag of the Russian Federation is a tricolour of three equal horizontal bands: white at the top, blue in the middle and red at the bottom. The flag became officially adopted in 1896 but was discontinued after the Russian Revolution of 1917. For the period of the Union of Soviet Socialist Republics a red flag of various forms flew instead of the tricolour. With the fall of the communist USSR in 1991 the tricolour returned as the official flag of the Russian Federation.

JACK TRAVERS CORNWELL:
THE BOY VC BY ALISTAIR MACLEAN

Jack Travers Cornwell won Britain's highest award for valour, the Victoria Cross, during the naval battle of Jutland in 1916. He was only sixteen himself at the time. Cornwell was a gunner aboard the light cruiser HMS Chester. *Here Alistair MacLean tells the story of the youngest person ever to be awarded the VC.*

On 30 May 1916, Admiral Jellicoe, the British commander-in-chief, received information from the Admiralty that the German Battle Cruiser Squadron, under Admiral Hipper, had put to sea, and was instructed to steam out with the Grand Fleet to intercept it. Accordingly he ordered his ships to get under way and instructed Admiral Beatty, commander of the battle cruiser squadrons, to put out from Rosyth and steam on sixty-five miles ahead of the main body of the fleet. Both the battle and the battle cruiser fleet were to proceed in the direction of Heligoland Bight until 2 p. m. on 31 May when, if no enemy had been encountered, Beatty was to effect visual contact with Jellicoe's ships and the combined forces were to make a sweep towards the Horn's Reef before returning to their bases.

The *Chester* was attached to the Third Battle Cruiser Squadron under Admiral Hood. With her consorts she took up a position some twenty miles ahead of the main body of the Grand Fleet, and it was the task of these ships to scout ahead and report the presence of the enemy to the British flagship, *Iron Duke*.

All through the night of the 30th, the mighty armada steamed down the North Sea in the agreed direction, but nothing occurred to excite any suspicion. An occasional steamer was stopped and examined, for the British had to be on constant guard against enemy scouts disguised as trawlers or merchant ships.

Meanwhile Beatty, in a position about seventy miles south of the battle fleet, had met with no better luck. At 2 p.m. on the 31st he had still sighted no enemy, and was just about to give orders for his battle cruisers to turn north and join up with the Grand Fleet as arranged when the *Galatea*, one of his cruiser screen, announced the appearance of smoke on the horizon and set off to investigate. Twenty minutes later she signalled "Enemy in sight" and reported that she could see two cruisers bearing E.S.E. At 2.28 p.m. she opened fire, and Beatty seeing his cruiser screen engaged moved up in support. Although he did not know it at the time the enemy ships that had been sighted were the scouting cruisers attached to the German Battle Cruiser Squadron which was following them up behind, and consequently it was not long before the two battle cruiser forces came to grips.

Hipper, being inferior in gun power and ships to the British, immediately turned about and retraced his steps: coming up some fifty miles behind him was the German High Seas Fleet, and the German admiral saw a good chance of leading Beatty into a trap. By 3.45 p.m. the British ships, with their superior speed, had got within range of the German battle cruisers and Beatty ordered his squadron to form line on a course E.S.E. in order to get his guns to bear on the enemy. Seeing this, the Germans opened fire and in a few minutes the British ships were replying.

Steaming through giant columns of water and spray from each other's shell fire, both fleets hurled masses of metal across the eleven miles that separated them. The firing at first was a little erratic, but soon improved, and in the first ten minutes the Germans had scored hits both on the *Lion* and *Tiger*. At 4.00 p.m. first blood was drawn. The *Indefatigable*, the last ship in the British line, was hit by a salvo from the German ship *Von der Tann*. A burst of flame and smoke hid her completely from view, and she staggered out of the line sinking fast by the stern.

A moment later a second salvo hit her; another terrible explosion rent the ship and she turned over and sank. In a few minutes all trace of this great cruiser was gone.

Twenty-six minutes later another disaster befell the British. The *Queen Mary* was struck by a salvo on her forward deck. A huge pillar of smoke ascended to the sky and she sank bow first taking with her a crew of fifty-seven officers and 1,209 men.

At 4.33 p.m. Commodore Goodenough, commanding the Second Light Cruiser Squadron in the *Southampton*, disposed some miles ahead of the battle cruisers, reported that battleships were in sight to the S.S.E., and a few minutes later the dim outlines of the German High Seas Fleet were visible. Beatty could not hope to engage such a large force with any success so, at 4.40 p.m., he gave the order for his ships to turn sixteen points to the N.W. from which direction he knew the Grand Fleet was steaming with all haste to his aid.

Meanwhile in the British battle fleet there was great excitement. The *Galatea*'s signals heralding the opening of the battle cruiser action had been received in the *Iron Duke* at 2.20 p.m. Although these messages only indicated the presence of enemy light cruisers, Jellicoe ordered full steam to be raised in case of emergency, but did not increase his speed. Later reports, however, made it evident that serious action was impending, and at 2.55 p.m. he ordered his light cruisers to take up a position sixteen miles ahead and altered his course S.E. by S. At 3.30 p.m. an urgent message was received from the *Lion* informing Jellicoe that the German battle cruisers had been sighted, and a further report twenty-five minutes later told him that the action had begun.

Jellicoe at once ordered speed to be increased to twenty knots and sent the Third Battle Cruiser Squadron with the light cruisers *Chester* and *Canterbury* on in all haste to reinforce the battle cruiser fleet.

According to the Official History of the War (Naval Operations, Vol. III), "The *Invincible* in which Admiral Hood's flag was flying was then about twenty-five miles on the port bow of the *Iron Duke*, and a little ahead of station, for when at 3.15 p.m. Admiral Hood heard from the *Galatea* of the enemy's light cruisers coming northward, he had inclined to the eastward at twenty-two knots to head them off. Half an hour later, when he knew they had turned to the southward, he altered back to S. 26 E., and when the welcome order came to push ahead he was about forty-three miles from the position the *Lion* had given S. by W. of him. But as he had no margin of speed there was little hope of overtaking Admiral Beatty on that course. He had therefore altered to S.S.E. . . . and sped away at twenty-five knots."

When the order came through to push ahead young Cornwell in the *Chester*, together with the rest of the gun crew, was ordered to take up his position at the forward gun. The prospect of an early encounter with the enemy must have produced a strange mixture of emotions in him as he scanned the horizon in search of the German ships. But the sight of the other ships of his squadron, smoke pouring from their funnels, their bows cutting through the waters of the North Sea like knives, sending up huge bow waves as they rushed southwards, must have filled his heart with pride and confidence.

The squadron was steaming in line ahead with the destroyers *Shark, Christopher, Ophelia* and *Acasta* disposed ahead as a submarine screen and the *Chester* and *Canterbury* scouting five miles ahead of the destroyers. The visibility was decreasing rapidly, and by five o'clock objects could be distinguished at a distance of sixteen thousand yards in some directions, but in others at only two thousand yards.

At 5.30 p.m. the sound of gunfire was plainly heard by the *Chester* to the S.W. and she immediately turned in that direction to investigate. Six minutes later she sighted a three-funnelled light cruise-on her starboard bow, accompanied by one or two destroyers. She immediately challenged but, receiving no reply closed with them. A moment or so later two more light cruisers appeared out of the mist astern of the first and the leading enemy ship opened fire on the *Chester*.

Cornwell was stationed at the forward gun. Fixed across his head and over his ears was what is known as a telepad, a sort of telephone, which was connected up with the fire control officer. Through this instrument came all the instructions for the gun crew – orders as to when and how to fire. Cornwell, as sight-setter, had a very important task to perform for upon him more than anyone else depended the accuracy of his gun's aim. When he received his orders from the gunnery officer he had to make certain adjustments to the mechanism of the gun. In front of him was a brass disc, pinned through the centre, and in some respects resembling a telephone dial. This disc was calibrated in yards, and as it was turned it raised and lowered the gun's muzzle, thus altering the range. It was essentially a job that required coolness and presence of mind. Moreover, the position in which Cornwell was obliged to stand in order to carry out his duties without interfering with the work of the gun crew, was almost entirely exposed. It was on the left-hand side of the gun just by the side of the protective shield.

The visibility at the time the enemy opened fire could not have been more than eight thousand yards, i.e. about four and a half miles, which, in naval warfare, amounts almost to point blank range, and from the moment the fight began the forward turret of the *Chester* received the full force of the enemy's fire. One by one the gun crew, consisting of ten men, fell, struck by splinters of shell, until only two were left. But still young Cornwell stood calmly at his post, never flinching, ready to carry out his orders. The enemy's fourth salvo scored a direct hit and put the gun port right out of action. It also mortally wounded Cornwell.

All alone, with practically no shelter from the fierce tornado of enemy fire, he stood. All around him lay the dead and dying. He himself was torn and bleeding and faint from the pain and horror of the sights and sounds of battle. His job was done, his gun was no longer capable of firing, no orders came through the wire from the control room; they could not have been carried out even if they had, but through his mind echoed the old naval order "a gun must be kept firing so long as there is one man left who is able to crawl." So he hung on. He thought he might be needed; it was his duty to remain at his post until he dropped.

Captain Lawson of the *Chester*, as soon as he realized the superiority of the force to which he was opposed, altered his course to the N.E. and towards the Third Battle Cruiser Squadron. This incident is vividly described by the Naval History of the War in the following words:

The *Chester* seemed doomed, but rescue was at hand. Directly Admiral Hood heard the firing abaft his starboard beam he swung round north-west (5.37). As the German cruisers were closing to the eastward the courses quickly converged. In a few minutes our battle cruisers could see emerging from the mist the *Chester* zigzagging in a storm of shell splashes that were drenching her. A minute later her eager pursuers came suddenly into view. Immediately they saw their danger they swung round to starboard on the opposite course to Admiral Hood, but it was too late. As they passed his guns crashed into them, while the *Chester* escaped across the *Invincible*'s bows, firing her last shots as she ran northward into safety. As for Admiral Boedicker, he only escaped the twelve-inch salvoes that were smothering him by recourse to his torpedoes. To avoid them Admiral Hood had to turn away, and the enemy was soon lost in the mist, but not before the *Wiesbaden* was a wreck and both the *Pillau* and *Frankfurt* badly hit.

The *Chester* then took up a station to the north-east of the Third Battle Cruiser Squadron, and at a later stage in the action joined the Second Cruiser Squadron.

During the unequal action between the *Chester* and the enemy light cruisers, which proved to belong to the German Second Scouting Group under Admiral Boedicker, the ship had suffered considerable casualties, having thirty-one killed and fifty wounded. Three guns and her fire control circuits were disabled, and she had four shell holes in her side just above the water line. But damaged as she was, she was still in fighting condition.

Cornwell had remained at his post throughout the whole action, and he was still standing there when the British battle cruisers drew off the enemy fire. When the fight was over the wounded were carried below, but it soon became apparent to the doctors that there was little hope of saving the brave young gunner's life. They bandaged his wounds, and made him as comfortable as possible, and although he must have been in terrible agony, he bore his suffering like a man and never complained.

Throughout the evening, and at intervals during the night the battle continued. The *Invincible* was struck by a salvo and sank, taking with her the gallant Admiral Hood and all but a few of her officers and men. But when the Grand Fleet came to grips with the High Seas Fleet the enemy were forced to flee. They were cut off from their ports, and twice they tried to break through the rear of the British Fleet and twice they failed. At last, under the cover of darkness they succeeded. Admiral Scheer, the German commander-in-chief had handled his fleet magnificently against superior forces, and the way that he extricated his ships from a position that looked like certain annihilation will go down in naval history as one of the greatest feats of tactics ever achieved.

On the morning of 1 June, the *Chester* was ordered to proceed to the Humber and the wounded were taken off and transferred to hospital at Grimsby. Jack Cornwell was amongst them. He could still talk in whispers but was very weak and in great pain. But his cheerfulness never left him. The matron of the hospital asked him how the battle had gone and he replied in simple, sailor-like fashion, "Oh, we carried on all right." But he never mentioned the part he had played – never boasted of his heroism. Indeed, it seems that he was quite unaware of the fact that he had done anything extraordinary: all he had done was to carry out his orders to the best of his ability and anyone else, he probably thought, if he thought about it at all, would have done the same.

These words to the matron were almost the last ever spoken by Jack. Occasionally he made a whispered request that he might see his mother, and at the end, just before he died on 2 June he said to the matron: "Give mother my love, I know she is coming." He was right, his mother was coming. She had received a telegram from the Admiralty and was hurrying to her son's side. But by the time she reached the hospital it was too late.

Although Jack Cornwell's action was not spectacular and was done with little prospect of being seen, there was one keen-eyed man who witnessed this splendid example of devotion to duty. Captain Lawson, the *Chester*'s commander, had noticed Cornwell's little figure at his post by the forward gun. He had noted how, with the dead and dying all round him and the enemy shells bursting thick and fast, he had never flinched. So Captain Lawson gave a full account of Jack's heroism when he made his report to his commander-in-chief, Admiral Jellicoe, who, in his official report to the Admiralty on the Battle of Jutland included the following paragraph:

A report from the commanding officer of the *Chester* gives a splendid instance of devotion to duty. Boy (First Class) John Travers Cornwell, of *Chester*, was mortally wounded early in the action. He nevertheless remained standing alone at a most exposed post, quietly awaiting orders till the end of the action, with the gun crew dead and wounded all around him. His age was under sixteen and a half years. I regret that he has since died, but I recommend his case for your special recognition in justice to his memory, and as an acknowledgment of the high example set by him.

This recommendation did not pass unheeded. There had been many heroes at the Battle of Jutland, but Cornwell was the only one, apart from officers, mentioned in the original despatches, and he was awarded the Victoria Cross.

In a letter to Mrs Cornwell the *Chester*'s commander told her how her son met his death: it was a fine letter, and she must have been proud to know that although she had lost her son, she was the mother of such a hero. It read:

I know you would wish to hear of the splendid fortitude and courage shown by your boy during the action of May 31. His devotion to duty was an example to us all. The wounds which resulted in his death within a short time were received in the first few minutes of the action. He remained steady at his most exposed post, waiting for orders. His gun would not bear on the enemy: all but two of the crew of ten were killed or wounded, and he was the only one who was in such an exposed position. But he felt he might be needed, as indeed he might have been; so he stayed there, standing and waiting, under heavy fire, with just his own brave heart and God's help to support him. I cannot express to you my admiration of the son you have lost from this world. No other comfort would I attempt to give to the mother of so brave a lad but to assure her of what he was and what he did and what an example he gave. I hope to place in the boys' mess a plate with his name on and the date, and the words "Faithful unto Death." I hope some day you may be able to come and see it there. I have not failed to bring his name prominently before my Admiral.

The prompt award of the Victoria Cross to Jack Cornwell only partly satisfied the desire of the public to pay homage to the dead hero. His body, which had been buried privately, was exhumed and reinterred with full naval honours. The funeral took place on 29 July 1916, at Manor Park Cemetery. The coffin, covered with the Union Jack, rested on a gun carriage drawn by a team of boys from the Crystal Palace Naval Depot. Vast crowds of people lined the route, and in the carriages that followed were many famous sailors and other notabilities including Dr T. J. MacNamara, Financial Secretary to the Admiralty.

Six boys from the *Chester*, all of whom had themselves been in the battle, walked in the procession carrying wreaths from his old ship's company, and there were countless other floral tributes including one from the Lord Mayor of London and one from Admiral Beatty. On the latter were inscribed the simple words, "With Deep Respect."

TOP SECRET: THE 007 FILE

BRIEFING DOCUMENT: COMMANDER JAMES BOND, AKA 007.
PREPARED FOR THE READER: EYES ONLY: 2008

WARNING: This is a TOP SECRET – EYES ONLY document containing information on the British spy Commander James Bond CMG, RNVR. ACCESS to the material herein is strictly limited to those boys possessing the highest grade security clearance.

NOTE: The subject is an agent of the British Intelligence Service. He is sometimes known as "007". The "double-o" prefix signifies that the subject holds a licence to kill.

The Creator

Commander James Bond, CMG, RNVR was created in January 1952 by British journalist Ian Fleming while on holiday at his Jamaican estate, Goldeneye. Fleming came up with the name James Bond after glancing at a bird book on his desk, *Birds of the West Indies* written by an American naturalist called . . . James Bond. In many ways Fleming based the super-suave fictional spy on himself. Fleming had been a spy for Naval Intelligence during the Second World War. Bond's likes were Fleming's likes: cigarettes, fine food, girls. They even went to the same British private schools, Eton and Fettes. The first novel featuring Bond, *Casino Royale*, appeared in 1953. When Fleming died in 1964 James Bond was a worldwide phenomenon and had made a successful move to the movie screen. Since Fleming's death a number of other authors have written official Bond novels. The adventures of the young Bond, James Bond, have been recorded by the British author Charlie Higson. All known appearances of James Bond in book and film are detailed below in APPENDICES A & B.

The Character: Essential James Bond Data

Place of Birth: Wattenscheid in Germany (some sources suggest Vienna, Austria).

Year of birth: 1924.

Parents: Andrew Bond, a Scotsman, Monique Delacroix, a Swiss national. Both parents killed in 1932 in climbing accident near Chamonix, after which Bond was placed in care of an aunt, Miss Charmian Bond.

Family motto: *Orbis non sufficit* ("The world is not enough").

Education: Eton College, from which he was expelled after an affair with a maid; Fettes College, the University of Geneva, the University of Cambridge.

Career as a spy: Subject entered Royal Naval Volunteer Reserve in 1941, rising to rank of Commander. Naval service however was a cover for subject's real occupation, working for the British Secret Intelligence Service (SIS), usually known as MI6. Bond gained his licence to kill in 1950 after a double assassination in *Casino Royale*. In confirmation of the "licence to kill" he was given a "double-o" prefix: 007.

Personal life: He is linked with a series of beautiful women, one of whom, Teresa "Tracy" di Vicenzo, he married. However, Teresa was killed on their wedding day by Bond's arch enemy, Ernst Stavro Blofeld; Bond has a child with Kissy Suzuki in *You Only Live Twice*.

Appearance: Bond is 6 feet tall with black hair, blue-grey eyes.

Distinguishing feature: Scar on right cheek.

Favourite weapon: Walther PPK.

Linguistic abilities: Fluent in German, French, Russian and Japanese (which he studied at the University of Cambridge).

Favourite drink: Vodka martini, "shaken not stirred".
Favourite food: Scrambled eggs.
Habits: Heavy smoker. His preferred brand are "Morland Specials", which blend Balkan and Turkish tobacco. These cigarettes are easily identified by the three gold bands on the filter, signifying Bond's rank as Commander Royal Naval Volunteer Reserve.
Home address: Unknown, but off the King's Road, Chelsea, London.

Appendix A: The James Bond Books

WARNING: Some of these books contain scenes unsuitable for those under 12.

After careful collation of information from our agents, we are able to list herein all official Bond novels and their authors:

Casino Royale, 1953 Author: Ian Fleming/*Live and Let Die*, 1954 Author: Ian Fleming/*Moonraker*, 1955 Author: Ian Fleming/*Diamonds Are Forever*, 1956 Author: Ian Fleming/*From Russia, With Love*, 1957 Author: Ian Fleming/*Dr No*, 1958 Author: Ian Fleming/*Goldfinger*, 1959 Author: Ian Fleming/ *For Your Eyes Only*, a short story collection consisting of "From A View To A Kill", "For Your Eyes Only", "Quantum of Solace", "Risico" and "The Hildebrand Rarity", 1960 Author: Ian Fleming/*Thunderball*, 1961 Author: Ian Fleming/*The Spy Who Loved Me*, 1962 Author: Ian Fleming/*On Her Majesty's Secret Service*, 1963 Author: Ian Fleming/*You Only Live Twice*, 1964 Author: Ian Fleming/*The Man With The Golden Gun*, 1965 Author: Ian Fleming/*Octopussy and The Living Daylights*, a short story collection consisting of "Octopussy" and "The Living Daylights", 1966 ("The Property of A Lady" added in 1967, "007 in New York" added 2002) Author: Ian Fleming/*Colonel Sun*, 1968 Author: Robert Markham aka Kingsley Amis/*The Spy Who Loved Me*, 1977 Author: Christopher Wood (novelization of movie)/*Moonraker*, 1979, Christopher Wood/*Licence Renewed*, 1981 Author: John Gardner/ *For Special Services*, 1982 Author: John Gardner/*Icebreaker*, 1983 Author: John Gardner/*Role of Honour*, 1984 Author: John

Gardner/*Nobody Lives For Ever*, 1986 Author: John Gardner/
No Deals, Mr Bond, 1987 Author: John Gardner/*Scorpius*, 1988
Author: John Gardner/*Win Lose or Die*, 1989 Author: John
Gardner/*Brokenclaw*, 1990 Author: John Gardner/*Licence to
Kill*, 1990 Author: John Gardner (novelization of movie)/*The
Man From Barbarossa*, 1991 Author: John Gardner/*Death is
Forever*, 1992 Author: John Gardner/*Never Send Flowers*, 1993
Author: John Gardner/*SeaFire*, 1994 Author: John Gardner/
Cold, 1995 Author: John Gardner/*GoldenEye*, 1995 Author:
John Gardner (novelisation of movie)/*Zero Minus Ten*, 1997
Author: Raymond Benson/*The Facts of Death*, 1998 Author:
Raymond Benson/*Tomorrow Never Dies*, 1997 Author Ray-
mond Benson (novelization of movie)/*High Time to Kill*,
1999 Author: Raymond Benson/*Doubleshot*, 2000 Author: Ray-
mond Benson/*Never Dream of Dying*, 2001 Author: Raymond
Benson/*The Man With The Red Tattoo*, 2002 Author: Raymond
Benson/*Silverfin* (Young Bond), 2005 Author: Charlie Higson/
Blood Fever (Young Bond), 2006 Author: Charlie Higson/
Double or Die (Young Bond), 2007 Author: Charlie Higson/
Hurricane Gold (Young Bond), 2007 Author Charlie Higson/
Devil May Care, 2008 Author: Sebastian Faulks.

Appendix B: The James Bond Movies

**WARNING: Please check censor's classification to
determine suitability for your eyes**.

Herewith are recorded all the official James Bond movies
together with the actor playing Bond:

Dr No 1962 Sean Connery/*From Russia with Love* 1963 Sean
Connery/*Goldfinger* 1964 Sean Connery/*Thunderball* 1965 Sean
Connery/*You Only Live Twice* 1967 Sean Connery/*On Her
Majesty's Secret Service* 1969 George Lazenby/*Diamonds Are
Forever* 1971 Sean Connery/*Live and Let Die* 1973 Roger
Moore/*The Man with the Golden Gun* 1974 Roger Moore/
The Spy Who Loved Me 1977 Roger Moore/*Moonraker* 1979
Roger Moore/*For Your Eyes Only* 1981 Roger Moore/*Octo-
pussy* 1983 Roger Moore/*A View to a Kill* 1985 Roger Moore/
The Living Daylights 1987 Timothy Dalton/*Licence to Kill* 1989

Timothy Dalton/*GoldenEye* 1995 Pierce Brosnan/*Tomorrow Never Dies* 1997 Pierce Brosnan/*The World Is Not Enough* 1999 Pierce Brosnan/*Die Another Day* 2002 Pierce Brosnan/ *Casino Royale* 2006 Daniel Craig.

CONCLUSION

The James Bond character in both books and film is dangerously addictive and poses a real enemy to teenage boredom. Recommended action: Read and watch.

ENDS > >.> >

EYES ONLY   TOP SECRET   EYES ONLY

HOW TO MAKE INVISIBLE INK

SMERSH about? Here's how to get a secret message past your parents/siblings (delete as appropriate) using invisible ink made from baking soda.

Mix equal amounts of baking soda and water in a small container. For a brief message a tablespoon of each will do.

Take an artist's thin paintbrush (if you can't find one, a cotton bud is fine) and dip it into the mixture. Write your message on a piece of white paper.

Let the paper dry completely.

Send paper to your fellow spy, whom you have previously tipped off as to the way of making the ink visible again.

Which is:

On receipt, he/she holds the paper near a lit light bulb (but not so close as to burn the paper or themselves). The message will appear in brown as the paper warms.

Of course, the arrival of a plain piece of paper will arouse anyone's suspicions. Much better then to write your secret message in a blank space on a "how are you" cover letter.

Baking soda is by no means the only household ingredient budding 007s can use for their top secret missives. Lemon juice works fine. So does vinegar. Neither needs to be shaken or stirred.

Scientifically minded boys may want to know the process behind the heat-activated secret ink spy craft. The baking soda/vinegar/lemon juice slightly weakens the paper where applied, which then burns (and turns brown) more quickly than the surrounding area.

SWIMMING GAMES

To become a fine swimmer means endless work and serious study but that need not prevent every bathe you take being full of enjoyment and fun, particularly when you are with friends. As a matter of fact, games and fun at the swimming pool have much to do with giving that ease, naturalness and good style which always mark the first-class swimmer. So here are some ideas for your enjoyment. *But don't be foolhardy*!

Leapfrog

This can be played in either shallow or deep water, and is performed as nearly as possible as on land. In deep water the front player must tread water, with arms folded and head bent forward. The other player then swims up from behind, puts hands on shoulders, and makes a leap with straddled legs – which ends with a head-first entry at the front. His companion will have been thrust downward and backward beneath the legs of the leaper, and after checking his descent by spreading his own limbs, he can rise to the surface and prepare for a leap in his turn. Any number can take part.

Tug and Liner

The leading swimmer, or *Tug*, uses an ordinary breast-stroke, pulling along the *Liner*, who floats horizontally on the surface, face upwards, with heels resting on the shoulders of his companion and feet gripping his head. The *Liner* may have his arms folded, held at his sides, or stretched beyond his head. The feat is not at all difficult, and is interesting and "showy".

Wrestling

Four boys usually enjoy this, in water that is breast-deep. Each wrestler is mounted on the shoulders of a companion, and the two mounted boys come to grips. The first to overturn his opponent wins the bout. The mount needs to be pretty sturdy, for, with the legs of his wrestler held firmly beneath his armpits he undergoes a good deal of strain.

Tag

This familiar land game is even more fun in the water, and can be played in almost any of its forms. One attractive variant is to have *It* chase the others in usual fashion, but with any player exempt from being tagged when his head is under water. You may play *Chain Tag* as well – each person touched joining hands with *It* and helping to catch the rest. Eventually, all the players are in the chain.

Crocodile Swimming

A *Crocodile* consists of four to eight swimmers, one behind the other, each with his hands on the hips of the one in front. Breast-stroke is most suitable, but only the leader can use his arms. A race between two or more *Crocodiles* can be quite exciting, especially if a number of sharp turns have to be made.

Tug-of-War

The best way of planning this is across a bath, with the rear member of each team standing on the bank with the rope tied round his waist. The other players should be in the water. The contest is over when the rear man is pulled in.

"Twenty ways of getting there"

This is best played across a bath, but you can enjoy it in any stretch of water, shallow or deep. Agree on a point at the other side of the "course", and then let each player in turn get there by a method which no one else has used. For instance, if the first sculls across no other is allowed to use that method. The second might swim breast-stroke, the third plunge right over. Other methods are the various strokes, swimming underwater, somersaulting, pretending to carry a baby, hopping, swinging arms windmill fashion. Any player who fails to follow on with some fresh idea drops out of the game.

Follow the Leader

This is even better in water than on land, for the leader may swim, dive, roll over, climb on the bank, jump in and so on.

Glide Ball

This is a more serious game, requiring some equipment. It must be played across a narrow stretch of water. Two teams take part, each of four to six players and of these one player stands on the bank at either side as goal-keeper. A cord or wire is fastened across the pool about six feet above the surface. On this wire a ring is threaded, and from the ring a large ball is suspended so that it nearly touches the water. To begin, the teams are lined up facing each other, each team facing its goal-keeper who is on the opposite bank. Players, wading or swimming, are allowed to punch or hit the ball in any fashion, their aim being to get it along through the opponents so that it can be caught by the goalie, who is waiting behind the opposing team. A goal is scored when he catches the ball. For a restart, teams spring from their respective sides towards the ball at the centre.

Rammers

A little stunt when you are in quite shallow water, perhaps at the seaside. You lie on your back, keeping yourself up by pressing with your hands on the bottom. Then you "walk" about like this, ramming unsuspecting friends – if you catch them behind the knees when they are standing up the chances are they will go over.

Tandem Swimming

There are two ways in which tandems can be formed: the two swimmers can be side by side or they can be in line – one behind the other. The side-by-side position is taken in most back-swimming methods. For instance, the partners may link their inner arms at the elbows and then swim along by performing an ordinary leg thrash and sculling with the outer arms. The one-behind-the-other position best fits breast-stroke, trudgen or crawl, the leading swimmer using arms alone and having his legs hooked under his friend's armpits. In these single-file formations it is the second swimmer who times his actions with the leader.

Back-crawl tandem is particularly graceful. The leading swimmer hooks his feet under the armpits of his fellow. The second swimmer is able to use both arms and legs, and the leader watches and fits in his arm strokes.

Mind the Shark

Here is another game played most conveniently across a bath. One swimmer remains in the middle, standing or treading water while the others travel backwards and forwards, trying not to be caught.

There are two ways of planning the game – anyone caught may either change places with the *Shark*, so that there is always just one to catch the rest, or each one caught may stay in the middle as a new *Shark* until everyone has been caught.

By Sid G. Hedges. Reprinted from the *Boy's Own Companion No. 2*, edited by Jack Cox, 1960.

THE WORLD

Facts and Figures

The Earth is one of nine planets in the solar system which revolves around the Sun. The other planets are Mercury, Venus, Mars, Jupiter, Saturn, Uranus, Neptune and Pluto.

The Earth is a sphere but is slightly flattened at the poles and slightly bulging at the middle, the Equator. The Equatorial circumference of the Earth is 40,076 km (24,901.8 miles). The distance from pole to pole through the centre of the earth is 12,700 km or (7,900 miles). The weight of the Earth is approximately 6,694,000,000,000,000,000,000 tonnes.

It takes a year for the Earth to revolve around the Sun, from which it is 149,000 km (93,0000 miles) in distance away. This revolution, together with the angle at which the Earth is tilted, produces the seasons.

At the same time as the Earth revolves around the Sun it spins on its own axis, which can be likened to an imaginary rod from pole to pole. One spin takes twenty-four hours and is what produces night and day; when your side of the Earth has turned away from the Sun's light you are in shadow, when it is turned towards the Sun you are in daylight.

Of the surface of the Earth 148,437,500 sq. km is land. The seven continents are: Asia, Africa, Europe, North America, South America, Antarctica, Oceania.

Nearly 70 per cent (361,666,020 sq. km or 139,638,000 sq. miles) of the Earth's surface is covered by water, forming the main oceans and seas. The seas and oceans are one vast mass but for reasons of navigation we divide it into the Atlantic, Arctic, Pacific and Indian Ocean. The oceans are further divided into seas, such as the Caribbean and Baltic.

Capital Cities of the World

There are presently 194 official countries in the world. They and their capitals are:

Afghanistan – Kabul
Albania – Tirana
Algeria – Algiers
Andorra – Andorra-la-Vella
Angola – Luanda
Antigua and Barbuda – Saint John's
Argentina – Buenos Aires
Armenia – Yerevan
Australia – Canberra
Austria – Vienna
Azerbaijan – Baku
The Bahamas – Nassau
Bahrain – Al Manamah
Bangladesh – Dhaka
Barbados – Bridgetown
Belarus – Minsk
Belgium – Brussels
Belize – Belmopan
Benin – Porto-Novo
Bhutan – Thimphu
Bolivia – La Paz (seat of government); Sucre (judicial)
Bosnia and Herzegovina – Sarajevo
Botswana – Gaborone
Brazil – Brasilia
Brunei – Bandar Seri Begawan
Bulgaria – Sofia
Burkina Faso – Ouagadougou
Burma (Myanmar) – Yangon
Burundi – Bujumbura
Cambodia – Phnom Penh

Cameroon – Yaounde
Canada – Ottawa
Cape Verde – Praia
Central African Republic – Bangui
Chad – N'Djamena
Chile – Santiago
China – Beijing
Colombia – Bogota
Comoros – Moroni
Congo, Republic of the – Brazzaville
Congo, Democratic Republic of the – Kinshasa
Costa Rica – San Jose
Cote d'Ivoire – Yamoussoukro
Croatia – Zagreb
Cuba – Havana
Cyprus – Nicosia
Czech Republic – Prague
Denmark – Copenhagen
Djibouti – Djibouti
Dominica – Roseau
Dominican Republic – Santo Domingo
East Timor (Timor-Leste) – Dili
Ecuador – Quito
Egypt – Cairo
El Salvador – San Salvador
Equatorial Guinea – Malabo
Eritrea – Asmara
Estonia – Tallinn
Ethiopia – Addis Ababa
Fiji – Suva
Finland – Helsinki
France – Paris
Gabon – Libreville
The Gambia – Banjul
Georgia – Tbilisi
Germany – Berlin
Ghana – Accra
Greece – Athens
Grenada – Saint George's
Guatemala – Guatemala City

Guinea – Conakry
Guinea-Bissau – Bissau
Guyana – Georgetown
Haiti – Port-au-Prince
Honduras – Tegucigalpa
Hungary – Budapest
Iceland – Reykjavik
India – New Delhi
Indonesia – Jakarta
Iran – Tehran
Iraq – Baghdad
Ireland – Dublin
Israel – Jerusalem
Italy – Rome
Jamaica – Kingston
Japan – Tokyo
Jordan – Amman
Kazakhstan – Astana
Kenya – Nairobi
Kiribati – Tarawa Atoll
Korea, North – Pyongyang
Korea, South – Seoul
Kuwait – Kuwait
Kyrgyzstan – Bishkek
Laos – Vientiane
Latvia – Riga
Lebanon – Beirut
Lesotho – Maseru
Liberia – Monrovia
Libya – Tripoli
Liechtenstein – Vaduz
Lithuania – Vilnius
Luxembourg – Luxembourg
Macedonia – Skopje
Madagascar – Antananarivo
Malawi – Lilongwe
Malaysia – Kuala Lumpur
Maldives – Malé
Mali – Bamako
Malta – Valletta

Marshall Islands – Dalap-Uliga-Darrit
Mauritania – Nouakchott
Mauritius – Port Louis
Mexico – Mexico City
Micronesia, Federated States of – Palikir
Moldova – Chisinau
Monaco – Monaco-Ville
Mongolia – Ulaanbaatar
Montenegro – Podgorica
Morocco – Rabat
Mozambique – Maputo
Namibia – Windhoek
Nauru – Yaren District (seat of government)
Nepal – Kathmandu
Netherlands – Amsterdam
New Zealand – Wellington
Nicaragua – Managua
Niger – Niamey
Nigeria – Abuja
Norway – Oslo
Oman – Muscat
Pakistan – Islamabad
Palau – Melekeok
Panama – Panama City
Papua New Guinea – Port Moresby
Paraguay – Asuncion
Peru – Lima
Philippines – Manila
Poland – Warsaw
Portugal – Lisbon
Qatar – Doha
Romania – Bucharest
Russia – Moscow
Rwanda – Kigali
Saint Kitts and Nevis – Basseterre
Saint Lucia – Castries
Saint Vincent and the Grenadines – Kingstown
Samoa – Apia
San Marino – San Marino
Sao Tomé and Principe – Sao Tomé

Saudi Arabia – Riyadh
Senegal – Dakar
Serbia – Belgrade
Seychelles – Victoria
Sierra Leone – Freetown
Singapore – Singapore
Slovakia – Bratislava
Slovenia – Ljubljana
Solomon Islands – Honiara
Somalia – Mogadishu
South Africa – Pretoria (administrative); Cape Town
   (legislative); Bloemfontein (judicial)
Spain – Madrid
Sri Lanka – Colombo
Sudan – Khartoum
Suriname – Paramaribo
Swaziland – Mbabane
Sweden – Stockholm
Switzerland – Bern
Syria – Damascus
Taiwan – Taipei
Tajikistan – Dushanbe
Tanzania – Dodoma
Thailand – Bangkok
Togo – Lome
Tonga – Nuku'alofa
Trinidad and Tobago – Port-of-Spain
Tunisia – Tunis
Turkey – Ankara
Turkmenistan – Ashgabat
Tuvalu – Vaiaku village, Funafuti province
Uganda – Kampala
Ukraine – Kiev
United Arab Emirates – Abu Dhabi
United Kingdom – London
United States of America – Washington D.C.
Uruguay – Montevideo
Uzbekistan – Tashkent
Vanuatu – Port-Vila
Vatican City (Holy See) – Vatican City

Venezuela – Caracas
Vietnam – Hanoi
Yemen – Sanaa
Zambia – Lusaka
Zimbabwe – Harare

The World's Largest Cities (by population)

City	Population	Country
Mumbai (Bombay)	13,073,929	India
Karachi	12,207,254	Pakistan
Delhi	11,505,196	India
Sao Paulo	11,016,703	Brazil
Moscow	10,654,000	Russia
Seoul	10,297,004	South Korea
Istanbul	10,121,102	Turkey
Shanghai	9,838,400	China
Lagos	9,229,944	Nigeria
Mexico City	8,658,576	Mexico

New York with a population of 8,143,197 is the thirteenth largest city in the world. London's population of 7,554,236 makes it the sixteenth largest city in the world.

The World's Largest Countries (by area)

Rank	Country	Area sq km	sq miles
1	Russia	17,075,400	6,592,811
2	Canada	9,970,610	3,849,652
3	China	9,572,900	3,695,942
4	USA	9,372,615	3,618,766
5	Brazil	8,511,965	3,286,469
6	Australia	7,682,300	2,966,136
7	India	3,166,829	1,222,713
8	Argentina	2,780,092	1,073,393
9	Kazakhstan	2,717,300	1,049,150
10	Sudan	2,505,800	967,489

The World's Smallest Countries (by area)

Rank	Country	Area	
		sq km	*sq miles*
1	Vatican City State	0.4	0.2
2	San Marino	61	24
3	Liechtenstein	160	62
4	Marshall Islands	181	70
5	St Kitts and Nevis	262	101
6	Maldives	298	115
7	Malta	320	124
8	Grenada	344	133
9	St Vincent and the Grenadines	388	150
10	Barbados	430	166

The World's Biggest Deserts

Desert	Location	Area	
Sahara	northern Africa	9,065,000	3,500,000
Gobi	Mongolia/northeastern China	1,295,000	500,000
Patagonian	Argentina	673,000	260,000
Rub al-Khali	southern Arabian peninsula	647,500	250,000
Kalahari	south-western Africa	582,800	225,000
Chihuahuan	Mexico/southwestern USA	362,600	140,000
Taklimakan	northern China	362,600	140,000
Great Sandy	north-western Australia	338,500	130,000
Great Victoria	south-western Australia	338,500	130,000
Kyzyl Kum	Uzbekistan/Kazakhstan	259,000	100,000

The World's Longest Rivers

River	km	miles	Location
Nile	6,695	4,160	North Africa
Amazon	6,571	4,083	South America
Chang Jiang (Yangtze)	6,300	3,915	China
Mississippi-Missouri-Red Rock	6,020	3,741	USA
Huang He (Yellow River)	5,464	3,395	China
Ob-Irtysh	5,410	3,362	China/Russia

Amur	4,416	2,744	Northern Asia
Lena	4,400	2,734	Russia
Congo (Zaire)	4,374	2,718	Central Africa
Mackenzie	4,241	2,635	Canada
Mekong	4,180	2,579	South East Asia

The World's Biggest Oceans and Seas

Ocean/sea	Area	
	sq km	sq miles
Pacific Ocean	166,242,000	64,186,000
Atlantic Ocean	86,557,000	33,420,000
Indian Ocean	73,429,000	28,351,000
Arctic Ocean	13,224,000	5,106,000
South China Sea	2,975,000	1,149,000
Caribbean Sea	2,754,000	1,063,000
Mediterranean Sea	2,510,000	969,000
Bering Sea	2,261,000	873,000

The World's Highest Mountains

Mountain	m	ft	Location	First Ascent
Everest	8,848	29,028	Nepal/Tibet	1953
K2	8,611	28,251	Pakistan/China	1954
Kanchenjunga	8,598	28,208	Nepal/India	1955
Lhotse	8,516	27,940	Nepal/Tibet	1956
Makalu	8,481	27,824	Nepal/Tibet	1955
Cho Oyu	8,201	26,906	Nepal/Tibet	1954
Dhaulagiri	8,172	26,811	Nepal	1960
Manaslu	8,156	26,759	Nepal	1956
Nanga Parbat	8,125	26,660	Pakistan	1953
Annapurna I	8,078	26,502	Nepal	1950

GREAT SPEECHES II

"Their Finest Hour"
by Winston Churchill MP

These are excerpts from Churchill's famous speeches to the British House of Commons in June 1940. The Second World War was eight months old, France was teetering on the very verge of defeat, and Britain was the only opponent of Hitler still standing. But cometh the hour, cometh the man. Churchill offered "blood, toil, tears and sweat" and through his leadership and oratory steeled the British people to fight on alone.

I have, myself, full confidence that if all do their duty, if nothing is neglected, and if the best arrangements are made, as they are being made, we shall prove ourselves once again able to defend our island home, to ride out the storm of war, and to outlive the menace of tyranny, if necessary for years, if necessary alone. At any rate, that is what we are going to try to do. That is the resolve of His Majesty's Government — every man of them. That is the will of Parliament and the nation. The British Empire and the French Republic linked together in their cause and in their need, will defend to the death their native soil, aiding each other like good comrades to the utmost of their strength. Even though large tracts of Europe and many old and famous States have fallen or may fall into the grip of the Gestapo and all the odious apparatus of Nazi rule, we shall not flag or fail. We shall go on to the end. We shall fight in France, we shall fight on the seas and oceans, we shall fight with growing confidence and growing strength in the air, we shall defend our island, whatever the cost may be. We shall fight on the beaches, we shall fight on the landing grounds, we shall fight in the fields and in the streets, we shall fight in the hills; we shall never surrender, and even if, which I do not for a moment believe, this island or a large part of it were subjugated and starving, then our Empire beyond the seas, armed and guarded by the British Fleet, would carry on the struggle, until, in God's good time, the new world, with all its power and might, steps forth to the rescue and the liberation of the old.

* * *

What General Weygand called the "Battle of France" is over. I expect that the battle of Britain is about to begin. Upon this battle depends the survival of Christian civilization. Upon it depends our own British life and the long continuity of our institutions and our Empire. The whole fury and might of the enemy must very soon be turned on us. Hitler knows that he will have to break us in this island or lose the war. If we can stand up to him all Europe may be free, and the life of the world may move forward into broad, sunlit uplands; but if we fail then the whole world, including the United States, and all that we have known and cared for, will sink into the abyss of a new dark age made more sinister, and perhaps more prolonged, by the lights of a perverted science. Let us therefore brace ourselves to our duty and so bear ourselves that if the British Commonwealth and Empire lasts for a thousand years men will still say, "This was their finest hour."

KNOTS

Here are six knots every boy should know.

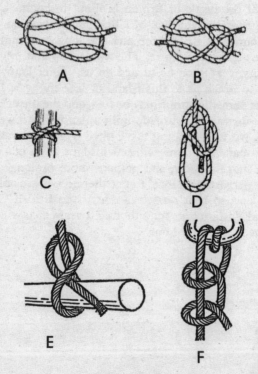

A

B

C

D

E

F

A Reef Knot

Used for tying two ropes together.

B Sheet Bend

The standard knot for tying two ropes of different thicknesses together.

C Clove Hitch

Used to make a rope fast to another rope or to a pole.

D Bowline

Pronounced "bowlin", this knot is best for making a loop which won't slip. It makes a good animal halter.

E Half Hitch

Another knot to tie ropes to poles

F Round Turn and Two Half Hitches

This knot firmly secures a rope to a post or ring

KEEPING GUINEA-PIGS

The guinea-pig, or, as it is sometimes termed, the domestic cavy, is a mild, gentle little creature of which few civilised people knew anything until it was introduced into Europe by the Dutch in the early part of the sixteenth century.

When Francisco Pizarro conquered Peru in 1531 the guinea-pig, or, as the Spaniards termed it, *cochinillo das Indias*, was as wild and plentiful as the llama and alpaca, and occupied the same position in the Peruvian market that the rabbit does in England.

The word "cavy" is a corruption of "coni" or "cony," the name given by an ancient Indian tribe who inhabited Peru previous to the coming of the Spaniards.

Many early travellers to South America have left testimony in their writings that in most Brazilian and Peruvian households the cavy was sufficiently domesticated to run about the house as freely as poultry, and that the cat amiably shared her place of honour at the hearth with this bright-eyed creature, which was, indeed, her bosom friend.

The squaw, or Indian housewife, when called upon suddenly to provide a meal for unexpected visitors, was frequently known to resort to the cavy, a dish much appreciated by her guests, and even more dainty and nutritious than the rabbit.

In England and many other countries the guinea-pig is regarded as uninteresting and stupid, whereas it is really of a very intelligent and even affectionate disposition.

There are three different tones in its voice – the shrill pipe, denoting fear, hunger, or thirst; the lower-pitched squeak, signifying placid content and welcome; and the grunt, expressing displeasure.

The cavy soon knows and becomes attached to its feeder, and will whisk forward at his approach with every sign of recognition and delight that a dumb animal can show.

It is quite an inexpensive pet, and, provided the hutch be kept clean, dry, and warm, it will thrive and multiply abundantly.

Homesteads are quite easy of manipulation, and a pair of cavies need very little space. When, however, there are more than two, it is better to have sufficient room to allow them exercise.

The guinea-pig revels in the sunlight, yet is extremely fond of snow. In severe winter weather it will devour a pan of snow with relish, and at

FIG. 1.—The Guinea-pig.

those times needs nothing else to quench its thirst, Fig. 1.

The home of a couple of cavies may be an old cask or a candle-box, where they will be perfectly happy, provided everything is kept sweet and clean.

Damp and cold are fatal, and those who wish to keep their pets from disease and death must shelter them carefully during the winter months.

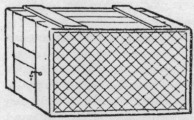

FIG. 2.—Hutch for Guinea-pigs.

A packing-case makes a handsome domicile. Fine-netted wire should be nailed over the front, and a small wooden door fixed at one end for the purpose of feeding and cleansing. When possible, the wood should be lined with zinc, as this keeps the interior from absorbing the damp. The box, Fig. 2, should always be painted, so that it does not warp or rot.

The most convenient way of keeping the cage sanitary is to fit in a zinc or wooden tray, Fig. 3. This should frequently be sprinkled with a mixture of clean sawdust and dry sand, and

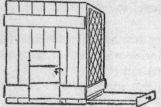

FIG. 3.—Cage with Moveable Tray.

removed as often as necessary, scalded and left in the air for a few hours.

Cavies need constant feeding, but it is not wise to provide the whole day's supply in the morning, for the cavy is very apt to lie on its food, thus rendering it dirty and unwholesome. This is injurious to its health, whilst the fur becomes clotted and discoloured.

Although the cavy loves to bask in the sunlight, it needs shelter, so that during the summer months, when the light is too dazzling, it may retire at pleasure to the shade. In Fig. 4 is shown another type of hutch.

A plank fixed across one end of the box, and not too high for the cavy to reach, is very necessary, for this provides exercise and a resting-place after feeding.

FIG. 4.—A Type of Hutch.

There should also be a supply of shelters for breeding purposes, as well as clean water in well-washed pans, which will not overturn and wet the cage when the cavy drinks. A partitioned trough, to hold his bran and drink, with a high back pierced for nails, to keep it from overturning, is the best article, Fig. 5. Saucers are easily upset, and not only wet the flooring, but deprive the cavies of that supply of water which they constantly need.

When Mr. and Mrs. Cavy have babies to look after, great care must be taken to prevent the parents from unintentionally trampling upon their young. Should it happen that there are several couples and families of varying ages, it would be well to remove the little ones with their mother to a nursery until they are strong enough to hold their own against larger relations.

Growing boars are apt to give themselves airs as they near maturity, and often cause constant breaches in the happiness of the home life. Papa Cavy makes a vain attempt to retain his authority and importance, but, alas! he is frequently one against many, and for this reason a large family should be divided into different homes.

Sometimes a deadly vendetta occurs between two cavies, who feel that the world is too small to contain them both. At such times the bigger boar naturally has matters all his own way, and will pursue his enemy with remorseless enmity, biting him so severely that before long the foe's head and back are covered with bleeding wounds. Before matters become so serious, the keeper must, of course, remove one of them to another hutch if he wishes to avoid the expense of a funeral.

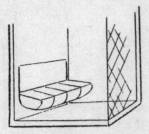

FIG. 5.—Trough for Hutch.

The cavy's foe is the rat, whom, strange to say, he does not in the least fear. This young gentleman, a very fox in cunning, will use all his strength and might to force his way into Mrs. Cavy's cottage. Wood is as digestible to him as sponge-cake to a baby; he gnaws and scratches until he has entered and committed a cowardly crime upon his defenceless prey.

Zinc or small-meshed wire, Fig. 6, surrounding the cage at a sufficient height from the ground is the only means of baulking this treacherous foe of his prey. Traps may, of course, be set; but prevention is always better than cure.

The larder of the cavy household is quite economically supplied. Cabbage leaves, groundsel, brock, carrot-tops, and other kinds of green meat will be very much appreciated.

Some guinea-pigs turn up their small noses at turnip-tops, and will only eat them when nothing else is forthcoming, yet they may be trained to eat most things in season.

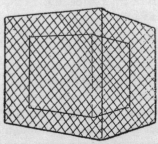

FIG. 6.—Wire-netting as a Protection against Rats.

Green refuse from the kitchen or garden, providing it is fresh, is very welcome, and the cavies' trough should always contain a supply of bran mixed with water. When Mother Cavy is weaning her young, which sometimes occurs before they are three weeks old, they must be removed and supplied with milk and special fare until this stage is over.

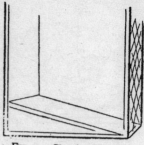

FIG. 7.—Slanting Floor for Hutch.

Babies need a slanted floor, Fig. 7, so that they are not crushed beneath the feet of their parents and relations.

The cavy that sulks in a corner, refuses his food, and shows signs of extreme unsociability, is not a hermit or genius planning some great work, and therefore preferring solitude – he is ill. A sluggish liver or the beginnings of dropsy may be troubling him, caused either by indiscreet feeding or damp. At the first symptoms he should be isolated and treated to light and dainty fare, with only a little food at a time. Warm milk and care will soon restore him to his normal condition.

Vermin are even more deadly than the rat, and attack the poor little creatures when they have been overcrowded or neglected. Vermin spread fast, and means must at once be taken to stop the invasion. Keating's powder, change of diet, and the removal of those infected are the only means of restoring the cavies to a wholesome condition.

Cavies love grass, and it is a good plan to have a bottomless box always at hand, and from time to time give them a chance of feeding on the lawn.

When a cavy has suffered from the enmity of his fellows, his wounds should be cleansed in lukewarm water and soothed with a mixture of oil and sulphur.

Those who pay especial attention to breeding, and desire to maintain a certain type of cavy, or exhibit animals at shows, must take care to prevent all chances of inter-breeding.

Sows and boars of pure pedigree should, of course, be kept separate from their fellows.

There are three kinds of fancy breeds, Fig. 8 – the Smooth cavy, the Abyssinian, and the Peruvian. The variety of colours usual to the Smooth cavy are six in number, the Abyssinian has ten, and the Peruvian five.

Of the Smooth kind, the pure white red-eyed cavies are the best subjects for experiments in transmission, although some of the spotted tribe show promise of reproducing their colours.

FIG. 8.—Abyssinian, Peruvian, and Smooth Guinea-pigs.

The Abyssinian differs very much from the Smooth cavy, and cannot be mistaken. Its head is crested with fur, which grows in clumps and makes it somewhat resemble a long-haired spaniel. Its face is plentifully whiskered, its nose broad and distinct, and the ears are more crinkled than those of the Smooth cavy.

The Peruvian is the most delicate and the rarest species. It has long, thick hair, which reaches below its feet in a heavy fringe, and bears a plentiful crest on its head. Care should be taken to keep the coat glossy and free from tangles and mats.

Occasional bathing with a damp sponge and gentle combings would reward the owner who wishes to exhibit his pets in the show pen.

It is a mistaken policy to have too many boars in a cage, for each has a masterful spirit which is apt to destroy the harmony of the home and lead to fierce civil warfare. Some hostile fathers have been known to destroy their young, perhaps with an eye to their future incursions. Concord is established when one boar shares his home with several sows. The latter are usually friendly, and often, when two of them litter at the same time, will share their duties in nourishing their young.

From *Every Boy's Book of Hobbies* by Cecil H. Bullivant, 1911.

SEMAPHORE

The semaphore signalling code is performed by the arms and is invaluable for signalling across country. It is important that arm and wrist are held in a straight line while signalling. To make certain of this, press your first finger along the flag stick. Obviously, the sky makes the best background to signal against, so if possible stand on a hill or prominent point.

The rules for semaphoring are straightforward: at the end of each word, you must drop your arms straight down in front of you and pause. This is the "ready position". Before you give a number you use the "numeral" sign. When you go back to letters you give the "alphabet" sign. If you make a mistake you signal "annul", meaning cancel, and do the word or number again.

Semaphore is far from being the only method of visually signalling over distance. Morse code can be signalled by flags and mirrors. Smoke can also be used for basic signals.

For smoke signals you need to get a good dry fire going, and then heap on green leaves or grass. Dense volumes of smoke will issue forth. By holding a wet blanket over the smouldering leaves and then removing it, you will get a puff of smoke. The number and regularity of the puffs constitutes the code. Three small puffs followed by three long puffs followed by three small puffs would make the Morse equivalent of $\cdots / --- / \cdots$ Or SOS. Save Our Souls.

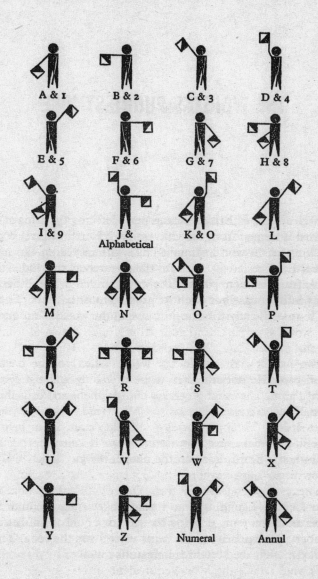

THE WORLD'S FUNNIEST JOKE

In 2001 a team of British researchers, led by psychologist Dr Richard Wiseman from the University of Hertfordshire, began searching for the world's funniest joke. After a year in which the "LaughLab" tested 40,000 jokes the researchers concluded that people from different parts of the world tended to find different things humorous – but one joke crossed most borders. Therefore it was officially the funniest joke in the world. And here it is:

> Two hunters are out in the woods when one of them collapses. He doesn't seem to be breathing and his eyes are glazed. The other guy takes out his phone and calls the emergency services. He gasps: "My friend is dead! What can I do?" The operator says: "Calm down, I can help. First, let's make sure he's dead." There is a silence, then a gunshot is heard. Back on the phone, the guy says, "OK, now what?"

According to LaughLab the hunter joke contains three key elements of humour: it helps reduce anxiety about a difficult situation; it surprises; and it helps us feel superior to others.

Incidentally, the second funniest joke was:

> Sherlock Holmes and Dr Watson go on a camping trip. After a good dinner and a bottle of wine, they retire for the night, and go to sleep.

Some hours later, Holmes wakes up and nudges his faithful friend. "Watson, look up at the sky and tell me what you see."

"I see millions and millions of stars, Holmes," replies Watson.

"And what do you deduce from that?"

Watson ponders for a minute.

"Well, astronomically, it tells me that there are millions of galaxies and potentially billions of planets. Astrologically, I observe that Saturn is in Leo. Horologically, I deduce that the time is approximately a quarter past three. Meteorologically, I suspect that we will have a beautiful day tomorrow. Theologically, I can see that God is all powerful, and that we are a small and insignificant part of the universe. What does it tell you, Holmes?"

Holmes is silent for a moment. "Watson, you idiot!" he says. "Someone has stolen our tent!"

According to LaughLab jokes stimulate a part of the brain called the prefrontal cortex and if this is damaged you lose your sense of humour.

Another joke which really got the prefrontal cortex going was:

Two goldfish in a tank. One turns to the other and says "Do you know how to drive this thing?"

http://www.laughlab.co.uk/

GOOD MANNERS

George Washington, the first President of the United States, wrote these "Rules of Civility" in a notebook in 1745, when he was fourteen. He followed them in life and didn't go far wrong. And nor will you if you do. They still make an excellent guide to proper behaviour and proper manners.

1. Every action in company ought to be with some sign of respect to those present.
2. In the presence of others sing not to yourself with a humming voice, nor drum with your fingers or feet.
3. Speak not when others speak, sit not when others stand, and walk not when others stop.
4. Turn not your back to others, especially in speaking; jog not the table or desk on which another reads or writes; lean not on anyone.
5. Be no flatterer, neither play with anyone that delights not to be played with.
6. Read no letters, books, or papers in company; but when there is a necessity for doing it, you must ask leave. Come not near the books or writings of anyone so as to read them unasked; also look not nigh when another is writing a letter.
7. Let your countenance be pleasant, but in serious matters somewhat grave.
8. Show not yourself glad at the misfortune of another, though he were your enemy.
9. They that are in dignity or office have in all places precedency, but whilst they are young, they ought to respect

those that are their equals in birth or other qualities, though they have no public charge.

10. It is good manners to prefer them to whom we speak before ourselves, especially if they be above us, with whom in no sort we ought to begin.

11. Let your discourse with men of business be short and comprehensive.

12. In visiting the sick do not presently play the physician if you be not knowing therein.

13. In writing or speaking give to every person his due title according to his degree and the custom of the place.

14. Strive not with your superiors in argument, but always submit your judgment to others with modesty.

15. Undertake not to teach your equal in the art he himself professes; it savors of arrogancy.

16. When a man does all he can, though it succeeds not well, blame not him that did it.

17. Being to advise or reprehend anyone, consider whether it ought to be in public or in private, presently or at some other time, also in what terms to do it; and in reproving show no signs of choler, but do it with sweetness and mildness.

18. Mock not nor jest at anything of importance; break no jests that are sharp or biting; and if you deliver anything witty or pleasant, abstain from laughing threat yourself.

19. Wherein you reprove another be unblamable yourself, for example is more prevalent than precept.

20. Use no reproachful language against anyone, neither curses nor revilings.

21. Be not hasty to believe flying reports to the disparagement of anyone.

22. In your apparel be modest, and endeavor to accommodate nature rather than procure admiration. Keep to the fashion of your equals, such as are civil and orderly with respect to time and place.

23. Play not the peacock, looking everywhere about you to see if you be well decked, if your shoes fit well, if your stockings set neatly and clothes handsomely.

24. Associate yourself with men of good quality if you esteem your own reputation, for it is better to be alone than in bad company.

25. Let your conversation be without malice or envy, for it is a sign of tractable and commendable nature; and in all causes of passion admit reason to govern.

26. Be not immodest in urging your friend to discover a secret.

27. Utter not base and frivolous things amongst grown and learned men, nor very difficult questions or subjects amongst the ignorant, nor things hard to be believed.

28. Speak not of doleful things in time of mirth nor at the table; speak not of melancholy things, as death and wounds; and if others mention them, change, if you can, the discourse. Tell not your dreams but to your intimate friends.

29. Break not a jest when none take pleasure in mirth. Laugh not aloud, nor at all without occasion. Deride no man's misfortunes, though there seem to be some cause.

30. Speak not injurious words, neither in jest or earnest. Scoff at none, although they give occasion.

31. Be not forward, but friendly and courteous, the first to salute, hear and answer, and be not pensive when it is time to converse.

32. Detract not from others, but neither be excessive in commending.

33. Go not thither where you know not whether you shall be welcome or not. Give not advice without being asked; and when desired, do it briefly.

34. If two contend together, take not the part of either unconstrained, and be not obstinate in your opinion; in things indifferent be of the major side.

35. Reprehend not the imperfection of others, for that belongs to parents, masters, and superiors.

36. Gaze not on the marks or blemishes of others, and ask not how they came. What you may speak in secret to your friend deliver not before others.

37. Speak not in an unknown tongue in company, but in your own language; and that as those of quality do, and not as the vulgar. Sublime matters treat seriously.

38. Think before you speak; pronounce not imperfectly, nor bring out your words too hastily, but orderly and distinctly.

39. When another speaks, be attentive yourself, and disturb not the audience. If any hesitate in his words, help him not, nor

prompt him without being desired; interrupt him not, nor answer him till his speech be ended.

40. Treat with men at fit times about business, and whisper not in the company of others.

41. Make no comparisons; and if any of the company be commended for any brave act of virtue, commend not another for the same.

42. Be not apt to relate news if you know not the truth thereof. In discoursing of things you have heard, name not your author always. A secret discover not.

43. Be not curious to know the affairs of others, neither approach to those that speak in private.

44. Undertake not what you cannot perform; but be careful to keep your promise.

45. When you deliver a matter, do it without passion and indiscretion, however mean the person may be you do it to.

46. When your superiors talk to anybody, hear them; neither speak or laugh.

47. In disputes be not so desirous to overcome as not to give liberty to each one to deliver his opinion, and submit to the judgment of the major part, especially if they are judges of the dispute.

48. Be not tedious in discourse, make not many digressions, nor repeat often the same matter of discourse.

49. Speak no evil of the absent, for it is unjust.

50. Be not angry at table, whatever happens; and if you have reason to be so show it not; put on a cheerful countenance, especially if there be strangers, for good humor makes one dish a feast.

51. Set not yourself at the upper end of the table; but if it be your due, or the master of the house will have it so, contend not, lest you should trouble the company.

52. When you speak of God or his attributes, let it be seriously, in reverence and honor, and obey your natural parents.

53. Let your recreations be manful, not sinful.

54. Labor to keep alive in your breast that little spark of celestial fire called conscience.

Reprinted from *The Book of Virtues* by William J. Bennett, 1993. Copyright © 1993 William J. Bennett.

MAKE A CRYSTAL RADIO RECEIVER

To make the crystal receiver you will need the following parts and tools:

A 0A90 diode
1 tin can of 7.0 cm diameter
1 tin can of 7.6 mm diameter
A crystal earpiece
A wooden board 15 × 10 cm
A 7 cm square of thin card
7–10 metres of aerial wire
Sticky tape
Plasticine
Four screws with metal cup washers
350 cm of 36 swg enamelled copper wire
50 cm thin insulated wire

A flathead screwdriver
A pinhead hammer and pin nail
A sheet of fine sandpaper

Instructions

The Baseboard:
1) Mark out the baseboard as shown in Figure 1.
2) Fit the screws into the cup washers and secure in baseboard as Figure 2.

The Tuning Capacitor:
1) Cover the outside of the small can with sticky tape (sticky side down).
2) Make a very small hole in the bottom of each can with the pinhead hammer and pin.
3) Attach 30 cm of connecting wire to the end of each can and secure the wires with a blob of plasticine.
4) Put the smaller can inside the larger can.

The Coil:
1) Roll the 7 cm square card into a 1 cm diameter tube.
2) Wind the enamelled wire 100 times tightly round the 1 cm tube leaving 10 cm at each end.
3) Cover the wire on the tube with sticky tape, leaving the end wires uncovered.
4) Take the sandpaper and remove the enamel from the ends of the wire; this is to ensure a good connection.

Assembly:
Attach the parts to the baseboard as in Figure 2. The tins can be secured with plasticine. Take care to insert the diode as shown in the diagram, with the end with the red spot (the cathode) facing towards the earpiece.

To operate:
1) Attach the earth wire to the copper pipe on a cold water tap.
2) Suspend the aerial wire somewhere high, such as the top of a wardrobe or closet.
3) Put the ear piece in your ear and slowly move the small can in and out of the larger can – until you can hear a radio programme.

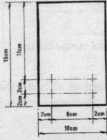

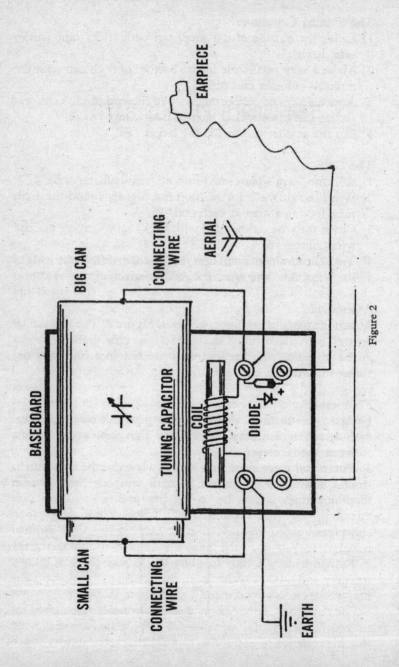

Figure 2

TEN WORLD FAMOUS BATTLES

Cannae

Where: Cannae, southern Italy.
Who: 86,000 Romans under Consuls Lucius Aemilius Paulus and Gaius Terentius versus 50,000 Carthaginians and mercenaries under Hannibal.
When: 216 BC.

After the Second Punic War exploded between Carthage and Rome in 218 BC, the Carthaginian army under Hannibal crossed the Alps into northern Italy. To the astonishment of Rome Hannibal achieved this feat in winter, using elephants as transports. Moving down through Italy, Hannibal won victories at Trebbia and Lake Trasimene, and by late summer he had reached the corn-rich province of Apulia in southern Italy, where he intended to secure provisions for his troops. More, he hoped that by occupying the vital Roman food depot at Cannae he would provoke the Romans into attacking him. The citizens of Rome, faced with food shortages, urged their leaders to attack the Carthaginian invader. In response, the Senate mustered the largest army in Roman history so far. Leading the Roman force of 80,000 infantry and 6,000 cavalry were the consuls, Varro and Paulus, who exercised command on alternate days.

For days the Carthaginians and the Romans skirmished on the coastal plain until Varro decided to force the issue, believing that his superiority in numbers would guarantee victory, since

Hannibal's army was considerably smaller, at 50,000 strong. Paulus, a more experienced campaigner urged caution, but Varro ignored him and ordered a full frontal attack, with troops deployed in the traditional Roman manner: a massive phalanx of foot soldiers with a wing of cavalry to each side. Varro intended to break Hannibal's line with sheer force. The Romans faced south-west, with their right cavalry wing on the bank of the Aufidus.

Hannibal, meanwhile, deployed his main body of troops in a convex shape, with columns of elite Carthaginian infantry at the tips of the crescent. On his left flank, Hannibal placed his heavy Celtic and Spanish cavalry, and on the right flank his Numidian light cavalry.

The battle began with a clash between Hannibal's heavy cavalry and the opposing Roman horse under Consul Paulus on the bank of the Aufidus. It was an engagement the Carthaginians won, and the Roman cavalry were driven off the field with the Carthaginians following round to the rear of the Roman cavalry on the right wing.

Meanwhile, the Roman legions advanced, shoulder to shoulder behind a wall of shields. This juggernaut drove in to the centre of Hannibal's crescent line, which was held by his weakest troops, Gallic and Spanish swordsmen. As Hannibal anticipated, his line began to buckle inwards under the weight of the Roman advance. Scenting victory, the Romans pushed into the seemingly disintegrating Carthaginian centre. In fact, the Romans were trapping themselves in an encirclement. Hannibal now ordered the Gauls and Spaniards to stand their ground, the Carthaginian infantry on the tips of the half-moon to advance inwards. The Romans' only avenue of escape to the rear was closed by the cavalry. Like a python constricting its prey, Hannibal's army encircled and squeezed the Roman army to death. So tightly did the Carthaginians press on the Romans that the latter were unable to swing their swords. Hacked by Carthaginian swords and pierced by Carthaginian spears, the Romans fell by the thousand. According to the Roman historian Livy, 50,000 Romans died at Cannae. Hannibal's losses were 6,000.

Hastings

Where: Hastings in southern England.
Who: 6,000 Normans commanded by Duke William of Normandy versus 6,000 English led by King Harold.
When: 9.00 a.m. to 5.00. p.m., 14 October 1066.

On the death of the childless Edward the Confessor the Anglo-Saxon council, the Witan, elected Harold Godwineson to the throne of England. The 44-year-old Harold had no noble blood but he was the mightiest earl in the kingdom and is thought to have been Edward's own choice of successor.

There were, however, other claimants to the throne. One of these was Hadrada of Norway, the other was Duke William of Normandy. William claimed that during a visit to England in 1051 Edward had promised the throne to him. William's claim was regarded by many in Europe, including the Pope, as the better claim.

Nonetheless Harold was determined to fight to keep the throne. On hearing that Hadrada had landed with troops in the north-east of England, Harold together with his housecarles (bodyguard) and part of the fyrd (the militia or part-time army) marched north, covering 190 miles in five days. At Stamford Bridge, Yorkshire, on 25 September 1066, Harold beat Hadrada's force, killing Hadrada himself.

The victory party was short lived. On 29 September the other claimant to the English throne, William of Normandy, landed at Pevensey on the south coast, so back down England Harold marched.

On Friday, 13 October Harold and his men appeared on the top of Senlac Hill, above the Norman's fortified camp at Hastings. Senlac Hill dominated the road to London (a cart track) and for William to make progress into England he had to go past Harold.

At about 9.00 a.m. the next day, the battle was joined when the Norman bowmen began firing shoals of arrows at the English. Next William launched his men-at-arms at the English shield wall, and there was a brutal melee of hacking and stabbing. Some of William's inferior troops, on the left of his line, panicked and ran down the hill, with English fyrdmen in full chase. The panic began to spread but William rallied his men. According to the chronicler William of Poitiers:

> Seeing a large part of the hostile host pursuing his own troops, the prince [William] thrust himself in front of those in flight, shouting at them and threatening them with his spear. Staying their retreat, he took off his helmet, and standing before them bareheaded the cried: "Look at me well. I am still alive and by the grace of God I shall yet prove victor. What is this madness which makes you fly, and what way is open for your retreat? You are allowing yourselves to be pursued and killed by men whom you could slaughter like cattle. You are throwing away victory and lasting glory, rushing into ruin and incurring abiding disgrace. And all for naught since by flight none of you can escape destruction." With these words he restored their courage, and, aleaping to the front and wielding his death-dealing sword, he defied the enemy who merited death for their disloyalty to him their prince. Inflamed by his ardour the Normans then surrounded several thousand of their pursuers and rapidly cut them down so that not one escaped.

Turning once more to the massed English line above him, William launched another attack – again to no avail. It was now that William employed a cunning *ruse de guerre* (trick of war); he ordered a pretend retreat so as to draw Harold's men off the ridge. The trick worked and many of Harold's ill-disciplined fyrdmen chased after what they thought was a fleeing army, only to be surrounded and cut down.

With the light of day disappearing, William ordered his archers to aim their arrows high in the air so they would fall like rain on the weakened English line. As William hoped the English raised their shields above their heads to protect themselves, so leaving their bodies open to attacks by his infantry and knights.

In the close combat which ensued, King Harold was hacked down by a knight (and not felled by an arrow in the eye as the Bayeux Tapestry suggests). Leaderless, the English army began to disintegrate and flee the field of battle.

Harold has been criticized for not assembling a larger force to engage William, yet the real problem for the English at Hastings was not numbers but out-datedness. About 2,000 of William's troops were mounted on horseback; all the English fought on foot. The role of William's cavalry in encircling the fyrd was crucial to the outcome of the battle.

William of Normandy's victory at Hastings was absolute. Ten weeks later he was crowned King of England in Westminster Abbey. William forced the English off their lands and gave them to his Norman followers. He tied his Norman and English kingdoms together, and a century later the Anglo-Norman Empire would be the greatest power in Europe.

Crécy

Where: Crécy, France
Who: 10,000 English under King Edward III versus 30,000 French under Philip VI
When: 6.00. to 9.00. p.m., 26 August 1346

Crécy was the first of the great English victories in the long conflict with France known as the Hundred Years' War.

On 11 July 1346, King Edward III of England landed in St Vaast, Normandy, with 10,000 troops, determined to pursue his claim to the French throne. However, Edward's navy mistakenly abandoned the invasion force, leaving Edward no option but to fight across northern France towards Flanders, which was allied to him. By the time the English reached the River Somme, Philip of France had assembled a force of 30,000 to meet the invaders.

Early in the morning of 26 August, Edward deployed his force along a 2,000-yard ridge between the villages of Crécy and Wadicourt. Along the front line Edward positioned formations of archers, as many as 1,000 in number, who jutted forward of his foot soldiers and dismounted men-at-arms. Behind the front line was drawn up a smaller line of men-at-arms, mounted and on foot, with archers on the flanks. Edward's archers, highly paid (at six pence a day) and highly trained, used a longbow of yew or elm. The longbow was extremely accurate and powerful enough to pierce armour.

Throughout the morning and into the afternoon, the English stood patiently waiting for the French to appear before them. In the late afternoon a lookout announced that the French army was approaching. Philip's plan was to camp and give battle on the morrow, but some hotheads in his army pushed on towards the English line. On seeing the strength of the English position, however, these hotheads fell back, crashing into troops who had followed them. To prevent his army becoming infected with pessimism Philip decided to give battle at once, and ordered his Genoese mercenaries to the fore. These mercenaries were equipped with crossbows, which Philip considered superior to the longbow. He was tragically mistaken. An English/Welsh bowman could fire up to ten arrows a minute with his longbow; the Genoese crossbowman struggled to fire two.

After the Genoese crossbowmen fired their volley of bolts, the English/Welsh archers stepped forward and loosed off flights and flights of arrows. The Genoese broke and ran. A slight change of angle, then Edward's bowmen targeted the French mounted men-at-arms. The French line became a congested mass of retreating Genoese mercenaries, dead and wounded men-at-arms and rearing horses. None of this, however, deterred the mounted French knights who literally cut their way through their own line with their swords. On emerging free of the chaos the French knights charged headlong at the English men-at-arms. This Edward had anticipated and the French cavalry were cut down by enfilade fire from his archers. Again and again, French knights charged uphill at the English to be slaughtered by arrow fire, with just handfuls of them reaching the English line to engage in the sort of close-quarters combat they sought.

As darkness fell, Philip's knights launched their fifteenth attack. It went the way of all its predecessors. When the French left the field of battle, they left behind them as many as 10,000 dead. Some chroniclers recorded Edward's losses as low as 100.

The French feudal nobility refused to learn the lesson of Crécy: that the longbow was a superior weapon to the crossbow. As a result, the English were assured of a string of victories culminating in the historic battle of Agincourt in 1415.

Trafalgar

Where: Off Cape Trafalgar, Spain.
Who: Thirty-seven ships of the Royal Navy, commanded by Admiral the Lord Nelson versus forty ships of the combined French-Spanish fleet commanded by Admiral Pierre-Charles Villeneuve.
When: 12.00 noon to 5.00 p.m., 21 October 1805.

"England Expects That Every Man Will Do His Duty."

So famously fluttered Admiral Nelson's signal on the leaden morning of 21 October 1805, as his ships closed in on the French-Spanish fleet. But the key to the man and his victories was in the next flag signal he had run up: *"Engage the enemy more closely".*

Horatio Nelson was a ruthless fighter and patriot. Many officers in the Royal Navy pursued the war against Napoleon as though it was a sport similar to fox-hunting, but Nelson wanted the "annihilation" of France.

There was little in Nelson's background to suggest such military single-mindedness; he was the son of a Norfolk vicar and as a boy he was frail. But he was courageous. When Nelson's mother died in 1767, when he was nine years old, he offered to go to sea "to provide for himself". His father kept him at school until Nelson was twelve, when he entered the Royal Navy as a midshipman, the most junior rank of commissioned officer. Within eight years Nelson's daring, determination and enthusiasm saw him promoted to captain. The King's son, Prince William, remembered Nelson as "the merest boy of a Captain I ever beheld".

In 1792 Britain went to war against France, and Nelson received the chance to do what he had long wanted to do: fulfil his patriotic duty on the blue sea of battle. Nelson commanded the naval brigade which bombarded Bastia and Calvi (where a blow from gravel, fragmented by cannon shot destroyed his right eye) and in 1796 he was instrumental in defeating the Spanish fleet off Cape St Vincent. Two years later, by which time Nelson had been promoted to rear admiral, he destroyed a French fleet in the Battle of the Nile. In gratitude, the British

Parliament raised him to the peerage as Baron Nelson of the Nile. In 1801 he was promoted to vice admiral and sent as second in command to the Baltic. There he famously disobeyed orders to retire (putting the telescope to his blind eye, he said, "I really do not see the signal") and won a great victory at Copenhagen.

Nelson's enthusiasm for fighting the French was contagious. He passed it to his captains, his "band of brothers", who passed it down to the men. Wrote one ordinary seaman of Nelson, "men adored him and in fighting under him, every man thought himself sure of success."

There is an important sense in which the Battle of Trafalgar was over before it began. The thirty-seven ships of the Royal Navy sailed into action full of confidence, they had an inspirational commander and they were highly trained; the forty ships of the French-Spanish fleet, by contrast, were full of demoralized sailors, many of them landsmen "pressed" into service and their commander, Villeneuve, was competent, but nothing more than that.

The Royal Navy had also been gifted an original and audacious battle plan by their commander. The "Nelson Touch" ordered the British fleet to attack the line of French-Spanish ships into two columns from the side. The first column cut into the French-Spanish line in the middle, while the second column attacked the rear of the line.

At 12.00 noon the French ship *Fougueux* began firing on HMS *Royal Sovereign* as she sailed towards her side. The Battle of Trafalgar had opened. Many of the engagements were at exactly the close-quarters Nelson wanted, thus enabling the Royal Navy to exploit its better guns and better crews to deadly effect. Jean Lucas, the captain of the French ship *Redoubtable* at Trafalgar, recalled one such action:

> The three-decker [HMS] *Temeraire* . . . came down, full sail, on our starboard side. We were almost immediately under the full fire of her artillery, discharged almost with muzzles touching.
>
> It is impossible to describe the carnage produced by the murderous broadside of this ship. More than two hundred

of our brave men were killed or wounded by it . . . A short time afterwards another ship . . . placed herself across the stern of the *Redoubtable* and fired on us within pistol shot. In less than half an hour our ship had been so fearfully mauled that she looked like little more than a heap of debris . . . The hull itself was riddled, shot through from side to side: deck beams were shattered, port lids torn away or knocked to pieces . . . Everywhere the decks were strewn with dead men, lying beneath the debris. Out of a crew of 634 men we had 522 *hors de combat* [dead and injured] . . . really I know of nothing on board that had not been hit by shot.

Many of the other French and Spanish ships suffered similar fates. By 5.00 p.m. the battle was over, when the last French ship still fighting, the *Intrepide*, struck her colours. As if to signal the end of battle, the magazine of the French *Achilles* caught fire and blew up in a tremendous explosion over the darkening sea.

Nelson had wanted the annihilation of the French-Spanish fleet. He got it. Eighteen French-Spanish ships were taken, eleven limped off the battlegound (never to sail again) and four fled, only to surrender the next day. No British ships were sunk or taken.

Some 4,400 French and Spanish sailors died at Trafalgar. The Royal Navy lost 449 men.

The most famous of these British casualties was Nelson himself, felled by a musket ball as he walked the quarter deck of his flagship, HMS *Victory*. His last words were, "Thank God, I have done my duty." On hearing of Nelson's death, people in Britain cried openly in the streets.

While Nelson's death was a tragedy for Britain, the Battle of Trafalgar itself was the nation's making. The last great fleet action of the age of sail, Trafalgar obliged Napoleon to abandon his plan for a Europe-wide military dictatorship. By contrast the British sailed from Trafalgar the ruler of the world's waves and free to build the greatest Empire the world has ever seen.

Little Big Horn

Where: Little Big Horn River, Montana, USA.
Who: 611 officers and men from the US 7th Cavalry led by
             Lieutenant Colonel George Armstrong Custer versus
             approximately 3,000 Sioux, Arapaho and Cheyenne
             warriors led by Sitting Bull and Crazy Horse.
When: 25 June 1876.

You might know the story of the Battle of Little Big Horn better
as "Custer's Last Stand".

In the morning of 25 June 1876 scouts from the US 7th
Cavalry climbed up a hill in what is modern Montana and
looked ahead towards the Little Big Horn mountain 15 miles
away. As the light improved the scouts saw gathered before
them the greatest camp of "hostile" Plains Indians ever gathered. Inside the tipis were as many as 7,000 Sioux, Cheyenne
and Arapaho.

The scouts reported back to their commanding officer, Colonel George Armstrong Custer, thirty-six years old and the
Army's most celebrated Indian-fighter. Undaunted by the size
of the Indian camp or the knowledge that the same Indian force
had just defeated the seasoned General Crook, Custer ordered
the 611 officers and men of the 7th Cavalry towards Little Big
Horn with the intention of attacking the Indian encampment.
This was directly contrary to the orders given Custer by his
commanding officer, which were to wait for reinforcements at
the mouth of the Little Big Horn River before giving battle, but
Custer wanted the glory of victory all for himself.

As he rode his horse down the Little Big Horn valley, Custer
may well have reflected on the series of events which led to the
present war between the US government and the Sioux. Events
Custer was directly responsible for. By the terms of a 1868 US
treaty with the Sioux, the Black Hills of Dakota had been given
exclusively to the Indians, but almost as the ink was still drying
Custer had led an expedition into the hills to determine whether
they contained gold. They did and soon the Black Hills were
flooded with white miners. In contravention of the treaty the
US government allowed the miners to stay – and ordered the
cavalry to drive the Sioux onto reservations. Any Indians

refusing to enter the reservations were deemed to be "hostile" and turned over to the Army "for such action as you may deem proper". What the US Army deemed proper was an all-out assault on the Plains Indians gathered in the Powder River country of Montana in the summer of 1876 for a buffalo hunt. Although the US Army in the 1870s was generally in pitiful condition, beset by bullying, poor pay and disease, the capability and morale of the cavalry was high. This was especially true of Custer's 7th Cavalry, an elite unit full of veteran troopers.

Nearing the great Indian camp, Custer made a fateful decision. Not knowing the terrain or the disposition of the enemy, he decided on reconnaissance in force, and split the regiment into three columns. Thinking the Indians might escape, Custer sent Captain Frederick Benteen with 125 troopers off to scout the hills to the south. Major Marcus Reno and his battalion was ordered to cross the Little Big Horn and attack the Indian village from the south. Custer and the remainder of the regiment, some 200 men, would proceed parallel to Reno and support his action.

Fording the Little Big Horn at around two o'clock in the afternoon, Reno began advancing along the open valley bottom. Ahead he could see a huge dust cloud caused by the hooves of waiting Indian war ponies. Reno signalled the charge, but as his command raced forward he could see no sign of the supporting Custer. Afraid of plunging into superior Indian numbers, Reno threw up his hand to halt the galloping charge which ground to a confused halt, with Reno then ordering his men to dismount and fight on foot. They began firing ragged volleys at the milling Indian horsemen in front of them before withdrawing into woods and brush along the river.

Without informing Reno, Custer had changed his battle plan. Instead of supporting Reno's charge, he rode north, screened by hills, and circled the Indian village so that it was between him and Reno. Presumably his intention was to attack the village through a gap in the hills, thus forcing the Indians to fight on two mini-fronts.

Custer and his men never reached the Indian village. As they descended a coulee, 1,500 Huncpapa Sioux warriors led by Chief Gall rode up to meet them, war cries screaming from their lips. Custer's men began to fall back, trying to seek higher ground. The situation was not entirely without hope, despite the size and ferocity of Gall's attack. But hope died for Custer and his men when they were attacked from the rear by 1,000 Oglala and Cheyenne warriors led by Crazy Horse. It was supposed by many army soldiers that American Indians had no tactical sense; but Crazy Horse and Sitting Bull, the overall chief of the Indian forces at Little Big Horn, were proof they did. Crazy Horse outflanked Custer by leading his warriors out from the camp in a downstream direction before doubling back in a vast sweeping arc which came in behind Custer's detachment. Custer was caught in a pincer movement between Crazy Horse and Gall.

Trapped on the hilltop Custer and his men fought desperately, shooting their horses to form breastworks from which they would shelter from the Indians. Some troopers fought to the last. Some were killed trying to make a break for the river. Some probably killed themselves to avoid torture. The battle took an hour, perhaps slightly less. And then Custer and all his men were dead.

An eyewitness view of "Custer's Last Stand" from the Indian side was later given by Two Moons, a Cheyenne chief:

Then the Sioux rode up the ridge on all sides, riding very fast. The Cheyenne went up the left way. Then the shooting was quick. Pop-pop-pop very fast. Some of the soldiers were down on their knees, some standing. Officers all in front. The smoke was like a great cloud, and everywhere the Sioux went the dust rose like smoke. We circled all round him – swirling like water round a stone. We shoot, we ride fast, we shoot again. Soldiers drop, and horses fall on them. Soldiers in line drop, but one man rides up and down the line – all the time shouting. He rode a sorrel horse with white face and white forelegs. I don't know who he was. He was a brave man.

Indians keep swirling round and round, and the soldiers killed only a few. Many soldiers fell. At last all horses killed but five. Once in a while some man would break out and run towards the river, but he would fall. At last about a hundred men and five horsemen stood on the hill all bunched together. All along the bugler kept blowing his commands. He was very brave too. Then a chief was killed. I hear it was Long Hair [Custer], I don't know; and then the five horsemen and the bunch of men, may be forty, started toward the river. The man on the sorrel horse led them, shouting all the time. He wore a buckskin shirt, and had long black hair and mustache. He fought hard with a big knife. His men were all covered with white dust. I couldn't tell whether they were officers or not. One man all alone ran far down towards the river, then round up over the hill. I thought he was going to escape, but a Sioux fired and hit him in the head. He was the last man. He wore braid on his arms [sergeant].

All the soldiers were now killed, and the bodies were stripped. After that no one could tell which were officers. The bodies were left where they fell. We had no dance that night. We were sorrowful.

Next day four Sioux chiefs, two Cheyennes and I, Two Moon, went upon the battlefield to count the dead. One man carried a little bundle of sticks. When we came to dead men we took a little stick and gave it to another man so we counted the dead. There were 388. There were thirty-nine Sioux and seven Cheyennes killed and about a hundred wounded.

Some white soldiers were cut with knives, to make sure they were dead; and the war women had mangled some. Most of them were left just where they fell. We came to man with the big mustache; he lay down the hills towards the river. The Indians did not take his buckskin shirt. The Sioux said, "That is a big chief. That is Long Hair." I don't know. I had never seen him. The man on the white-faced horse was the bravest man.

Three miles south of Custer, Reno had been mauled and retreated up a hill. Benteen arrived in time to save him, and the combined companies held out for another scorching day before they were relieved by the soldiers Custer had been ordered to wait for, Colonel Gibbon's infantry column. Reno and Benteen would have their share of blame for the debacle at Little Big Horn; Benteen, an able officer but public in his dislike of Custer, failed to respond to messages sent out by

Custer to hurry to join him for the attack; Reno was indecisive, failed to keep a front at the river and failed to send Benteen, his subordinate, forward to a possible relief of Custer, whose battle he could hear.

But the greatest blame for the defeat at Little Big Horn lies with Custer himself. His decision to split the regiment into three columns fatally weakened his attack. He also made the most basic mistake in warfare: underestimation of the enemy.

Late in the afternoon of 26 June the exultant Indians withdrew, leaving behind their dead warriors on burial scaffolds, surrounded by a circle of dead ponies to serve the braves in the spirit land. The Battle of the Little Big Horn was over.

Examining the battlefield the next day Colonel Gibbon found the ghastly piles of Custer's mutilated dead. "Long Hair" himself had been shot twice, once through the left temple, once through the heart. According to Kate Bighead, a Cheyenne woman who was on the battlefield, his ear was punctured to enable him to hear better in the afterworld.

The Sioux and Cheyenne had won an astounding victory. All five of Custer's companies, 225 men, had been killed. Reno and Benteen had lost 53. It was the worst defeat in US military history to that date.

It took eight days for the news of the massacre to reach the town of Helena, Montana, and from there to be flashed by telegraph all over the world. Most Americans found out on reading their newspaper on the morning of 5 July, just a day after they had celebrated the centennial of independence.

Yet, although the Indians won the battle, they lost the war. An enraged nation demanded immediate vengeance. All reservations in the northern plains were placed under military control. Throughout the rest of the year the free Indians of the northern plains were harassed by Crook, Mackenzie, Colonel Nelson A. Miles, and just about every seasoned Indian fighter the Army could get into the field. Small bands of Sioux and Cheyenne limped into the Red Cloud Agency, among them the lodges led by Crazy Horse. Some Huncapapa Sioux, led by Sitting Bull and Chief Gall, fled to Canada but there, instead of sanctuary, they found famine. The Huncapapa "holdouts" began to trickle back over the border and on to the reservations. At midday on 19 July 1881, near starving and dressed in rags, the mighty Sitting Bull himself rode into Fort Buford in Dakota. With him were just 143 followers. The last chief of the free Indians of the Plains had surrendered. It was the end of an era.

The First Battle of the Marne

Where: North-eastern France.
Who: The German First and Second Armies versus the French Fifth and Sixth Armies, together with the British Expeditionary Force.
When: 6–12 September 1914.

Having invaded Belgium and north-eastern France, the German Army made rapid progress, either pushing aside Allied forces sent to stop it or causing them to retreat. By early September the German steamroller had reached the Marne River, just 30 miles from the capital of France itelf. The French government, expecting Paris' downfall at any moment, left for Bordeaux.

Fortunately for the Allies, the French Commander-in-Chief, Joseph Joffre, was made of unflappable stuff, and ordered the French Sixth Army (comprising 150,000 men) to attack the right flank of the First German Army. After their series of relentless victories the Germans had virtually discounted the possibility of a counter-attack. French surprise was near total. Consequently, the Germans met the French onslaught of 6 September with uncharacteristic cumbersomeness and allowed a 30-mile wide gap to appear in their line – which Joffre gleefully exploited, sending the French Fifth Army together with elements of the British Expeditionary Force pouring through it. However, on 7 September, the French Sixth Army, which had been the hammer to hit the Germans, began to show signs of cracking apart. The situation was saved only by the aid of 6,000 French reserve troops ferried from Paris in taxi cabs. By the next day the French Fifth Army was mauling the flank of the German Second Army, thus widening the hole in the German line. Fearing a mass Allied breakthrough, the German Chief of Staff, Helmuth von Moltke, ordered a retreat from the Marne. After withdrawing 40 miles the German First and

Second Armies dug in along the River Aisne, beginning the trench warfare which would characterize the First World War.

Casualties in the First Battle of the Marne were heavy. The French incurred 250,000 casualties and the Germans around 200,000. The British Expeditionary Force recorded 12,733 casualties.

The Marne was more than a battle won. It was a strategic triumph, for it ended German hopes of a quick victory in the West. Many military historians argue that Germany could no longer win the war after their defeat on the Marne in 1914.

The Battle of Britain

Where: England and the English Channel.
Who: 2,500 RAF pilots versus 4,000 Luftwaffe pilots and air crew.
When: 10 July 1940 to 31 October 1940.

In April 1940, Hitler launched his "lightning war" (blitzkrieg) on the countries of Western Europe. Denmark and Norway fell rapidly. On 10 May, the Germans invaded the Low Countries and France; in just two weeks German panzers reached the English Channel, cutting the French Army in two and encircling the British Expeditionary Force, which was forced to evacuate from Dunkirk. On 16 June France surrendered.

Britain now stood alone against the Germans. Hitler determined that Britain should be conquered. But before Operation Sealion – the German invasion of Britain – could be put into effect, Germany needed control of the skies over the English Channel, across which the German invasion barges would need to sail. Göring, the head of the Luftwaffe (the German air force), informed Hitler that his fighters, now operating from bases in France, would require just four days to defeat the Royal Air Force's Fighter Command. Certainly, the Luftwaffe had numbers on their side: records show that Göring had 1,480 bombers, 989 fighters and 140 reconnaissance aircraft at his command. The principal German fighter was the superb Messerschmitt Bf109.

Against the Nazi's aerial armada, the RAF could muster some 700 combat-ready fighters, with 513 under repair. The majority of the RAF's fighters were Hawker Hurricanes, with sizeable numbers of aged Defiants and Blenheim night-fighters. Only some 20 per cent of the RAF's fighter force were the new Spitfires. Slower by 15 mph than the Bf 109, it could turn faster and its eight wing-mounted Browning machine-guns were capable of destroying a plane in a two-second burst of fire. Perhaps most seriously for Fighter Command, it was desperately short of pilots, being 154 pilots below establishment, despite the addition of volunteers from France, Poland, Czechoslovakia, the USA and the Commonwealth. One advantage, however, that the RAF did boast was a highly developed radar system which allowed for early warning of the enemy's approach. Another was that it was building aircraft at a faster rate than the enemy.

The first phase of the Battle of Britain began on 10 July with the Luftwaffe attacking shipping and ports in the English Channel, as a prelude to the German Navy mining Britain's south coast harbours. Unfortunately for the Luftwaffe it was obliged to use the Ju-87 "Stuka" for many of its sorties against Channel shipping; slow and cumbersome because of its externally hung bombs, the Stuka made easy prey for Spitfires and Hurricanes. Although the Luftwaffe achieved dominance of the sky over the Straits of Dover it did so at a high cost, losing twice as many aircraft as the RAF.

After this indecisive skirmish, the German High Command decided on 12 August to switch the focus of the attack to the RAF and its airfields in the South of England. Soon German fighter squadrons were flying as many as three low-level strafing raids a day against RAF airfields, but encountered fierce resistance from anti-aircraft guns and "scrambled" RAF fighters. To the frustration of the German 109 pilots, the size of their aircraft's fuel tank meant that they had as little as ten minutes operational time over the target area, the RAF fighter bases in southern England. A steady loss of planes and pilots caused a dip in Luftwaffe fighter morale.

With the failure of his fighters to achieve air supremacy, Göring looked to his bombers and ordered bombing raids on the RAF's southern airfields. Day after day, the airfields were battered by bombs, but nearly all continued to operate. To protect their airfields, RAF fighter pilots were scrambled as many as six times a day. Generally, their tactic was to climb high above the attacking formations of Luftwaffe bombers and their Messerschmitt 109 and 110 fighter escorts, and swoop from above in a line-astern formation. Bombers were generally attacked head on and at point-blank range before the RAF pilot pulled up and away at the last moment. After the one squadron attack that their limited numbers permitted, RAF pilots then found themselves in private battles or "dogfights" as the German fighter escorts peeled off to attack them. Pilot officer Roger Hall RAF, describes one such attack on a Luftwaffe formation during the Battle of Britain:

We were ready to attack. We were now in the battle area and three-quarters of an hour had elapsed since we had taken off.

The two bomber formations furthest from us were already being attacked by a considerable number of our fighters. Spitfires and Hurricanes appeared to be in equal numbers at the time. Some of the German machines were already falling out of their hitherto ordered ranks and floundering towards the earth. There was a little ack-ack fire coming from up somewhere on the ground although its paucity seemed pathetic and its effect was little more than that of a defiant gesture.

We approached the westernmost bomber formation from the front port quarter, but we were some ten thousand feet higher than they were and we hadn't started to dive yet. Immediately above the bombers were some twin-engined fighters, M.E. 110's. Maida Leader let the formation get a little in front of us then he gave the order "Going down now Maida aircraft," turning his machine upside-down as he gave it. The whole of "A" Flight, one after the other, peeled off after him, upside-down at first and then into a vertical dive.

When they had gone "B" Flight followed suit. Ferdie and I turned over with a hard leftward pressure to the stick to bring the starboard wing up to right angles to the horizon, and some application to the port or bottom rudder pedal to keep the nose from rising. Keeping the controls like this, the starboard wing fell over until it was parallel to the horizon

again, but upside-down. Pulling the stick back from this
position the nose of my machine fell towards the ground and
followed White one in front, now going vertically down on
to the bombers almost directly below us. Our speed started
to build up immediately. It went from three hundred miles
per hour to four and more. White one in front, his tail wheel
some distance below me but visible through the upper part
of my windscreen, was turning his machine in the vertical
plane from one side to the other by the use of his ailerons.
Red Section had reached the formation and had formed into
a loosened echelon to starboard as they attacked. They were
coming straight down on top of the bombers, having gone
slap through the protective M.E. 110 fighter screen, ignor-
ing them completely.

Now it was our turn. With one eye on our own machines I
slipped out slightly to the right of Ferdie and placed the red
dot of my sight firmly in front and in line with the starboard
engine of a Dornier vertically below me and about three
hundred yards off. I felt apprehensive lest I should collide
with our own machines in the mêlée that was to ensue. I
seemed to see one move ahead what the positions of our
machines would be, and where I should be in relation to
them if I wasn't careful. I pressed my trigger and through
my inch thick windscreen I saw the tracers spiralling away
hitting free air in front of the bomber's engine. I was
allowing too much deflection. I must correct. I pushed
the stick further forward. My machine was past the vertical
and I was feeling the effect of the negative gravity trying to
throw me out of the machine, forcing my body up into the
perspex hood of the cockpit. My Sutton harness was biting
into my shoulders and blood was forcing its way to my head,
turning everything red. My tracers were hitting the bomber's engine and bits of metal were beginning to fly off it. I
was getting too close to it, much too close. I knew I must
pull away but I seemed hypnotised and went still closer,
fascinated by what was happening. I was oblivious to
everything else. I pulled away just in time to miss hitting
the Dornier's starboard wingtip. I turned my machine to
the right on ailerons and heaved back on the stick, inflicting
a terrific amount of gravity on to the machine. I was pressed

down into the cockpit again and a black veil came over my eyes and I could see nothing.

I eased the stick a little to regain my vision and to look for Ferdie. I saw a machine, a single Spitfire, climbing up after a dive about five hundred yards in front of me and flew after it for all I was worth. I was going faster than it was and I soon caught up with it – in fact I overshot it. It was Ferdie all right. I could see the "C" Charlie alongside our squadron letters on his fuselage. I pulled out to one side and back again hurling my machine at the air without any finesse, just to absorb some speed so that Ferdie could catch up with me. "C" Charlie went past me and I thrust my throttle forward lest I should lose him. I got in behind him again and called him up to tell him so. He said: "Keep an eye out behind and don't stop weaving." I acknowledged his message and started to fall back a bit to get some room. Ferdie had turned out to the flank of the enemy formation and had taken a wide sweeping orbit to port, climbing fast as he did so. I threw my aircraft first on to its port wing-tip to pull it round, then fully over to the other tip for another steep turn, and round again and again, blacking out on each turn. We were vulnerable on the climb, intensely so, for we were so slow.

I saw them coming quite suddenly on a left turn; red tracers coming towards us from the centre of a large black twin-engined M.E. 110 which wasn't quite far enough in the sun from us to be totally obscured, though I had to squint to identify it. I shouted to Ferdie but he had already seen the tracers flash past him and had discontinued his port climbing turn and had started to turn over on his back and to dive. I followed, doing the same thing, but the M.E. 110 must have done so too for the tracers were still following us. We dived for about a thousand feet, I should think, and I kept wondering why my machine had not been hit.

Ferdie started to ease his dive a bit. I watched him turn his machine on to its side and stay there for a second, then its nose came up, still on its side, and the whole aircraft seemed to come round in a barrel-roll as if clinging to the inside of some revolving drum. I tried to imitate this manoeuvre but I didn't know how to, so I just thrust open the throttle and aimed my machine in Ferdie's direction and eventually caught him up.

The M.E. 110 had gone off somewhere. I got up to Ferdie and slid once more under the doubtful protection of his tail and told him that I was there. I continued to weave like a pilot inspired, but my inspiration was the result of sheer terror and nothing more.

All the time we were moving towards the bombers; but we moved indirectly by turns, and that was the only way we could move with any degree of immunity now. Four Spitfires flashed past in front of us, they weren't ours, though, for I noticed the markings. There was a lot of talking going on on the ether and we seemed to be on the same frequency as a lot of other squadrons. "Hallo Firefly Yellow Section – 110 behind you" – "Hallo Cushing Control – Knockout Red leader returning to base to refuel." "Close up Knockout 'N' for Nellie and watch for those 109's on your left" – "All right Landsdown Squadron – control answering – your message received – many more bandits coming from the east – over" – "Talker White two where the bloody hell are you?" – "Going down now Sheldrake Squadron – loosen up a bit" – "You clumsy clot – Hurricane 'Y' Yoke – what the flaming hades do you think you are doing?" – "I don't know Blue one but there are some bastards up there on the left – nine o'clock above" – Even the Germans came in intermittently: "Achtung, Achtung – drei Spitfeuer unter, unter Achtung, Spitfeuer, Spitfeuer." "Tally Ho – Tally Ho – Homer Red leader attacking now." "Get off the bastard air Homer leader" – "Yes I can see Rimmer leader – Red two answering – Glycol leak I think – he's getting out – yes he's baled out he's o.k."

And so it went on incessantly, disjointed bits of conversation coming from different units all revealing some private little episode in the great battle of which each story was a small part of the integral whole.

Two 109's were coming up behind the four Spitfires and instinctively I found myself thrusting forward my two-way radio switch to the transmitting position and calling out "Look out those four Spitfires – 109's behind you – look out." I felt that my message could hardly be of less im-

portance than some that I had heard, but no heed was taken
of it. The two 109's had now settled themselves on the tail of
the rear Spitfire and were pumping cannon shells into it.
We were some way off but Ferdie too saw them and changed
direction to starboard, opening up his throttle as we closed.
The fourth Spitfire, or "tail end Charlie", had broken
away, black smoke pouring from its engine, and the third
in line came under fire now from the same 109. We approached the two 109's from above their starboard rear
quarter and, taking a long deflection shot from what must
have been still out of range, Ferdie opened fire on the
leader. The 109 didn't see us for he still continued to fire
at number three until it too started to trail Glycol from its
radiator and turned over on its back breaking away from the
remaining two. "Look out Black one – look out Black
Section Apple Squadron – 109's – 109's" came the belated
warning, possibly from number three as he went down. At
last number one turned steeply to port, with the two 109's
still hanging on to their tails now firing at number two.
They were presenting a relatively stationary target to us
now for we were directly behind them. Ferdie's bullets were
hitting the second 109 now and pieces of its tail unit were
coming away and floating past underneath us. The 109
jinked to the starboard. The leading Spitfire followed by its
number two had now turned full circle in a very tight turn
and as yet it didn't seem that either of them had been hit.
The 109 leader was vainly trying to keep into the same turn
but couldn't hold it tight enough so I think his bullets were
skidding past the starboard of the Spitfires. The rear 109's
tail unit disintegrated under Ferdie's fire and a large chunk
of it slithered across the top surface of my starboard wing,
denting the panels but making no noise. I put my hand up to
my face for a second.

The fuselage of the 109 fell away below us and we came
into the leader. I hadn't fired at it yet but now I slipped
out to port of Ferdie as the leader turned right steeply and
over on to its back to show its duck-egg blue belly to us. I
came up almost to line abreast of Ferdie on his port side
and fired at the under surface of the German machine,
turning upside-down with it. The earth was now above

my perspex hood and I was trying to keep my sights on the 109 in this attitude, pushing my stick forward to do so. Pieces of refuse rose up from the floor of my machine and the engine spluttered and coughed as the carburettor became temporarily starved of fuel. My propeller idled helplessly for a second and my harness straps bit into my shoulders again. Flames leapt from the engine of the 109 but at the same time there was a loud bang from somewhere behind me and I heard "Look out Roger" as a large hole appeared near my starboard wing-tip throwing up the matt green metal into a ragged rent to show the naked aluminium beneath.

I broke from the 109 and turned steeply to starboard throwing the stick over to the right and then pulling it back into me and blacking out at once. Easing out I saw three 110's go past my tail in "V" formation but they made no attempt to follow me round "Hallo Roger – Are you O.K.?" I heard Ferdie calling. "I think so – where are you?" I called back.

"I'm on your tail – keep turning" came Ferdie's reply. Thank God, I thought. Ferdie and I seemed to be alone in the sky. It was often like this. At one moment the air seemed to be full of aircraft and the next there was nothing except you. Ferdie came up in "V" on my port side telling me at the same time that he thought we had better try to find the rest of the squadron.

From *Clouds of Fear* by Roger Hall, 1975. Copyright © 1975 RMD Hall.

Despite the bravery of RAF pilots, by the end of August the battle was beginning to wear down Fighter Command. From 31 August to 6 September the Luftwaffe lost 255 bombers and fighters, the British 185 fighters. The reserve of RAF fighters was dwindling, as was the reserve of pilots. The strain of flying every day, sometimes several times a day, began to tell on Fighter Command's pilots.

Relief was at hand. On 7 September Göring switched the main focus of the Luftwaffe attack away from the RAF's airfields to London. A little after 5.00 p.m. over 300 German bombers, escorted by 600 fighters, converged on London and dropped their bombs on the East End and the docklands. The fires which were started acted as a beacon for a night raid by 250 bombers. When morning broke amidst the smoke 306 Londoners were dead.

Even so, Göring's decision to target London was a colossal strategic mistake. It allowed RAF Fighter Command to repair its airfields and reorganize its dwindled squadrons. More raids on London followed. The Luftwaffe believed that the RAF was down to its last 200 fighters. Some German bombers arrived over London unescorted and were picked off by the RAF.

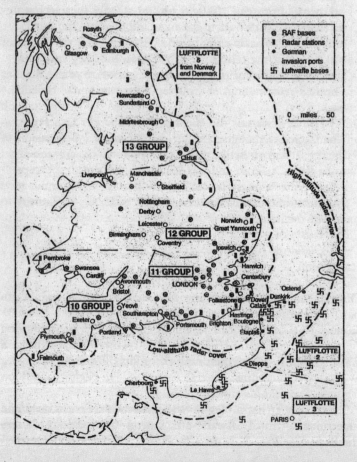

The climax of the battle came on 15 September when a mass raid by German bombers, stacked twenty storeys high, was badly mauled by RAF fighters at midday. Another raid in the early afternoon was also repulsed. The Germans lost sixty aircraft to the RAF's twenty-six.

It was clear that the Luftwaffe had not achieved air supremacy. Neither was it likely to. On 17 September Hitler abandoned his plan for the invasion of Britain. Increasingly the Luftwaffe turned to night bombing of London – a tacit admission that it had lost the daylight battle. The British Prime Minister Winston Churchill said of the Battle of Britain, "Never in the course of human history has so much been owed by so many to so few." "The few", the 2,500 pilots of Fighter Command, deserved their plaudits. Over the course of the battle, which officially ended on 31 October, the RAF had shot down 1,733 German aircraft for the loss of 915.

The Battle of Britain had far-reaching consequences, besides the saving of Britain from invasion. The battle destroyed the myth of Nazi military invincibility and required Hitler to keep thirty-five divisions in the West in case of British intervention on the Continent. Consequently, his force for his invasion of Russia was substantially reduced – so that it too ended in failure.

At the end of the Second World War Field Marshal von Rundstedt, one of Hitler's main commanders, was asked to name the decisive battle of the war. Unhesitatingly he replied, "The Battle of Britain".

Midway

Where: Midway Island, the Hawaiian archipelago, South Pacific.

Who: 161 ships of the Japanese Imperial Navy (including four aircraft carriers) versus fifty-three ships of the US Pacific Fleet (including three aircraft carriers).

When: 4–7 June 1942.

After their surprise attack on the US base at Pearl Harbor in December 1941, the Japanese advanced remorselessly though the Pacific, seizing Malaysia, the Dutch East Indies, Singapore, the Philippines and numerous island groups in the central and western Pacific. In spring 1942, the Japanese identified the US-owned Midway Island as a key strategic target; the island could be both a base for another phase of conquest and an outer shield in the event of counter-attack. Moreover, the Commander-in-Chief of the Japanese Combined Fleet, Admiral Isoruku Yamamoto, believed that he could use Midway as a trap to destroy the US Pacific Fleet. When the US Pacific Fleet rushed to the aid of invaded Midway, a Japanese carrier and battleship task force, waiting unseen, would fall upon the unsuspecting US Navy.

Unknown to the Japanese, however, their Midway plan had been rumbled. American cryptanalysts – code-breakers – had deciphered crucial Japanese military messages and knew that Midway was an intended target. The Americans also knew when the Japanese attack would fall: 4 June 1942.

In early June, American naval reconnaissance planes observed a Japanese armada of 185 ships 966 km (600 miles) from Midway. Two American naval task forces, spearheaded by the aircraft carriers *Enterprise, Hornet* and *Yorktown*, were already at sea. Just after midnight on 4 June US Admiral Chester W. Nimitz, on analysing patrol plane reports, advised his task forces of the course and speed of the Japanese invasion fleet. And ordered the interceptiom.

Even as Nimitz was relaying his orders, Japanese armourers and air mechanics were readying the planes aboard the four carriers in the Japanese invasion fleet. A little after dawn on 4 June, 108 Japanese planes roared down the decks of their carriers, their destination Midway. At 6.15 a.m. ordnance from Japanese "Kate" and "Val" bombers landed on Midway. Clouds of dust and smoke bloomed up, and most Japanese pilots believed that they had wiped out US defences and storage facilities. However, the more sagacious Lieutenant Tomonga radioed back to the Japanese fleet, "There is need for a second attack." Accordingly, on board the carriers *Akagi* and *Kaga* the armourers were ordered to load the reserve Kates with bombs.

While the Japanese armourers were hauling bombs to the waiting Kates, the Japanese fleet received a dread signal from the pilot of a reconnaissance plane. He had sighted enemy [US] surface ships and they were accompanied "by what appears to be a carrier". The pilot was a third right. There were in fact three US carriers steaming towards the Japanese fleet. The hunter had become the hunted.

Absolute pandemonium broke out in the hangars of the Japanese carriers, because the Kates now had to have their bombs unloaded and replaced by torpedoes. Meanwhile, the Japanese planes which had attacked Midway were returning to the carriers, needing to land, rearm and refuel. One Japanese officer later described the mayhem aboard the carriers:

> We had about one hundred Zeros (fighters), Vals and Kates in the air, low on fuel, the Zeros out of ammunition too, some of them damaged. They all had to be recovered and serviced. That would take one hour. And we could not launch an attack meanwhile. The Zeros that had not gone to Midway were . . . half out of fuel as a result of defending our carriers. Some of our bombers were armed with bombs, some with torpedoes, some unarmed. It was not a good situation – not good at all.

Meanwhile, US Admiral Fletcher commanding Task Force 17 launched Devastator torpedo bombers from all three of his carriers. The Devastator was ill-named; it was slow and clumsy. Three waves flew in at the Japanese carriers, but almost all were shot down by anti-aircraft fire or circling Zeros. But then three US Douglas Dauntless dive-bombers suddenly swooped on the Japanese ships. A 1,000 lb high-explosive bomb hit the *Akagi* bang in the centre of the flight deck. Another Dauntless-delivered bomb hit the *Akagi* on the port side of the flight deck. Multiple explosions destroyed the heart of the ship, which had to be abandoned.

The second wave of Dauntless dive-bombers zeroed in on the *Kaga*, which received two hits on the bridge. Fire spread to the hangar, where explosives and aviation fuel combined to produce an inferno that within minutes melted metal and men together.

Dauntlesses then dropped down towards the *Soryu*, which was dealt the same fate as the *Akagi* and *Kaga*.

The only surviving Japanese carrier was now the *Hiryu*, from which the Japanese launched their retaliation. Forty Japanese bombers and Zeros duly attacked the USS *Yorktown*. Three

Vals broke through the anti-aircraft "flak" to bomb the ship, which caught fire. Desperate work by firefighting crews, however, got the blaze damped down. To no avail. A following wave of Kates hit the *Yorktown* with torpedoes, causing her to list in the water with her flight deck at too steep an angle to be used.

The battle was not quite finished. The Americans then sent up twenty-four Dauntlesses on a hunt for the remaining Japanese carrier, the *Hiryu*. They found her. And sunk her.

Two days later *Yorktown* finally gave up her personal battle for survival, after being hit by torpedoes from a Japanese submarine.

Despite the loss of the *Yorktown*, Midway was a decisive victory for the Americans, and turned the tide of war in the Pacific. The Japanese never recovered from the loss of carriers, aircraft and pilots.

Midway also merits attention for being a milestone in the history of warfare. It was the first naval battle in which the opposing fleets never sighted each other. All the fighting was done by aircraft.

D-day

Where: Normandy, France.
Who: 180,000 British, American, Canadian, Free French, Polish troops commanded by General Dwight Eisenhower versus approximately 100,000 German troops commanded by Field Marshal Rommel.
When: 12.30 a.m. to 12 midnight, 6 June 1944.

D-Day, the Allied invasion of German-occupied France, was the biggest seaborne invasion in history. Some 156,000 Allied troops sailed in 5,000 craft from ports in southern England across the Channel to land at five beaches in Normandy. The Americans had the most westerly beaches, code-named Utah and Omaha, the British and the remainder of the Allies landed at Sword, Juno and Gold beaches. The left flank of the British beaches was to be protected by 8,500 troops from the British 6th Airborne Division; the right flank of the American beaches was to be protected by 13,000 parachutists from the US 82nd and 101st Airborne Divisions.

In the early minutes of 6 June 1944 the Allied paratroopers began dropping out over the Normandy sky like so much confetti in the night. The Airborne drops, which were reinforced by glider landings, caused chaos and confusion amongst the occupying German troops, many of whose senior officers were inconveniently away from the front line on a course or leave. Field Marshal Rommel, in command of Army Group B and the "Atlantic Wall" defences, was in Germany celebrating his wife's fiftieth birthday.

As dawn opened that morning of 6 June, German Army lookouts on the cliffs of Normandy were astonished to see the sea before them full of craft. Some of these were battleships – at 05.45 they began to bombard German coastal positions, which were also pounded from above by RAF and USAAF bombers. (Over 14,000 sorties were flown by the RAF and USAAF on D-Day.) At around the same time, Allied troops began transferring into landing craft to make the final approach to the invasion beaches.

The Americans began landing on Omaha and Utah beaches at 06.25, struggling through the waves to the sand. The landing at Utah beach was relatively uneventful, but Omaha beach was dominated by a low cliff on which were ensconced first-rate Wehrmacht troops from the 352nd Division. Soon hundreds of US troops from the assault waves lay dead in the surf and on the sand, with thousands more troops pinned down by German machine-gun and rifle fire. Not until 10.30 did the US 1st Infantry Division "neutralize" German machine-gun emplacements. Captain Joseph T. Dawson was one of the American soldiers responsible for "knocking out" the German positions:

Above me, right on top of the ridge, the Germans had a line of defences with an excellent field of fire. I kept the men behind and, along with my communications sergeant and his assistant, worked our way slowly up to the crest of the ridge. Just before the crest was a sharp perpendicular drop, and we were able to get up the crest without being seen by the enemy. I could now hear the Germans talking in the machine-gun nest immediately above me. I then threw two grenades, which were successful in eliminating the enemy and silencing the machine gun which had been holding up our approach.

Meanwhile, the British and other Allied troops began landing on their beaches from 07.30 onwards. The experience of these troops as they struggled ashore differed widely. To get off Gold Beach the 1st Battalion The Hampshire Regiment fought an eight-hour battle; only hundreds of yards further down the beach the Green Howards landed almost unopposed. By midday most Allied lead units had broken through Hitler's "Atlantic Wall" and were moving inland. In their wake, thousands of other troops were landing on the beaches, along with tanks, vehicles and supplies.

Not until late afternoon were the Germans able to mount a serious counterattack, since their movements were constantly harried by Allied aircraft, the airborne parachutists and the French resistance. The German response was also delayed by the fact that Hitler – whose permission was needed to commit the panzer [tank] divisions stationed in France to battle – slept late and his staff feared to wake him. At 5.00 p.m., the 21st Panzer Division were told by General Marks "the future of Germany may very well rest on your shoulders. If you don't push the British back to the sea, we've lost the war." Only minutes after starting their charge to the sea, 21st Panzer were met by heavy fire from Sherman Fireflies of the Staffordshire Regiment. Thirteen panzers were knocked out almost immediately. The 21st Panzer Division failed to push back the British, although it did foil their attempt to reach their D-Day objective of Caen.

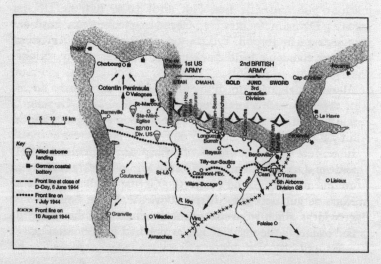

On the American beaches, progress inland from Utah was rapid, and the 4th Infantry Division was able to link up with the American airborne divisions around Ste Mère Eglise. At Omaha, immediately nicknamed "Bloody Omaha" by GIs, every yard inland had to be fought for against dogged resistance from remnants of the Wehrmacht's 352nd and 716th Divisions, which used the high hedges and ditches of the Normandy *bocage* to great defensive effect. Around 12,000 Allied soldiers perished in the landings (and a similar number of Germans) but by midnight 100,000 Allied soldiers were on French soil holding a bridgehead 60 miles in length.

If the landings had failed, the whole course of the Second World War would have been different. In the event, D-Day was the beginning of the end of the Nazis' "Third Reich".

Desert Storm

Where: Kuwait/Iraq.
Who: 450,000 Coalition troops led by US General H. Norman Schwarzkopf versus 500,000 Iraqi troops led by Saddam Hussein.
When: 16 January to 28 February 1991.

In the vast winter silence of the desert night the ominous keening of aircraft high overhead could be heard. Everywhere along the Saudi-Kuwaiti border troops looked anxiously skywards from their foxholes. The jets were flying east, and mud soldiers of the Coalition shivered a sigh of relief. Ours. At the wet, temporary HQ of Britain's First Armoured Division a single voice rang out clear into the sandy darkness: "Yellow Alert. We are at war."

It was 11.30 p.m. on the evening of 16 January 1991. Operation Desert Storm, the effort to remove Saddam Hussein from his occupation of Kuwait, and the biggest concerted military action since the Second World War, had begun – just five months and 13 days after the Iraqi dictator had sent his tanks rolling across the Kuwaiti border. If the invasion of Kuwait had been a military success, it had also proved to be the biggest political mistake of Saddam's career.

No sooner had Saddam ordered his 500,000 victorious invasion troops to dig-in along the Kuwaiti–Saudi Arabian border, than the Americans had, under the flag of the United Nations, garnered together a considerable Coalition of anti-Saddam forces dedicated to ejecting him from Kuwait.

The bulk of these forces, some 450,000 men and women, were provided by the USA; in recognition of America's contribution, the command of Operation Desert Storm was given to US General H. Norman Schwarzkopf and his CENTCOM staff.

"Stormin Norman", as he became dubbed, was a 56-year-old Vietnam veteran, of some irascibility. Whether by luck or design, in him the Americans had appointed a commander who was a canny user of the media – many American officers still blamed TV for defeat in Vietnam – and a master of the soundbite. At the end of the campaign, Schwarzkopf was asked by a journalist what he thought of Saddam Hussein as a military strategist. Using the fingers of his left hand to count off Saddam's "attributes", Schwarzkopf replied: "As far as Saddam Hussein being a great military strategist, he is neither a strategist, nor is he schooled in the operational arts, nor is he a tactician, nor is he a general, nor is he a soldier. Other than that, he is a great military man. I want you to know that."

Schwarzkopf himself, however, was all the above. A near-genius at battlefield strategy and tactics, his Operation Desert Storm would draw comparisons with Cannae and El Alamein.

Following his arrival in Saudi Arabia in August 1990, Schwarzkopf had initially been concerned only to secure the east Saudi border (Operation Desert Shield) against Iraqi incursions. Two months later Washington, mindful that economic and diplomatic sanctions might well fail to persuade Saddam to withdraw his forces from Kuwait, directed the General to prepare contingency plans for an offensive.

On paper, at least, the Iraqi Army was a formidable opponent and CENTCOM planned for the worst. Intelligence suggested that the Iraqi Army was as big and as dangerous as Saddam Hussein himself claimed. It contained over a million men, and possessed a devil's feast of modern weaponry: around 6,000 tanks (including a number of Soviet T-72s), 4,000 armoured personnel carriers, between 800 and 1,000 combat aircraft and 3,200 artillery pieces, including some which could outgun those of the Coalition. Moreover, the Iraqi Army was reputed to be battle-hardened after its grinding 1980–8 war with Iran, and extremely adept at defence. It had already fortified the border with Saudi Arabia with a continuous belt of obstacles, including sand berms and oil-filled trenches which could, with the touch of a torch, be turned into a wall of fire. Most dangerous of all the Iraqi forces were the armoured divisions of the "elite" Republican Guard, held as a theatre reserve in southern Iraq and northern Kuwait. Uncomfortable at not having the classic three to one ratio of advantage that military wisdom says an attacker should have in order to guarantee victory, and worried that an offensive might break down into an attrition battle or *slugfest*, Schwarzkopf decided to exploit the Coalition's huge air force to reduce Saddam's military capability, especially in the Kuwaiti Theatre of Operations (KTO). This would be the preliminary to a ground offensive with air support (in line with the AirLand Battle Doctrine adopted by the Pentagon in 1982) which would outflank the main Iraqi defences in the west beyond the point at which the Iraqi, Saudi and Kuwaiti borders meet – and where the Iraqis had failed inexplicably to build fortifications. This massive outflanking drive into the KTO from the west would be accompanied by direct attacks from the south and a feint amphibious landing from the east, where 17,000 US Marines were waiting offshore. The Iraqis would be crushed and caught in a massive envelopment. Though it was apparently bitterly contested by some of his staff, Schwarzkopf stuck to the essentials of his plan, finally getting it approved in mid-January 1991.

The plan was no sooner approved than it was called into use. The deadline for the implementation of United Nations Resolution 660 (Iraqi withdrawal from Kuwait) ex-

pired on midnight 15 January. The first Coalition aircraft
were in the air twenty-four hours later, flying the first of
a total of 110,000 sorties against targets across Iraq and
Kuwait. Radar-guided American Stealth bombers executed
pinpoint attacks with so-called smart bombs, accurate
enough to be deposited down the airshafts of Iraqi bun-
kers. Other planes, wave after wave of them, F-15Es, F-
A18 Hornets, A-6E Intruders and RAF Tornadoes
bombed Iraqi military and communications targets and
destroyed much of Saddam's air force before it could
leave the runway. In the first day of the air campaign,
US warships in the Gulf launched more than 100 Toma-
hawk Cruise missiles (each armed with half a ton of high
explosive); observers in the Iraqi capital, Baghdad,
watched in wonder as the Cruise missiles flew between
buildings and turned corners before hitting their targets.
Baghdad shook under the weight of the bombardment.
Iraqi anti-aircraft fire turned the sky white.

Over the following weeks the air campaign drastically
degraded Saddam's ability to fight a battle, destroying his
highly centralized communications and command system,
his arms and his army's morale. The Coalition achieved
complete air supremacy. In Schwarzkopf's phrase, the
removal of the Iraqis from the skies "blinded" Saddam.
For this, the Allies were to lose a total of 67 aircraft.

The one black cloud in the Coalition's silver-lined air
campaign was Iraq's Scud missile capability. Saddam
began firing his Soviet-built Scud missiles on the second
night of the air war, the first targets being Tel Aviv and
Haifa in Israel. Although the six missiles which landed in
Israel killed no one, and did not contain the feared
chemical or nuclear warheads, the impact was psycholo-
gically and politically explosive. Israel threatened to take
unilateral retaliatory action, something which would have
wrecked the anti-Iraqi alliance, even perhaps starting a
new Arab–Israeli war. Frantic diplomacy by the Americans, together with the dispatch of Patriot ground-to-air
missile systems to shoot down Scuds, managed to persuade Israel from immediate punitive measures. The Pa-
triots, though, were only of minimal effectiveness, failing,

even when they intercepted incoming Scuds, always to destroy the warhead. Covert operations by British SAS and US Special Forces teams, dropped behind Iraqi lines, and the hunting of mobile Scud launchers by the Coalition air force did better. In the end, the Israelis suffered only 13 fatalities from Scuds. The Iraqis' most effective Scud launch was one of those aimed at Saudi Arabia. In the dying hours of the war a Scud landed on a US barracks in Dhahran, killing 28.

Such was the effectiveness of the air campaign that senior Coalition air force officers began to question whether a ground offensive was necessary. Schwarzkopf, however, along with the army and the Marines, was mindful that a war has never been won by airpower alone. Consequently, as the air campaign continued its attrition of enemy units, Schwarzkopf continued the deployment of the coalition army, most crucially of all the move west of the bulk of his forces: the US XVIII Airborne Corps, including the French Light Armoured *Division Daguet*, farthest west, its task a lightning drive to the Euphrates which would simultaneously protect the left flank of the invasion and cut off an Iraqi escape; then, to the right of XVIII Airborne, VII Corps, including British 1st Armoured Division, the steel *schwerpunkt* of the offensive which would smash north and then north-east towards Kuwait, hitting the Republican Guard in the flank. This remarkable movement of XVIII Airborne and VII Corps to their start positions was accomplished across several hundred miles of desert by thousands of tanks, trucks and other support vehicles. In order both to tie down Iraqi troops and confirm Iraqi expectations of a frontal attack on Kuwait City, Coalition Arab forces and the US 1st and 2nd Marines, together with the 1st (Tiger) Brigade of the US 2nd Armoured Division were deployed in the south of the battlefield, along the Kuwaiti–Saudi border.

While Schwarzkopf made ready, time was trickling away for Saddam Hussein. If the air war had degraded his military capacity it had done nothing to diminish his rhetoric or his will to hold onto Kuwait, promising the Coalition "the Mother of All Battles" should it try to force him out. A Soviet attempt to broker talks failed. On 22 February US President Bush gave Saddam the ultimatum to withdraw from Kuwait or face the consequences. In the best fashion of the Western, Bush's deadline expired at noon–noon (EST) on Saturday 23 February. Saddam refused to blink. That night, with singular appropriateness, American Forces network radio in the Gulf played "Saturday Night's All Right (For Fighting)". As Elton John sang, soldiers along the front line were making ready for combat, Marine bulldozers breaching Iraqi defences. Sand berms were demolished, trenches filled with oil burned off, and minefields cleared.

As Saturday night edged into Sunday morning, Coalition air force and navy began a massive bombardment of the Iraqi lines. It started raining. And then at 4 a.m., US and Saudi Marines in the coastal area that was the easternmost point of the battlefield began moving forward through the Iraqi defences, the vaunted "Saddam Line". The ground war had begun.

The Marines breached the Iraqi barriers with relative ease, the minefields posing fewer problems than expected: many mines had become exposed by shifting sand, while some Marines crossed the minefields by walking on anti-tank mines, knowing that they could not be detonated by the weight of a man. By the end of the first day of the ground war (G-Day) the 1st Marine Division had secured Al-Jaber airfield, halfway to Kuwait City, having bypassed some Iraqi units who were poised to fight but failed to counter-attack. The battlefield, eerily quiet and shrouded in acrid smoke from the Kuwaiti oil wells set on fire by the Iraqis on 22 February, was littered with burnt-out wrecks of Iraqi trucks and tanks, victims of the Coalition air force.

At the opposite end of the Allied line, the French *Division Daguet* and its attached US 82nd Airborne Division (the Screaming Eagles), given the task of sweeping around the Saddam Line and securing the offensive's left flank, penetrated rapidly into Iraq, brusquely subduing the Iraqi 45th Infantry Division with artillery and HOT anti-tank missiles from French-built Gazelle helicopters. The 101st Airborne Division, immediately to the east, after a hold-up due to poor weather, mounted one of the biggest airmobile operations in history with some 300 Chinook helicopters ferrying troops to establish an advance position, FOB Cobra, 70 miles inside Iraqi territory.

Iraqi resistance to the Coalition incursions was everywhere so minimal that by late morning Schwarzkopf decided to deal the enemy a further reeling blow, bringing the second phase of the offensive forward to the afternoon of G-Day instead of the morning of G + 1. The US 24th Mechanized Infantry Division – Schwarzkopf's old division – along with the 3rd Armoured Cavalry began rolling forward at midday, its mission to cross nearly 250 miles of Iraqi rock and sand and establish itself near the town of Basra, where it would cut off Iraqi forces and engage the Republican Guards. As the 24th roared across the desert it passed weary US Long Range Surveillance Detachments, who had been in Iraq for weeks sending back HUMINT (human intelligence). Also at midday, VII Corps – with 1,300 tanks the biggest armoured corps in history – led by the "Big Red One", the US 1st Infantry Division (Mechanized), began its breach of the Iraqi line, with the divisions of the Corps following through over the next 24 hours. The British 1st Armoured Division went through the breach in the morning of G + 1, the "anvil" on which the rest of the Corps would hammer the Republican Guards.

To the right of VII Corps, east of Wadi al-Batin, Arab forces from Egypt, Syria, Saudi Arabia and Kuwait began their advance in the afternoon of G-Day, proceeding more circumspectly than their neighbours, the US Marines, in part because they faced one of the most fortified sections of the Saddam Line. The Egyptians found themselves in front of walls of burning oil, but managed the breach in less than five hours after pushing sand into the trenches with their tanks and bulldozers.

By evening all Coalition forces had advanced well beyond their schedule, progress only improved by the Coalition's continuing deception operation, with thousands of Marines – apparently set for a seaborne invasion – waiting off Kuwait's shore, and a highly visible demonstration by the famous 1st Armoured Cavalry Division (the Air Cav) in the Wadi al-Batin. Casualties had been minimal. Among the worst losses of the day were those suffered by the British in a "friendly fire" incident, when an American A-10 "Tankbuster" mistakenly eliminated a British Warrior Armoured Vehicle; nine soldiers died.

As dawn broke on 25 February, G + 1, the scale of the Iraqi rout and disorientation became more apparent. The fast-moving *Division Daguet* had hardly encountered a living soul and continued its spectacular dash throughout the day, reaching As-Salman airfield, 70 miles inside Iraq, by evening, where it had to be ordered to pause. Eastward down the line the 24th Infantry Division (the Victory Division) rolled ever onwards, also without opposition, while the British 1st Armoured Division engaged and defeated the Iraqi 12th Armoured Division before becoming delayed by the throngs of Iraqi soldiers eager to surrender. Elsewhere over the battlefield it was the same story of Iraqis throwing down their weapons. The crush of POW's, indeed, posed more of a problem than the Iraqis who tried to fight; 25,000 prisoners were captured during the day. Only in a handful of places did the Iraqis put up serious resistance. An armoured division counter-attacked the US 2nd Marine Division near Al-Jaber but was heavily repulsed. Iraqi armour which tried to block the path of the 2nd Marine Division and the Tiger Brigade also fared badly. Perhaps the fiercest encounter of the day was at the Burgan oil field near Kuwait International Airport, where the 1st Marine Division met with well-entrenched Iraqi units. These were flushed out by a massive "time on time" artillery bombardment and then decimated by USMC tanks and Cobra attack helicopters. The Iraqis lost 50 tanks for no USMC loss.

If the Coalition needed any proof that things were going well, it came on the morning of the next day, Tuesday 26 February (G + 2), when Baghdad Radio announced that Iraq was prepared to withdraw from Kuwait. Washington's response was brusque: "The war goes on." In Kuwait City itself, panic-stricken Iraqis began to commandeer vehicles and flee northwards on the road to the Mutla Gap causing, as one commentator quipped, "the mother of all traffic jams". A dozen Coalition F-15s bombed the front of a 1,000-vehicle Iraqi convoy, and then bombed its rear. Coalition aircraft then swarmed down on the luckless trapped Iraqis in a turkey-shoot reminiscent of the destruction of the Wehrmacht as it tried to escape through the Falaise Gap in 1944.

The reason for the Iraqi haste in quitting Kuwait City was that the Coalition's southern groupings were now only miles from the suburbs, although the US 1st Marine Division had run into a sizeable formation of Iraqi armour determined to make a fight for the International Airport. The battle would last throughout the day and into the next, the sky so dark with smoke from oil well fires that flashlights had to be used to read charts. The Tiger Brigade and 2nd Marine Division also met opposition as they curled north around Kuwait City to prevent any retreat.

Meanwhile, far to the west, with the *Division Daguet* holding the left flank secure against Iraqi reinforcements, the XVIII Airborne Corps had consolidated its hold on the Euphrates valley, with the 24th Infantry Division reaching Highway 8 and then surging eastwards down it towards Basra, its helicopter attack regiment in the van. The 24th had the smell of success in its nostrils and was now riding towards the Republican Guard. A brigade of 57 Iraqi T-72 tanks unlucky enough to cross the 24th's path was decimated, the T-72s no match for the 24th's M1A1s and Apache attack helicopters.

Likewise closing on the Republican Guards was VII Corps, with the 2nd Armoured Cavalry making contact with the Guard late in the evening. After completing its rout of the 12th Iraqi Armoured Division, the British 1st Armoured Division had overrun the 17th and 52nd Armoured Divisions, eliminating 300 enemy tanks and armoured vehicles in the process. At midnight the British division reached its main objective, codenamed Waterloo, at the south end of Phase Line Smash. Caught between an anvil and a descending hammer, the Republican Guard realized too late that the target of XVIII Airborne and VII Corps was not Kuwait but the Guard itself.

Over the next 32 hours, by 8 a.m. Thursday 28 February (G + 4), the Iraqi Army disintegrated. They surrendered in their thousands, waving anything white they could find. The Iraqi force at Kuwait International Airport was finally overcome, with the triumphant Marines opening their lines to give the honour of liberating Kuwait City to the Kuwait 35th Mechanized Brigade, who entered the city at 9 a.m. on 27 February to an ecstatic welcome. Much of the city was anyway already in the control of Kuwaiti resistance fighters.

Along the Iraq–Kuwait border, meanwhile, XVIII Airborne and VII Corps engaged the Republican Guard in what would be the classic tank battle of the campaign, lasting into the morning of G + 4. Although some of the Iraqi units in the Basra Pocket put up a brave fight, especially those from the Guard's best-equipped divisions (Tawakalna, Medina and Hammurabi), it was always a one-sided contest. The Iraqis had no air cover and very poor communications, while the attack–attack tactic of the US forces never allowed them time to consolidate. The Coalition was fighting a multi-dimensional modern war while the Iraqis wanted a static war of First World War vintage. The Republican Guard left the field with its pretensions to military elitism in tatters. In truth the Guard was never the force Saddam claimed it to be, or the Coalition feared it to be. Its experience fighting the Iranians had left it not so much combat-ready as combat-fatigued. Moreover, the Guard – its primary function being the protection of Saddam's Ba'athist dictatorship – selected most of its officers for political reliability, not military ability. What was arguably the best Guard unit, *Amn al-Khas* (special security), was judged too important by Saddam to fight in the war, and was kept in Baghdad. Other Iraqi units, made up overwhelmingly of conscripts, had second-rate equipment and little desire to die for Saddam's lost cause. Nor were there as many Iraqi soldiers in the KTO as the Coalition had estimated (500,000); in all probability they numbered fewer than 300,000–200,000 fewer than the Coalition.

With the Iraqi Army almost completely encircled, Schwarzkopf would have liked to have continued the war to ensure its destruction. As it was, 700 Iraqi tanks escaped the net. The Coalition's Arab members had no wish to see the complete disintegration of Iraq – which would have unleashed a wave of protest in their countries, where support for Saddam was sizeable – and at 9 p.m. (EST), in a televised address, President Bush announced a ceasefire from midnight

– 8 a.m. on 28 February in the Gulf. By the close of the ground war the Iraqis had suffered around 8,000 casualties; another 86,000 Iraqis had surrendered to the Coalition. The Iraqi Army had not only been driven from Kuwait, it had been routed. Coalition casualties during the ground war were minimal: 150 KIA, a quarter of these victims in "friendly fire" incidents. The Mother of All Battles had taken exactly 100 hours.

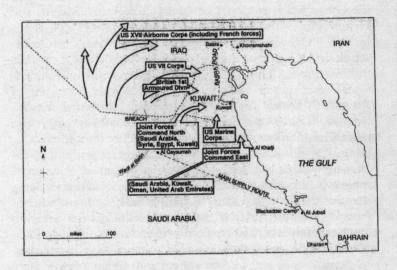

THREE SIMPLE MAGIC TRICKS

The Sack Trick

This trick is probably best done under adult supervision. You'll need to make sure that the sack selected for the trick is made from material which allows the "disappearing boy" to breathe easily.

Many mysterious conjuring tricks can be performed with very simple apparatus that any handy lad can make at small cost – in fact – most of the necessary material can probably be found in the house. For example, if you can find or acquire a large clean sack and a few yards of stout cord you can easily rig up an effective trick. The sack must be big enough to allow a boy to stand inside it, because

you are going to tie up a boy in the sack, as in Fig. 1, and let the audience tie as many knots in the cords as they please, then within a few seconds of tying him up securely in the sack he will be free. First of all you must prepare the sack – as shown in Fig. 2

Fig 1.—The sack trick.

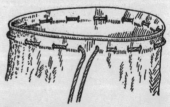

Fig 2.—Arrangement of cord in sack.

– by making holes in it about every four inches apart and about two to three inches from the edge. Run a cord in and out of these holes and leave the two ends loose as shown in the diagram, Fig. 2, then borrow a sheet or a large tablecloth and you are ready to perform the trick. You should tie up a boy to whom you have entrusted the secret – under dire threats of severe punishment if he "tells" how it is done!

This is how you perform the trick; first you let the audience examine the sack very thoroughly, then you put the boy in the sack – draw the sack up over

Fig. 3.—How the trick is worked.

his head – then draw the two cords tight and knot them. Next you get the audience to tie as many knots in the cord as they like – but do not let them twist the loose ends around the neck of the sack. You must not let the audience know you are stopping them from doing this – all you have to do is to tell them to tie knots in the cord – they will not think of doing anything else. As soon as the knots are securely tied, take the sheet or tablecloth – throw it over the sack and take out your watch. Tell the audience that within thirty seconds from the word "go" – and of course a wave of your magic wand! the boy will appear with the sack in his hand and the knots untied. Now you will want to know how the boy gets out – of course it is really very simple. Directly the boy is in the sack and while you are closing the neck of the sack over his head he grabs hold of the cord on the inside of the sack and pulls in about 18 inches of the cord and holds it tightly, as shown in Fig. 3, and directly you cover him with the sheet he lets go of the cord, pushes the sack open – lets it slip down enough for him to unfasten the knots, which he does quite easily because the cord is slack, then he steps out of the sack and throws off the sheet.

From "Simple Apparatus For Amateur Conjurers" by E.W. Hobbs, *Modern Wonders for Boys*, 1938.

Rising Card Trick

To "appear" any card chosen by the audience – you can work this simple trick with a specially prepared card.

Prepare the "card" as shown in Fig. 4 by putting a piece of thin rubber band through two cards – and fasten the rubber with a pin. Then cover the backs of these cards with two other

cards so that the ends of the rubber are hidden. Put this prepared card in the pack – then taking out a card, show it face forwards to the audience so that you cannot see which card it is, then put it in the pack; pretend to shuffle or mix up the cards in any way you please – then hold the pack – up face to the audience – and gradually the selected card will rise from the pack. All you have to do is to put the chosen card into the prepared "card", then when you square up the cards in the

Fig. 4.—Elastic fitted to cards.

pack – press the card down into line with the others and grip the pack tightly. Make a few "passes" with the hand, slacken your grip a little and the rubber band will then push the card up.

From "Simple Apparatus For Amateur Conjurers" by E.W. Hobbs, *Modern Wonders for Boys*, 1938.

Mind Reading

In this trick you appear to be able to read someone's mind. It is from a branch of magic known as "mentalism".

You need five differently coloured crayons, preferably with soft leads, and a box or opaque bag.

Give the pencils to the person you want to play the trick on and then turn away from them but with your hands behind your back. Ask them to choose one pencil, remember its colour and then put in in your waiting hands. Tell them to put the remaining pencils in the box or bag so that you cannot see them. Keeping your hands and the pencil behind you turn around to face your victim.

Now tell them to concentrate very hard and think of the colour of the pencil. While they are doing this you, behind your back, craftily put the pencil in your right hand and rub the sharpened end of the pencil against the thumbnail of your left hand. (If you're left handed reverse the process). A fleck of colour will stay on the left thumb nail. With the pencil still in your right hand behind bring your left hand up towards your mouth or forehead – making sure to keep the thumbnail towards you, not the audience – as if you were thinking very hard. As your thumb comes up you will see the fleck of rubbed-off colour. Pretend to think for a moment before announcing, "The colour you chose is . . ."

Don't be tempted to do the trick more than once or twice, because the victim will become suspicious of your attempt to impersonate Rodin's famous sculpture "The Thinker".

FIFTY MOVIES EVERY BOY SHOULD SEE

The Adventures of Robin Hood (1938)

Classic swashbuckler with Errol Flynn as the Saxon lord who leads the merry men from Sherwood Forest in a fight against the cruel overseer of England, Prince John.

American Graffiti (1973)

In 1962 two high-school graduates and their friends cruise the strip for one last night before going their separate ways. The definitive coming-of-age movie, complete with an evocative rock'n'roll soundtrack. For early/mid teens.

Apollo 13 (1995)

Houston, we have a problem . . . a movie version of the true story to bring the astronauts of Apollo 13 home safely when their spacecraft suffers a near-fatal accident.

Babe (1995)

Barnyard fable about a pig that herds sheep; a movie that did wonders for vegetarianism.

Back to the Future (1985)

Time-travel comedy/actioner starring Michael J. Fox.

Ben-Hur (1959)

In the first century AD a Jewish prince, Judah Ben-Hur, is framed by Messala, his one-time Roman friend, and is sent to be a galley slave. Eventually Ben-Hur gains his freedom and seeks his revenge on Messala. The ensuing chariot race between Ben-Hur and Messala may well be the greatest action sequence ever filmed without use of special effects. The epic *Ben-Hur* won no less than eleven Oscars.

Das Boot (1981) aka *The Boat*

German movie about a U-boat crew during the Second World War. One of the most realistic pictures of men at war. For rising fourteens.

Bringing Up Baby (1938)

Fast-paced "screwball comedy" about a palaeontologist (played by Cary Grant) who meets a scatterbrained girl (Katherine Hepburn) who uses a leopard – among other means – to keep him from marrying anyone else.

Bugsy Malone (1976)

Improbably successful mobster musical for kids in which the sub-machine guns fire cream pies.

Butch Cassidy and the Sundance Kid (1969)

Paul Newman and Robert Redford teamed together to play two outlaws on the run in a Western that combined comedy with action. For early-mid teens.

Chariots of Fire (1981)

Dramatization of the true story of the British Olympic runners Harold Abrahams and Eric Liddle. Guaranteed to make you want to take up track.

A Christmas Story (1983)

In 1940 in the Indiana town of Hohman, nine-year-old Ralph "Ralphie" Parker wants only one thing for Christmas – an official Red Ryder BB rifle with a compass in the stock. Unfortunately, his parents and teacher and even Santa Claus say No, because "You'll shoot your eye out". Does Ralphie get his gun? A comedy with a moral.

Duck Soup (1933)

All four Marx brothers – Groucho, Harpo, Chico and Zeppo – starred in this madcap comedy about the dictator of fictitious Fredonia.

ET: The Extra-Terrestrial (1982)

One boy and his pet alien. Directed by Steven Spielberg.

Fantasia (1940)

Disney animations set to music by Tchaikovsky, Schubert and others.

Ferris Bueller's Day Off (1986)

Teen comedy in which Bueller skips high school for a day to live an adult high life – including driving a Ferrari.

Garfield: The Movie (2004)

The fat cat (voiced by Bill Murray) kicks puppy Odie out of the house, only for Odie to be dog napped. Worth the price of admission for Garfield's dance class alone.

The Great Dictator (1940)

Charlie Chaplin plays dictator Adenoid Hynkel in a satire (send up) on Hitler's Nazi Germany.

The Great Escape (1963)

Thrilling Second World War-based movie in which Allied prisoners break out from a German POW camp. Steve McQueen played Hilts, the "cooler king".

High Noon (1952)

In the Western town of Hadleyville, Marshal Will Kane (Gary Cooper) fights for his life against a gunman seeking revenge.

The Incredibles (2004)

Cartoon family of superheroes want a quiet life but are obliged to save the world.

It's a Wonderful Life (1946)

When overburdened George Bailey (played by James Stewart) tries to commit suicide an angel called Clarence steps in to save his life and show him how grim life in Bedford Falls would have been without him.

Jason and the Argonauts (1963)

The legendary Greek hero takes his men on an intrepid quest to find the fabled Golden Fleece.

Jungle Book (1967)

Disney cartoon, based on Rudyard Kipling's book, about Mowgli, a boy living in the Indian jungle, where his life is threatened by tiger Shere Khan, snake Kaa and ape King Louie. Luckily for Mowgli, his friends Bagheera (a panther) and Baloo (a bear) are on hand to help him.

King Kong (1933)

Faye Wray starred as the beauty captured by the beast with a heart.

The Lavender Hill Mob (1951)

An "Ealing Comedy" about a daring bullion raid.

Lawrence of Arabia (1962)

Epic movie biography of the First World War British officer T.E. Lawrence and his exploits in the desert.

The Lord of the Rings (2001–3)

In the Shire a young Hobbit called Frodo is entrusted with the dangerous quest of travelling to the Crack of Doom to destroy the Ring. A trilogy of films based on Tolkien's novel which effortlessly takes the viewer to a far-off land where heroism rules.

March of the Penguins (2005)

Oscar-winning documentary about Emperor penguins and how they raise their young in the snowy wastes of Antarctica.

Mr Smith Goes to Washington (1939)

Stars Jimmy Stewart as Jefferson Smith, an idealist who cleans up the corruption in Washington DC. A movie hymn to the virtue and value of democracy. For thirteen(+).

Monsieur Hulot's Holiday (1953)

It might be French, but so are croissants. Jacques Tati directs and stars as the accident-prone M. Hulot.

Monty Python and the Holy Grail (1975)

Offbeat comedy from British TV's Monty Python team. King Arthur and his knights seek the Holy Grail but encounter very odd obstacles (such as killer rabbits) on the way.

The Muppet Movie (1979)

Kermit is a country frog who determines to make it big in Hollywood – but to do so has to evade a bad guy who wants him as a mascot for the Frog's Legs Restaurant chain. Comedy movie featuring Jim Henson's famous TV puppets.

Oliver Twist (1948)

Adaptation of Charles Dickens' novel in which a young boy leaves a workhouse and becomes entangled with a gang of pickpockets on Victorian London's mean streets.

Pirates of the Caribbean: The Curse of the Black Pearl (2003)

Jack Sparrow, an eccentric pirate captain, helps a young blacksmith to rescue a damsel captured by the cursed, undead Captain Barbarossa. For twelve/thirteen and above.

Raiders of the Lost Ark (1981)

Starring Harrison Ford as daredevil archeologist Indiana Jones.

The Railway Children (1970)

When the father of a comfortable Victorian family suddenly disappears his wife and children fall on hard times and move to a cottage in Yorkshire. There the children bravely keep their spirits up and endear themselves to the locals – and begin to untangle the mystery of their father's vanishing. Based on E. Nesbit's much-loved novel.

Rocky (1976)

Sylvester Stallone plays Rocky "Italian Stallion" Balboa, a New York boxer edging over the hill but who has an outside shot at the championship of the world. For twelve and above.

Sen To Chihiro No Kamikakushi (2001)
aka *Spirited Away*

A fantastical Japanese animation about a girl, Chihiro, whose family is on their way to a new home but take a wrong turn down a mysterious track. Emerging from a tunnel they find a strange world in which Chihiro's parents are magically transformed into pigs. At night, as spirits descend, Chihiro must overcome her fears, rescue her parents and find the way home.

Shane (1953)

Legendary Western in which a gunman helps a homesteader protect his land against an evil rancher.

Snow White and the Seven Dwarfs (1937)

Disney's version of the classic fairy tale.

Some Like It Hot (1959)

Two jazz musicians (played by Tony Curtis and Jack Lemmon) witness the 1929 St Valentine's Day Massacre and flee Chicago dressed as girls. Selected by the American Film Institute as the Best Comedy of All Time. Marilyn Monroe also starred.

The Sound of Music (1965)

Musical based on the true story of the Von Trapp family and their flight from Nazi-occupied Austria.

Stand By Me (1986)

Despite being based on a Stephen King story, this is no horror movie; instead it explores boyhood, its hopes and fears. Set in the summer of 1959, the movie stars River Phoenix as Chris.

Star Wars (1977)

The film that launched a thousand franchises was really an old-time Western shoot-'em-up set on the final frontier of space.

To Kill a Mockingbird (1962)

Gregory Peck stars as the lawyer who fights for justice in a racially intolerant small town.

Toy Story (1995)

A blockbuster from the Pixar studio, this is a computer-generated kid's adventure about playthings which come alive when six-year-old Andy is not in his bedroom.

Willy Wonka and the Chocolate Factory (1971)

A dark comedy, based on Roald Dahl's novel, about five children who get to tour the fantastic chocolate factory of Willy Wonka.

The Wizard of Oz (1939)

A film fairy tale based on the children's novel by L. Frank Baum. Judy Garland plays Dorothy, the girl transported from Kansas to the Land of Oz.

Zulu (1964)

Outnumbered British soldiers do battle with Zulu warriors at Rorke's Drift.

SAS SURVIVAL SKILLS II: TRAPPING GAME

Meat is the most nourishing food for man, and is certainly the most satisfying for the fugitive who is surviving for any length of time in the wild. Collecting and eating grubs may be an easier option than trapping larger animals, but you have to get through a lot of worms and caterpillars to beat a decent rabbit or duck. Here we describe how to set about catching whatever you find.

The first thing to know is that all animals are edible (but not necessary the whole of the beast). The second thing is that they're nearly all very difficult to catch and you'll have to use all your skills to be successful; and that means understanding the animal's way of life.

Daily Habits

They're usually fairly regular in their habits, using the same paths and trails, drinking at the same places on the river bank and from pools, sleeping in the same sheltered places. They also have a timetable, and stick to it; if an animal went to a certain place to drink at dawn this morning, there's a very good chance that it will do the same again tomorrow. Spend time looking for signs of animals.

If there's a lot of animal activity going on, find a hiding place and stay in it until you recognize the local wildlife patterns. It will make trapping or hunting them a great deal easier. All you've got going for you is your intelligence; they've lived there all their lives!

Unless you have an accurate weapon, such as a rifle, shotgun or crossbow, hunting will be a lot less likely to provide you with dinner than trapping. In a hostile environment, where there are enemy forces or natives, hunting is almost certain to be impossible anyway, but let's look at some of the basic skills you'll need to hunt game in the wild.

Always assume that any small animals in the area will be wary and quick to run away. If they spot you, hear you or smell you (remember that their sense of smell may be a thousand times better than yours), they will either go to ground or disappear off into the distance. Seeing them before they become aware of you greatly increases your chances of catching them.

DEADFALLS

The figure-four deadfall is simple to make and surprisingly sensitive. The props should be as thin as you can make them, the fall itself as heavy as possible. The one shown here is relatively small, but you can make larger ones too, to stun larger animals.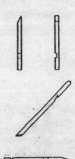

Cut two sticks of roughly equal length, and trim and notch them as shown. Sharpen one end of each stick, one to go into the ground and the other to take the bait.

Cut and notch a third, longer stick to form the third side of the triangle.

Pay careful attention to the notches. Cut them too shallow and they won't hold for very long.

You may find it frustrating, trying to set the trap up. But remember, the harder it is to get it to stay together, the more sensitive it will be in use.

They often use the same pathways and drinking places, and make permanent homes. Look for their signs – tracks, paths in grass, faeces, dens, feeding places – and use that intelligence to help you set up a plan to catch them.

Camouflage and Approach

Remember, the fieldcraft that makes you a good foot-soldier can also make you a good hunter. Always obey the rules of camouflage and approach. Never silhouette yourself against the skyline, even in woodland. Always move upwind or across wind. Approach streams, rivers and waterholes very carefully, especially around dawn and dusk. Find cover and get into it, and wait for the animals.

And stay still! Fidgeting may cost you a meal – and that may end up costing you your life.

Larger game, even if it sees you, may not take flight straight away. Stop and keep still until it loses interest, and then approach in a wide zigzag. In hills and mountains, always try to get above the animal you're stalking.

Best Target Areas

If you are shooting game, the best targets are the head, neck and the spine just behind the shoulder. Take your time, and make

A POLE TO CATCH SQUIRRELS

Take a pole, fix some wire snares to it and lean it up against a tree where you've seen squirrels. It may seem too simple to be true, but these inquisitive creatures are quite likely to get caught up before too long.

the first shot count – because you're not likely to get a second chance. If you hit and wound the animal and it runs off, follow the blood trail. A badly wounded creature won't have the strength to run far. Give it the chance to go to ground before following it up. Approach slowly and then make the kill. Don't waste ammunition if you can finish it off by clubbing it.

Hunting, however, should take second place to making and setting traps. Traps are much more likely to provide you with a lasting supply of meat. Simple ones are very easy to make and set: the simplest of all is a snare – a slip noose firmly pegged into the ground or anchored to a rock or tree. Make them from wire if it's available, or use plastic fishing line, string or even line made up from natural fibres.

These snares are especially effective when you set them at the entrance to burrows and dens. Set them in trees to catch

squirrels, or make a "squirrel pole": an eight to 12 ft (2.5 to 3.5m) pole with perhaps half-a-dozen snares around it, leaned up against a tree used by squirrels. It may sound too easy, but squirrels are inquisitive creatures and will often investigate something new just for the fun of it.

You're not likely to be able to kill anything larger than a rabbit or a small cat with a wire snare, though you may slow down larger animals so that you have a better chance of clubbing them to death.

Trapping, even more than hunting, depends on how well you can read the signs. There is no point in placing a trap just anywhere hoping that an animal will stumble into it by chance! Entrances to burrows and tunnels are the best place. Look for signs that they are occupied – fresh droppings, signs of feeding and movement in and out.

HANGING SNARES

Hanging snares are a more secure way of holding on to the animal that you've caught. They use the creature's own weight to keep it from wriggling out of the noose. Apart from the wire noose itself, to make a hanging snare you need a sapling close to the run you've chosen, and a forked stick, or one bent over into a hoop. The forked stick is used as part of the trigger, holding the wire noose down in the animal's way and presenting the bait. The example here uses a half-hoop, for increased sensitivity.

You can even scare off large animals this way – cats and bears, for instance. Building a fire when you've frightened them off will often make them stay away long enough for them to forget you've robbed them of their meal. But unless you're well armed, don't be too ready to take on these large predators yourself.

Unless you're using wire for the snare, which may stand up on its own, you will have to make a stand to hold the noose open. Two twigs, one each side of the mouth of the burrow or the path will do, with another one perhaps placed across the top to support the trap.

Human Scent

Don't forget to cover your scent; both on the snare itself and on the surrounding ground: soaking the snare in a stream after you've made it and before setting it is one way. Or you can rub it with cold ashes, or disguise your own scent with something stronger – urine from the bladder of a dead animal, for example. Animals are usually attracted to urine from their own kind.

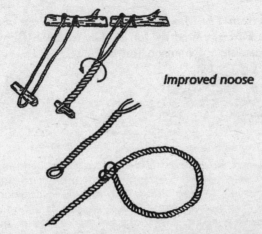

Improved noose

You can improve on the simple noose, and make it more difficult for the animal to escape from the trap, by intertwining two lengths of wire. Use the two strands that are left at the end to make up a double running loop. These two loops will naturally catch in the twists of the wire that makes the body of the line and noose, and will make it much more difficult for the animal to wriggle out of the noose.

SKINNING SMALL ANIMALS

1 Lay the animal down on its back, spread all four legs wide, and cut from the anus up to the breastbone, taking care not to rupture the intestine.
2 Cut the skin through around all four paws at the first joint. Remove the guts, starting from the throat and working downwards. Do not eat these innards.
3 Now you can peel the skin off. You may find it necessary to remove the tail first.
4 Take the skin off in one piece. A firm grip and a quick pull are all that is needed.
5 The last thing to do is to remove the head. Keep the skin for making clothing.

You can always let predators do your hunting for you. Watch until you can work out their pattern of activity, then wait for them to make a kill. If you rush them you'll often cause them to drop their prey.

Adapted from *The Mammoth Book of The Secrets of the SAS and Elite Forces*, edited by Jon E. Lewis, 2002. Copyright © 2002 Constable & Robinson/Jon E. Lewis.

THE KINGS AND QUEENS
OF ENGLAND/BRITAIN

The House of Wessex

The House of Wessex was a Saxon kingdom which came to have
effective overlordship of England.
Egbert (802–39)
Aethelwulf (839–55)
Aethelbald (855–60)
Aethelbert (860–6)
Aethelred (866–71)
Alfred the Great (871–99)
Edward the Elder (899–925)
Athelstan (925–40)
Edmund the Magnificent (940–6)
Eadred (946–55)
Eadwig (Edwy) All-Fair (955–9)
Edgar the Peaceable (959–75)
Edward the Martyr (975–8)
Aethelred the Unready (978–1016)
Edmund Ironside (1016)

The Danish Line

This became effective with the conquest of England in 1013 by
the Vikings by Svein Forkbeard; the House of Wessex continued to claim the throne but was decisively defeated by the

Danes at Abingdon in 1016.
Svein Forkbeard (1014)
Canute (Cnut) the Great (1016–35)
Harald Harefoot (1035–40)
Hardicanute (1040–42)

House of Wessex, Restored

The restoration followed the death of Hardicanute and the lack of an obvious Danish successor, at which the Anglo-Saxon council, the Witan, replaced the House of Wessex on the throne.
Edward the Confessor (1042–66)
Harold II (1066)

Norman Line

Began with the conquest of England by William Duke of Normandy in 1066.
William I the Conqueror (1066–87)
William II Rufus (1087–1100)
Henry I Beauclerc (1100–35)
Stephen (1135–54)
Empress Matilda (1141)

Plantagenet, Angevin Line

Henry II Curtmantle (1154–89)
Richard I the Lionheart (1189–99)
John Lackland (1199–1216)
Henry III (1216–72)
Edward I Longshanks (1272–1307)
Edward II (1307–27)
Edward III (1327–77)
Richard II (1377–99)

Plantagenet, Lancastrian Line

Henry IV Bolingbroke (1399–1413)
Henry V (1413–22)
Henry VI (1422–61, 1470–1)

Plantagenet, Yorkist Line

This was the era of the wars of the Roses, a dynastic struggle between the royal houses of York and Lancaster. Edward IV came to power in a coup d'etat against the schizophrenic Henry VI but was temporarily deposed himself later. The Wars of the Roses only came to an end with the 1485 coup of the Lancastrian adventurer Henry Tudor, who unified the lines by marrying Elizabeth of York.

Edward IV (1461–70, 1471–83)
Edward V (1483)
Richard III Crouchback (1483–5)

House of Tudor

Henry VII Tudor (1485–1509)
Henry VIII (1509–47)
Edward VI (1547–53)
Lady Jane Grey (1553)
Mary I Tudor (1553–58)
Elizabeth I (1558–1603)

House of Stuart

By Elizabeth's bequest the English throne passed to the Scottish King James Stuart VI; henceforth England (and Wales) were unified with Scotland. At first the union was a personal one under the monarch, but became a proper legal entity with the Act of Union of 1707. This was the birth of Great Britain.

James I (1603–25), formerly James VI of Scotland
Charles I (1625–49)

The Commonwealth

Also known as the Interregnum, meaning the interval between royal reigns. This followed the rebellion by the nation against the autocratic Stuarts, who were deposed by Parliament's Army. For a decade England was a republic.

Oliver Cromwell (1649–58)
Richard Cromwell (1658–9)

House of Stuart, Restored

Charles II (1660–85)
James II (1685–8)

House of Orange and Stuart

Another rebellion against the pro-Catholic, dictatorial Stuarts
prompted Parliament to offer the English throne to James II's
protestant daughter Mary and her Dutch husband William.
William III, Mary II (1689–1702)

House of Stuart

Having no children, William and Mary bequeathed the throne
of Mary's Protestant sister Anne.
Anne (1702–14)

House of Brunswick, Hanover Line

Anne died without heirs and the line of succession passed to the
German-speaking Hanoverians.
George I (1714–27)
George II (1727–60)
George III (1760–1820)
George IV (1820–30)
William IV (1830–37)
Victoria (1837–1901)

House of Saxe-Coburg-Gotha
Edward VII (1901–10)

House of Windsor
The Windsors were the Saxe-Coburg-Gotha under a new
name; Saxe-Coburg-Gotha was judged too German-sounding
in an era of strife with Germany.
George V (1910–36)
Edward VIII (1936)
George VI (1936–52)
Elizabeth II (1952–present)

There's a useful rhyme to remember the order of the kings and queens of England from the Norman conquest onwards. It is:

> Willy, Willy, Harry, Steve
> Harry, Dick, John, Harry three,
> One, two, three Neds, Richard two,
> Henries four, five, six – then who?
> Edwards four, five, Dick the bad,
> Harries twain and Ned the lad,
> Mary, Bessie, James the vain,
> Charlie, Charlie, James again,
> William & Mary, Anna Gloria,
> Four Georges, William and Victoria,
> Edward, George, then Ned the eighth
> quickly goes and abdicat'th,
> leaving George, then Liz the second,
> and with Charlie next it's reckoned.
>
> That's the way our monarchs lie
> since Harold got it in the eye!
>
> PS. Sorry, Lady Jane Grey – you got the chop!

A SIMPLE KITE

There's nothing better to do on a fresh, windy, autumn day than flying a kite. There's also a great deal of satisfaction to be had from making your own, rather than buying from the store. To make a kite you need:

1 metre of bamboo
String
Glue
Tissue paper
Nylon fishing line.

If using bamboo, split the metre of bamboo lengthways. Take one piece for the upright, notching a third of the way down. Saw the remaining piece of bamboo in half with a fire-toothed saw. Fit one 50 cm piece across the upright where you have notched it and tie tightly with string. Make sure that the two sides of this cross spar protrude equally from the upright. Fix a piece of string round the outside of the frame to provide rigidity (as in Figure 1). Now cut out the shape of the kite in tissue paper, allowing an extra 3 cm round the edges. Put the kite frame on top of this tissue paper and fold in the edges. Cut out the shape of the kite from another piece of tissue paper, but this time do not allow an extra 3cm. Glue this tissue paper to the first piece.

While the tissue paper is drying, you can make the tail. Cut off two metres of string and tie bows of tissue paper into it at 10 cm intervals. Now tie the tail to the bottom of the kite frame.

Finally, attach about 1.3 metres of heavy fishing line to the top and bottom of the kite. To the middle of this loop attach the line which will fly the kite.

The virtue of this kite is that it is very light and catches the wind easily. Any tears to the tissue fabric can easily be repaired by simply glueing a square of tissue over the top. If you can't find bamboo, a length of very thin dowling will do.

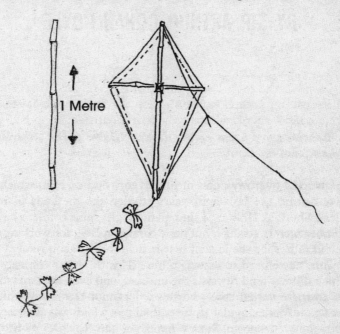

1 Metre

STORY: "THE SPECKLED BAND" BY SIR ARTHUR CONAN DOYLE

A detective story featuring the sleuth of Baker Street, Sherlock Holmes, and his trusty assistant, Dr John Watson.

In glancing over my notes of the seventy odd cases in which I have during the last eight years studied the methods of my friend Sherlock Holmes, I find many tragic, some comic, a large number merely strange, but none commonplace; for working as he did rather for the love of his art than for the acquirement of wealth, he refused to associate himself with any investigation which did not tend towards the unusual, and even the fantastic. Of all these varied cases, however, I cannot recall any which presented more singular features than that which was associated with the well-known Surrey family of the Roylotts of Stoke Moran. The events in question occurred in the early days of my association with Holmes, when we were sharing rooms as bachelors, in Baker Street. It is possible that I might have placed them upon record before, but a promise of secrecy was made at the time, from which I have only been freed during the last month by the untimely death of the lady to whom the pledge was given. It is perhaps as well that the facts should now come to light, for I have reasons to know there are widespread rumours as to the death of Dr Grimesby Roylott which tend to make the matter even more terrible than the truth.

It was early in April, in the year '83, that I woke one morning to find Sherlock Holmes standing, fully dressed, by the side of my bed. He was a late riser as a rule, and, as the clock on the mantelpiece showed me that it was only a quarter past seven, I blinked up at him in some surprise, and perhaps just a little resentment, for I was myself regular in my habits.

"Very sorry to knock you up, Watson," said he, "but it's the common lot this morning. Mrs Hudson has been knocked up, she retorted upon me, and I on you."

"What is it, then? A fire?"

"No, a client. It seems that a young lady has arrived in a considerable state of excitement, who insists upon seeing me. She is waiting now in the sitting-room. Now, when young ladies wander about the Metropolis at this hour of the morning, and knock sleepy people up out of their beds, I presume that it is something very pressing which they have to communicate. Should it prove to be an interesting case, you would, I am sure, wish to follow it from the outset. I thought at any rate that I should call you, and give you the chance."

"My dear fellow, I would not miss it for anything."

I had no keener pleasure than in following Holmes in his professional investigations, and in admiring the rapid deductions, as swift as intuitions, and yet always founded on a logical basis, with which he unravelled the problems which were submitted to him. I rapidly threw on my clothes, and was ready in a few minutes to accompany my friend down to the sitting-room. A lady dressed in black and heavily veiled, who had been sitting in the window, rose as we entered.

"Good morning, madam," said Holmes cheerily. "My name is Sherlock Holmes. This is my intimate friend and associate, Dr Watson, before whom you can speak as freely as before myself. Ha, I am glad to see that Mrs Hudson has had the good sense to light the fire. Pray, draw up to it, and I shall order you a cup of hot coffee, for I observe that you are shivering."

"It is not cold which makes me shiver," said the woman in a low voice, changing her seat as requested.

"What then?"

"It is fear, Mr Holmes. It is terror." She raised her veil as she spoke, and we could see that she was indeed in a pitiable state of agitation, her face all drawn and grey, with restless, frightened eyes, like those of some hunted animal. Her features and figure were those of a woman of thirty, but her hair was shot with premature grey, and her expression was weary and haggard. Sherlock Holmes ran her over with one of his quick, all-comprehensive glances.

"You must not fear," said he soothingly, bending forward and patting her forearm. "We shall soon set matters right, I have no doubt. You have come in by train this morning, I see."

"You know me, then?"

"No, but I observe the second half of a return ticket in the palm of your left glove. You must have started early, and yet you had a good drive in a dog-cart, along heavy roads, before you reached the station."

The lady gave a violent start, and stared in bewilderment at my companion.

"There is no mystery, my dear madam," said he, smiling. "The left arm of your jacket is spattered with mud in no less than seven places. The marks are perfectly fresh. There is no vehicle save a dog-cart which throws up mud in that way, and then only when you sit on the left-hand side of the driver."

"Whatever your reasons may be, you are perfectly correct," said she. "I started from home before six, reached Leatherhead at twenty past, and came in by the first train to Waterloo. Sir, I can stand this strain no longer, I shall go mad if it continues. I have no one to turn to – none, save only one, who cares for me, and he, poor fellow, can be of little aid. I have heard of you, Mr Holmes; I have heard of you from Mrs Farintosh, whom you helped in the hour of her sore need. It was from her that I had your address. Oh, sir, do you not think you could help me too, and at least throw a little light through the dense darkness which surrounds me? At present it is out of my power to reward you for your services, but in a month or two, I shall be married, with the control of my own income, and then at least you shall not find me ungrateful."

Holmes turned to his desk, and unlocking it, drew out a small case-book which he consulted.

"Farintosh," said he. "Ah, yes, I recall the case; it was concerned with an opal tiara. I think it was before your time, Watson. I can only say, madam, that I shall be happy to devote the same care to your case as I did to that of your friend. As to reward, my profession is its reward; but you are at liberty to defray whatever expenses I may be put to, at the time which suits you best. And now I beg that you will lay before us everything that may help us in forming an opinion upon the matter."

"Alas!" replied our visitor. "The very horror of my situation lies in the fact that my fears are so vague, and my suspicions depend so entirely upon small points, which might seem trivial to another, that even he to whom of all others I have a right to look for help and advice looks upon all that I tell him about it as the fancies of a nervous woman. He does not say so, but I can read it from his soothing answers and averted eyes. But I have heard, Mr Holmes, that you can see deeply into the manifold wickedness of the human heart. You may advise me how to walk amid the dangers which encompass me."

"I am all attention, madam."

"My name is Helen Stoner, and I am living with my step-father, who is the last survivor of one of the oldest Saxons families in England, the Roylotts of Stoke Moran, on the western border of Surrey."

Holmes nodded his head. "The name is familiar to me," said he.

"The family was at one time among the richest in England, and the estate extended over the borders into Berkshire in the north, and Hampshire in the west. In the last century, however, four successive heirs were of a dissolute and wasteful disposi-tion, and the family ruin was eventually completed by a gam-bler, in the days of the Regency. Nothing was left save a few acres of ground and the two-hundred-year-old house, which is itself crushed under a heavy mortgage. The last squire dragged out his existence there, living the horrible life of an aristocratic pauper; but his only son, my stepfather, seeing that he must adapt himself to the new conditions, obtained an advance from a relative, which enabled him to take a medical degree, and went out to Calcutta, where, by his professional skill and his force of character, he established a large practice. In a fit of anger, however, caused by some robberies which had been perpetrated in the house, he beat his native butler to death, and narrowly escaped a capital sentence. As it was, he suffered a long term of imprisonment, and afterwards returned to England a morose and disappointed man.

"When Dr Roylott was in India he married my mother, Mrs Stoner, the young widow of Major-General Stoner, of the

Bengal Artillery. My sister Julia and I were twins, and we were only two years old at the time of my mother's re-marriage. She had a considerable sum of money, not less than a thousand a year, and this she bequeathed to Dr Roylott entirely whilst we resided with him, with a provision that a certain annual sum should be allowed to each of us in the event of our marriage. Shortly after our return to England my mother died – she was killed eight years ago in a railway accident near Crewe. Dr Roylott then abandoned his attempts to establish himself in practice in London, and took us to live with him in the ancestral house at Stoke Moran. The money which my mother had left was enough for all our wants, and there seemed no obstacle to our happiness.

"But a terrible change came over our stepfather about this time. Instead of making friends and exchanging visits with our neighbours, who had at first been overjoyed to see a Roylott of Stoke Moran back in the old family seat, he shut himself up in his house, and seldom came out save to indulge in ferocious quarrels with whoever might cross his path. Violence of temper approaching to mania has been hereditary in the men of the family, and in my stepfather's case it had, I believe, been intensified by his long residence in the tropics. A series of disgraceful brawls took place, two of which ended in the police-court, until at last he became the terror of the village, and the folks would fly at his approach, for he is a man of immense strength, and absolutely uncontrollable in his anger.

"Last week he hurled the local blacksmith over a parapet into a stream, and it was only by paying over all the money that I could gather together that I was able to avert another public exposure. He had no friends at all save the wandering gipsies, and he would give these vagabonds leave to encamp upon the few acres of bramble-covered land which represent the family estate, and would accept in return the hospitality of their tents, wandering away with them sometimes for weeks on end. He has a passion also for Indian animals, which are sent over to him by a correspondent, and he has at this moment a cheetah and a baboon, which wander freely over his grounds, and are feared by the villagers almost as much as their master.

"You can imagine from what I say that my poor sister Julia and I had no great pleasure in our lives. No servant would stay with us, and for a long time we did all the work of the house. She was but thirty at the time of her death, and yet her hair had already began to whiten, even as mine has."

"Your sister is dead, then?"

"She died just two years ago, and it is of her death that I wish to speak to you. You can understand that, living the life which I have described, we were little likely to see anyone of our own age and position. We had, however, an aunt, my mother's maiden sister, Miss Honoria Westphail, who lives near Harrow, and we were occasionally allowed to pay short visits at this lady's house. Julia went there at Christmas two years ago, and met there a half-pay Major of Marines, to whom she became engaged. My step-father learned of the engagement when my sister returned, and offered no objection to the marriage; but within a fortnight of the day which had been fixed for the wedding, the terrible event occurred which has deprived me of my only companion."

Sherlock Holmes had been leaning back in his chair with his eyes closed, and his head sunk in a cushion, but he half opened his lids now, and glanced across at his visitor.

"Pray be precise as to details," said he.

"It is easy for me to be so, for every event of that dreadful time is seared into my memory. The manor house is, as I have already said, very old, and only one wing is now inhabited. The bedrooms in this wing are on the ground floor, the sitting-rooms being in the central block of the buildings. Of these bedrooms, the first is Dr Roylott's, the second my sister's, and the third my own. There is no communication between them, but they all open out into the same corridor. Do I make myself plain?"

"Perfectly so."

"The windows of the three rooms open out upon the lawn. The fatal night Dr Roylott had gone to his room early, though we knew that he had not retired to rest, for my sister was troubled by the smell of the strong Indian cigars which it was his custom to smoke. She left her room, therefore, and came into mine, where she sat for some time, chatting about her approaching wedding. At eleven o'clock she rose to leave me, but she paused at the door and looked back.

"'Tell me, Helen,' said she, 'have you ever heard anyone whistle in the dead of the night?'

" 'Never,' said I.

" 'I suppose that you could not possibly whistle yourself in your sleep?'

" 'Certainly not. But why?'

" 'Because during the last few nights I have always, about three in the morning, heard a low clear whistle. I am a light sleeper, and it has awakened me. I cannot tell where it came from – perhaps from the next room, perhaps from the lawn. I thought that I would just ask you whether you had heard it.'

" 'No, I have not. It must be those wretched gipsies in the plantation.'

" 'Very likely. And yet if it were on the lawn I wonder that you did not hear it also.'

" 'Ah, but I sleep more heavily than you.'

" 'Well, it is of no great consequence at any rate,' she smiled back at me, closed my door, and a few moments later I heard her key turn in the lock."

"Indeed," said Holmes. "Was it your custom always to lock yourselves in at night?"

"Always."

"And why?"

"I think that I mentioned to you that the Doctor kept a cheetah and a baboon. We had no feeling of security unless our doors were locked."

"Quite so. Pray proceed with your statement."

"I could not sleep that night. A vague feeling of impending misfortune impressed me. My sister and I, you will recollect, were twins, and you know how subtle are the links which bind two souls which are so closely allied. It was a wild night. The wind was howling outside, and the rain was beating and splashing against the windows. Suddenly, amidst all the hubbub of the gale, there burst forth the wild scream of a terrified woman. I knew that it was my sister's voice. I sprang from my bed, wrapped a shawl round me, and rushed into the corridor. As I opened my door I seemed to hear a low whistle, such as my sister described, and a few moments later a clanging sound, as if a mass of metal had fallen. As I ran down the passage my sister's door was unlocked, and revolved slowly upon its hinges. I stared at it horror-stricken, not knowing what was about to issue from it. By the light of the corridor lamp I saw my sister appear in the opening, her face blanched with terror, her hands groping for help, her whole figure swaying to and fro like that of a drunkard. I ran to her and threw my arms round her, but at that moment her knees seemed to give way and she fell to the ground. She writhed as one who is in terrible pain, and her limbs were dreadfully convulsed. At first I thought that she had not recognized me, but as I bent over her she suddenly shrieked out in a voice which I shall never forget, 'O, my God! Helen! It was the band! The speckled band!' There was something else which she would have fain have said, and she stabbed with her finger into the air in the direction of the Doctor's room, but a fresh convulsion seized her and choked her words. I rushed out, calling loudly for my step-father, and I met him hastening from his room in his dressing-gown. When he reached my sister's side she was unconscious, and though he poured brandy down her throat, and sent for medical aid from the village, all efforts were in vain, for she slowly sank and died without having recovered her consciousness. Such was the dreadful end of my sister."

"One moment," said Holmes; "are you sure about this whistle and metallic sound? Could you swear to it?"

"That was what the county coroner asked me at the inquiry. It is my strong impression that I heard it, and yet among the crash of the gale, and the creaking of an old house, I may possibly have been deceived."

"Was your sister dressed?"

"No, she was in her nightdress. In her right hand was found the charred stump of a match, and in her left a match-box."

"Showing that she had struck a light and looked about her when the alarm took place. That is important. And what conclusions did the coroner come to?"

"He investigated the case with great care, for Dr Roylott's conduct had long been notorious in the county, but he was unable to find any satisfactory cause of death. My evidence showed that the door had been fastened upon the inner side, and the windows were blocked by old-fashioned shutters with broad iron bars, which were secured every night. The walls were carefully sounded, and were shown to be quite solid all round, and the flooring was also thoroughly examined, with the same result. The chimney is wide, but is barred up by four large staples. It is certain, therefore, that my sister was quite alone when she met her end. Besides, there were no marks of any violence upon her."

"How about poison?"

"The doctors examined her for it, but without success."

"What do you think that this unfortunate lady died of, then?"

"It is my belief that she died of pure fear and nervous shock, though what it was which frightened her I cannot imagine."

"Were there gipsies in the plantation at the time?"

"Yes, there are nearly always some there."

"Ah, and what did you gather from this allusion to a band – a speckled band?"

"Sometimes I have thought that it was merely the wild talk of delirium, sometimes that it may have referred to some band of people, perhaps to these very gipsies in the plantation. I do not know whether the spotted handkerchiefs which so many of them wear over their heads might have suggested the strange adjective which she used."

Holmes shook his head like a man who is far from being satisfied.

"These are very deep waters," said he; "pray go on with your narrative."

"Two years have passed since then, and my life has been until lately lonelier than ever. A month ago, however, a dear friend, whom I have known for many years, has done me the honour to ask my hand in marriage. His name is Armitage – Percy Armitage – the second son of Mr Armitage, of Crane Water, near Reading. My step-father has offered no opposition to the match, and we are to be married in the course of the spring. Two days ago some repairs were started in the west wing of the building, and my bedroom wall has been pierced, so that I have had to move into the chamber in which my sister died, and to sleep in the very bed in which she slept. Imagine, then, my thrill of terror when last night, as I lay awake, thinking over her terrible fate, I suddenly heard in the silence of the night the low whistle which had been the herald of her own death. I sprang up and lit the lamp, but nothing was to be seen in the room. I was too shaken to go to bed again, however, so I dressed, and as soon as it was daylight I slipped down, got a dog-cart at the Crown Inn, which is opposite, and drove to Leatherhead, from whence

I have come on this morning, with the one object of seeing you and asking your advice."

"You have done wisely," said my friend. "But have you told me all?"

"Yes, all."

"Miss Roylott, you have not. You are screening your step-father."

"Why, what do you mean?"

For answer Holmes pushed back the frill of black lace which fringed the hand that lay upon our visitor's knee. Five little livid spots, the marks of four fingers and a thumb, were printed upon the white wrist.

"You have been cruelly used," said Holmes.

The lady coloured deeply, and covered over her injured wrist. "He is a hard man," she said, "and perhaps he hardly knows his own strength."

There was a long silence, during which Holmes leaned his chin upon his hands and stared into the crackling fire.

"This is very deep business," he said at last. "There are a thousand details which I should desire to know before I decide upon our course of action. Yet we have not a moment to lose. If we were to come to Stoke Moran today, would it be possible for us to see over these rooms without the knowledge of your stepfather?"

"As it happens, he spoke of coming into town today upon some most important business. It is probable that he will be away all day, and that there would be nothing to disturb you. We have a housekeeper now, but she is old and foolish, and I could easily get her out of the way."

"Excellent. You are not averse to this trip, Watson?"

"By no means."

"Then we shall both come. What are you going to do yourself?"

"I have one or two things which I would wish to do now that I am in town. But I shall return by the twelve o'clock train, so as to be there in time for your coming."

"And you may expect us early in the afternoon. I have myself some small business matters to attend to. Will you not wait and breakfast?"

"No, I must go. My heart is lightened already since I have confided my trouble to you. I shall look forward to seeing you again this afternoon." She dropped her thick black veil over her face, and glided from the room.

"And what do you think of it all, Watson?" asked Sherlock Holmes, leaning back in his chair.

"It seems to me to be a most dark and sinister business."

"Dark enough and sinister enough."

"Yet if the lady is correct in saying that the flooring and walls are sound, and that the door, window, and chimney are impassable, then her sister must have been undoubtedly alone when she met her mysterious end."

"What becomes, then, of these nocturnal whistles, and what of the very peculiar words of the dying woman?"

"I cannot think."

"When you combine the ideas of whistles at night, the presence of a band of gipsies who are on intimate terms with this old doctor, the fact that we have every reason to believe that the doctor has an interest in preventing his step-daughter's marriage, the dying allusion to a band, and finally, the fact that Miss Helen Stoner heard a metallic clang, which might have been caused by one of those metal bars which secured the shutters falling back into their place, I think there is good ground to think that the mystery may be cleared along those lines."

"But what, then, did the gipsies do?"

"I cannot imagine."

"I see many objections to any such a theory."

"And so do I. It is precisely for that reason that we are going to Stoke Moran this day. I want to see whether the objections are fatal, or if they may be explained away. But what, in the name of the devil!"

The ejaculation had been drawn from my companion by the fact that our door had been suddenly dashed open, and that a huge man framed himself in the aperture. His costume was a peculiar mixture of the professional and of the agricultural, having a black top hat, a long frock-coat, and a pair of high gaiters, with a hunting-crop swinging in his hand. So tall was he that his hat actually brushed the crossbar of the doorway, and his breadth seemed to span it across from side to side. A large face, seared with a thousand wrinkles, burned yellow with the sun, and marked with every evil passion, was turned from one to the other of us, while his deep-set, bile-shot eyes, and the high, thin, fleshless nose, gave him somewhat the resemblance to a fierce old bird of prey.

"Which of you is Holmes?" asked this apparition.

"My name, sir, but you have the advantage of me," said my companion quietly.

"I am Dr Grimesby Roylott, of Stoke Moran."

"Indeed, Doctor," said Holmes blandly. "Pray take a seat."

"I will do nothing of the kind. My step-daughter has been here. I have traced her. What has she been saying to you?"

"It is a little cold for the time of the year," said Holmes.

"What has she been saying to you?" screamed the old man furiously.

"But I have heard that the crocuses promise well," continued my companion imperturbably.

"Ha! You put me off, do you?" said our new visitor, taking a step forward, and shaking his hunting-crop. "I know you, you scoundrel! I have heard of you before. You are Holmes the meddler."

My friend smiled.

"Holmes the busybody!"

His smile broadened.

"Holmes the Scotland-yard Jack-in-office."

Holmes chuckled heartily. "Your conversation is most entertaining," said he. "When you go out close the door, for there is a decided draught."

"I will go when I have had my say. Don't you dare to meddle with my affairs. I know that Miss Stoner has been here – I traced her! I am a dangerous man to fall foul of! See here." He stepped swiftly forward, seized the poker and bent it into a curve with his huge brown hands.

"See that you keep yourself out of my grip," he snarled, and hurling the twisted poker into the fireplace, he strode out of the room.

"He seems a very amiable person," said Holmes, laughing. "I am not quite so bulky, but if he had remained I might have shown him that my grip was not much more feeble than his own." As he spoke he picked up the steel poker, and with a sudden effort straightened it out again.

"Fancy his having the insolence to confound me with the official detective force! This incident gives zest to our investigation, however, and I only trust that our little friend will not suffer from her imprudence in allowing this brute to trace her. And now, Watson, we shall order breakfast, and afterwards I shall walk down to Doctors' Commons, where I hope to get some data which may help us in this matter."

It was nearly one o'clock when Sherlock Holmes returned from his excursion. He held in his hand a sheet of blue paper, scrawled over with notes and figures.

"I have seen the will of the deceased wife," said he. "To determine its exact meaning I have been obliged to work out the present prices of the investments with which it is concerned. The total income, which at the time of the wife's death was little short of £1,100, is now through the fall in agricultural prices not more than £750. Each daughter can claim an income of £250, in case of marriage. It is evident, therefore, that if both girls had married this beauty would have had a mere pittance, while even one of them would cripple him to a serious extent. My morning's work has not been wasted, since it has proved that he has the very strongest motives for standing in the way of anything of the sort. And now, Watson, this is too serious for dawdling, especially as the old man is aware that we are interesting ourselves in his affairs, so if you are ready we shall call a cab and drive to Waterloo. I should be very much obliged if you would slip your revolver into your pocket. An Eley's No. 2 is an excellent argument with gentlemen who can twist steel pokers into knots. That and a toothbrush are, I think, all that we need."

At Waterloo we were fortunate in catching a train for Leatherhead, where he hired a trap at the station inn, and drove for four or five miles through the lovely Surrey lanes. It was a perfect day, with a bright sun and a few fleecy clouds in the heavens. The trees and wayside hedges were just throwing out their first green shoots, and the air was full of the pleasant smell of the moist earth. To me at least there was a strange contrast between the sweet promise of the spring and this sinister quest upon which we were engaged. My companion sat in front of the trap, his arms folded, his hat pulled down over his eyes, and his chin sunk upon his breast, buried in the deepest thought. Suddenly, however, he started, tapped me on the shoulder, and pointed over the meadows.

"Look there!" said he.

A heavily-timbered park stretched up in a gentle slope, thickening into a grove at the highest point. From amidst the branches there jutted out the grey gables and high roof-tree of a very old mansion.

"Stoke Moran?" said he.

"Yes, sir, that be the house of Dr Grimesby Roylott," remarked the driver.

"There is some building going on there," said Holmes; "that is where we are going."

"There's the village," said the driver, pointing to a cluster of roofs some distance to the left; "but if you want to get to the house, you'll find it shorter to go over this stile, and so by the foot-path over the fields. There it is, where the lady is walking."

"And the lady, I fancy, is Miss Stoner," observed Holmes, shading his eyes. "Yes, I think we had better do as you suggest."

We got off, paid our fare, and the trap rattled back on its way to Leatherhead.

"I thought it as well," said Holmes, as we climbed the stile, "that this fellow should think we had come here as architects, or on some definite business. It may stop his gossip. Good afternoon, Miss Stoner. You see that we have been as good as our word."

Our client of the morning had hurried forward to meet us with a face which spoke her joy. "I have been waiting so eagerly for you," she cried, shaking hands with us warmly. "All has turned out splendidly. Dr Roylott has gone to town, and it is unlikely that he will be back before evening."

"We have had the pleasure of making the Doctor's acquaintance," said Holmes, and in a few words he sketched out what had occurred. Miss Stoner turned white to the lips as she listened.

"Good heavens!" she cried, "he has followed me, then."

"So it appears."

"He is so cunning that I never know when I am safe from him. What will he say when he returns?"

"He must guard himself, for he may find that there is someone more cunning than himself upon his track. You must lock yourself from him tonight. If he is violent, we shall take you away to your aunt's at Harrow. Now, we must make the best use of our time, so kindly take us at once to the rooms which we are to examine."

The building was of grey, lichen-blotched stone, with a high central portion, and two curving wings, like the claws of a crab, thrown out on each side. In one of these wings the windows were broken, and blocked with wooden boards, while the roof was partly caved in, a picture of ruin. The central portion was in little better repair, but the right-hand block was comparatively modern, and the blinds in the windows, with the blue smoke curling up from the chimneys, showed that this was where the family resided. Some scaffolding had been erected against the end wall, and the stonework had been broken into, but there were no signs of any workmen at the moment of our visit. Holmes walked slowly up and down the ill-trimmed lawn, and examined with deep attention the outsides of the windows.

"This, I take it, belongs to the room in which you used to sleep, the centre one to your sister's, and the one next to the main building to Dr Roylott's chamber?"

"Exactly so. But I am now sleeping in the middle one."

"Pending the alterations, as I understand. By the way, there does not seem to be any very pressing need for repairs at that end wall."

"There were none. I believe that it was an excuse to move me from my room."

"Ah! that is suggestive. Now, on the other side of this narrow wing runs the corridor from which these three rooms open. There are windows in it, of course?"

"Yes, but very small ones. Too narrow for anyone to pass through."

"As you both locked your doors at night your rooms were unapproachable from that side. Now, would you have the kindness to go into your room, and to bar your shutters."

Miss Stoner did so, and Holmes, after a careful examination through the open window, endeavoured in every way to force the shutter open, but without success. There was no slit through which a knife could be passed to raise the bar. Then with his lens he tested the hinges, but they were of solid iron, built firmly into the massive masonry. "Hum!" said he, scratching his chin in some perplexity, "my theory certainly presents some difficulty. No one could pass these shutters if they were bolted. Well, we shall see if the inside throws any light upon the matter."

A small side-door led into the whitewashed corridor from which the three bedrooms opened. Holmes refused to examine the third chamber, so we passed at once to the second, that in which Miss Stoner was now sleeping, and in which her sister had met her fate. It was a homely little room, with a low ceiling and a gaping fire-place, after the fashion of old country houses. A brown chest of drawers stood in one corner, a narrow white-counterpaned bed in another, and a dressing-table on the left-hand side of the window. These articles, with two small wicker-work chairs, made up all the furniture in the room, save for a square of Wilton carpet in the centre. The boards round and the panelling of the walls were brown, worm-eaten oak, so old and discoloured that it may have dated from the original building of the house. Holmes drew one of the chairs into a corner and sat silent, while his eyes travelled round and round and up and down, taking in every detail of the apartment.

"Where does that bell communicate with?" he asked at last, pointing to a thick bell-rope which hung down beside the bed, the tassel actually lying upon the pillow.

"It goes to the housekeeper's room."

"It looks newer than the other things?"

"Yes, it was only put there a couple of years ago."

"Your sister asked for it, I suppose?"

"No, I never heard of her using it. We used always to get what we wanted for ourselves."

"Indeed, it seemed unnecessary to put so nice a bell-pull there. You will excuse me for a few minutes while I satisfy myself as to this floor." He threw himself down upon his face with his lens in his hand, and crawled swiftly backwards and forwards, examining minutely the cracks between the boards. Then he did the same with the woodwork with which the chamber was panelled. Finally he walked over to the bed and spent some time in staring at it, and in running his eye up and down the wall. Finally he took the bell-rope in his hand and gave it a brisk tug.

"Why, it's a dummy," said he.

"Won't it ring?"

"No, it is not even attached to a wire. This is very interesting. You can see now that it is fastened to a hook just above where the little opening of the ventilator is."

"How very absurd! I never noticed that before."

"Very strange!" muttered Holmes, pulling at the rope. "There are one or two very singular points about this room. For example, what a fool a builder must be to open a ventilator in another room, when, with the same trouble, he might have communicated with the outside air!"

"This is also quite modern," said the lady.

"Done about the same time as the bell-rope," remarked Holmes.

"Yes, there were several little changes carried out about that time."

"They seem to have been of a most interesting character – dummy bell-ropes, and ventilators which do not ventilate. With your permission, Miss Stoner, we shall now carry our researches into the inner apartment."

Dr Grimesby Roylott's chamber was larger than that of his stepdaughter, but was as plainly furnished. A camp bed, a small wooden shelf full of books, mostly of a technical character, an arm-chair beside the bed, a plain wooden chair against the wall, a round table, and a large iron safe were the principal things which met the eye. Holmes walked slowly round and examined each and all of them with the keenest interest.

"What's in here?" he asked, tapping the safe.

"My stepfather's business papers."

"Oh! you have seen inside, then!"

"Only once, some years ago. I remember that it was full of papers."

"There isn't a cat in it, for example?"

"No. What a strange idea!"

"Well, look at this!" He took up a small saucer of milk which stood on the top of it.

"No; we don't keep a cat. But there is a cheetah and a baboon."

"Ah, yes, of course! Well, a cheetah is just a big cat, and yet a saucer of milk does not go very far in satisfying its wants, I dare say. There is one point which I should wish to determine." He squatted down in front of the wooden chair, and examined the seat of it with the greatest attention.

"Thank you. That is quite settled," said he, rising and putting his lens in his pocket. "Hullo! here is something interesting!"

The object which had caught his eye was a small dog lash hung on one corner of the bed. The lash, however, was curled upon itself, and tied so as to make a loop of whipcord.

"What do you make of that, Watson?"

"It's a common enough lash. But I don't know why it should be tied."

"That is not quite so common, is it? Ah, me! it's a wicked world, and when a clever man turns his brain to crime it is the worst of all. I think that I have seen enough now, Miss Stoner, and, with your permission, we shall walk out upon the lawn."

I had never seen my friend's face so grim, or his brow so dark, as it was when we turned from the scene of this investigation. We had walked several times up and down the lawn, neither Miss Stoner nor myself liking to break in upon his thoughts before he roused himself from his reverie.

"It is very essential, Miss Stoner," said he, 'that you should absolutely follow my advice in every respect."

"I shall most certainly do so."

"The matter is too serious for any hesitation. Your life may depend upon your compliance."

"I assure you that I am in your hands."

"In the first place, both my friend and I must spend the night in your room."

Both Miss Stoner and I gazed at him in astonishment.

"Yes, it must be so. Let me explain. I believe that that is the village inn over there?"

"Yes, that is the 'Crown',"

"Very good. Your windows would be visible from there?"

"Certainly."

"You must confine yourself to your room, on pretence of a headache, when your step-father comes back. Then when you hear him retire for the night, you must open the shutters of your window, undo the hasp, put your lamp there as a signal to us, and then withdraw with everything which you are likely to want into the room which you used to occupy. I have no doubt that, in spite of the repairs, you could manage there for one night."

"Oh, yes, easily."

"The rest you will leave in our hands."

"But what will you do?"

"We shall spend the night in your room, and we shall investigate the cause of this noise which has disturbed you."

"I believe, Mr Holmes, that you have already made up your mind," said Miss Stoner, laying her hand upon my companion's sleeve.

"Perhaps I have."

"Then for pity's sake tell me what was the cause of my sister's death."

"I should prefer to have clearer proofs before I speak."

"You can at least tell me whether my own thought is correct, and if she died from some sudden fright."

"No, I do not think so. I think that there was probably some more tangible cause. And now, Miss Stoner, we must leave you, for if Dr Roylott returned and saw us, our journey would be in vain. Goodbye, and be brave, for if you will do what I have told you, you may rest assured that we shall soon drive away the dangers that threaten you."

Sherlock Holmes and I had no difficulty in engaging a bed-room and sitting-room at the Crown Inn. They were on the upper floor, and from our window we could command a view of the avenue gate, and of the inhabited wing of Stoke Moran Manor House. At dusk we saw Dr Grimesby Roylott drive past, his huge form looming up beside the little figure of the lad who drove him. The boy had some slight difficulty in undoing the heavy iron gates, and we heard the hoarse roar of the Doctor's voice, and saw the fury with which he shook his clenched fists at him. The trap drove on, and a few minutes later we saw a sudden light spring up among the trees as the lamp was lit in one of the sitting-rooms.

"Do you know, Watson," said Holmes, as we sat together in the gathering darkness, "I have really some scruples as to taking you tonight. There is a distinct element of danger."

"Can I be of assistance?"

"Your presence might be invaluable."

"Then I shall certainly come."

"It is very kind of you."

"You speak of danger. You have evidently seen more in these rooms than was visible to me."

"No, but I fancy that I may have deduced a little more. I imagine that you saw all I did."

"I saw nothing remarkable save the bell-rope, and what purpose that could answer I confess is more than I can imagine."

"You saw the ventilator, too?"

"Yes, but I do not think that it is such a very unusual thing to have a small opening between two rooms. It was so small that a rat could hardly pass through."

"I knew that we should find a ventilator before ever we came to Stoke Moran."

"My dear Holmes!"

"Oh, yes, I did. You remember in her statement she said that her sister could smell Dr Roylott's cigar. Now, of course that suggests at once that there must be a communication between the two rooms. It could only be a small one, or it would have been remarked upon at the coroner's inquiry. I deduced a ventilator."

"But what harm can there be in that?"

"Well, there is at least a curious coincidence of dates. A ventilator is made, a cord is hung, and a lady who sleeps in the bed dies. Does not that strike you?"

"I cannot as yet see any connection."

"Did you observe anything very peculiar about that bed?"

"No."

"It was clamped to the floor. Did you ever see a bed fastened like that before?"

"I cannot say that I have."

"The lady could not move her bed. It must always be in the same relative position to the ventilator and to the rope – for so we may call it, since it was clearly never meant for a bell-pull."

"Holmes," I cried, "I seem to see dimly what you are hitting at. We are only just in time to prevent some subtle and horrible crime."

"Subtle enough and horrible enough. When a doctor goes wrong he is the first of criminals. He has nerve and he has knowledge. Palmer and Pritchard were among the heads of their profession. This man strikes even deeper, but I think, Watson, that we shall be able to strike deeper still. But we shall have horrors enough before the night is over: for goodness' sake let us have a quiet pipe, and turn our minds for a few hours to something more cheerful."

About nine o'clock the light among the trees was extinguished, and all was dark in the direction of the Manor House. Two hours passed slowly away, and then, suddenly, just at the stroke of eleven, a single bright light shone out right in front of us.

"That is our signal," said Holmes, springing to his feet; "it comes from the middle window." As we passed out he exchanged a few words with the landlord, explaining that we were going on a late visit to an acquaintance, and that it was possible that we might spend the night there. A moment later we were out on the dark road, a chill wind blowing in our faces, and one yellow light twinkling in front of us through the gloom to guide us on our sombre errand.

There was little difficulty in entering the grounds, for unrepaired breaches gaped in the old park wall. Making our way among the trees, we reached the lawn, crossed it, and were about to enter through the window, when out from a clump of laurel bushes there darted what seemed to be a hideous and distorted child, who threw itself on the grass with writhing limbs, and then ran swiftly across the lawn into the darkness.

"My God!" I whispered, "did you see it?"

Holmes was for the moment as startled as I. His hand closed like a vice upon my wrist in agitation. Then he broke into a low laugh, and put his lips to my ear.

"It is a nice household," he murmured, "that is the baboon."

I had forgotten the strange pets which the Doctor affected. There was a cheetah, too; perhaps we might find it upon our shoulders at any moment. I confess that I felt easier in my mind when, after following Holmes's example and slipping off my shoes, I found myself inside the bedroom. My companion noiselessly closed the shutters, moved the lamp onto the table, and cast his eyes round the room. All was as we had seen it in the day-time. Then creeping up to me and making a trumpet of his hand, he whispered into my ear again so gently that it was all that I could do to distinguish the words:

"The least sound would be fatal to our plans."

I nodded to show that I had heard.

"We must sit without a light. He would see it through the ventilator."

I nodded again.

"Do not go to sleep; your very life may depend upon it. Have your pistol ready in case we should need it. I will sit on the side of the bed, and you in that chair."

I took out my revolver and laid it on the corner of the table.

Holmes had brought up a long thin cane, and this he placed upon the bed beside him. By it he laid the box of matches and the stump of a candle. Then he turned down the lamp and we were left in darkness.

How shall I ever forget that dreadful vigil? I could not hear a sound, not even the drawing of a breath, and yet I knew that my companion sat open-eyed, within a few feet of me, in the same state of nervous tension in which I was myself. The shutters cut off the least ray of light, and we waited in absolute darkness. From outside came the occasional cry of a night-bird, and once at our very window a long drawn, cat-like whine, which told us that the cheetah was indeed at liberty. Far away we could hear the deep tones of the parish clock, which boomed out every quarter of an hour. How long they seemed, those quarters! Twelve o'clock, and one, and two, and three, and still we sat waiting silently for whatever might befall.

Suddenly there was the momentary gleam of a light up in the direction of the ventilator, which vanished immediately, but was succeeded by a strong smell of burning oil and heated metal. Someone in the next room had lit a dark lantern. I heard a gentle sound of movement, and then all was silent once more, though the smell grew stronger. For half an hour I sat with straining ears. Then suddenly another sound became audible – a very gentle, soothing sound, like that of a small jet of steam escaping continually from a kettle. The instant that we heard it, Holmes sprang from the bed, struck a match, and lashed furiously with his cane at the bell-pull.

"You see it, Watson?" he yelled. "You see it?"

But I saw nothing. At the moment when Holmes struck the light I heard a low, clear whistle, but the sudden glare flashing into my weary eyes made it impossible for me to tell what it was at which my friend lashed so savagely. I could, however, see that his face was deadly pale, and filled with horror and loathing.

He had ceased to strike, and was gazing up at the ventilator, when suddenly there broke from the silence of the night the most horrible cry to which I have ever listened. It swelled up louder and louder, a hoarse yell of pain and fear and anger all mingled in the one dreadful shriek. They say that away down in the village, and even in the distant parsonage, that cry raised the sleepers from their beds. It struck cold to our hearts, and I stood gazing at Holmes, and he at me, until the last echoes of it had died away into the silence from which it rose.

"What can it mean?" I gasped.

"It means that it is all over," Holmes answered. 'And perhaps, after all, it is for the best. Take your pistol, and we shall enter Dr Roylott's room."

With a grave face he lit the lamp, and led the way down the corridor. Twice he struck at the chamber door without any reply from within. Then he turned the handle and entered, I at his heels, with the cocked pistol in my hand.

It was a singular sight which met our eyes. On the table stood a dark lantern with the shutter half open, throwing a brilliant beam of light upon the iron safe, the door of which was ajar. Beside this table, on the wooden chair, sat Dr Grimesby Roylott, clad in a long grey dressing-gown, his bare ankles protruding beneath, and his feet thrust into red heelless Turkish slippers. Across his lap lay the short stock with the long lash which we had noticed during the day. His chin was cocked upwards, and his eyes were fixed in a dreadful rigid stare at the corner of the ceiling. Round his brow he had a peculiar yellow band, with brownish speckles, which seemed to be bound tightly round his head. As we entered he made neither sound nor motion.

"The band! the speckled band!" whispered Holmes.

I took a step forward. In an instant his strange headgear began to move, and there reared itself from among his hair the squat diamond-shaped head and puffed neck of a loathsome serpent.

"It was a swamp adder!" cried Holmes, "the deadliest snake in India. He has died within ten seconds of being bitten.

Violence does, in truth, recoil upon the violent, and the schemer falls into the pit which he digs for another. Let us thrust this creature back into its den, and we can then remove Miss Stoner to some place of shelter, and let the county police know what has happened.''

As he spoke he drew the dog whip swiftly from the dead man's lap, and throwing the noose round the reptile's neck, he drew it from its horrid perch, and carrying it at arm's length, threw it into the iron safe, which he closed upon it.

Such are the true facts of the death of Dr Grimesby Roylott, of Stoke Moran. It is not necessary that I should prolong a narrative which has already run to too great a length by telling how we broke the sad news to the terrified girl, how we conveyed her by the morning train to the care of her good aunt at Harrow, of how the slow process of official inquiry came to the conclusion that the Doctor met his fate while indiscreetly playing with a dangerous pet. The little which I had yet to learn of the case was told me by Sherlock Holmes as we travelled back next day.

"I had," said he, "come to an entirely erroneous conclusion, which shows, my dear Watson, how dangerous it always is to reason from insufficient data. The presence of the gipsies, and the use of the word 'band', which was used by the poor girl, no doubt, to explain the appearance which she had caught a horrid glimpse of by the light of her match, were sufficient to put me upon an entirely wrong scent. I can only claim the merit that I instantly reconsidered my position when, however, it became clear to me that whatever danger threatened an occupant of the room could not come either from the window or the door. My attention was speedily drawn, as I have already remarked to you, to this ventilator, and to the bell-rope which hung down to the bed. The discovery that this was a dummy, and that the bed was clamped to the floor, instantly gave rise to a suspicion that the rope was there as a bridge for something passing through the hole, and coming to the bed. The idea of a snake instantly occurred to me, and when I coupled it with my knowledge that the Doctor was furnished with a supply of creatures from India, I felt that I was probably on the right track. The idea of using a form of poison which could not possibly be discovered by any chemical test was just such a one as would occur to a clever and ruthless man who had had an Eastern training. The rapidity with which such a poison would take effect would also, from his point of view, be an advantage. It would be a sharp-eyed coroner indeed who could distinguish the two little dark punctures which would show where the poison fangs had done their work. Then I thought of the whistle. Of course, he must recall the snake before the morning light revealed it to the victim. He had trained it, probably by the use of the milk which we saw, to return to him when summoned. He would put it through the ventilator at the hour that he thought best, with the certainty that it would crawl down the rope, and land on the bed. It might or might not bite the occupant, perhaps she might escape every night for a week, but sooner or later she must fall a victim.

"I had come to these conclusions before ever I had entered his room. An inspection of his chair showed me that he had been in the habit of standing on it, which, of course, would be necessary in order that he should reach the ventilator. The sight of the safe, the saucer of milk, and the loop of whipcord were enough to finally dispel any doubts which may have remained. The metallic clang heard by Miss Stoner was obviously caused by her father hastily closing the door of his safe upon its terrible occupant. Having once made up my mind, you know the steps which I took in order to put the matter to the proof. I heard the creature hiss, as I have no doubt that you did also, and I instantly lit the light and attacked it."

"With the result of driving it through the ventilator."

"And also with the result of causing it to turn upon its master at the other side. Some of the blows of my cane came home, and roused its snakish temper, so that it flew upon the first person it saw. In this way I am no doubt indirectly responsible for Dr Grimesby Roylott's death, and I cannot say that it is likely to weigh very heavily upon my conscience."

WEIGHTS AND MEASURES

Units in the Imperial System

Length

1 foot	= 12 inches
1 yard	= 3 feet
1 rod	= 5½ yards (= 16½ feet)
1 chain	= 4 rods (= 22 yards)
1 furlong	= 10 chains (= 220 yards)
1 mile	= 5,280 feet
1 mile	= 1,760 yards
1 mile	= 8 furlongs

Nautical

1 fathom	= 6 feet
1 cable length	= 120 fathoms
1 nautical mile	= 6,076 feet

Area

1 square foot	= 144 square inches
1 square yard	= 9 square feet
1 square rod	= 30¼ square yards
1 acre	= 4 roods
1 acre	= 4,840 square yards
1 square mile	= 640 acres

Volume

1 cubic foot	= 1,728 cubic inches
1 cubic yard	= 27 cubic feet
1 bulk barrel	= 5.8 cubic feet

Weight (avoirdupois)

1 ounce	= 437½ grains
1 ounce	= 16 drams
1 pound	= 16 ounces
1 stone	= 14 pounds
1 quarter	= 28 pounds
1 hundredweight	= 4 quarters
1 ton	= 20 hundredweight

Shipping

1 register ton	= 100 cubic feet

Capacity

1 fluid ounce	= 8 fluid drams
1 gill	= 5 fluid ounces
1 pint	= 4 gills
1 quart	= 2 pints
1 gallon	= 4 quarts
1 peck	= 2 gallons
1 bushel	= 4 pecks
1 quarter	= 8 bushels
1 bulk barrel	= 36 gallons

Units in the Metric System

Length

1 centimetre	= 10 millimetres	
1 decimetre	= 10 centimetres	= 100 millimetres
1 metre	= 10 decimetres	= 1,000 millimetres
1 decametre	= 10 metres	
1 hectometre	= 10 decametres	= 100 metres
1 kilometre	= 10 hectometres	= 1,000 metres

Area

1 square centimetre	= 100 square millimetres	
1 square metre	= 10,000 square centimetres	= 1,000,000 square millimetres
1 are	= 100 square metres	
1 hectare	= 100 ares	= 10,000 square metres
1 square kilometre	= 100 hectares	= 1,000,000 square metres

Mass (avoirdupois)

1 centigram	= 10 milligrams	
1 decigram	= 10 centigrams	= 100 milligrams
1 gram	= 10 decigrams	= 1,000 milligrams
1 decagram	= 10 grams	
1 hectogram	= 10 decagrams	= 100 grams
1 kilogram	= 10 hectograms	= 1,000 grams
1 metric ton	= 1,000 kilograms	

Capacity

1 centilitre	= 10 millilitres	
1 decilitre	= 10 centilitres	= 100 millilitres
1 litre	= 10 decilitres	= 1,000 millilitres
1 decalitre	= 10 litres	
1 hectolitre	= 10 decalitres	= 100 litres
1 kilolitre	= 10 hectolitres	= 1,000 litres

Volume

1 cubic centimetre	= 1,000 cubic millimetres	
1 cubic decimetre	= 1,000 cubic centimetres	= 1,000,000 cubic millimetres
1 cubic metre	= 1,000 cubic decimetres	= 1,000,000,000 cubic millimetres

Conversion Imperial to Metric/Metric to Imperial

To convert from imperial to metric	Multiply by	To convert from metric to imperial	Multiply by
Length			
inches	25.4	millimetres	0.0393701
feet	0.3048	metres	3.28084
yards	0.9144	metres	1.09361
furlongs	0.201168	kilometres	4.97097
miles	1.609344	kilometres	0.621371
Area			
square inches	6.4516	square centimetres	0.1550
square feet	0.092903	square metres	10.7639
square yards	0.836127	square metres	1.19599
square miles	2.589988	square kilometres	0.386102
acres	4046.856422	square metres	0.000247
acres	0.404685	hectares	2.471054
Volume/capacity			
cubic inches	16.387064	cubic centimetres	0.061024
cubic feet	0.028317	cubic metres	35.3147
cubic yards	0.764555	cubic metres	1.30795
cubic miles	4.1682	cubic kilometres	0.239912
fluid ounces (imperial)	28.413063	millilitres	0.035195
fluid ounces (US)	29.5735	millilitres	0.033814
pints (imperial)	0.568261	litres	1.759754
pints (US)	0.473176	litres	2.113377
quarts (imperial)	1.136523	litres	0.879877
quarts (US)	0.946353	litres	1.056688
gallons (imperial)	4.54609	litres	0.219969
gallons (US)	3.785412	litres	0.364172
Mass/weight			
ounces	28.349523	grams	0.035274
pounds	0.453592	kilograms	2.20462
stone (14 lb)	6.350293	kilograms	0.157473
tons (imperial)	1016.046909	kilograms	0.000984
tons (US)	907.18474	kilograms	0.001102
tons (imperial)	1.016047	metric tonnes	0.984207
tons (US)	0.907185	metric tonnes	1.10231
Speed			
miles per hour	1.609344	kilometres per hour	0.621371
feet per second	0.3048	metres per second	3.28084

THE SEVEN WONDERS
OF THE ANCIENT WORLD

Colossus of Rhodes

A giant bronze statue of the god Helios, erected on the Greek island of Rhodes by the sculptor Chares of Lindos between 304 to 292 BC. Some 33 metres high, the Colossus was destroyed by an earthquake which hit Rhodes in around 226 BC.

The Hanging Gardens

The Hanging Gardens of Babylon (near present-day Baghdad, Iraq) were laid out by King Nebuchadnezzar II for one of his wives in 600 BC. The Gardens were 75 feet above the ground and watered by a screw system which lifted water from the nearby Euphrates. It is possible that the gardens were a fable.

The Tomb of Mausolus

Built between 353 and 350 BC at Halicarnassus (present Bodrum, Turkey) for Mausolus, a provincial king in the Persian Empire, by his wife Artemisia. Designed by the Greek architects Bryaxis, Leochares, Scopas and Timotheus, the wonder is the origin of our word "mausoleum".

The Pharos of Alexandria

A lighthouse built around 250 BC on the island of Pharos in Alexandria Harbour, Egypt. Variously estimated at between 115 and 135 metres (383–440 ft) it was among the tallest man-made structures on Earth for many centuries. It ceased operating in the fourteenth century AD.

Statue of Zeus at Olympia

A statue of the father of the gods, sculpted by Phidias in 435 BC in Olympia, Greece, and made of marble inlaid with ivory and gold.

Great Pyramid of Giza

Constructed over a 20-year period concluding around 2560 BC, the Great Pyramid of Giza is generally believed to have been the tomb of the Egyptian pharaoh Khufu (Cheops). It is the only Ancient Wonder still in existence.

The Temple of Artemis

A marble temple erected in around 550 BC in honour of the Greek goddess and huntress Artemis (known as Diana to the Romans). It was sited at Ephesus, in present-day Turkey.

THE LIFE OF GALILEO GALILEI
BY JOHN HALL

The cathedral of Pisa, capital of the State of Tuscany, 1581. A young man enters by the great Gothic portal, out of the blazing sun into the shade and coolness of the House of God, the pride of a proud city under the domination of the great and powerful family of the Medicis.

The young man is a brilliant student of medicine at the University of Pisa, under the celebrated physician, Andrea Cesalpini. A great career is prophesied for him.

He crosses himself, student's bonnet in hand, and makes his way slowly across the church, until finally he comes to a quiet place between two pillars where he can stand at ease and meditate in the peace of the vaulted nave, and watch the brilliant play of the sunlight through the stained-glass windows.

His was an inquiring and a reasoning mind. He had it from his father, Vincenzio Galilei, a skilful musician and writer on the theory of music, a great player of the lute, a philosopher, born in the first flush of the Renaissance in Italy, when new ideas were lauded and accepted by all men of learning. He had taught his eldest son Greek and Latin; schooled him well, and instructed him never to accept without questioning the opinions even of the ancients, but to test even the greatest with his own reason, the better to understand them.

This, then, was the training and habit of mind of the young Galileo Galilei.

Born of an ancient and noble family, in his ancestry there were already many learned men. In 1450, there had been another celebrated Galileo Galilei, Professor of Physics and Medicine at the University of Florence. This man's brother had a great grandson, Vincenzio, who was Galileo's father. The family, though, had fallen on evil days; Vincenzio lacked the necessary means to place his eldest son in one of the famous seats of learning of Italy, where he might pursue his literary, medical and philosophic bent, at ease. He had to choose for him a profession, that of a cloth dealer, but the boy showed no aptitude for business, either at school or at the monastery of Vallombrosa, where his father had sent him to complete his classical education. Hence it was that, casting about for some paying profession not demeaning to one of ancient birth, Vincenzio remembered his son's famous ancestor, and, when he was eighteen, put him to study medicine and philosophy at Pisa.

The young Galileo often went alone to the cathedral. Within its walls was beauty and peace; and there a young and forceful soul could retire into itself to think out those things which, in the practical experience of daily life, puzzle the will. There too, there were no other students to mock him and call him the Wrangler for his habit of vehemently questioning any accepted theory which he could find no reason to believe, and no interfering professor to endeavour to force his mind to think in terms of tradition rather than curiosity.

This day in 1581 was the culmination of many weeks of thought and calculation. Aristotle . . . How could he accept wholesale that great man's conception of the Universe? He could hear the drone of the professor's voice in the classroom, in his imagination, and picture the minutes reserved for questions at the end of the lecture; hear his own voice rising hotly from the back of the room, questioning a theory here, contesting a point there, all the time impeded by the flippancies of his more careless fellow students, bored by his earnestness, waiting to escape to their laughing banter outside in the sunlight under the blue sky and the almond trees. The professor? . . . A wise man, but tedious . . . infinitely tedious . . . dispensing dry and untested theory from memory; never applying to it the test of intelligence!

The youth looked up at the vaulted roof of the cathedral, and laughed to himself quietly, flinging back his long reddish hair with a toss of the head. His features were fine and strong, with very bright, dark eyes; a fighter's face, lively, sanguine and shrewd.

"He would show them," he thought. "His philosophy would be one of knowledge: knowledge of the past, with criticism of it, that it might be the better appraised and valued in the future . . . he would—"

He stopped short, his attention fixed on a great lamp, swung from the ceiling of the aisle above him. Quick as light, his mood changed. The lamp was swinging . . . swinging round and round in a monotonous circle . . . swinging . . . swinging.

Always, he had viewed the world in two ways, philosophically and mechanically; the problems of the mind and those of the physical universe; the mechanics of things.

"What knowledge could be extracted from this swinging lamp? . . . what knowledge?"

He watched it attentively. "Curious . . . the circles of the lamp . . . constant speed . . . same timing . . . watch it while the arc gets smaller . . . wait! What can we time it with?"

His hand moved to his pulse, and he felt its steady, constant beat under his fingers. "Now, the swing of the lamp!"

For five minutes, he timed it, while the circles got smaller and smaller. By the end of it, he had determined that the timing of the swing was practically constant, no matter how small the arc. Seized with the excitement of discovery, he hurried from the church and went home.

All the next night, he worked, drawing and calculating. He had calculated the time of the swing by means of the beat of his pulse. He had left the cathedral in triumph because from this he had instantly deduced the real lesson of the lamp – the checking of the regularity of the human pulse by means of a swinging pendulum!

In the calm of Pisa Cathedral then, was born the first invention of Galileo. He called it the Pulsilogia, and the leading doctors of Italy welcomed his discovery with delight, though it brought him in little money. Nor did it advance his medical career, for his mind was turning to its true bent, mathematics.

His parents had returned to Florence, leaving him to his

studies at Pisa. Among their friends there was a mathematician of note attached to the Tuscan Court, one Ricci.

When the court was in residence at Pisa, during his second year at the university, came another turning point in Galileo's life. He went to call on Ricci, who happened to be lecturing on Euclid to the grand ducal pages. He listened at the door without entering the classroom. His inquiring spirit ever awake, the young man absorbed the new ideas, enthralled. He left the building without announcing himself to Ricci and, on succeeding days, secretly returned. At last he plucked up courage to ask the teacher to help him, which the latter gladly promised to do.

Galileo plunged into the study of mathematics with his usual passionate energy, but neglected his medical studies to such an extent that his father felt it impossible to maintain his son at the university in the faculty of medicine, which was costly and seemed to be giving no results, and recalled him to Florence.

At the age of twenty-one, therefore, Galileo, with the help of Ricci and the encouragement of his father, began to devote himself entirely to the study of mathematics and physics. He encountered the works of the great Greek mathematician, Archimedes, and in exploring his celebrated problem connected with the varying displacements in water of various solids, invented his hydrostatic balance, called the *Bilancetta*, which attracted the attention of a certain Marquis del Monte, himself an able mathematician, who recommended him to the Grand Duke of Tuscany. At last, his patience and work were rewarded by an appointment to a professorship of mathematics at the University of Pisa.

The salary was only five shillings a week, but he also received pupils' fees, and it sufficed for his immediate needs. It also gave him a forum in which to express, forcibly and emphatically, his views concerning the ancients.

This habit made him both enemies and friends; enemies among the professors who had best hated him as a student, friends among the learned, the broadminded and the young.

Galileo never lacked respect for the opinions of the dead. Were they not all scientists who worked and judged according to their time? He was of the present and of the future; therefore, with respect, in order that science might advance, he would question the past. He did not pillory Aristotle's system of mechanics; he quite simply refuted it, and then continued to lecture on him, as before.

The celebrated Leaning Tower of Pisa was the scene of one of the most famous of these refutations.

Galileo was in his classroom, packed with students of all ages. He was becoming famous.

Before him were two weights, one of a hundred pounds, one of one pound. In the presence of all, he had decided to challenge by experiment, Aristotle's contention that the velocity of falling bodies is proportional to their weight.

He was addressing his pupils:

"I tell you, gentlemen, and will furthermore put it to the test of practice, the only yardstick for philosophers and men of understanding, that were it not for the varying resistance of the air, due to the shape of these two bodies, were the one as large as the moon and the other as small as a pin, they would fall at the same speed. We will therefore go to the great tower, and drop from it these two weights, and see which travels the faster, small or large."

A murmur rose from the room. Those present were by now used to Galileo's challenges, and knew that he rarely undertook such a demonstration without good reason. The company rose and went out, pleased at the diversion.

An hour later, they returned in triumph, the heavy weight having beaten the light by only a fraction of a second. It should have travelled a hundred times as fast, according to Aristotle!

An aged professor stood up to question Galileo. He was ironical.

"Master Galileo, your pupils are misled. We cannot accept your contention against that of the great master of antiquity. His was only an error of degree. Yours is total and complete. The heavy weight reached the ground first."

Galileo was on his feet in a second, caustic and biting:

"Nay, sir; peace to your grey hairs, but neither you nor any other man shall cover up Aristotle's ninety-nine inches by my one! Does any man else contradict me?"

The answer was a second's respectful silence.

Such incidents, and there were many of them, swelled the ranks of his opponents among the professors. The university was against him and his growing reputation. He earned the animosity, too, of Giovanni dei Medici, the grand duke's natural son, an engineer, who had designed a mechanical dredger, to clear Leghorn Harbour. Galileo examined it at the request of the Grand Duke, and pronounced it useless, which it was. This incident, however, combined with official academic pressure was enough to force him to resign his professorship and return to Florence.

Galileo's return to his family was to a position of difficulty and hardship. In 1581, he pledged himself to provide a marriage dowry for his sister, Virginia, and had now no means to fulfil his pledge. His father had died, leaving him head of the family. He had to support his mother and two younger sisters, as well as his good for nothing musician brother, Michelangelo.

In the nick of time, again through the good offices of the Marquis del Monte, he obtained a mathematical professorship at the University of Padua, at a salary of forty pounds a year, under the great republican government of Venice. It brought him in more pupils than ever; in addition, at his house, he employed a staff of mechanics to manufacture his inventions, among them, in 1596, the geometrical and military compass, now known as the sector.

In seven years at Padua, his fame grew to such an extent that his friends pestered the Doge until his salary was raised to seventy pounds a year. His reputation became European. The Archduke Ferdinand, future Emperor of Germany, was among his pupils. He moved into a larger house and took in resident students.

Galileo needed every penny of the money he earned. For his family, he provided everything. His brother, Michelangelo, sponged on him mercilessly all his life. He obtained for him posts as court musician, first in Poland, then in Bavaria, providing him with an outfit and expenses, on loan, none of which Michelangelo ever repaid. His sister Virginia's husband threatened to sue him for the unpaid balance of her dowry. Another sister, Livia, married in 1601, and Galileo had to find her dowry too.

Furthermore, he himself set up an irregular household with a Venetian lady of lower station than his own, Marina Gamba, by whom he had three children.

To meet all these additional expenses, in 1601, he undertook the holiday tuition of the son of the Grand Duke of Tuscany, in

Florence. In addition, he acted as astrologer to the Grand Duchess Cristina.

His lecture rooms at Padua were always crowded out; sometimes he was even forced to lecture in the open air, so great was the press. Finally, in 1604, his salary was raised to a hundred and fifteen pounds a year, the highest ever paid to a professor of mathematics in the Republic. All about him were envious tongues and many defamatory accusations were made against him.

The attacks were useless, but his caustic wit in rebutting them did him no good. In reply to one attack mentioning his mistress, he angrily retorted:

"They say I live in sin. A great man gives to the woman he favours, whatever her station, something of his essence. Many of those men who live in virtue have nothing to give. Which woman's station then is the more honourable, that of the empty or the richly endowed?"

The most momentous year of the life of Galileo, 1609, was also the source of all his disasters. It began with his telescope, which he produced in that year, having heard of such an instrument in Flanders the year before. He thought its construction out as a scientific problem, from the meagre data which he had been sent from the Low Countries, and soon produced independently an instrument which magnified to three diameters and showed objects twenty-two miles distant on the earth's surface.

The Council of Venice called him to show them his discovery, and when he did so, as a reward for seventeen years' brilliant service to the state, he was granted a life professorship at a new salary of two hundred and twenty pounds a year. The stipend was magnificent and his future secure. All over Europe, copies of his telescope were sent as gifts to ruling princes, potentates and learned men. But Galileo accepted his success coolly, and turned his instrument on the heavens.

There began his greatness, his immortal fame, and his downfall.

Up to this time, there had been one principal system of astronomy, the Ptolemaic, which was based on the earth being the centre of the universe, all the planets, stars and the sun revolving round it, the "immutable sphere." Twenty years before the birth of Galileo, however, another great astronomer, Copernicus, had arisen, and his system, with greater truth, had shown the sun as the centre of the universe, with the earth revolving round it.

The system of Copernicus had been accepted by many learned men, but not by the Church. It had been founded largely on inspired observation, needing proof. Galileo had already espoused the Copernican cause as opposed to the Ptolemaic. Now, with his telescope and his brilliant deductive mind, he turned a new eye to the stars and completed the Copernican revolution.

Alone, night after night, he swept the heavens. The moon he first saw as a world, all hills and valleys; the structure of the Milky Way, the planets – all came under his avid gaze, and their movements and positions were interpreted by his great intelligence. In January, 1610, he first saw Jupiter's satellites, the four moons, which he called the Medicean Stars, in honour of the Grand Duke of Tuscany and his three brothers. Then he discovered the "Ring" of Saturn. Under his hand, the "changeless" heavens were changing. This, as he was to discover to his cost, could not happen without the consent of Holy Church. The Scriptures said: "He hath made the round world so fast that it cannot be moved." By confirming the earth's movement, Galileo was setting his foot on the road to becoming a heretic.

Already a subject for envy among the professors of all Italy, he was now, unwittingly and unwillingly, making enemies among the Jesuits, and attracting the fearful attention of the Holy Inquisition. Finally, he made a fatal mistake which paved the way to the ultimate triumph of his enemies.

At this time, Venice was the only part of Italy which was entirely free from Jesuit influence. Before Galileo entered the service of the Republic, the Senate, finding the Jesuits scheming to gain control of education in its territories, had declared that they were not to teach there. Only in the Republic was freedom of thought complete. With the growth of Galileo's fame it was fitting for him to serve his own Grand Duke, Cosmo II dei Medici. Besides, he needed time for his researches: in Venice and Padua he was too occupied with his pupils, now legion, to follow them properly. When, at length, he was offered the post of first mathematician at the University of Pisa, and philosopher and mathematician to the grand duke, at the same salary as in Padua, and in addition with no obligation to lecture or live at Pisa, he accepted it. In 1610, he left the Venetian Republic, and his security.

Henceforward, whatever he did was attacked by the Jesuits, Aristotelians and traditionalists of all kinds; what was worse, he defended himself brilliantly and successfully, with pungent satire.

Deeming it prudent, none the less, to beware of offending the Church openly, he early journeyed to Rome in order to forestall any possible theological accusations. The Pope, Paul V, received him cordially. His "Celestial Novelties", as they were called, were accepted by the Church as real observations, yet without giving them official sanction. The great scientific academy, "Dei Lincei", honoured Galileo by electing him a member. He returned in triumph to Pisa, fearing nothing. In Rome, among those who had supported him and shown himself greatly in sympathy with his cause, was Cardinal M. Barberini, afterwards Pope Urban VIII, later to be one of his chief accusers.

On his return, controversy followed controversy. In April 1611, Galileo discovered the existence of "sun-spots", announcing that they were actually "blemishes" on the face of the sun, an idea highly repugnant to accepted tradition, which held that the sun was a "perfect body". In the same year a Jesuit, Christopher Scheiner, claimed to have made the same discovery, explaining that the spots were really planets revolving round the sun, a thesis already dropped by Galileo. The Jesuits championed Scheiner's view on theological grounds.

Roused to anger, finally, by these and other doctrinal objections to what he regarded as purely scientific truths, Galileo wrote his famous letter to his pupil Castelli, taking the view that the "language of the Scriptures is suited to the intelligence of those for whom it is written, and that the interpretation must be revised in the light of new facts".

Castelli rashly circulated copies of this letter, and the Inquisition, obtaining one, prepared to attack. Galileo, his fighting spirit roused, went to Rome, determined to defend himself and his doctrines equally. He did not believe his voyage to be dangerous either to himself or his integrity as a teacher. He was wrong.

In February 1616, the Inquisition reported on Galileo's work on sun-spots, embodying the doctrine that the sun is the fixed centre of the world. To his amazement and uneasiness, they condemned this view as false philosophically and formally heretical, and similarly the doctrine that the earth rotates and also revolves round the sun. At the same time, Copernicus's own book on his system was suspended.

Cardinal Bellarmine sent for Galileo and solemnly warned him of the error of his opinions, and Galileo, as a good son of the Church, bowed his acknowledgement of this error. What he did not know, however, was that when he signed the written copy of the cardinal's admonition, the Commissary of the Inquisition secretly amplified it, adding that from henceforth he "must not hold, teach or defend the opinions in question".

When he returned to Florence, it was with the uneasy knowledge that in future he must be more circumspect in dealing with the Copernican doctrine, but he did not realize that from now on the Inquisition was only waiting for an occasion to suppress him entirely, remove his liberty, and if they could, his life.

The next fifteen years were therefore years of caution and decision. Galileo was growing old. He was one of the most celebrated figures in Christendom, but ill-health and family troubles were for ever with him.

Ever since the far-off days in Padua, he had been a sick man. In his first year under the Venetian Republic, he had gone with some friends to rest in a cave near the city. They slept there, in a cold, possibly a poisonous draught. Two of his friends died of their exposure. Galileo had suffered ever since from a constitutional weakness and tendency to catch chills, colds and ague.

From 1616 until the end of his life, he was constantly weak, constantly in the shadow of death. Only his indomitable spirit and boundless enthusiasm kept him alive, writing of his discoveries and attacking his enemies. When he saw his friends, or his beloved pupil, Castelli, he was the great man, the philosopher, wit and musician, fond of good wine and good company. But he rarely discussed his work with strangers, and alone he was an æsthete and a hermit.

Always tortured by money cares, he supported all his parasitic family with truly philosophic calm and extraordinary generosity. His son by Marina Gamba, Vincenzio, had turned out selfish, idle and good for nothing, like his uncle, Michelangelo. Marina Gamba herself, Galileo married off to a man in her own station in life, providing for her generously and gratefully.

His two daughters he had made nuns. They were his great solace, particularly the elder of the two, Marie Celeste. They had taken the veil because their father, with all his other pressing cares, had not the money to provide for them, and their birth barred them from marriage in their own rank. Marie Celeste was her father's dearest human interest.

When she died in 1634, he wrote to his friend Elia Diodati: "I paid frequent visits to the neighbouring convent where I had two daughters who were nuns and whom I loved dearly; but the eldest in particular, who was a woman of exquisite mind, singular goodness and most tenderly attached to me . . . now she is dead."

Above all family matters, however, in the years following his first condemnation by the Inquisition, Galileo studied, observed, worked and schemed for the publication of his work; schemed, because now publication was for him an act of diplomacy. He had to please his supporters and avoid the ban or too close attention of the hunting, ferreting Inquisition.

In 1623, he obtained the papal sanction to publish his book, *Il Saggiatore*, the Assayer. It was a reply to a Jesuit attack on a work of his concerning comets, which he maintained were atmospheric phenomena. He dedicated it to Cardinal M. Barberini, his former sympathizer, who had lately become Pope Urban VIII. The Pope was well pleased with the work, though the General of the Jesuits forbade even the mention of it to the members of the Order.

Urban VIII was between two fires: his own critical appreciation of Galileo's greatness, and the power of the Jesuits. When Galileo went to Rome in 1624 to pay his respects to the new Pope, the latter received him generously, with gifts and the promise of a pension for his son, while refusing for reasons of policy to remove the embargo of 1616 on the doctrines of Copernicus. He did, however, add a rider that the Church had not condemned these doctrines as heretical, but rash.

Encouraged by the attitude of the Pope, Galileo, between desperate bouts of illness, and overwhelmed by his brother

Michelangelo's sending his whole family to live with him in Florence, concentrated his energies on the work which was to be his glory and downfall, the *Dialogues on the Two Principal Systems of the World*.

Month after month he worked at it, until his daughter, Marie Celeste, knowing how his knowledge and concentration was an anodyne to his family cares, beseeched him in letter after letter not to weaken himself and thereby lay himself open to sickness, for on him the whole family depended.

By the time the book was ready, Galileo was an invalid in all save his spirit and mind. His strong face with its white beard and piercing eye remained, but his poor body was a torture. None the less, in 1629, he again journeyed to Rome, where he actually obtained the papal permission to print his masterpiece.

Castelli, his favourite pupil, was now Papal Mathematician. Riccardi, the Chief Censor, encouraged him, by telling him that the Pope was still a Copernican at heart, and sure enough, he returned to Florence in 1630 with the coveted permission to print, provided only that he made it clear that the subject of the dialogues was purely hypothetical, and furthermore, that if anything in the Scriptures appeared to present insuperable difficulties according to the new theory, the Scriptures must not because of this be called impossible.

Nature, however, now took a hand in delaying the publication of the dialogues. The plague was raging in Florence and throughout Italy when he returned. Communications between all the great cities were interrupted, and Galileo decided to have the work published in Florence instead of in Rome. New permission had to be obtained from the censor, and this was not forthcoming until the end of 1631. The Jesuits in Rome, in the absence of Galileo, fought tooth and nail to prevent its publication. It did not appear until February 1632.

The book was an immense and immediate success. Only by the Jesuits was it received with a howl of execration, headed by Galileo's old enemy, Scheiner. On every possible occasion, the most cunning and persuasive men in the Order were put to work on the mind of the Pope, trying to turn him against Galileo. At last they succeeded.

The scheme of the dialogues is that of an argument between two supporters of the Ptolemaic and Copernican systems, respectively. A third party is introduced as their judge and commentator, supposed to represent the view of the man in the street. To him is given the name of Simplicio.

It was cleverly noted by the Inquisition that the Pope's arguments, the inclusion of which the latter had demanded when granting the permission to print, were put into the mouth of Simplicio, and it was claimed that Galileo wished to insinuate thereby that the Pope was a simpleton. This childish argument struck home. Galileo's publisher received an order from the Inquisition forbidding the sale of the book until further notice. A commission was set up to examine and report on the dialogues. Its composition was grossly unfair. Even the intervention of the Grand Duke of Tuscany himself did not succeed in obtaining the representation of any man of science, such as Castelli. Niccolini, the grand duke's ambassador, in Rome, was told that His Holiness believed himself to have been deliberately deceived into granting his licence to publish, and that furthermore, in the book, Galileo "did not fear to make game of me".

Galileo, sick and in the depths of despair, knowing that he had found truth, yet cursing the light of his mind which had led him to it, awaited his unjust condemnation.

In due course, the whole of the Inquisition proceedings of 1616 were brought up against him, and, principally on account of the false minute forbidding him to "hold, teach or defend" the doctrines of Copernicus, he was condemned and summoned to Rome by the commissary general to recant of his heresy.

The plague was still raging. Niccolini endeavoured without success to arrange for Galileo to be examined in Florence, for he was gravely ill. Ophthalmia and the threat of blindness was on him. The summons was for October. In December, the Pope, impatient at the delay, ordered that he should be brought to Rome immediately, "in irons if necessary". Helpless, the grand duke arranged for his transport in litters to the Eternal City, and for him to be lodged there in the Tuscan Embassy. He left in cold and bitter rain, at the worst season of the year, sick probably to death. He did not expect to see Florence again, but his spirit never failed him. To a friend who came to bid him farewell, he said:

"I go to my death, but what is death to immortal achievement? My dishonour, as a faithful son of the Church, must one day be the Church's shame. Would that it were otherwise. I shall defend myself to the end."

But once in Rome, Niccolini, who knew that there were plans to torture the old man, to discover "his true opinions", managed to dissuade him from this dangerous determination, making him promise to submit to the tribunal.

April 12, 1633: the day fixed for the trial of Galileo. He went to it as to execution, in the full knowledge that he had not long to live, being in his seventieth year and very infirm. His real concern was not for his frail life, but for the coming suppression of his life's work.

He went to the court in mental anguish, aching with revolt, the last words of Niccolini echoing resentfully in his ears:

"Submit: the more completely the better."

He appeared before the commissary general and the procurator fiscal, hard and bitter men, in silent triumph. His spirit and person dominated theirs: white-haired and venerable, thoughtful and strong of face, sublimely simple in his answering of questions.

They asked him: "You know why you are here?"

"On account of my book, the authorship of which I must freely admit, though it be to my own scandal."

"Did you, Galileo Galilei, take cognizance of the admonition of his late Eminence, Cardinal Bellarmine, in the process of 1616, that the doctrine that the sun is the fixed centre of the universe, and that the terrestrial globe rotates and revolves round the sun, is absurd in philosophy and formally heretical?"

"I did, and furthermore submitted to the admonition and signed it as an obedient son of the Church."

"And did you then promise not to hold, teach or defend these doctrines?" The old man hesitated, too wily to walk into a trap.

"Did I promise such a thing," he replied, "my conscience is clear that I have been obedient: but the infirmity of my age makes memory insecure. . . . Besides, it has ever been my contention that by publishing my last work, of which you complain, far from glorying in the truth of Copernican doctrines, I have refuted them as weak, and inconclusive, according to the views of our Holy Father Himself." He had promised submission, and therefore, heart wrung with bitterness, he gave it. For reward, and because the eyes of the whole learned world were on Galileo and his tribunal, the procurator fiscal had him confined in his own house, and Niccolini was allowed to send in meals to him.

Three days later, the counsellors of the holy office pronounced his guilt. Next, they demanded, as was the practice in cases of heresy, his full admission of this guilt. The commissary general therefore came to Galileo and persuaded him to promise a full confession "so that the Court could deal leniently with him".

Accordingly, on April 30, with a humility altogether foreign to his nature, he was called to speak a colourless admission of guilt to the assembled court. He still had the strength to deliver his speech in his own manner, not impersonal enough for his soulless accusers:

"Sure, sirs, I have fully examined my work and conscience since last I appeared before you . . . I know well of the untruth latent in my defence of the system of Copernicus, witness the fact that in my teachings at various universities throughout my life, I have not neglected assiduously to pay tribute to Ptolemy and Aristotle. Yet I do find that carried away by false pride in my own subtlety, in my present work, I put a lying cause too strongly, so that to the untutored mind, it might appear true. Of this I do repent in all humility, and offer, to satisfy the holy office, to add to my dialogues, with all my poor skill, a full and complete refutation of Copernicus, that men's minds may no longer be in danger."

After this humiliation, Galileo was allowed to return to the Tuscan Embassy. On May 10, however, he was summoned again and forced to sign a written confession of the truth of the minute of 1616, with an appeal for clemency on account of his age and sickness.

Perjury was thus added to the crimes which he was forced to commit against his own conscience and lifelong beliefs.

On June 16, the Pope presided at a meeting of the sacred congregation, at which it was decided that Galileo should be put to the question, under threat of torture, as to his real beliefs; that he should be made to recant before the plenary assembly of the Inquisition; that he should be imprisoned, and forbidden thereafter to discuss the motion of the earth and sun, under pain of death by burning, as a relapsed heretic.

On June 21, Galileo suffered this penultimate indignity at the hands of the court: it saved him from torture. Under close question, a reply was wrung from him which cost him untold agony:

"You order me to abandon these doctrines: gentlemen, I have never held them as true, in my heart. How then can I recant further? I am ready to do so if only you will point the way."

The day of sentence came at last. Bodily utterly broken, yet still unbowed in spirit, he was led before the court to receive his deserts at the hands of the Church.

Ten cardinals' names were prefixed to the account of his trial and works, damning him and them completely. It ended with sentence on the man Galileo, "vehemently suspected of heresy, who will be absolved of his crimes only if he will abjure, curse and detest the said errors and heresies in the form hereunder prescribed . . . and furthermore, as a warning to himself and all others, his works will be prohibited by public edict, he will be formally imprisoned in the Inquisition at the judges' pleasure, and will recite once a week the seven Penitential Psalms; the judges alone reserving the right to mitigate the above penalties."

Grovelling on his knees, therefore, before the Inquisition, in plenary council assembled, Galileo, the greatest man of his age, read aloud the prescribed form of abjuration, then signed it.

By intervention of Niccolini, the Pope permitted Galileo's place of imprisonment to be changed from the Inquisition to one of the grand duke's villas, near Rome. As Niccolini conducted him thither, the grand old man laid a hand on that of the ambassador:

"Do not grieve, Master Niccolini," he said. "My condemnation is nothing. . . . The earth moves for all that."

A year after his departure to Rome for trial, he was allowed to return to his villa at Arcetri, near Florence, still under conditions of close confinement. Until the end of his life he was pestered by restrictions. His bitterness over his fate was terrible. In 1632, he wrote to a friend:

"When I think that the end of all my labours, after having gained for myself a name not obscure among the learned, has been finally to bring upon me a citation to appear before the Tribunal of the Holy Office . . . I detest the remembrance of the time I have consumed in study. I regret ever having published what I wrote, and I have a mind to burn every composition that I have yet by me."

But despite illness and disappointment, sorrow in the death of his beloved daughter, resentment at his treatment by the Church whose faithful son he had always believed himself to be, he still worked. Worked until blindness took away from him, in December 1637, the infinite joy of contemplating the unfettered heavens.

His blindness drew forth from him a piteous letter to his friend, Diodati:

"Alas, your dear friend and servant Galileo, has been for the last month hopelessly blind; so that this heaven, this universe, which I by marvellous discoveries and clear demonstrations had enlarged a thousand times, beyond the belief of wise men of bygone ages, henceforward for me is shrunk into such a small space as is filled by my own bodily sensations."

Yet when he knew that he would never see again, this man to whom sight was life never complained, only asking his friends to remember him in their prayers.

Broken, weary, blind, he died in 1642 on January 8. His last mechanical suggestion was the application of the pendulum principle to regulate a clock, but his mortal illness interrupted his work on it.

His enemies, unappeased, even struck at him beyond the grave. He was to have been given a public funeral in Florence and a monument in marble, by order of the Grand Duke Ferdinand dei Medici. The Pope forbade it.

But his monument was more lasting than marble, his name imperishably greater than those of his accusers, popes, cardinals and princes. When, a century later, they were all dead and his name still lived, in the church of Santa Croce, in Florence, with money left for the purpose by his last pupil, Viviani, a monument was erected to his memory. His bones were brought thither and laid to rest with Viviani's own, but Galileo no longer stood in need of this recognition. He was immortal.

Reprinted from *Fifty World Famous Heroic Deeds*, Odhams, n.d.

COLLECTING ANIMAL TRACKS

This is a good way to enliven a country walk. It also makes for a rewarding, informative hobby.

First buy some plaster of Paris from a craft store and a tub of Vaseline from the pharmacy. Then cut some "collars" of cards about 5 cm high and 20 cm long. Find a child's plastic bucket (or something similar), a large spoon and a roll of sticky tape. Fill a plastic bottle with water. Put everything in a small backpack and set out into the wild yonder. The best place to look for clear, deep impressions of animal tracks is somewhere slightly damp.

Select the track to be collected. Lightly grease the inside of a collar of card with Vaseline, then put the collar (greasy side in) around the track. Adjust the collar so that it just fits around the track, fixing it in place with sticky tape. In the bucket mix plaster of Paris with water to the consistency of whipping cream. You need just enough of the mixture to fill the collar about 3 cm deep. After the plaster has set – which only takes a few minutes – gently lift the collar off, then carefully dig out the impression.

You now have an exact impression of the foot that made the track.

For tracks in snow, gently sprinkle dry plaster of Paris into the track. Allow to dry. Then top up with the usual plaster of Paris mixture.

Only one thing remains – to identify the animal that made the track. Most animal encyclopaedias should have information on animal "spoors" (tracks). The tracks of some common European and North American animals and birds are shown below.

Animal Tracks

These tracks are not to scale. F = Front Track; H = Hind Track. The "track pattern" is the way the animal walks.

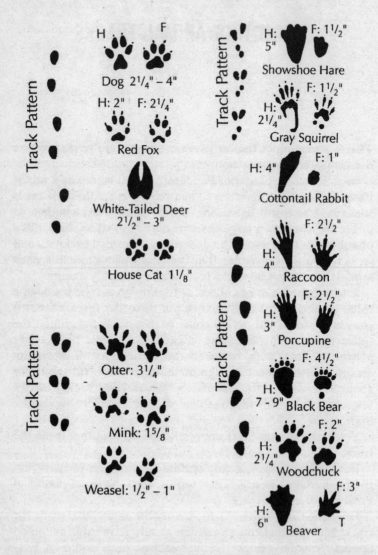

Track Pattern

H   F

Dog 2¹⁄₄" – 4"

H: 2"   F: 2¹⁄₄"

Red Fox

White-Tailed Deer
2¹⁄₂" – 3"

House Cat 1¹⁄₈"

Track Pattern

H: 5"   F: 1¹⁄₂"

Snowshoe Hare

H: 2¹⁄₄"   F: 1¹⁄₂"

Gray Squirrel

H: 4"   F: 1"

Cottontail Rabbit

Track Pattern

H: 4"   F: 2¹⁄₂"

Raccoon

H: 3"   F: 2¹⁄₂"

Porcupine

H: 7 – 9"   F: 4¹⁄₂"

Black Bear

H: 2¹⁄₄"   F: 2"

Woodchuck

H: 6"   F: 3"   T

Beaver

Track Pattern

Otter: 3¹⁄₄"

Mink: 1⁵⁄₈"

Weasel: ¹⁄₂" – 1"

Adapted from *Mass Wildlife Pocket Guide to MA Animal Tracks*.

MOTORWAY CRICKET

This is a version of the car game known as pub cricket, where the "batsman" scores runs corresponding to the legs in a public house's name. So, for instance, if the car passes a public house named "The Queen Victoria" he gets two runs. "The Dog" is four runs and so on. If the public house had a name with no legs ("The Wheatsheaf") the batsman is out and the next occupant of the car is in to bat.

As there are next to no public houses on motorways the game falls flat. Hence this alternative version.

For every car passing in the opposite direction the batsman scores one run. Every van passing in the opposite direction is four runs. Every motor home or caravan is six runs.

The batman is out when a lorry or coach passes in the opposite direction. Each player can have as many innings as you like. Obviously the winner is the batsman with the most runs at the end of the previously determined number of innings.

PEN AND PAPER GAMES

These are games to while away car journeys, rainy days and waits at the dentist. All you need is a piece of paper, a pen or pencil, and your wits about you.

Battleships

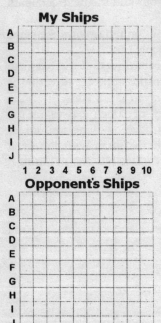

My Ships

Opponent's Ships

This is a game for two players.

Draw two 10-square grids as below. Label the columns on the grids A–J and the rows 1–10. Mark the top grid "My Ships" and the bottom grid "Opponent's Ships".

Each player puts five ships on his top grid, horizontally or vertically but not diagonally. Make sure your opponent can't see what you are doing. The ships should be represented with letters, a letter to a square:

Aircraft Carrier – AAAAA

Battleship – BBBB

Cruiser – CCC

Submarine – SS

Destroyer – DD

When this is done, the players take turns at calling out a spot on the grid which they identify by letter and number – for example"B7". If the other player has a ship on that spot they say "hit" and if not they say "miss". Each player needs to keep track of their guess by writing H or M on the nominated square. You should also keep note of your opponent's guesses. If a player guesses correctly for all the squares of a ship that ship is considered sunk and this must be announced by his opponent. The first player to sink all the opponent's ships wins.

Hangman

This game can be played with several players, but two is best. It can be adapted for just about any spelling age.

The first person thinks of a dictionary word, and draws a series of dashes on paper, one for each letter in the word. The opponent takes guesses at letters in the word. When a guess is correct, the first person writes the letter above each corresponding dash. If a guess is wrong (that is, the letter isn't in the chosen word) then a line of the gallows and stick man is drawn. Below is the traditional sequence of how the gallows and hanged man is drawn.

The first person is the winner if the "man" is hanged before the second player can guess the word.

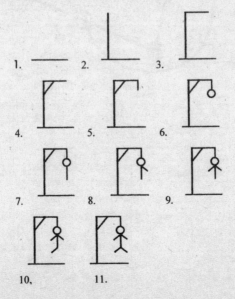

Sprouts

Sprouts is a two-player pencil and paper game designed in 1967 by John Conway and by Michael S. Paterson. It is a more advanced game than battleships or hangman and is suitable for boys aged 11 +.

Draw three dots on a piece of paper. Take turns to connect any two dots (or one dot to itself) with a curve which doesn't cross other curves. After that, the player must mark a new spot on the just-drawn curve. To every spot can be attached a maximum three curves of the new line. The last one who can draw a line is the winner.

The strategy in sprouts lies in using your lines to divide the paper up into parts that trap dots. If the three-dot game gets too easy for you, start with more dots. This game is a good tool for building your sense of spatial perception.

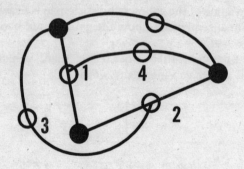

ESSENTIAL SPEECHES FROM SHAKESPEARE

William Shakespeare was born in Stratford-upon-Avon in England in 1564 and died there in 1616. Little else is known about his life, save that he lived and worked in London for many years as an actor, playwright and poet. What can safely be said about Shakespeare is that he is the most important and illuminating writer in the English language. Although he died nearly 400 years ago his words and thoughts are still part of our lives. He also tended to write about basic human themes and emotions – things which will endure for ever. It is worth not only reading this selection of speeches from "the Bard's" plays, but reading them aloud as they were intended. And then memorizing them. A knowledge of Shakespeare is the mark of the civilized boy and man.

"All the World's A Stage" from *As You Like It*

The speaker is Jacques, a lord attending the usurped Duke Senior, who considers the stages of a man's life.

All the world's a stage,
And all the men and women merely players:
They have their exits and their entrances;
And one man in his time plays many parts,
His acts being seven ages. At first the infant,
Mewling and puking in the nurse's arms.
And then the whining school-boy, with his satchel
And shining morning face, creeping like snail
Unwillingly to school. And then the lover,

Sighing like furnace, with a woeful ballad
Made to his mistress' eyebrow. Then a soldier,
Full of strange oaths, and bearded like the pard,
Jealous in honour, sudden and quick in quarrel,
Seeking the bubble reputation
Even in the cannon's mouth. And then the justice,
In fair round belly with good capon lin'd,
With eyes severe, and beard of formal cut,
Full of wise saws and modern instances;
And so he plays his part. The sixth age shifts
Into the lean and slipper'd pantaloon,
With spectacles on nose and pouch on side,
His youthful hose, well sav'd, a world too wide
For his shrunk shank; and his big manly voice,
Turning again toward childish treble, pipes
And whistles in his sound. Last scene of all,
That ends this strange eventful history,
Is second childishness and mere oblivion,
Sans teeth, sans eyes, sans taste, sans everything.

"The Quality of Mercy"
from The Merchant of Venice

*The scene is a courtroom in old venice. Portia, an heiress, is trying
to convince the moneylender Shylock to give up his legal claim to a
pound of Antony's flesh. Portia argues that mercy is a divine
attribute and that when we give it we are closer to God.*

The quality of mercy is not strain'd.
It droppeth as the gentle rain from heaven
Upon the place beneath. It is twice blest:
It blesseth him that gives, and him that takes.
'Tis mightiest in the mightiest; it becomes
The throned monarch better than his crown.
His scepter shows the force of temporal power,
The attribute to awe and majesty,
Wherein doth sit the dread and fear of kings;
But mercy is above this sceptered sway;
It is enthroned in the hearts of kings;
It is an attribute to God himself;

And earthly power doth then show likest God's
When mercy seasons justice.

"Before the Battle of Agincourt" from *Henry V*

*Henry V's small English army, trapped by a superior French force,
expects defeat. King Henry encourages them to think of victory
instead.*

Westmoreland: O that we now had here But one ten thousand of
those men in England That do no work to-day!
King Henry V: What's he that wishes so?
My cousin Westmoreland? No, my fair cousin:
If we are mark'd to die, we are enow
To do our country loss; and if to live,
The fewer men, the greater share of honour.
God's will! I pray thee, wish not one man more.
By Jove, I am not covetous for gold,
Nor care I who doth feed upon my cost;
It yearns me not if men my garments wear;
Such outward things dwell not in my desires:
But if it be a sin to covet honour,
I am the most offending soul alive.
No, faith, my coz, wish not a man from England:
God's peace! I would not lose so great an honour
As one man more, methinks, would share from
me
For the best hope I have. O, do not wish one
more!
Rather proclaim it, Westmoreland, through my
host,
That he which hath no stomach to this fight,
Let him depart; his passport shall be made
And crowns for convoy put into his purse:
We would not die in that man's company
That fears his fellowship to die with us.
This day is called the feast of Crispian:
He that outlives this day, and comes safe home,
Will stand a tip-toe when the day is named,
And rouse him at the name of Crispian.

He that shall live this day, and see old age,
Will yearly on the vigil feast his neighbours,
And say "To-morrow is Saint Crispian:"
Then will he strip his sleeve and show his scars.
And say "These wounds I had on Crispin's
    day."
Old men forget: yet all shall be forgot,
But he'll remember with advantages
What feats he did that day: then shall our names.
Familiar in his mouth as household words
Harry the king, Bedford and Exeter,
Warwick and Talbot, Salisbury and
    Gloucester,
Be in their flowing cups freshly remember'd.
This story shall the good man teach his son;
And Crispin Crispian shall ne'er go by,
From this day to the ending of the world,
But we in it shall be remember'd;
We few, we happy few, we band of brothers;
For he to-day that sheds his blood with me
Shall be my brother; be he ne'er so vile,
This day shall gentle his condition:
And gentlemen in England now a-bed
Shall think themselves accursed they were not
    here,
And hold their manhoods cheap whiles any
    speaks
That fought with us upon Saint Crispin's day.

The Battle of Agincourt, 1415, really happened and King Henry must have said something very similar to his troops to rouse them to fight. And fight they did. And won.

"To Be Or Not To Be" from
The Tragedy of Hamlet, Prince of Denmark

In what is possibly the most quoted piece of literature outside of the Bible, the troubled Hamlet wonders whether death is an escape from life's troubles:

Hamlet: To be, or not to be: that is the question:
Whether 'tis nobler in the mind to suffer
The slings and arrows of outrageous fortune,
Or to take arms against a sea of troubles, And by
opposing end them? To die: to sleep;
No more; and by a sleep to say we end
The heart-ache and the thousand natural shocks
That flesh is heir to, 'tis a consummation
Devoutly to be wish'd. To die, to sleep;
To sleep: perchance to dream: ay, there's the rub;
For in that sleep of death what dreams may come
When we have shuffled off this mortal coil,
Must give us pause: there's the respect
That makes calamity of so long life;
For who would bear the whips and scorns of time,
The oppressor's wrong, the proud man's
    contumely,
The pangs of despised love, the law's delay,
The insolence of office and the spurns
That patient merit of the unworthy takes,
When he himself might his quietus make
With a bare bodkin? who would fardels bear,
To grunt and sweat under a weary life,
But that the dread of something after death,
The undiscover'd country from whose bourn
No traveller returns, puzzles the will
And makes us rather bear those ills we have
Than fly to others that we know not of?
Thus conscience does make cowards of us all;
And thus the native hue of resolution
Is sicklied o'er with the pale cast of thought,
And enterprises of great pith and moment
With this regard their currents turn awry,
And lose the name of action. – Soft you now!
The fair Ophelia! Nymph, in thy orisons
Be all my sins remember'd.

"Romeo sees Juliet at her window" from *Romeo and Juliet*

The young Romeo and Juliet have met at a party, and Romeo has fallen hopelessly in love. Later, the same evening he creeps into Juliet's garden hoping to see her.

Romeo: But, soft! what light through yonder window breaks?
It is the east, and Juliet is the sun.
Arise, fair sun, and kill the envious moon,
Who is already sick and pale with grief,
That thou her maid art far more fair than she:
Be not her maid, since she is envious;
Her vestal livery is but sick and green
And none but fools do wear it; cast it off.
It is my lady, O, it is my love!
O, that she knew she were!
She speaks yet she says nothing: what of that?
Her eye discourses; I will answer it.
I am too bold, 'tis not to me she speaks:
Two of the fairest stars in all the heaven,
Having some business, do entreat her eyes
To twinkle in their spheres till they return.
What if her eyes were there, they in her head?
The brightness of her cheek would shame those stars,
As daylight doth a lamp; her eyes in heaven
Would through the airy region stream so bright
That birds would sing and think it were not night.
See, how she leans her cheek upon her hand!
O, that I were a glove upon that hand,
That I might touch that cheek!

"This sceptre'd isle" from *Richard II*

John of Gaunt describes England:

John of Gaunt: This royal throne of kings, this scepter'd isle,
This earth of majesty, this seat of Mars,
This other Eden, demi-paradise,
This fortress built by Nature for herself

Against infection and the hand of war,
This happy breed of men, this little world,
This precious stone set in the silver sea,
Which serves it in the office of a wall,
Or as a moat defensive to a house,
Against the envy of less happier lands,
This blessed plot, this earth, this realm, this
    England,
This nurse, this teeming womb of royal kings,
Fear'd by their breed and famous by their birth,
Renowned for their deeds as far from home,
For Christian service and true chivalry,
As is the sepulchre in stubborn Jewry,
Of the world's ransom, blessèd Mary's Son,
This land of such dear souls, this dear dear land,
Dear for her reputation through the world,
Is now leased out, I die pronouncing it,
Like to a tenement or pelting farm:
England, bound in with the triumphant sea
Whose rocky shore beats back the envious siege
Of watery Neptune, is now bound in with
    shame,
With inky blots and rotten parchment bonds:
That England, that was wont to conquer others,
Hath made a shameful conquest of itself.
Ah, would the scandal vanish with my life,
How happy then were my ensuing death!

"To-morrow, and to-morrow and to-morrow" from *Macbeth*

Macbeth has become King of Scotland after murdering his rival. He was supported in his evil deed by his wife, who then went mad. Macbeth has learned that she has just died. Macbeth also knows that an army is approaching, one which likely beat him in battle. These are the reflections of a man who had much but because of excess ambition wanted more. In the end, he is left with nothing.

Macbeth: She should have died hereafter;
          There would have been a time for such a word.

To-morrow, and to-morrow, and to-morrow,
Creeps in this petty pace from day to day
To the last syllable of recorded time,
And all our yesterdays have lighted fools
The way to dusty death. Out, out, brief candle!
Life's but a walking shadow, a poor player
That struts and frets his hour upon the stage
And then is heard no more: it is a tale
Told by an idiot, full of sound and fury,
Signifying nothing.

SAS SURVIVAL SKILLS III:
NAVIGATION WITHOUT A COMPASS

Navigation without a compass begins with one task: finding one natural indicator of direction.

The Sun

This is your most obvious indicator of direction, so long as it is not covered by cloud. It rises in the east and sets in the west; this is always true, no matter what hemisphere you are in. Near the Equator, the sun appears to be almost overhead; further north the sun will always be south of you, and further south it will be north of you.

Find out where true north is by measuring the shadow cast by a vertical stick. To do this, find a piece of level ground, preferably bare earth, and put a 30-cm straight stick vertically into the ground. Using a short marker stick, record the end of the shadow cast by the vertical stick. As the sun moves west the shadow will move east. Wait until the shadow has moved a few centimetres and mark its end again. By drawing a line between the two markers you will have a west to east line. If you need a north/south reference, simply draw a line that cuts the west/east line at a right angle.

The Moon

Like the sun, the moon moves in a regular and predictable manner. If the moon rises before the sun sets, the illuminated

USING YOUR WATCH TO FIND NORTH

Northern temperate zone

1 Place a small stick in the ground so that it casts a definite shadow.
2 Put your watch on the ground so that the hour hand points along the shadow.
3 Find the point on the watch midway between the hour hand and 12 o'clock. A line from the centre of the face to this point indicates due south.

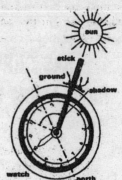

Southern temperate zone

1 Place the stick in the ground.
2 Put the watch on the ground so that 12 o'clock points along the shadow.
3 A line drawn from the centre of the watch to a point midway between the hour hand and 12 o'clock points north.

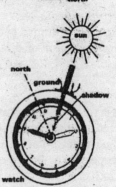

NOTE: If your watch is on British Summer Time (Daylight Saving Time) you must take the mid point of the hour hand and 1 o'clock. You can still use this method with a digital watch, simply draw out the clock face in the dirt with the hands representing the correct time GMT.

side is the west. If the moon rises at the same time as the sun sets, it will be a full moon and you will need to know the time to attain the direction. If the moon rises after the sun has set, the illuminated side is the east side.

When there is a crescent moon in the sky, you can gain an approximate cardinal point (south in the northern hemisphere, north in the southern hemisphere) by imagining a line joining the points of the crescent reaching to the horizon.

Using the Moon

The moon can be used to find direction in the following way in the northern hemisphere: imagine a line joining the tips of the crescent of the moon or bisecting the full moon and continuing to the horizon; this line is south. In the southern hemisphere use the same method to find north.

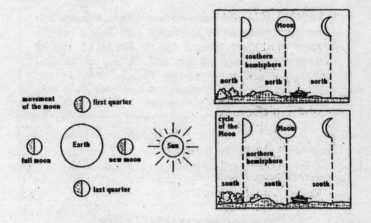

The stars

Gaining an approximate fix on north or south from the stars is an ancient and easy skill. The technique differs between the northern and southern hemispheres:

1. In the northern hemisphere, the star Polaris (the pole star) is your guide to true north. This is because it is never more than 1° from the North Celestial Pole. If you are facing the pole star, you are facing true north. To find Polaris, first find the easily recognized constellations "The Plough" or "Cassiopeia" which will guide you to Polaris.

2. In fact, the South Celestial Pole is so devoid of stars it is called the Coal Sack. If you are facing the South Celestial Pole you are facing true south. To find the pole, draw an imaginary line from the Southern Cross (do not confuse this

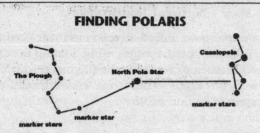

FINDING POLARIS

On a clear night in the northern hemisphere, the direction of north is indicated by the north star. This is not the brightest star in the sky and can be difficult to find. All other stars revolve around the north star. Or you can find the group of stars known as the "Plough" or Ursa Major which is usually fairly prominent. A line joining the stars forming the blade of the plough points to the north star.

with the "false cross") and another imaginary line at 90° to the two bright stars east of the Southern Cross. The point at which these two lines intersect is a point approximately 5–6° off true south.

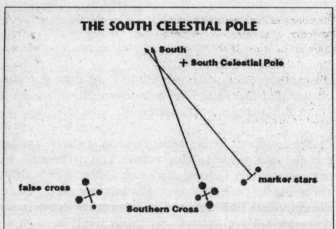

THE SOUTH CELESTIAL POLE

In the southern hemisphere you can find the direction of true south by finding the south celestial pole. Unfortunately there are no convenient star markers and you have to work out the position from the southern cross and two adjacent bright stars.

Natural landmarks

If you are on the move and in a hurry you will need quicker references. Because the landscape and vegetation is shaped by the local environmental conditions you can gain rough indications of direction by simple observation. However, you will find these indicators to be unreliable guides, and you should never rely upon one indicator alone.

Wind

The generally prevailing wind in England is south-westerly (and in north-west Europe north-westerly).

Lone trees and isolated new plantations will lean away from the prevailing wind direction.

Make sure you are aware of the prevailing wind direction in any area in which you are operating.

Lone trees lean away from the wind, as do tussocks of grass and other forms of upright vegetation such as ferns. Small isolated woods, especially near the coast, have stunted trees on their windward sides.

In sandy areas, tails of sand form behind small bushes and plants, pointing directly away from the wind. Sand dunes and snow cornices are gently sloping on their windward side and steep on their lee (sheltered) side.

Sun

The sun also greatly affects vegetation, in particular isolated trees, whose branches should be more numerous and foliated on the sunny side: (south in the northern hemisphere and north in the southern hemisphere). Because of this you will also usually find, that the decaying vegetation at the base of the trunk is drier on the sunny side a good night-time guide. The stumps of felled trees will show their growth rings more tightly packed on the sunny side.

Using natural landmarks

Remember that prevailing weather conditions vary from region to region and are especially unpredictable in hilly or heavily wooded areas. Success in navigation depends on your choice of landmark; lone isolated trees in flat country are the ideal choice.

By comparing the results of several differing natural navigation aids for example, grass tufts, the way a star moves and the moisture of leaf litter at the base of a tree, you should be able to move over unfamiliar country in any direction you want.

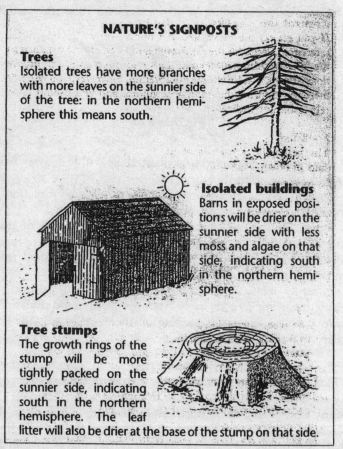

NATURE'S SIGNPOSTS

Trees
Isolated trees have more branches with more leaves on the sunnier side of the tree: in the northern hemisphere this means south.

Isolated buildings
Barns in exposed positions will be drier on the sunnier side with less moss and algae on that side, indicating south in the northern hemisphere.

Tree stumps
The growth rings of the stump will be more tightly packed on the sunnier side, indicating south in the northern hemisphere. The leaf litter will also be drier at the base of the stump on that side.

Adapted from *The Mammoth Book of Secrets of the SAS and Elite Forces*, ed. Jon E. Lewis, 2002.

TOP 10 SINGLES OF ALL TIME

Artist/Title	Released	Sales
1) Elton John "Candle in the Wind"/ "Something About the Way You look Tonight"	1997	37,000,000
2) Bing Crosby "White Christmas"	1942	30,000,000
3) Bill Haley and His Comets "Rock Around the Clock"	1954	17,000,000
4) The Beatles "I Want to Hold Your Hand"	1963	12,000,000
5) Elvis Presley "It's Now or Never"	1960	10,000,000
= The Beatles "Hey Jude"	1968	10,000,000
= Whitney Houston "I Will Always Love You"	1992	10,000,000
8) Paul Anka "Diana"	1957	9,000,000
= Elvis Presley "Hound Dog/Don't Be Cruel"	1956	9,000,000
10) Bryan Adams "(Everything I Do) I Do it for You"	1991	8,000,000
= The Monkees "I'm a Believer"	1966	8,000,000

THE BEAUFORT SCALE

The Beaufort Scale is a scale of wind force, which was devised by Francis Beaufort, an officer in the Royal Navy, in 1805. Initially the scale was for use of sailing ships in the Royal Navy only, and described the amount of sails a frigate could carry in different wind conditions, from 0 (calm) to 13 (storm). However, the passing of the age of sail made such specifications impractical so in the early twentieth century the British meteorologist George Simpson revised Beaufort's scale to use the appearance of the sea as the descriptor. The revised Beaufort Scale was adopted by the International Meteorological Organization in 1939 and extended by the British military in 1944 to include Forces 13–17. However, the additional points were intended to apply to specific cases such as typhoons, and for all practical intents and purposes the Beaufort Scale is still ranged 1–12.

For the record, the highest surface wind speed ever recorded was in 1934 on Mount Washington, New Hampshire, USA. The wind speed reached 231 mph (372 kph).

Specifications and equivalent speeds

Beaufort wind scale	Mean Wind Speed		Limits of wind speed		Wind descriptive terms	Probable wave height in metres*	Probable maximum wave height in metres*	Seastate	Sea descriptive terms
	Knots	m/s	Knots	m/s					
0	0	0	<1	0-0.2	Calm	-	-	0	Calm (glassy)
1	2	0.8	1-3	0.3-1.5	Light air	0.1	0.1	1	Calm (rippled)
2	5	2.4	4-6	1.6-3.3	Light breeze	0.2	0.3	2	Smooth (wavelets)
3	9	4.3	7-10	3.4-5.4	Gentle breeze	0.6	1.0	3	Slight
4	13	6.7	11-16	5.5-7.9	Moderate breeze	1.0	1.5	3-4	Slight-Moderate
5	19	9.3	17-21	8.0-10.7	Fresh breeze	2.0	2.5	4	Moderate
6	24	12.3	22-27	10.8-13.8	Strong breeze	3.0	4.0	5	Rough
7	30	15.5	28-33	13.9-17.1	Near gale	4.0	5.5	5-6	Rough-Very rough
8	37	18.9	34-40	17.2-20.7	Gale	5.5	7.5	6-7	Very rough-High
9	44	22.6	41-47	20.8-24.4	Severe gale	7.0	10.0	7	High
10	52	26.4	48-55	24.5-28.4	Storm	9.0	12.5	8	Very High
11	60	30.5	56-63	28.5-32.6	Violent storm	11.5	16.0	8	Very High
12	-	-	64+	32.7+	Hurricane	14+	-	9	Phenomenal

* i. These values refer to well-developed wind waves of the open sea.
   ii. The lag effect between the wind getting up and the sea increasing should be borne in mind.

STORY: "THE LOCUM TENENS"
BY LIEUTENANT COLONEL A. LLOYD-OWEN

As the clock in the quadrangle tower started chiming, the Head closed his *Thucydides*, and the Classical Sixth followed suit. Morning school was over.

"There will, of course, be the usual half this afternoon for those of you who are sitting for the exam to-morrow," the Head Master announced, when he had put away his book in his desk. "And may I suggest," he added, "that you spend it in getting a breath of fresh air, rather than with your books. There's nothing so fatal to one's chances of success in an exam as last-minute studying."

He paused, as if an idea was occurring to him.

"By the way," he went on, after a moment, "Mr. Grazebrook is arriving to-day, and it would be an act of friendliness if one of you would take a walk over to Hesgarth to meet him. If he's travelling by train, as I expect he is, he's almost certain to come by the one that gets in soon after three o'clock. There's no other suitable train from town."

"I'll do that, sir. I've an accumulator being charged in the village, and it'll give me an opportunity of picking it up."

It was Fladgate, Senior Prefect of School House and one of the candidates for the morrow's exam, that spoke.

"That's very good of you, Fladgate," responded the Head, "and I'm sure Mr. Grazebrook will appreciate your meeting him. Will you tell him that I would have done so myself had I been able to spare the time."

A newcomer in mid-term to the staff of Hesgarth College was something unusual. But a wave of influenza had played rather more than havoc among the masters, and the Head had been constrained to advertise for a *locum tenens* to fill one of the gaps in his seriously depleted staff. A Mr. Grazebrook, recently "down" from Oxford, had been chosen from a host of applicants for the post, and, as the Head had just announced, was expected to make his appearance that afternoon.

As soon as dinner was over, Fladgate was swinging through the main gateway of the college to set out upon his four-mile tramp across the moors to Hesgarth. And slung over his shoulders, it might have been observed, was a leather case containing his field-glasses.

For Fladgate was by way of being something of a naturalist – birds were his especial line – and he never moved over the moors without having his glasses hanging from a shoulder, in readiness when required for distant observation of what was going on in the wild.

To-day, however, he guessed there would be little chance for doing anything in the way of observing. He had barely an hour for the walk to Hesgarth, if he was to reach the station by the time the London train was due, which would allow no opportunity for lingering by the wayside. Still, he was carrying his glasses as usual – more out of habit than anything else, perhaps. And, of course, there was always the likelihood that Mr. Grazebrook might not be travelling by train, in which case he would no doubt make a leisurely return to the college and put the binoculars to the best of use.

A ten minutes' uphill climb from the gates brought him to the fringe of a wild stretch of Yorkshire moorland, that was cut in two by the stonewall bounded road that led to Hesgarth – a stretch of moorland whose every square yard, almost, he had tramped in his searchings after nature in the raw. But to-day, rather strangely, as he mounted the edge of this naturalist's paradise, he had not a thought for his birds. His mind was engrossed on a subject altogether different.

The exam that was to open to-morrow was flooding his thoughts. So much – practically his life's career – hung on its result.

Once a year, about midway in the spring term, the exams for the college prizes in Latin and Greek were held, and this was the exam that was about to take place. But it was no ordinary examination this, such as brings prestige and handsomely bound books, and nothing else, to the most successful. It brought infinitely more than that.

To the boy who made the highest aggregate of marks in the two subjects was awarded the Hesgarth Scholarship at Oxford – a scholarship that was worth a hundred pounds a year for three years. And from the very day that Fladgate had left his prep. school to go to Hesgarth his mind had been set upon winning this.

Time and time and time again his father had impressed upon him that he was to keep the idea of winning the Hesgarth always before him – that, without it, Oxford for him was an impossibility. There simply was not the money to send him there if he failed to pull off the schol., he told him, and he would have to be content with

Next moment his glasses were out of their case.

an office stool as a starting point to a career.

But Fladgate had turned out to be no great classical scholar – that is, as brains were generally appraised in the Classical Sixth in Hesgarth. However, to use the Head Master's own words, when he was explaining the situation to Fladgate senior some few weeks previously, it was an unusually lean year for brains in the Sixth – and therein lay Fladgate's chance. He was very nearly as strong a candidate, if not quite as strong, the Head had said, as the best of those that would be competing against him.

He knew his weak point well enough, did Fladgate – and the

Head, of course, knew it too. It was in Greek Unseen translation. That was where he was likely to flounder.

And the prospect of his so floundering was worrying him more than enough as he tramped along the road.

"By jingo, the Head was right!" he exclaimed presently, when a whiff of scent from the heather, that was gorgeously redolent after a recent shower, was wafted across his nostrils. "There's nothing like a breath of fresh air before an exam. To Hades with Greek Unseen till to-morrow, say I! I'll not give the stuff another thought till then. No, by jove, I won't! If that accumulator's ready for me I'll get the wireless going again to-night, an' I'll tune in to . . . Hullo! There's a curlew!"

The sight of a curlew, circling low at a distance and dropping to the heather with its wild, mournful note, drove Greek Unseen from his thoughts on the instant. Next moment his glasses were out of their case, and he was focusing on the spot where the long-billed wader had dropped.

"Wonder if she's pairing yet," he muttered, as he steadied the glasses by resting his elbows on the top of the wall that skirted the roadside. "Trifle soon yet, I should imagine. Still, she might be. I wish I had time to watch her for a bit. Anyhow, I'll mark the spot, so that if by chance Mr. Grazebrook doesn't turn up on the train, and I have to walk back, I might pick her up again."

Having marked the spot by dislodging a couple of loose stones from the top of the wall, he returned the glasses to their case and set off again.

Half an hour later he was on the platform of Hesgarth station, watching the train from London steam in.

It is a pretty little station, is Hesgarth, and, except on the first and last days of term, precious few passengers depart from it or alight there. On this occasion the number that left the train was but two; and neither of these, even by the widest stretch of the imagination, could have been taken for a 'varsity graduate.

"Well, he's not come on this one," Fladgate said to himself, when he had surveyed the two arrivals. "Probably he's travelling by coach, or he may have a car. Anyhow, the Head won't expect me to wait for the next, for that doesn't get in till after seven. I'll buzz round to the garage and collect my accumulator, and then saunter back. And, with luck, I'll pick up that curlew again."

In ten minutes, having recovered his accumulator, he was on the road again. And presently he was back at the spot that he had marked.

He clambered over the wall, and set off across the heather towards a distant clump of gorse that was growing somewhere near where the wader had dropped to ground.

"Make a first-class hide, that patch of gorse," he said to himself, as he opened his binocular case again. "I'll put in a good hour there, and find out just what's going on in the curlew world."

"Infernally skiddy surface!"

The remark, uttered to himself, came from the driver of an open touring car that was travelling over the moorland road in the direction of Hesgarth College.

In spite of the treacherous state to which the recent shower had brought the surface, the car was moving at no mean speed. However, when it came to a point where the road began to dip and to zigzag, with a blind corner not twenty-five yards ahead – quite close to the spot where Fladgate had dropped the stones from the wall – the driver took his foot off the accelerator pedal.

Probably he realised he was going a bit too fast. Or he might even have heard the exhaust of the motor-cycle that was coming towards him from the farther side of that blind corner. One cannot say.

But there is one thing certain – the rider of the motor-cycle did not hear *him* coming. Otherwise he would never have taken the corner at thirty-five miles an hour on the wrong side of the road.

They saw each other, these two, almost at the moment the cyclist was rounding the bend. The motorist swerved. So did the cyclist. But they could not miss one another. The front wheel of the motor-cycle struck a glancing blow at the off-side front wheel of the car, and an instant later rider and machine were sprawling.

The car made a violent skid, righted itself, and skidded again. Such was the driver's skill, however, he would probably have righted it a second time, had not his near-side wheel mounted the grass margin at the foot of the wall just where the stones that Fladgate had dislodged were lying.

Striking first one stone and then the other, the car gave a mighty lurch and overturned.

"Jerusalem! I don't believe I'm even scratched!"

This gasp of amazement at being uninjured came from the motorcyclist, who had already picked himself up.

"Bike's pretty well done in, though," he went on, as soon as he glimpsed the twisted mass of metal into which his machine had been converted through crashing into the wall of stone on the outside of the bend. "That's a bit awkward, just as I was getting nicely away. Wonder who was in the wrong? Couldn't say, myself, rightly. . . . Hullo! He's hurt, by the look of it!"

Turning, he had discovered the figure of the motorist lying in a motionless heap a couple of yards from his upturned car.

He went over to him.

"Goodness! He's badly knocked!" he exclaimed, as he dropped on a knee beside him.

Obviously badly knocked. The wretched man was bleeding from an ugly scalp wound, and he was quite unconscious.

The motor-cyclist, whose ideas of first aid were somewhat sketchy, took a handkerchief from his pocket and bound it over the wound.

"Blest if I know what I ought to do next," he muttered to himself when he had completed that operation. "Wish somebody'd come along in a car so that we could get him to a hospital. But on a lonely stretch like this nobody's likely to . . . Ho! Schoolmaster, eh?"

A suitcase, that had been flung out of the car, had opened itself and spread its contents in the roadway; and a 'varsity cap and gown had caught his eye.

"I wonder who the fellow is," he said to himself after a moment. "P'raps he's got something about him that will tell one. Better have a look, I sh'd think."

He thrust a hand into the injured man's pocket, and promptly pulled out a letter. It was addressed to John Grazebrook Esq., M.A., at an address in London. He opened it and began to read:

"DEAR MR. GRAZEBROOK (the letter ran),

"I am glad to learn that you are able to take up the temporary appointment on my staff that has been offered to you, and I am looking forward to meeting you on the sixth of the month.

"We have none of your contemporaries at Cambridge here at present. But no doubt you will quickly strike friendship with those who are assisting me.

> "Believe me,
> > "Yours sincerely,
> > > "JAMES RIDDELL, Head Master,"

Having read the letter through once, he ran over it quickly a second time. Then he looked at the address from which it had been sent.

"Hesgarth College, Yorkshire. Why, that must be just close here," he muttered, and for a moment he paused in thought. "Hesgarth College? Name sounds familiar. Hesgarth Coll—" And then a gasp of excitement suddenly broke from him. " 'Pon my Sam! Why, of course! That's the place where they've got a genuine Hol!"

Till that moment he had been resting the injured man's head on his knee. Releasing himself quickly from his burden, he sprang to his feet. His eyes were gleaming, and his whole frame was a-quiver.

For a third time he glanced at the Head Master's letter.

"*Am looking forward to meeting you on the sixth*. Why, this is the sixth!" he breathed excitedly. "Then he's on his way there! And of all the places I've wanted to visit, this Hesgarth College . . . Heavens! It's the chance of a lifetime! And there're none of his Cambridge contemporaries there to bowl me out. Oh, it's the chance of a lifetime, upon my Sam it is!"

Giving a vigorous hand-clap to mark his rejoicing, he bent again over the form of the still unconscious Mr. Grazebrook, and slipped an arm under his shoulders and another under his knees. Then, lifting him bodily, he carried him to where his own crippled machine was lying.

"You'll be better there than in the road, anyway," he remarked, as he laid him down on the grass beside the cycle. "And don't you think it would be as well if we exchanged our coats? I do. Might help things a bit if you were taken for me, y'know. Lucky we're both wearing flannel bags, so we needn't bother about them."

For the next few moments he was looking keenly about him to make certain he had the moor to himself. And when he was quite sure that he had, off came Mr. Grazebrook's coat and waistcoat and then his own. The exchange was effected speedily, and when it was completed he crammed the Head Master's letter into his trousers' pocket.

"I don't think they'll have much doubt who you are when they get you into hospital," he said, with a facetious chuckle. "There's my name on the tab of your jacket, and a bill or two in one of your pockets to convince 'em. Oh, they'll be pleased to see you, right enough!"

He was still chuckling merrily over the joke he was perpetrating, when a voice called out behind him:

"Hullo! What's happened here? Accident?"

He turned round with a start, and saw a man, evidently a country doctor by his cut and by the bag that he held in his hand, stepping out of a car that had noiselessly driven up that moment.

"Why, ye – yes. B – bit of a smash-up," he stammered, a little uncertain whether he had been spotted making the change of garments.

But a glance at the other's face soon put him at ease on that score.

"Pretty badly hurt, by the look of him," observed the doctor – it was the doctor from Hesgarth – as he knelt beside the injured Mr. Grazebrook, and began to undo his bandage. "What happened?"

The motor-cyclist told him. He was nearing the corner in his car on his way to the college, he said, when the fellow came blinding round on his cycle on the wrong side of the road, and they crashed nearly head on. He, himself, he added, overturned in his car, but was luckily not hurt. Just what happened to him – meaning Mr. Grazebrook – he did not know; but he imagined he must have been flung head-first at the wall.

"Evidently, by the look of his skull," said the doctor, producing a dressing and lint from his bag. "I shall be very surprised if it is not fractured. In any case he'll be unconscious for some hours – days, I should think."

"Just what I thought," remarked the motor-cyclist, giving himself a metaphorical pat on the back for his astuteness in gauging the extent of the unconsciousness. "You'll take him to hospital, I suppose."

"We've a cottage hospital in Hesgarth, and I'll take him there," said the doctor. "If you care to come with me, you'll be able to make arrangements at the local garage for salvaging your car, and pick up a taxi to take you on to your destination. Going to the college, I think you said."

The man nodded.

"You're the young fellow that's going there as *locum tenens*, then, I suppose," remarked the doctor, as he put the finishing touch to the temporary dressing he was applying.

"That's it," said the man.

Mr. Grazebrook was then carried by the two to the doctor's car, and placed comfortably in the back. And as soon as the one that was now impersonating him had repacked the suitcase with the scattered garments, and taken his seat beside the doctor, the car drove off.

"Must have been something of a smash, I sh'd think. Not much use my going over to see what's happened, though, now they've taken the fellow away. But I *would* like to know what the deuce those two were changing coats for!"

Fladgate, crouching in his "hide" some hundreds of yards away, then swung his glasses away from the road and focused again on his curlew.

The Head Master was standing at the foot of the steps of the college main entrance, watching a taxi coming up the drive. When the vehicle drew up, a young man carrying a bulging suitcase stepped out of it.

"Mr. Grazebrook, I presume," said the Head, stretching out a hand.

"It is, sir," returned the young man.

There was a cordial greeting, and the Head explained that he was Doctor Riddell.

"I was expecting you to come by train, and I sent one of my boys to meet you," said the Head, as they went up the steps together.

"That was very kind of you, sir," Mr. Grazebrook said. "But I travelled by car – and I'm rather sorry I did now."

"Yes, yes, indeed," said the Head. "I've heard all about your accident. Our doctor telephoned me from the hospital a few minutes ago to say you were coming on by taxi, and he gave me an account of what happened. You were lucky to have escaped unhurt."

They were crossing the floor of the Great Hall now, on the way to the Head Master's study. Just as they were mid-

"That's a Holbein, a genuine Holbein."

way across, Mr. Grazebrook cast an interested glance at a portrait in oils that adorned one of the walls.

"So you've an eye for an old master, I see, Grazebrook," observed the Head, stopping in front of the picture.

"I'm nothing of a connoisseur, sir," said Mr. Grazebrook modestly. "But it certainly strikes me you have something unusually good there."

"You're quite right, Grazebrook. That's a Holbein, a genuine Holbein," the Head told him. "It's a portrait of our founder."

He was proud of exhibiting this picture, the greatest of all the college's possessions, and he stood for some moments to allow Mr. Grazebrook to admire it. Then they passed on, and up a flight of stairs.

At the top of the stairs they met a boy, who was hurrying to the sound of the tea bell.

"Ah! Here's Fladgate, whom I sent to meet you," exclaimed the Head, stopping the prefect. "Fladgate, you must make the acquaintance of Mr. Grazebrook."

"Sorry you went on a wild goose chase, Fladgate," said Mr. Grazebrook genially, as the two shook hands. "I came by car, you know."

"I see, sir," said Fladgate, looking rather closely at the *locum tenens*. "Still, I had a good walk."

He had an impression at once that this Mr. Grazebrook was one of the two men involved in the car smash that he had seen through his glasses on the Hesgarth road. He was on the point of asking if that was not so. But he was in a hurry, and a trifle shy to boot, so he refrained. And he was glad when the Head and the *locum* passed on again.

"My Senior House Prefect, that boy Fladgate," remarked the Head, as he led the way into his study. "One of my candidates for the Oxford Scholarship exam that begins to-morrow."

"A good candidate?" queried Mr. Grazebrook.

"Well, as good as most of them," returned the Head, dropping into his chair. "He might even get it; and there's no boy I would rather see succeed. But he has one woefully weak point."

"What is that, sir?"

"Greek Unseen," answered the Head. "It's the one thing that's likely to let him down. I have the papers here" – he tapped a sealed, unopened envelope on his table – "and when I look at them in the prep. hour this evening I shall know well enough what chance he has. Ah! I see you are looking at that picture behind me."

Mr. Grazebrook had fastened his gaze on a picture that was an exact replica of the Holbein portrait – even to the frame itself – that hung in the Great Hall.

"It's a copy, of course," smiled the Head, "and really quite valueless. Still, without close inspection there are few that could tell the two apart."

Fladgate had his wireless going again soon after tea. He was true to his resolve, and did not touch a book the whole evening. The examinees having been excused prep., he spent the hours of freedom in his study tuning in to various foreign stations.

After prayers he repaired again to his study to pick up the Second News Bulletin. It was a dull lot of news that the announcer had to give, however, and he was on the point of switching him off when the mention of the name Hesgarth made him prick up his ears again.

"The last item of news to-night concerns the village of Hesgarth, in the North Riding of Yorkshire," spoke the announcer. "There was a collision between a car and a motor-cycle on a moorland road near the village this afternoon, that involved the cyclist in serious injury. When he was taken to the local cottage hospital it was discovered, by correspondence that he was carrying and by the name inside his jacket, that the cyclist is none other than the young man, Seth Hickman, whose name has been so much in the news of late in connection with the series of picture thefts that has been taking place in the north.

"A policeman is sitting beside the bed of the injured man, waiting to effect his arrest the moment he recovers consciousness.

"That concludes the Second News Bulletin."

Fladgate switched off. Then he leaned back in his chair.

"So they've got that fellow Seth Hickman at last!" he exclaimed – he had read a good deal of those picture thefts. "And in Hesgarth, of all places! Must have been the smash I saw through the glasses. There'll be a bit of excitement locally about that to-morrow, I expect, and . . . and . . .oh! what the deuce *was* all that exchanging of coats about, I wonder?"

Slowly his brows knitted. He was definitely puzzled. And as he sat for some minutes in contemplation he grew more and more puzzled.

And he was still puzzled when he went to bed.

Something must have disturbed the Head. He was not given to waking in the middle of the night. But there he was, lying wide awake at half-past twelve and trying to persuade himself that it was only his imagination that somebody was prowling about beneath his sleeping quarters.

"No, by George! There *is* somebody moving about!" he exclaimed suddenly, when he distinctly heard a floor-board creak.

He was out of bed in a moment, and into slippers and a dressing-gown. Then, flashing a torch, he noiselessly opened his door and listened.

But not a sound was now to be heard.

In ordinary circumstances he would no doubt have gone back to bed again – in fact, would probably never have stirred from his bed, thinking some skylarking was afoot that the prefects would be capable of dealing with. But the truth was, he was apprehensive – apprehensive for the safety of the Holbein.

Ever since there had been so much in the papers concerning the sequence of thefts of valuable pictures he had been anxious concerning the Holbein, and he dreaded the thought of that Seth Hickman person paying a visit to the college. Strangely enough, withal, he had not listened to the late bulletin of news that night.

So he picked up the poker and went downstairs.

One flight brought him to a corridor that ran past his study to the stairs leading to the Great Hall.

As he neared the study door he saw it was just ajar, and that a light was shining within. Next instant the light went out, and the door was thrown open.

"Fladgate! So it's you!"

The exclamation came from him in a gasp of indescribable amazement. He was thunderstruck. And for several seconds he faced his Senior Prefect, with his torch shining full in his face, scarcely knowing what further to say.

"What . . . what has brought you to my study, Fladgate?" he inquired at length.

"I . . . I . . ."

Fladgate stuttered miserably, and got no further. His tongue clove to his palate, and he trembled in every limb.

"Go to your bed, Fladgate!" commanded the Head, in inexorable tones. "You will tell me to-morrow what has brought you here, boy."

Mute with agony, Fladgate obeyed.

When he had gone, the Head entered his study and switched on the light.

"Just as I thought!" he gasped, in almost as much agony as Fladgate had shown. "They *were* open on my table, those Greek Unseen papers! Oh, merciful heavens! What can have come over the boy?"

At half-past two the Head woke again. He was having a restless night. He almost thought he again heard somebody moving below his floor. But he was asleep once more before he could bring himself properly to listen.

Purposely Fladgate was late for breakfast the next morning. He felt little or no desire for the meal, and certainly he had no inclination for the company of his fellows – for somehow he had a feeling that it must already be known by everyone that he had been caught in the Head's study in the hours of darkness on the eve of the examination.

There were only a few tardy ones left in the dining-hall when he reached it, and, avoiding their glances, he took a seat as far removed from them as he could find. He had half expected to see Mr. Grazebrook presiding. But he was not there, and another master was in the chair at the top of the room.

When he was half-way through a plateful of porridge, the master spoke to him.

"I am to tell you, Fladgate," he said, "that you are to report to the Head Master's study at quarter to nine."

"Very good, sir," droned Fladgate, without looking up.

He glanced at his wrist-watch. It was twenty to nine already. Pushing his plate from him, he passed the next two minutes with his head between his hands.

At a minute to the quarter he was going along a corridor on his way to the Head Master's room. A junior prefect was coming towards him.

"Hullo, Fladgate!" said the younger boy. "Didn't see you at brekker this morning."

"No. I was late," remarked Fladgate, not stopping.

But the other caught hold of the lapel of his coat and made him stop.

"Here! You've heard about the Holbein, I s'pose," he burst out.

"No? What about it?" exclaimed Fladgate, lighting up.

"Why, it's gone, man! Cut out of its frame in the night! And so's our Mr. Grazebrook gone too!" cried the boy breathlessly. "And all the fellows are saying it wasn't really Mr. Grazebrook at all, but . . ."

But Fladgate had broken away, and was already knocking at the Head's door. "Come in!"

Fladgate, blanched like a sheet, turned the handle and entered.

"I have sent for you, Fladgate," said the Head Master, as soon as the door was closed again, "to learn what brought you to this room last night."

Fladgate moistened his quivering lips with the tip of his tongue. But he did not speak.

"Shall I help you, Fladgate?" said the Head frigidly, when he saw the boy's discomfiture. And then, dropping to his gravest tone and giving each word a dire emphasis, he went on, "On my table last night were lying open the Greek Unseen papers for to-day's exam. Was it to . . .?"

"On my solemn word of honour, sir, I did not go near your table," suddenly and passionately protested Fladgate.

The Head caught at a breath – a breath of infinite relief.

"If you tell me that on your word of honour, Fladgate," he said, "I believe you utterly . . . Then, what could have brought you to my room?"

"I came, sir . . . I came to . . ." Fladgate began.

But the wonderful ring of the Head's "I believe you utterly," had brought him to the verge of breaking down. Then, suddenly, he flung out a hand to point at the portrait behind the Head's chair.

"Oh, sir!" he panted hysterically. "That's our Holbein behind you! *I came to change the two pictures round!*"

Envoi.

The Greek Unseen proved unexpectedly to Fladgate's liking, and by a margin of twenty marks he landed the Hesgarth Scholarship. Mr. Grazebrook recovered in due course from his serious accident, and eventually took up permanent duty at the college.

But of the *locum tenens* nothing was heard again. Possibly, when he found how he had been "done" over the Hesgarth Holbein, and knowing the police were hot on his track, he gave up the game of picture thieving and slipped quietly out of the country.

Reprinted from *Modern Wonders for Boys*, 1938.

"That's our Holbein behind you."

THE PERIODIC TABLE

The Periodic Table is something science teachers put on the wall to scare you.

Or so it seems. Actually, if you stop to look at the Periodic Table you'll find that it's source of indispensable information. It was invented in 1869 by Dmitri Mendeleev.

The Table's full name is "The Perodic Table of the Elements". **Elements** are the building blocks of all matter. The Table is a useful way of arranging those elements to show which elements are similar to each other and which are not, and why not.

As far as scientists know, there are only so many basic elements. Up to this point in time over 100 elements have been discovered or created. These elements are the same wherever they come from: iron (which has the chemical symbol Fe) from earth is the same as iron from Mars.

In the Periodic Table, each row is considered to be a different "period" and all the elements in that row have the same number of **atomic orbitals**. And what are atomic orbitals you may well ask? Elements themselves are made up of a building material called **atoms**. Each tiny atom is made up of even smaller particles called **protons**, **neutrons** and **electrons**. These are made up of even smaller particles called **quarks**.

An atomic orbital is the shell in which the electron spins around the centre of the atom.

Every element in the top row (the first period) of the Periodic Table has one orbital for its electron. All of the elements in the second row (the second period) have two orbitals for their electrons. And so on down the table. The maximum number of orbitals for any element is seven.

So much for the rows of "periods". Now to the "groups" of columns of the table, which read up-down. The elements in a group have the same number of electrons in their outer orbital. Each element in the first column (group one) has one electron in its outer shell. Each element on the second column (group two) has two electrons in the outer shell. There are some exceptions to the order when you look at the transition metal elements but you get the idea. From the column an element occupies you can work out how many electrons there are in its outer shell.

Next, the "two at the top", Hydrogen (H) and Helium (He). These are special elements. Hydrogen can have the talents and electrons of two groups, I and VII. Hydrogen is sometimes missing an electron and sometimes it has an extra. Although Helium can only have two electrons in its outer shell it is grouped with elements which have eight, the 'inert gases'.

The Periodic Table below also shows the atomic weight of the elements. The amount of matter in an atom is called its **atomic mass**. Carbon-13 has a greater atomic mass than carbon-12. The average atomic mass of all of the different atoms of the same element is called the element's **atomic weight**. Every element has a different atomic weight.

It's easier to navigate your way around the Periodic Table if you know your chemical element symbols. These are.

Element name	Element symbol	Atomic number
Actinium	Ac	89
Silver	Ag	47
Aluminium (aluminum)	Al	13
Americium	Am	95
Argon	Ar	18
Arsenic	As	33
Astatine	At	85
Gold	Au	79
Boron	B	5
Barium	Ba	56

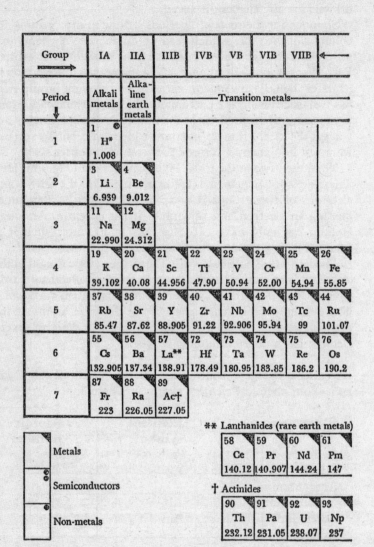

Group →	IA	IIA	IIIB	IVB	VB	VIB	VIIB	←
Period ↓	Alkali metals	Alka-line earth metals	←		Transition metals		→	
1	1 ◉ H* 1.008							
2	3 Li 6.939	4 Be 9.012						
3	11 Na 22.990	12 Mg 24.312						
4	19 K 39.102	20 Ca 40.08	21 Sc 44.956	22 Ti 47.90	23 V 50.94	24 Cr 52.00	25 Mn 54.94	26 Fe 55.85
5	37 Rb 85.47	38 Sr 87.62	39 Y 88.905	40 Zr 91.22	41 Nb 92.906	42 Mo 95.94	43 Tc 99	44 Ru 101.07
6	55 Cs 132.905	56 Ba 137.34	57 La** 138.91	72 Hf 178.49	73 Ta 180.95	74 W 183.85	75 Re 186.2	76 Os 190.2
7	87 Fr 223	88 Ra 226.05	89 Ac† 227.05					

	Metals
◉	Semiconductors
◉	Non-metals

** Lanthanides (rare earth metals)

58 Ce 140.12	59 Pr 140.907	60 Nd 144.24	61 Pm 147

† Actinides

90 Th 232.12	91 Pa 231.05	92 U 238.07	93 Np 237

←—VIII—→	IB	IIB	IIIA	IVA	VA	VIA	VIIA	O
	Noble metals						Halogens	Inert gases
								2 He 4.003
			5 B 10.811	6 C 12.011	7 N 14.007	8 O 15.999	9 F 18.998	10 Ne 20.183
			13 Al 26.982	14 Si 28.086	15 P 30.974	16 S 32.064	17 Cl 35.453	18 Ar 39.948
27 Co 58.93	29 Cu 63.54	30 Zn 65.37	31 Ga 69.72	32 Ge 72.59	33 As 74.92	34 Se 78.96	35 Br 79.909	36 Kr 83.80
45 Rh 102.91	47 Ag 107.87	48 Cd 112.40	49 In 114.82	50 Sn 118.69	51 Sb 121.75	52 Te 127.60	53 I 126.904	54 Xe 131.30
77 Ir 192.2	79 Au 196.97	80 Hg 200.59	81 Tl 204.37	82 Pb 207.19	83 Bi 208.98	84 Po 210	85 At 211	86 Rn 222

Note: Columns 28 Ni 58.71, 46 Pd 106.4, 78 Pt 195.09 appear in the VIII group area.

62 Sm 150.35	63 Eu 151.96	64 Gd 157.25	65 Tb 158.92	66 Dy 162.50	67 Ho 164.93	68 Er 167.26	69 Tm 168.93	70 Yb 173.04	71 Lu 174.97

94 Pu 239	95 Am 241	96 Cm 242	97 Bk 247	98 Cf 251	99 Es 254	100 Fm 253	101 Md 256	102 No 254	103 Lr 257

Beryllium	Be	4
Bohrium	Bh	107
Bismuth	Bi	83
Berkelium	Bk	97
Bromine	Br	35
Carbon	C	6
Calcium	Ca	20
Cadmium	Cd	48
Cerium	Ce	58
Californium	Cf	98
Chlorine	Cl	17
Curium	Cm	96
Cobalt	Co	27
Chromium	Cr	24
Caesium (Cesium)	Cs	55
Copper	Cu	29
Dubnium	Db	105
Darmstadtium	Ds	110
Dysprosium	Dy	66
Erbium	Er	68
Einsteinium	Es	99
Europium	Eu	63
Fluorine	F	9
Iron	Fe	26
Fermium	Fm	100
Francium	Fr	87
Gallium	Ga	31
Gadolinium	Gd	64
Germanium	Ge	32
Hydrogen	H	1
Helium	He	2
Hafnium	Hf	72
Mercury	Hg	80
Holmium	Ho	67
Hassium	Hs	108
Iodine	I	53
Indium	In	49
Iridium	Ir	77
Potassium	K	19
Krypton	Kr	36

Lanthanum	La	57
Lithium	Li	3
Lawrencium	Lr	103
Lutetium	Lu	71
Mendelevium	Md	101
Magnesium	Mg	12
Manganese	Mn	25
Molybdenum	Mo	42
Meitnerium	Mt	109
Nitrogen	N	7
Sodium	Na	11
Niobium	Nb	41
Neodymium	Nd	60
Neon	Ne	10
Nickel	Ni	28
Nobelium	No	102
Neptunium	Np	93
Oxygen	O	8
Osmium	Os	76
Phosphorus	P	15
Protactinium	Pa	91
Lead	Pb	82
Palladium	Pd	46
Promethium	Pm	61
Polonium	Po	84
Praseodymium	Pr	59
Platinum	Pt	78
Plutonium	Pu	94
Radium	Ra	88
Rubidium	Rb	37
Rhenium	Re	75
Rutherfordium	Rf	104
Rhodium	Rh	45
Radon	Rn	86
Ruthenium	Ru	44
Sulfur (Sulphur)	S	16
Antimony	Sb	51
Scandium	Sc	21
Selenium	Se	34
Seaborgium	Sg	106

Silicon	Si	14
Samarium	Sm	62
Tin	Sn	50
Strontium	Sr	38
Tantalum	Ta	73
Terbium	Tb	65
Technetium	Tc	43
Tellurium	Te	52
Thorium	Th	90
Titanium	Ti	22
Thallium	Tl	81
Thulium	Tm	69
Uranium	U	92
Ununbium	Uub	112
Ununhexium	Uuh	116
Ununoctium	Uuo	118
Ununpentium	Uup	115
Ununquadium	Uuq	114
Ununseptium	Uus	117
Ununtrium	Uut	113
Unununium?	Uuu	111
Vanadium	V	23
Tungsten	W	74
Xenon	Xe	54
Yttrium	Y	39
Ytterbium	Yb	70
Zinc	Zn	30
Zirconium	Zr	40

A DIY VOLCANO

Thar she blows!

Here's how to make a mini Mount Vesuvius in the kitchen. The recipe is safe – but messy. But then it's a volcano you're making so you would expect nothing else.

You need:

2 cups salt
6 cups flour
4 tablespoons of cooking oil
Warm water
1 plastic soda/mineral water bottle
Dishwasher detergent or washing-up liquid
Vinegar
Baking soda (bicarbonate of soda)
Red food colouring such as cochineal
A baking dish or large shallow pan.

It will take about thirty minutes before the "lava" comes flowing down the mountain.

Step 1. This is to make the volcanic cone from home-made play dough. Mix the 6 cups of flour, 2 cups of salt, 4 tablespoons of cooking oil and 2 cups of warm water into a firm dough. (Add more water if the mixture is to dry to be easily mouldable.)

Step 2. Stand the plastic bottle upright in the baking pan and place in the kitchen sink.

Step 3. Mould the dough around the bottle to form a volcanic mountain shape. Don't cover the open bottle top.

Step 4. Place a teaspoon of red food dye in the bottle. Fill the bottle with warm water to about 2 inches from the top.

Step 5. Add half a teaspoon of dishwasher detergent to the bottle, followed by 2 tablespoons of baking soda.

Step 6. Slowly add the vinegar.

Step 7. Watch the volcano erupt.

What's happening in your DIY kitchen volcano is similar to what happens in a real volcano.

When the vinegar encounters the baking soda they react together to form carbon dioxide. Carbon dioxide is an active agent in real volcanoes too. As more carbon dioxide is produced inside the bottle the pressure builds up until the gas forces its way out through the top of the "volcano".

BRITISH AND US MILITARY OFFICER RANKS

British Army and Royal Marines	US Army, USAF and USMC	Royal Navy	US Navy and US Coast Guard	RAF
Field Marshal (FM)	General of the Army General of the Air Force (no USMC enquiv)	Admiral of the Fleet	Fleet Admiral (FADM) US Navy only	Marshal of the Royal Air Force (MRAF)
General (Gen)	General (GEN/ Gen/Gen)	Admiral (Adm)	Admiral (ADM)	Air Chief Marshal (Air Chf Mshl)
Lieutenant General (Lt Gen)	Lieutenant General (LTG/Lt Gen/LtGen)	Vice Admiral (VAdm)	Vice Admiral (VADM)	Air Marshal (Air Mshl)
Major General (Maj Gen)	Major General (MG/Maj Gen/ MajGen)	Rear Admiral (RAdm)	Rear Admiral (Upper Half) (RADM)	Air Vice-Marshal (AVM)
Brigadier (Brig)	Brigadier General (BG/Brig Gen/ BGen)	Com-modore (Cdre)	Rear Admiral (Lower Half) (RDML)	Air Com-modore (Air Cdre)
Colonel (Col)	Colonel (COL/ Col/Col)	Captain (Capt)	Captain (CAPT)	Group Captain (Gp Capt)
Lieutenant Colonel (Lt Col)	Lieutenant Colonel (LTC/Lt Col/LtCol)	Com-mander (Cdr)	Commander (CDR)	Wing Com-mander (Wg Cdr)
Major (Maj)	Major (MAJ/Maj/ Maj)	Lieutenant Com-mander (Lt Cdr)	Lieutenant Commander (LCDR)	Squadron Leader (Sqn Ldr)
Captain (Capt)	Captain (CPT/ Capt/Capt)	Lieutenant (Lt)	Lieutenant (LT)	Flight Lieutenant (Flt Lt)

Lieutenant (Lt)	First Lieutenant (1LT/1Lt/1Lt)	Sub Lieutenant (SLt)	Lieutenant, Junior Grade (LTJG)	Flying Officer (Fg Off)
Second Lieutenant (2Lt)	Second Lieutenant (2LT/2Lt/2Lt)		Ensign (ENS)	Pilot Officer (Plt Off)
		Midship-man (Mid)		
Officer Cadet (OCdt)	Cadet/USMC Midshipman (MIDN)/Officer Candidate/Officer Trainee	Officer Cadet (O/C)	Midshipman/USN (MIDN), Cadet/USCG or Officer Candidate (OC)	Officer Cadet (OCdt)

THEORY AND FACTS OF FLIGHT

Why Does An Aeroplane Fly?

Early in the eighteenth century, about 1735, a Swiss scientist, Daniel Bernoulli, discovered that in any moving fluid the pressure is lowest where the speed is greatest. The air about us acts like a fluid and if we can increase the speed of air over a surface, such as a wing, the pressure should decrease and the wing should rise.

In actual practice, the wing of an aeroplane is shaped somewhat like a bow – the upper surface is curved while the lower part is straight. Since the air has to travel a greater distance over the top part of the wing, it must travel at a faster speed. As a result, the pressure is lower above the wing than below it and the wing rises, or *lifts*, into the air.

When an aeroplane flies horizontally, its engine must do two things. First, it must keep the plane from falling and, second, it must overcome the friction of the air in order to pull the plane forward. Moving the aircraft forwards increases the speed of the air over the wings. According to the Bernoulli principle, this creates *lift* – the upward pressure on the wing. Lift overcomes *gravity* – the downward pressure created by the weight of the plane.

A propeller slices through the air in the same way that a screw cuts into wood, and pulls the plane forward, whereas a jet engine pushes it. This forward motion is called *thrust*. It counteracts the *drag* of the atmosphere, the force that resists forward motion.

What Makes An Aeroplane Go Up and Down?

An aeroplane, like any moving object following the basic laws of physics, tends to continue in a straight line unless some force is exerted to change its direction. The speed at which the engine turns is governed by the *throttle*. Opening the throttle increases the propeller speed or jet thrust and lifts the plane higher.

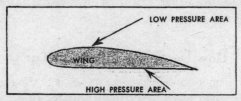

As the air rushes past the wing, or airfoil, it flows above and below the airfoil. The shape of the airfoil causes the air to travel a greater distance over the top of the foil. This results in a lowering of air pressure, which creates an upward lift on the airfoil.

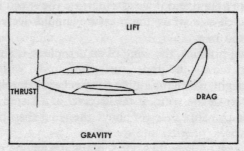

These four forces act upon a plane while in flight.

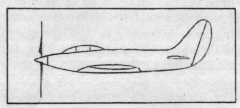

The propeller, sometimes called airscrew, provides the forward pulling or lifting power of an aeroplane.

Equally important is the *elevator* which controls the plane's upward and downward movement. It is a horizontal, hinged surface attached to the tail. When the pilot applies back pressure on the control stick, or column, the elevator is tilted upwards. The air, striking the raised elevator, forces the tail down and the nose upwards. The thrust of the engine pulls the plane upwards. Conversely, when the pilot pushes the control stick forward, the elevator is tilted downwards. This forces the tail up and the nose down.

How Does An Aeroplane Turn?

Two parts of an aeroplane control its turns to the right and left. The *rudder*, a vertical surface that is hinged to the tail, swings the tail to the right or left just in the same way as a section of the tail swings up or down. On the ground, it is used to make the plane turn just as a rudder of a boat does. In the air, however, the major purpose of the rudder is *not* to make the plane turn, but to assist the plane in entering and recovering from a turn.

The *ailerons*, small sections of the rear edge of the wing, near the tips, are hinged and are so connected that as one rises, the other lowers. This action tends to raise one wing and lower the other.

When the aileron on the right wing is lowered, the right wing rises and the plane will be tilted, or *banked*, to the left. The lifting force on the right wing is no longer completely upward –

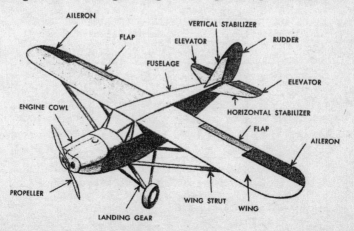

part of the force is pulling the plane to the left. This, in combination with the rudder, produces a left turn; that is, the plane is "lifted" around the turn.

How Can You Demonstrate Lift?

Take a piece of paper about 2 inches wide and about 5 inches long. Fold it an inch from the end. Hold the paper with your forefinger and thumb so that the fold is about an inch or two from your mouth. Blow with all your might over the top of the paper.

What happened? The paper moves up or *lifts*. By increasing the speed of the air over the top of the paper, you have reduced the pressure, causing the paper to rise.

Reprinted from *The How and Why Wonder Book of Flight*, 1964. Copyright © 1964 Wonder Books Inc.

STAR CHARTS

The Sun is one of 100,000 million stars in the Milky Way galaxy. Galaxies of stars are held together by gravity, the same force that keep us pushed down on planet Earth. Astronomers, scientists who study the stars, believe that the Milky Way is only one of millions of galaxies in the Universe.

Stars are formed from clouds of hydrogen, other gases and dust. Over time the gases are drawn towards the centre, which becomes hot and glows. Nuclear reactions, caused by the change of hydrogen into helium, create enormous amounts of energy. Soon a star is born. Its surface temperature is in excess of 60,000 degrees Centigrade. The Sun, with a diameter of 1.4 million kilometres, is a medium-sized star.

Eventually stars die, because the hydrogen supply runs out. In dying the star swells to become a red giant. In around 5,000 million years the Sun will become a red giant, possibly swallowing Earth in its death throes. Finally, the red giant cools down to become a small white dwarf star.

The nearest star to earth is Bungula which is 40,000,000,000,000 km (25,000,000,000,000 miles) away. On a cloudless night around 3,000 stars are visible at night with just the naked eye, although a pair of binoculars or a telescope will enable to you to see more and better. The brightness of stars, as seen from Earth, is measured in a unit called magnitude. Magnitude 0 is the brightest; a star of this brightness would be clearly visibly. The brightest star, as seen from Earth, is Sirius.

For the convenience of astronomers, stars are grouped together in "constellations". There are eighty-eight constella-

tions in all, which are named after people, animals and objects.
The constellations, with their scientific and English names are:

Latin	Abbreviation	English
Andromeda	And	Andromeda
Antlia	Ant	Air Pump
Apus	Aps	Bird of Paradise
Aquarius	Aqr	Water Carrier
Aquila	Aql	Eagle
Ara	Ara	Altar
Aries	Ari	Ram
Auriga	Aur	Charioteer
Boötes	Boo	Herdsman
Caelum	Cae	Chisel
Camelopardalis	Cam	Giraffe
Cancer	Cnc	Crab
Canes Venatici	CVn	Hunting Dogs
Canis Major	CMa	Big Dog
Canis Minor	CMi	Little Dog
Capricornus	Cap	Goat
Carina	Car	Keel
Cassiopeia	Cas	Cassiopeia
Centaurus	Cen	Centaur
Cepheus	Cep	Cepheus
Cetus	Cet	Whale
Chamaeleon	Cha	Chameleon
Circinus	Cir	Compasses
Columba	Col	Dove
Coma Berenices	Com	Berenice's Hair
Corona Australis	CrA	Southern Crown
Corona Borealis	CrB	Northern Crown
Corvus	Crv	Crow
Crater	Crt	Cup
Crux	Cru	Southern Cross
Cygnus	Cyg	Swan
Delphinus	Del	Dolphin
Dorado	Dor	Goldfish
Draco	Dra	Dragon
Equuleus	Equ	Little Horse
Eridanus	Eri	River

Fornax	For	Furnace
Gemini	Gem	Twins
Grus	Gru	Crane
Hercules	Her	Hercules
Horologium	Hor	Clock
Hydra	Hya	Hydra (Sea Serpent)
Hydrus	Hyi	Water Serpent (male)
Indus	Ind	Indian
Lacerta	Lac	Lizard
Leo	Leo	Lion
Leo Minor	LMi	Smaller Lion
Lepus	Lep	Hare
Libra	Lib	Balance
Lupus	Lup	Wolf
Lynx	Lyn	Lynx
Lyra	Lyr	Lyre
Mensa	Men	Table
Microscopium	Mic	Microscope
Monoceros	Mon	Unicorn
Musca	Mus	Fly
Norma	Nor	Square
Octans	Oct	Octant
Ophiucus	Oph	Serpent Holder
Orion	Ori	Orion
Pavo	Pav	Peacock
Pegasus	Peg	Winged Horse
Perseus	Per	Perseus
Phoenix	Phe	Phoenix
Pictor	Pic	Easel
Pisces	Psc	Fishes
Pisces Austrinus	PsA	Southern Fish
Puppis	Pup	Stern
Pyxis	Pyx	Compass
Reticulum	Ret	Reticle
Sagitta	Sge	Arrow
Sagittarius	Sgr	Archer
Scorpius	Sco	Scorpion
Sculptor	Scl	Sculptor
Scutum	Sct	Shield
Serpens	Ser	Serpent

Sextans	Sex	Sextant
Taurus	Tau	Bull
Telescopium	Tel	Telescope
Triangulum	Tri	Triangle
Triangulum Australe	TrA	Southern Triangle
Tucana	Tuc	Toucan
Ursa Major	UMa	Great Bear
Ursa Minor	UMi	Little Bear
Vela	Vel	Sails
Virgo	Vir	Virgin
Volans	Vol	Flying Fish
Vulpecula	Vul	Fox

What one sees from the Southern hemisphere in the night sky is, of course, different to what one sees in the Northern hemisphere.

Northern Hemisphere Star Chart

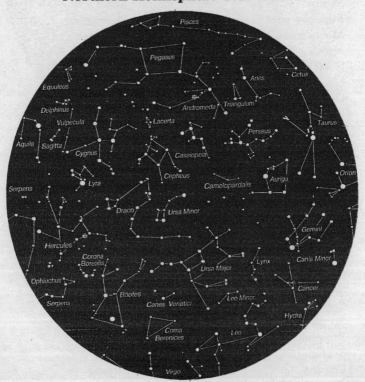

Southern Hemisphere Star Chart

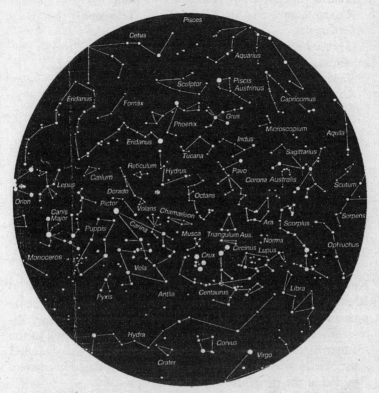

CROSSING THE EMPTY QUARTER
BY BERTRAM THOMAS

Bertram Thomas, a British explorer, was the first Caucasian to cross the fearsome Rub 'al Khali desert in Arabia, better known as "The Empty Quarter". The year was 1931.

Never before had the great South Arabian desert of Rub 'al Khali been crossed by a white man, and the ambition to be its pioneer seized me as it had seized every adventurous Englishman whose lot has been cast in Arabia. But before I tell of the manner of my camel crossing and of the things that befell, I must briefly introduce the reader who is uninitiated in matters Arabian to the lie of the land.

"The World," said the medieval Moslem geographer, "is in shape like a ball, and it floats in the circumambient ocean like an egg in water, half in and half out. Of the exposed portion one half constitutes the Inhabited Quarter, while the remaining half is the Empty Quarter, the Rub 'al Khali placed in the barren wastes of Arabia."

An extravagant estimate, this, of the place of our wanderings; yet it is no mean desert that approaches an area as big as England and France together. That it should have remained *terra incognita* till after the icy Polar regions, the tropic sources of the Amazon, and the vast interior spaces of Asia and Africa had been made to yield up their secrets to Western curiosity, is strange. An Arabian explanation was given to the traveller Charles Doughty, by his genial companion Zayed as Shaykhan, that worthy, with his finger upon a page of Arab script, declaring the matter in this wise: "God has given two of the four parts of the earth to the children of Adam, the third part He has given to Gog and Magog, the fourth is the Rub 'al Khali void of the breath of life."

Lack of rain and merciless heat indeed make of this a place where the Persian poet would have us believe "the panting sinner receives a foretaste of his future destiny." Certainly human life can be but spasmodically supported, and then mostly round the desert's fringes, where, among semi-barbarous nomadic tribes, hunger and the raid are Nature's pruning-hooks.

Native suspicion and an insular outlook combine with insecurity of life to keep the infidel intruder at arm's length, and he who would travel hopefully and usefully requires some apprenticeship and acclimatisation: needs must he speak the tongue, know the mind, grow a beard, dress and act like his desert companions, betraying, for instance, no squeamishness over drinking water, pestiferous though it might be, drawn from unsampled water-holes come upon in the burning sands, and not improved by churning in strong-smelling animal-skins carried on the march. But to our story!

On the 5th October, 1931, the S.S. *British Grenadier*, homeward bound from Persia, arrived off Muscat harbour at dawn, and there picked me up, by arrangement, from a small boat. Two nights later I was dropped, clothed in native dress, into an Arab dhow we sighted riding at anchor off the central-south Arabian shore. Landing, I made my way to the rendezvous where I had expected a trusted Arab chieftain who had served me on an earlier desert expedition, but I found neither him nor his promised string of riding camels.

Experience had taught me the need of not disclosing my plans to anyone in a land where secrecy of movement at the outset is imperative. My hopes of even making a start were thus dashed, and, sick at my bad luck, I turned up into the Qara Mountains to think and to scheme, while I explored and hunted their forested slopes. More than two impatient months passed before despair gave way to reviving hope.

It was the 10th December when at last I set out from Dhufar with a party of desert Arabs that included the famous Sheikh

Salih, of the Rashid (Kathir) tribe, 26 warriors – nearly all of whom could show the scars of wounds, none of whom had I set eyes on before – and 40 camels. The first day's march was as usual cut short, some of the men returning to the booths to buy a trifling gimcrack with which to gladden the eyes of their beauties far away in the black tents, some for a final watering at the sweet well of the mosque, while skins in which we carried our water were oiled and made watertight, and crude, improvised sacks, which did for pack-saddles, were given a final look over.

Our northerly course, on the morrow, led upward through the dense jungles of the Qara escarpment, where I had reaped a bountiful harvest for the Museum – hyenas, wolves, and coneys, snakes and lizards, chameleons, birds, and butterflies; and at Qatan I looked back for a last glimpse of the blue Indian Ocean 3,000 feet below. Waving yellow meadows that crowned the uplands gave place to libaniferous shrubs as we wended our way down the far side, amid red and rugged rocks wherein were groves of the frankincense and myrrh trees that gave rise to the fame of the Arabia of antiquity, of which we gain echoes in the Bible. Never could camp-fires have been more luxuriantly fragrant.

Soon we were to bid farewell to this pleasant countryside of rippling brooks and gay bird life, the decorative stork by day and the eerie sound of the tree-bat by night. The pebbly gorge of Dauka, by which we descended, grew shallower as we went, and became but a sandy, serpentine depression in the arid wilderness beyond. In such ancient dried-up river-beds as this is the secret of life, for the night dews that here collect give rise to an arterial way of desert flora across the barren plain and the route of the caravan.

The foothills of the southern mountains soon sank below our horizon in rear, and the vast clean spaces of a flint-strewn steppe stretched northward before us. Sand-devils, slender columns of whirling sand, sometimes swept hither and thither; sometimes the skyline danced before us in a hot, shimmering mirage, distorting a far-away bush into an expansive copse, an antelope into some monstrous creature, and generally playing tricks with lakes of illusory water.

For the next two months the stars were my only roof, for I travelled, like my companions, without a tent; and as the thermometer almost immediately fell to 45° Fahrenheit at night, one felt bitterly cold after the hot days in the saddle, wearing the same clothes day and night. The luxury of a tent had to be eschewed, in order to keep camel-loads at a minimum, for there were certain indispensable things to carry – rations of rice, sugar, native fat, and dates; mapping instruments: a compass, sextant, artificial horizon, chronometers, barometers, and hydrometer; natural-history skinning instruments, killing-bottles, and preserving chests; a rifle, for none goes unarmed in these parts, it being held neither safe nor respectable; and to pay my way, gunnybags stuffed with 3,000 Maria Theresa dollars, which I kept under my saddle by day and my pillow by night.

I had to be careful to conceal my sextant and keep my star observations unobserved, lest I be suspected of magic or worse, and to this end I always contrived to sleep some thirty or forty yards away from the camp and wait till my companions had settled down for the night. This they did after prayers and hobbling their camels over the best pastures available, lying sprawling around the flickering camp-fires with their rifle as their only bedding.

A few days' march northward across the gently declining steppe brought us to the waterhole of Shisur, where we dallied for two days to rest our camels preparatory to a nine-days' waterless and hungry stretch westward. This was to be the most dangerous part of my journey, for it is a no-man's-land with a bloody reputation for raiding and counter-raiding between the various tribes of these southern borderlands; and as I was moving with Rashidi tribesmen, I was particularly apprehensive of a collision with a party of the Sa'ar tribe, their hereditary enemies, for whom, moreover, the money I carried would doubtless have acted as a magnet.

Yellow sand-dunes rose tier upon tier, backing the western reaches of Umm al Hait, the mighty, dried-up river-system I had discovered and mapped on an earlier journey; and hummocky summits were crowned with tamarisk, which in these hungry marches brought our camels running up at the glad sight. It is impossible to carry fodder over these long trails, and camels have to fend for themselves, or rather, a small, well-mounted reconnaissance party goes off to discover the best pastures in the neighbourhood before a general move.

Hence the route taken by the desert traveller cannot with certainty be determined; his course will most likely not be the straightest and shortest one between two points, as with an aeroplane in the air or a ship at sea. And thus it came about that although my plan was to cross the sands northward from sea to sea, I here found myself travelling from east to west along the southern bulwark of the sands.

The full force of the tropical afternoon sun in our faces made me appreciate the Beduin headdress, the long kerchief which can be wound round the face being merciful indeed as a protection from the sun's burning rays, though my lips and nostrils rarely escaped. Glare glasses I never used, for the reason of possible queer effects on my companions' unaccustomed minds.

"Look, sahib!" said the Arabs riding at my side, one afternoon, and pointing to the ground. "There is the road to Ubar. Ubar was a great city that our fathers have told us existed in olden times; a city that possessed much treasure and had date gardens and a fort of red silver (gold); it now lies buried beneath the sands, men say in the Rumlait Shu'ait, maybe a few days to the north."

I had heard of Ubar, an ancient Atlantis of the sands, as it were, from Arab companions of an earlier expedition in the eastern desert, but none could tell of its location. Where my notice was now directed there were deep impressions as of ancient caravan tracks in the hard steppe surface, leading away only to be lost under a wall of sand.

Desiccation of climate through the ages and the extension of the sands, ever encroaching southward, could have brought about its disuse, for it can have led to nowhere worth leading to in historic times, and is now good for nothing. If this local tradition is well founded, Ubar may preserve a memory of the famed land of Ophir, long since lost in the mists of antiquity.

Our course, now trending more to the south, past the dunes of Yibaila and Yadila, was interesting for large, silvery patches in the hollows suggesting a dried-up sea, but which turned out to be sheets of gypsum; though, curiously enough, all along this borderland between sand and steppe, 1,000 feet and more above sea-level and to-day more than 100 miles from the coast, the surface was strewn with oyster and other shell fossils, suggesting that this desert was once an ocean bed.

Beyond Yadila I was next to experience what is extremely rare even for an Arabian explorer, and that was singing sands. As we were floundering along through heavy dune country, the silence were suddenly broken and I was startled for a moment, not knowing what the interruption was or whence it came. "Listen to that ridge bellowing," said a Badu* at my side, and looking to where he pointed I saw away on our right hand a steepish sand-cliff about a hundred feet high.

I was too deeply absorbed in the sound to talk, and there was nothing unusual to the eye. The hour was 4.15, and a slight northerly wind blew from the rear of the cliff. I must often have observed similar conditions, but never before heard any accompanying bellowing, only the spectacle of a film of sand smoking over the sand-ridges to build up a shape recalling a centurion's helmet. But here the leeward side of the cliff, facing us, was a fairly steep sloping wall, and maybe the surface sands were sliding; certainly some mysterious friction was in progress on a vast scale to produce such startling loud booming. The noise was comparable to a deep pedal-note of an organ, or the siren of a ship heard, say, from a couple of cables distant. It continued for about two minutes and then ended as abruptly as it had begun.

The term "singing sands" seems hardly the most satisfactory one to describe a loud and single note, but it is too firmly established to cavil over, for singing sands are mentioned by quite early Chinese writers, and Marco Polo, who crossed the Great Gobi Desert in the thirteenth century, wrote: "Sometimes you shall hear the sound of musical instruments and still more commonly the sound of drums."

We bade adieu to hungry and shivering steppe borderlands, and, turning northward, struck into the body of the sands. The scene before us was magnificent. The sands became almost Alpine in architectural structure, towering mountainously above us, and from the summits we were rewarded with the most glorious panoramas of purest rose-red colour. This Uruq region of the central south must surely be the loftiest throughout all the great ocean of sands.

* Singular of Beduin.

Our camels climbed arduously the soft slopes, and, slithering knee-deep, made slow progress. No one remained mounted. Indeed, there were places where we had to dig footholds in the sands to enable our animals to climb, other places where we turned back to find an easier way. No horse could have negotiated these southern sands, even if brought here, and the waterless marches behind us, with many consecutive days of ten hours in the saddle, would have made the bringing impossible. A motor-car, too, would surely have charged these slopes in vain.

"The gift of God" – that is the illuminating name by which the Arab nomad knows the camel; and how great is his consideration for her! Time and time again I found myself the only member of our party in the saddle, the Arabs preferring to walk and so spare their mounts, running hither and thither to collect a juicy tuft of camelthorn with which to feed the hungry brutes as we marched along. In the deserts, halts are called, not in accordance with a European watch, but where Nature has, for the nonce, blessed the site with camel pastures. The great ungainly beasts, which you start by despising and learn greatly to admire, are the only means by which you move forward to success or back and out to safety. If camels perish in the remoter waterless wastes, their masters must perish with them.

Christmas Eve was to be a night of excitement and false alarm. We had arrived late in camp, camels had been hobbled and shooed off to the scant bushes, from behind some of which came the brisk noises of merry camp-fire parties. There was a sudden scream. To me it was like the hooting of an owl or the whining of some wild beast.

"*Gom! Gom!* – Raiders! Raiders!" shouted the excitable Beduin, leaping to their feet, their rifles at the ready; and my Arab servant came running across to me with my Winchester and ammunition. Our *rabias* (safe-escorts) of the Awamir and Karab tribes rushed out in different directions into the night, shouting – "We are alert! We are alert! We are So-and-so (giving their names) of such-and-such tribes. These are our party and are under our protection."*

---

* The night's vigil proved to have been unnecessary, for at dawn the tracks of a sand-wolf were traced near by; its whoop had been mistaken for the war-cry of raiders in the final act.

The object of this was to save us from raiders of their own particular tribes, if such they were, for these would then stay their hand. The cry, I gathered, is never abused: certainly in 1928 I had owed my life, during a journey through the south-eastern borderlands, to my Harsusi *rabia*, who saved us from ambush by members of his own tribe after these had already opened fire at short range.

Our camels were now played out. Their humps, plump and large at the outset, told a story; for the hump is the barometer of the camel's condition, and ours had fallen miserably away. To move onwards involved raising fresh camels, a contingency that had been foreseen, and Shaikh Salih sent ahead to search the Rashidi habitat. He and I had at the outset counted on the need of four relays, but in the event three proved sufficient.

Propitious rains (over great areas rain does not fall through-out the year) of last season in the sands of Dakaka had given rise to superior pastures, and to that area, therefore, the herds had this year gravitated. At the waterhole of Khor Dhahiyah we acquired a new caravan and pushed leisurely westward towards where our third caravan for the final northward dash across the sands was to assemble.

My companions scanned the sands for sign of friend or foe. "Look, sahib! that's So-and-so," my men said, pointing to a camel's foot impression that looked, to me, like any other. "See! she is gone with calf: look how deep are the impressions of her tracks!" And so, following these in the sands, we came up with the object of our quest.

The accuracy of their divination was fascinating. Reading sand-imprints recalled finger-print identifying in the West, except that it is far less laborious and slow, and not at all the technical job of a highly trained specialist. In fact, every Badu bred in these sands reads the sand-imprints with the readiest facility, for all creation goes unshod, except on an occasion when a Badu wears socks against extreme heat or cold – this being rare, because it is considered effeminate.

The sands are thus an open diary, and he who runs may read. Every one of my companions not only knew at a glance the foot impression of every man and every camel in my caravan, but claimed to know every one of his tribe and not a few of his enemies. No bird may alight, no wild beast or insect pass but needs must leave its history in the sands, and the record lasts until the next wind rises and obliterates it. To tell-tale sand-tracks a sand-fox and many snakes, hares, and lizards, which I added to my collection, owed their undoing, for their hiding-places were in vain.

Whenever, in future, we halted for the night, generally just before sunset, Hamad, my Murra *rabia*, would slink back over our tracks for a few miles with my telescope to ensure that we were not being tracked by an enemy, and return just after nightfall with the good news that camp-fires could now be safely lighted.

I picked up fragments of ostrich eggs, often in a semi-petrified condition, and members of my party had shot ostriches hereabouts in their youth, though these birds appear now to be extinct. So also the *rim* or white gazelle is becoming rare, though I saw horns lying about, while the common red gazelle and the larger edible lizards are inhabitants of the bordering steppe rather than of the sands, as is the antelope, specimens of which I shot, besides bringing home a young live one.

It is the antelope whose long, straight horns occasionally appear to be a single spear when she runs across your front, thus giving rise, as some suppose, to the ancient myth of the unicorn. This legendary guardian of chastity allowed none but virtuous maidens to approach it, when its anger turned to joy; and, singularly, to-day in these southern marches the only musical instrument known is a pipe made of antelope horn, which the Arab maiden plays on the joyful occasions of marriage and circumcision.

Of animal life in the sands, a small sand-coloured wolf is said to be met with in parts where subsoil water, however brackish, can be reached by pawing; a sand-coloured fox and a lynx – relatively non-drinking varieties – are commoner; and the hare, the most widespread mammal, is hunted by the Beduin's *salugi*** dog. Of birds I saw very few – bustards, sand-larks, sand-grouse, owls, and the most common, a black raven, while old eggs in a gigantic nest show that the Abyssinian tawny eagle comes on important visits.

---

* Familiar to British breeders as the Salukhi hound.

The full moon before the fast month of Ramadhan found us at the waterhole of Shanna, where my third, last, and much-reduced caravan (13 men and 5 pack animals) was to rendez-vous. One of our old camels was ailing, and there is only one way with a worn-out camel in the desert – namely, to kill and eat it. The law of Leviticus is also the law of Islam: flesh not lawfully slaughtered is sinful to eat; wherefore the hats went round, and 56 dollars, plus her earnings due from me, satisfied the owner of the almost blind 40-year-old Fatira. The beast was slaughtered, jointed, and divided into heaps after the Arabs had all had a good swig at the contents of her bladder – they had done the same to the antelope's bladder – and for the joints the Beduin now cast lots.

In the steppe, where stones availed, they would have grilled the carcass on a heap of heated stones with a fire beneath – the Stone Age manner, surely! Here as much as sufficed for a meal was boiled in brackish water, and the rest they allowed to remain uncooked, and so carried it exposed on their saddles, where all the cooking that it received was drying from the heat of the sun. These saddle-dainties the Beduin were to nibble with great relish in the marches ahead, and to declare to be very good. My own view, I confess, was one to be concealed!

The zero hour for the dash northward had arrived. Star sights and traverse-plotting showed my position on the 10th January, 1932, to be lat. 19° N., long 50° 45′ E. My objective, Qatar, on the Persian Gulf, was thus bearing slightly to the east of north, about 330 miles in a straight line across the mysterious sands. Two only of my thirteen Beduin – the Murras – claimed to have been over this line of desert before. I had rations left for but twenty-five days.

Clearly, no one could afford to fall ill. A hold-up for ten days, an insufficient rate of progress, a meeting with a party of raiders outnumbering us – any of these might spell disaster. Throughout my journey I was screened from any Arab encampments, that, for all I knew, might have been just over the skyline, the single exception being a tiny encampment of Murra, kinsmen of my guide, where an old man lay dying.

It was made up of one or two miserably small tents, roughly spun – doubtless by the womenfolk – of brown and white camel's hair; tent-pegs that once had been the horns of an antelope; a hammer and a leathern bucket or two – these perhaps typical of the belongings of poor nomadic folk, among whom wealth is counted, primarily, in the noble possessions of camel herds and firearms.

Marching north, the character of the desert sands changed; from the sweeping red landscapes of Dakaka we passed through the region of Suwahib, of lighter hue and characteristic parallel ridges in echelon formation; then the white ocean calms of the central sands, succeeded by a rolling swell of redder colour; and with these changing belts the desert flora changed too, the height above sea-level falling progressively.

Contrary to expectation, the great central sand-ocean was found to be not waterless. We dug down to water at quite shallow depths – a fathom and a half or so; but it was so brackish as to be almost undrinkable – not unlike Epsom-salt both in taste and in its effect on man and beast. There are places where even the camel cannot drink the water, though normally when pastures bring nomads to these parts their camels play the part of distillers, for they drink the water and their masters drink their milk.

The shallow waterholes of the southern sands are sometimes filled in, after water, to hinder a possible pursuer, but in the low, shallowing sands of the north, where patches of hard floor made their first appearance, the waterholes were regular wells, sometimes seventeen fathoms and more deep. They are rare and precious, too, apart from their sweeter contents, for great labour and skill have gone to their making. Both making and cleaning out, which must be done periodically, exact a toll of life, for the soft sides are prone to slip in and entomb the miners, and all that avails for revetment is the branches of dwarf sand-bushes.

Onwards through these great silent wastes my little party moved ever northwards, and my bones no longer ached at the daily demand of eight hours in the saddle. On setting out in the morning the Badu with his first foot forward would mumble some pious invocation – a constant reminder of the great uncertainty and insecurity which shadows him:

In the name of God the Merciful, the Compassionate,
Reliance is upon Thee.
There is none other and none equal to Thee.
In the name of God the Merciful.
Deliverance from the slinking devil;
And on Him we rely.

Their inborn philosophy of life is strictly fatalistic, holding that whatever comes to pass is according to a Divine and inscrutable Will. Their attitude to me, at first sullen and suspicious, changed with growing intimacy as the days passed, and they could be, with a few exceptions, cheerful and friendly companions. Under the stimulating effects of a juicy patch of camel pasture come upon unexpectedly, they would break forth into merry chanting, while around the night camp-fire they never tired of telling me stories from their entrancing folklore.

January 22nd brought the first of a series of sandstorms, and I passed many fitful nights. The hissing of the sand-laden wind, the rattling of pack-cordage, and icy cold feet – for the night temperature often fell to within five degrees of freezing point – made sleeping out-of-doors, without a roof over one's head, intolerable.

Eagerly one waited for the dawn. The wind then dropped, and camp-fires were the scene of huddled, shivering Beduin who now roused their camels that had been rounded up overnight for safety, and the wretched beasts shuffled off to graze and feel the warmth of the rising sun. For me the nights had tragic results, the sand-drifts having buried my instruments, making some of them of little further use.

But I was on the last lap. And though for many days sweeping, stinging, blinding winds enveloped us in a blanket of yellow mist, a fine morning came when, climbing the towering sand-hill of Nakhala, I beheld before me a silver streak of sea along the faraway sky-line. Success was in sight. Keeping the coast a day's march, by report, on our right hand, our northerly course carried us through quarry-like country abounding in fossil shells, the aneroid recording below sea-level readings.

And here we came upon an interesting discovery – a lake in this wilderness. For several miles we marched along its western shore. The Beduin, walking to the edge, brought away large chunks of rock salt that for a width of twenty feet lined its border. There along the water's edge, too, was a line of dead-white locusts, desiccated specimens of the large red variety which, collected and thrown alive on to the hot ash of the camp-fire, sizzles into one of the few delicacies of the Beduin. Wretched creatures, these locusts, for they seem to delight in swarming out from the thirsty desert in spring-time, only to take a suicidal plunge into the first water they come to.

Our lake behind us, we trekked on through bleak stony country, the haunt of owl and wolf, that proved to be the base of the Qatar peninsula. A Gulf *shamal* was blowing, but its attendant cold and drizzling rain were powerless to damp the enthusiasm of my poor companions on the eve of a rare pay-day. They chanted the water-chants which, alas! I should be hearing for the last time, and our thirsty camels pricked up their ears with eager knowingness. And so, at last, we came to the fort of Qatar's ruler standing bold and beckoning on the rim of the sea. The dim luxury of a bath and a square meal was at hand. I had lost a stone and a half in weight on my 650-mile camel journey, but the great south Arabian desert, hitherto a blank on our maps, had ceased to be an enigma and a reproach.

THE GREEK ALPHABET

Name	Letter		English equivalent
Alpha	A	α	a
Beta	B	β	b
Gamma	Γ	γ	hard g
Delta	Δ	δ	d
Epsilon	E	ε	short e (as in "egg")
Zeta	Z	ζ	z, dz
Eta	H	η	long e (as in "bee")
Theta	Θ	θ	th
Iota	I	ι	i
Kappa	K	κ	k or hard c
Lambda	Λ	λ	l
Mu	M	μ	m
Nu	N	ν	n
Xi	Ξ	ξ	x
Omicron	O	o	short o (as in "box")
Pi	Π	π	p
Rho	P	ρ	r
Sigma	Σ	σ, s	s
Tau	T	τ	t
Upsilon	Y	υ	u or y
Phi	Φ	φ	ph, f
Chi	X	χ	kh or hard ch
Psi	Ψ	ψ	ps
Omega	Ω	ω	long o (as in "dome")

THE INDIAN TRIBES OF NORTH AMERICA

The first settlers of America arrived there about 30,000 years ago. It was a time when the world's sea levels were so low that they were able to walk there, crossing from Russia to America over a land bridge in what is now the Bering Strait. From the Yukon the pioneers fanned out until, thousands of years later, they reached the tip of South America. Always they were lured on by game, in the vast shapes of the mastodon, the giant buffalo and the like. However, the big game died out about 8,000 BC either through over-hunting or global warming, causing the pioneers to diversify into the hunting of smaller game and into farming. Wherever groups of these nomads settled they adapted to whatever nature locally had to offer: in the Great Lakes they harvested wild rice; on the North Pacific Coast they came to depend on salmon-hunting; in the South they began to grow corn.

Originally the pioneers spoke with one single voice, but as they spread and changed their ways of life, they developed many different languages and identities. By 1492, when Columbus stumbled upon America, there were around 300 distinct aboriginal tribes in North America. Thinking he was in the East Indies, Columbus called the natives he met "Indians". The name, though inaccurate, stuck. Under the impact of war and diseases carried by the white newcomers, the population of the Indians went into freefall. Those who survived conflict and deprivation were shunted onto "reservations" until by the 1890s there were no free Indians left in North America.

Here are the 300 main tribes and sub-tribes, together with area of settlement. A number of tribes are remembered because consumer goods have been named after them, such as the (Jeep) Cherokee 4 × 4 and the Winnebago motor home.

Abitbi (Sub-Arctic)

Abnaki (Eastern Woodlands)

Accohannock (East Coast)

Achomawi/Atsugewi (Northwest Plateau)

Alabama (Southeast)

Aleut (Alaska)

Alsea (Northwest Coast)

Apache (Southwest)

Arapaho (Great Plains)

Arikara (Great Plains)

Assiniboin (Great Plains)

Atakapa (Southeast)

Atsina (Great Plains)

Attiwandaronk (Eastern Woodlands)

Bannock (Great Basin)

Beaver (Sub-Arctic)

Bella Coola (Northwest Coast)

Biloxi (Southeast)

Blackfoot (Great Plains)

Caddo (Great Plains)

Cahuilla (California)

Calusa (Southeast)

Caribou (Sub-Arctic)

Carrier (Sub-Arctic)

Catawba (Southeast)

Cayuse (Northwest Plateau)

Chemehuevi (Great Basin)

Cherokee (Southeast)

Cheyenne (Great Plains)

Chickasaw (Southeast)

Chicora (Southeast)

Chilcotin (Northwest Plateau)

Chinook (Northwest Coast)

Chipewyan (Sub-Arctic)

Chitimacha (Southeast)

Choctaw (Southeast)

Chumash (California)

Coahuiltec (Southwest)

Cocopa (Southwest)

Coeur d'Alene (Northwest Plateau)

Coharie (Eastern Woodlands/Southeast)

Comanche (Great Plains)

Conoy (East Coast)

Coos (Northwest Coast)

Costanoa (California)

Cowlitz (Northwest Coast)

Cree (Sub-Arctic)

Creek (Southeast)

Crow (Great Plains)

Delaware (East Coast)

Dieguno (California)

Dogrib (Sub-Arctic)

Edisto (Southeast)

Erie (Eastern Woodland/Great Lakes)

Eskimo (Sub-Arctic/Arctic Circle)

Esselen (California)

Eyak (Northwest Coast)

Flathead (Northwest Plateau)

Fox (Eastern Woodlands/Great Lakes)

Gabrielino (California)

Gitskan (Northwest Coast)

Goshute (Great Basin)

Gros Ventres of the Prairie (Great Plains)

Gros Ventres of the River (Great Plains)

Haida (Northwest Coast)

Haisla (Northwest Coast)

Halchidhoma (Southwest)

Han (Sub-Arctic)

Heiltsuk (Northwest Coast)

Hohokam (Southwest)

Hopi (Southwest)

Houma (Southeast)

Hupa (California)

Huron (Eastern Woodland/Great Lakes)

Illinois (Eastern Woodlands)

Ingalik (Alaska)

Inupiaq (Alaska)
Iowa (Great Plains)
Iroquois (including Mohawk, Oneida,
    Onondaga, Cayuga, Seneca) (Eastern
    Woodlands/Great Lakes)
Jemez (Southwest)
Kalapuya (Northwest Coast)
Kalispel (Northwest Plateau)
Kansa (Great Plains)
Karankawa (Great Plains)
Karok (California)
Kaw (Great Plains)
Keres (Southwest)
Kickapoo (Eastern Woodlands/Great Lakes)
Kiowa (Great Plains)
Kiowa-Apache (Great Plains)
Klamath (Northwest Plateau)
Klikitat (Northwest Plateau)
Koyukon (Alaska)
Kutchin (Sub-Arctic)
Kutenai (Northwest Plateau)
Kwakiutl (Northwest Coast)
Lillooet (Northwest Plateau)
Lipan (Great Plains)
Luiseno (California)
Mahican (East Coast)
Maidu (California)
Makah (Northwest Coast)
Malisit (East Coast)
Mandan (Great Plains)
Maricopa (Southwest)
Mascouten (East Coast)
Massachuset (East Coast)
Mattabesic (East Coast)
Menomini (Eastern Woodlands/Great Lakes)
Metoac (East Coast)
Miami (Eastern Woodlands)
Micmac (East Coast)
Minga (Eastern Woodlands)
Missouri (Great Plains)
Miwok (California)
Modoc (Great Plains)
Mohegan (East Coast)

Mojave (Southwest)
Mono (California)
Montagnais (Sub-Arctic)
Mountain (Sub-Arctic)
Nansemond (Southeast)
Narragansett (East Coast)
Naskapi (Sub-Arctic)
Natchez (Southeast)
Navajo (Southwest)
Nespelem (Northwest Plateau)
Netsilik (Arctic Circle)
Nez Percé (Great Plains)
Notka (Northwest Coast)
Ojibwa (Eastern Woodlands/Great Lakes)
Okanagan (Northwest Plateau)
Omaha (Great Plains)
Osage (Great Plains)
Oto (Great Plains)
Ottawa (Eastern Woodlands/Great Lakes)
Paiute (Great Basin)
Palus (Northwest Plateau)
Pamlico (East Coast)
Pamunkey (Southeast)
Papago (Southwest)
Patwin (California)
Pawnee (Great Plains)
Pennacook (East Coast)
Penobscot (East Coast)
Pequot (East Coast)
Pericu (California)
Pima (Southwest/Mexico)
Plains Cree (Great Plains)
Plains Objiwa (Great Plains)
Pomo (California)
Ponca (Great Plains)
Potawatomi (Eastern Woodlands)
Powahatan (East Coast)
Quapaw (Southeast)
Quileute (Northwest Coast)
Quinault (Northwest Coast)
Salinan (California)
Salish (Northwest Coast)
Santee Sioux (East Coast Great Plains)

Sarsi (Great Plains)

Sauk (Eastern Woodlands/Great Lakes)

Secotan (Eastern Woodlands)

Sekani (Sub-Arctic)

Seminole (Southeast)

Seri (Southwest)

Serrano (California)

Shasta (California)

Shawnee (Eastern Woodlands/Great Plains)

Shoshoni (Great Basin)

Shuswap (Northwest Plateau)

Skidi (Great Plains)

Slave (Sub-Arctic)

Sobaipuri (Southwest)

Spokan (Southwest)

Susquehanna (Eastern Woodlands)

Sutaio (Great Plains)

Taensa (Southeast)

Tagish (Sub-Arctic)

Tahltan (Sub-Arctic)

Tanaina (Alaska)

Tanoan Pueblos (Southwest)

Tekesta (Southeast)

Teton Sioux (Great Plains)

Thompson (Northwest Plateau)

Timucua (Southeast)

Tionontati (Eastern Woodlands)

Tlingit (Northwest Coast)

Tobacco (Eastern Woodlands/Great Lakes)

Tolowa (Northwest Coast)

Tonkawa (Great Plains)

Tsetsaut (Sub-Arctic)

Tsimshian (Northwest Coast)

Tubatulabal (California)

Tunica (Southeast)

Tuscarora (East Coast)

Tutchone (Sub-Arctic)

Tutelo (Eastern Woodlands)

Umatilla (Northwest Plateau)

Ute (Great Basin)

Walapai (Southwest)

Wampanoag (Eastern Woodlands)

Wappinger (Eastern Woodlands)

Washo (Great Basin)

Wenro (Eastern Woodlands/ Great Lakes)

Wind River Shoshoni (Great Basin)

Winnebago (Eastern Woodlands/ Great Lakes)

Wintun (California)

Wishram (Northwest Plateau)

Witchita (Great Plains)

Wiyot (California)

Yakima (Northwest Plateau)

Yakutat (Northwest Coast)

Yana (California)

Yankton Sioux (Eastern Woodlands/ Great Plains)

Yaqui (Southwest/Mexico)

Yavapai (Southwest)

Yellowknife (Sub-Arctic)

Yokuts (California)

Yuchi (Southwest)

Yuma (Southwest)

Yurok (California)

Zuni (Southwest)

THE TEN COMMANDMENTS

According to the Bible, the Ten Commandments were revealed to Moses on Mount Sinai by God's fingers etching them onto stone. The Ten Commandments maintained a prominent place in Judeo-Christian culture as a moral code. The first commandment is of particular importance because it is the foundation of "monotheism", the worship of one God rather than the many Gods.

1. I am the Lord thy God. Thou shalt have no other gods before me.
2. Thou shalt not make unto thee any graven image.
3. Thou shalt not take the name of the Lord thy God in vain.
4. Remember the sabbath day, to keep it holy.
5. Honour thy father and thy mother.
6. Thou shalt not kill.
7. Thou shalt not commit adultery.
8. Thou shalt not steal.
9. Thou shalt not bear false witness against thy neighbour.
10. Thou shalt not covet.

From the King James Bible.

STORY: "HUNTER QUATERMAIN'S STORY"
BY H. RIDER HAGGARD

A story by H. Rider Haggard featuring his famous fictional explorer and big-game hunter, Allan Quatermain, the man who found King Solomon's Mines.

Sir Henry Curtis, as everybody acquainted with him knows, is one of the most hospitable men on earth. It was in the course of the enjoyment of his hospitality at his place in Yorkshire the other day that I heard the hunting story which I am now about to transcribe. Many of those who read it will no doubt have heard some of the strange rumours that are flying about to the effect that Sir Henry Curtis and his friend Captain Good, R.N., recently found a vast treasure of diamonds out in the heart of Africa, supposed to have been hidden by the Egyptians, or King Solomon, or some other antique person. I first saw the matter alluded to in a paragraph in one of the society papers the day before I started for Yorkshire to pay my visit to Curtis, and arrived, needless to say, burning with curiosity; for there is something very fascinating to the mind in the idea of hidden treasure. When I reached the Hall, I at once asked Curtis about it, and he did not deny the truth of the story; but on my pressing him to tell it he would not, nor would Captain Good, who was also staying in the house.

"You would not believe me if I did," Sir Henry said, with one of the hearty laughs which seem to come right out of his great lungs. "You must wait till Hunter Quatermain comes; he will arrive here from Africa tonight, and I am not going to say a word about the matter, or Good either, until he turns up. Quatermain was with us all through; he has known about the business for years and years, and if it had not been for him we should not have been here today. I am going to meet him presently."

I could not get a word more out of him, nor could anybody else, though we were all dying of curiosity, especially some of the ladies. I shall never forget how they looked in the drawing-room before dinner when Captain Good produced a great rough diamond, weighing fifty carats or more, and told them that he had many larger than that. If ever I saw curiosity and envy printed on fair faces, I saw them then.

It was just at this moment that the door was opened, and Mr Allan Quatermain announced, whereupon Good put the diamond into his pocket, and sprang at a little man who limped shyly into the room, convoyed by Sir Henry Curtis himself.

"Here he is, Good, safe and sound," said Sir Henry, glee-fully. "Ladies and gentlemen, let me introduce you to one of the oldest hunters and the very best shot in Africa, who has killed more elephants and lions than any other man alive."

Everybody turned and stared politely at the curious-looking little lame man, and though his size was insignificant, he was quite worth staring at. He had short grizzled hair, which stood about an inch above his head like the bristles of a brush, gentle brown eyes that seemed to notice everything, and a withered face, tanned to the colour of mahogany from exposure to the weather. He spoke, too, when he returned Good's enthusiastic greeting, with a curious little accent, which made his speech noticeable.

It so happened that I sat next to Mr Allan Quatermain at dinner, and, of course, did my best to "draw" him; but he was not to be drawn. He admitted that he had recently been a long journey into the interior of Africa with Sir Henry Curtis and Captain Good, and that they had found treasure; then he politely turned the subject and began to ask me questions about England, where he had never been before – that is, since he came to years of discretion. Of course, I did not find this very interesting, and so cast about for some means to bring the conversation round again.

Now, we were dining in an oak-panelled vestibule, and on the wall opposite to me were fixed two gigantic elephant tusks, and under them a pair of buffalo horns, very rough and knotted, showing that they came off an old bull, and having the tip of one horn split and chipped. I noticed that Hunter Quatermain's eyes kept glancing at these trophies, and took an occasion to ask him if he knew anything about them.

"I ought to," he answered, with a little laugh; "the elephant to which those tusks belonged tore one of our party right in two about eighteen months ago, and as for the buffalo horns, they were nearly my death, and were the end of a servant of mine to whom I was much attached. I gave them to Sir Henry when he left Natal some months ago;" and Mr Quatermain sighed and turned to answer a question from the lady whom he had taken down to dinner, and who, needless to say, was also employed in trying to pump him about the diamonds.

Indeed, all around the table there was a simmer of scarcely suppressed excitement, which, when the servants had left the room, could no longer be restrained.

"Now, Mr Quatermain," said the lady next to him, "we have been kept in an agony of suspense by Sir Henry and Captain Good, who have persistently refused to tell us a word of this story about the hidden treasure till you came, and we simply can bear it no longer; so, please, begin at once."

"Yes," said everybody, "go on, please."

Hunter Quatermain glanced round the table apprehensively; he did not seem to appreciate finding himself the object of so much curiosity.

"Ladies and gentlemen," he said at last, with a shake of his grizzled head, "I am very sorry to disappoint you, but I cannot do it. It is this way. At the request of Sir Henry and Captain Good I have written down a true and plain account of King Solomon's Mines and how we found them, so you will soon all be able to learn all about that wonderful adventure for yourselves; but until then I will say nothing about it, not from any wish to disappoint your curiosity, or to make myself important, but simply because the whole story partakes so much of the marvellous, that I am afraid to tell it in a piecemeal, hasty fashion, for fear I should be set down as one of those common fellows of whom there are so many in my profession, who are not ashamed to narrate things they have not seen, and even to tell wonderful stories about wild animals they have never killed. And I think that my companions in adventure, Sir Henry Curtis and Captain Good, will bear me out in what I say."

"Yes, Quatermain, I think you are quite right," said Sir Henry. "Precisely the same considerations have forced Good and myself to hold our tongues. We did not wish to be bracketed with – well, with other famous travellers."

There was a murmur of disappointment at these announcements.

"I believe you are all hoaxing us," said the young lady next to Mr Quatermain, rather sharply.

"Believe me," answered the old hunter, with a quaint courtesy and a little bow of his grizzled head; "though I have lived all my life in the wilderness, and amongst savages, I have neither the heart, nor the want of manners, to wish to deceive one so lovely."

Whereat the young lady, who was pretty, looked appeased.

"This is very dreadful," I broke in. "We ask for bread and you give us a stone, Mr Quatermain. The least that you can do is to tell us the story of the tusks opposite and the buffalo horns underneath. We won't let you off with less."

"I am but a poor storyteller," put in the old hunter, "but if you will forgive my want of skill, I shall be happy to tell you, not the story of the tusks, for it is part of the history of our journey to King Solomon's Mines, but that of the buffalo horns beneath them, which is now ten years old."

"Bravo, Quatermain!" said Sir Henry. "We shall all be delighted. Fire away! Fill up your glass first."

The little man did as he was bid, took a sip of claret, and began:

About ten years ago I was hunting up in the far interior of Africa, at a place called Gatgarra, not a great way from the Chobe River. I had with me four native servants, namely, a driver and voorlooper, or leader who were natives of Matabeleland, a Hottentot called Hans, who had once been the slave of a Transvaal Boer, and a Zulu hunter, who for five years had accompanied me upon my trips, and whose name was Mashune. Now near Gatgarra I found a fine piece of healthy, park-like country, where the grass was very good, considering the time of year; and here I made a little camp or headquarter settlement, from whence I went on expeditions on all sides in search of game, especially elephant. My luck, however, was bad; I got but little ivory. I was therefore very glad when some natives brought me news that a large herd of elephants were feeding in a valley about thirty miles away. At first I thought of trekking down to the valley, waggon and all, but gave up the idea on hearing that it was infested with the deadly "tsetse" fly, which is certain death to all animals, except men, donkeys, and wild game. So I reluctantly determined to leave the waggon in the charge of the Matabele leader and driver, and to start on a trip into the thorn country, accompanied only by the Hottentot Hans, and Mashune.

Accordingly on the following morning we started, and on the evening of the next day reached the spot where the elephants were reported to be. But here again we were met by ill luck. That the elephants had been there was evident enough, for their spoor was plentiful, and so were other traces of their presence in the shape of mimosa trees torn out of the ground, and placed topsy-turvy on their flat crowns, in order to enable the great beasts to feed on their sweet roots; but the elephants themselves were conspicuous by their absence. They had elected to move on. This being so, there was only one thing to do, and that was to move after them, which we did, and a pretty hunt they led us. For a fortnight or more we dodged about after those elephants, coming up with them on two occasions, and a splendid herd they were – only, however, to lose them again. At length we came up with them a third time, and I managed to shoot one bull, and then they started off again, where it was useless to try to follow them. After this I gave it up in disgust, and we made the best of our way back to the camp, not in the sweetest of tempers, carrying the tusks of the elephant I had shot.

It was on the afternoon of the fifth day of our tramp that we reached the little koppie overlooking the spot where the waggon stood, and I confess that I climbed it with a pleasurable sense of home-coming, for his waggon is the hunter's home, as much as his house is that of a civilized person. I reached the top of the koppie, and looked in the direction where the friendly white tent of the waggon should be, but there was no waggon, only a black burnt plain stretching away far as the eye could reach. I rubbed my eyes, looked again, and made out on the spot of the camp, not my waggon, but some charred beams of wood. Half wild with grief and anxiety, followed by Hans and Mashune, I ran at full speed down the slope of the koppie, and across the space of plain below to the spring of water, where my camp had been. I was soon there, only to find that my suspicions were confirmed.

The waggon and all its contents, including my spare guns and ammunition, had been destroyed by a grass fire.

Now before I started, I had left orders with the driver to burn off the grass round the camp, in order to guard against accidents of this nature, and here was the reward of my folly: a very proper illustration of the necessity, especially where natives are concerned, of doing a thing one's self if one wants it done at all. Evidently the lazy rascals had not burnt round the waggon; most probably, indeed, they had themselves carelessly fired the tall and resinous tambouki grass near by; the wind had driven the flames on to the waggon tent, and there was quickly an end of the matter. As for the driver and leader, I know not what became of them: probably fearing my anger, they bolted, taking the oxen with them. I have never seen them from that hour to this.

I sat down on the black veldt by the spring, and gazed at the charred axles and disselboom of my waggon, and I can assure you, ladies and gentlemen, I felt inclined to weep. As for Mashune and Hans they cursed away vigorously, one in Zulu and the other in Dutch. Ours was a pretty position. We were nearly three hundred miles away from Bamangwato, the capital of Khama's country, which was the nearest spot where we could get any help, and our ammunition, spare guns, clothing, food, and everything else, were all totally destroyed. I had just what I stood in, which was a flannel shirt, a pair of "veldt-schoons", or shoes of raw hide, my eight-bore rifle, and a few cartridges. Hans and Mashune had also each a Martini rifle and some cartridges, not many. And it was with this equipment that we had to undertake a journey of three hundred miles through a desolate and almost uninhabited region. I can assure you that I have rarely been in a worse position, and I have been in some queer ones. However, these accidents are natural to a hunter's life, and the only thing to do was to make the best of them.

Accordingly, after passing a comfortless night by the remains of my waggon, we started next morning on our long journey towards civilization. Now if I were to set to work to tell you all the troubles and incidents of that dreadful journey I should keep you listening here till midnight; so I will, with your permission, pass on to the particular adventure of which the pair of buffalo horns opposite are a melancholy memento.

We had been travelling for about a month, living and getting along as best we could, when one evening we camped some forty miles from Bamangwato. By this time we were indeed in a melancholy plight, footsore, half starved, and utterly worn out; and, in addition, I was suffering from a sharp attack of fever, which half blinded me and made me as weak as a babe. Our ammunition, too, was exhausted; I had only one cartridge left for my eight-bore rifle, and Hans and Mashune, who were armed with Martini Henrys, had three between them. It was about an hour from sundown when we halted and lit a fire – for luckily we had still a few matches. It was a charming spot to camp, I remember. Just off the game track we were following was a little hollow, fringed about with flat-crowned mimosa trees, and at the bottom of the hollow, a spring of clear water welled up out of the earth, and formed a pool, round the edges of which grew an abundance of watercresses of an exactly similar kind to those which were handed round the table just now. Now we had no food of any kind left, having that morning devoured the last remains of a little oribe antelope, which I had shot two days previously. Accordingly Hans, who was a better shot than Mashune, took two of the three remaining Martini cartridges, and started out to see if he could not kill a buck for supper. I was too weak to go myself.

Meanwhile Mashune employed himself in dragging together some dead boughs from the mimosa trees to make a sort of "skerm", or shelter for us to sleep in, about forty yards from the edge of the pool of water. We had been greatly troubled with lions in the course of our long tramp, and only on the previous night had very nearly been attacked by them, which made me nervous, especially in my weak state. Just as we had finished the skerm, or rather something which did duty for one, Mashune and I heard a shot apparently fired about a mile away.

"Hark to it!" sung out Mashune in Zulu, more, I fancy, by way of keeping his spirits up than for any other reason – for he was a sort of black Mark Tapley, and very cheerful under difficulties. "Hark to the wonderful sound with which the 'Maboona' (the Boers) shook our fathers to the ground at the battle of the Blood River. We are hungry now, my father; our stomachs are small and withered up like a dried ox's paunch, but they will soon be full of good meat. Hans is a Hottentot, and an *umfagozan* (that is, a low fellow), but he shoots straight – ah! he certainly shoots straight. Be of a good heart, my father, there will soon be meat upon the fire, and we shall rise up men."

And so he went on talking nonsense till I told him to stop, because he made my head ache with his empty words.

Shortly after we heard the shot, the sun sank in his red splendour, and there fell upon earth and sky the great hush of the African wilderness. The lions were not up as yet, they would probably wait for the moon, and the birds and beasts were all at rest. I cannot describe the intensity of the quiet of the night: to me in my weak state, and fretting as I was over the non-return of the Hottentot Hans, it seemed almost ominous – as though Nature were brooding over some tragedy which was being enacted in her sight.

It was quiet – quiet as death, and lonely as the grave.

"Mashune," I said at last, "where is Hans? My heart is heavy for him."

"Nay, my father, I know not; mayhap he is weary, and sleeps, or mayhap he has lost his way."

"Mashune, art thou a boy to talk folly to me?" I answered. "Tell me, in all the years thou hast hunted by my side, didst thou ever know a Hottentot to lose his path or to sleep upon the way to camp?"

"Nay, Macumazahn," (that, ladies, is my native name, and means the man who "gets up by night," or who "is always awake") "I know not where he is."

But though we talked thus, we neither of us liked to hint at what was in both our minds, namely, that misfortune had overtaken the poor Hottentot.

"Mashune," I said at last, "go down to the water and bring me of those green herbs that grow there. I am hungered, and must eat something."

"Nay, my father; surely the ghosts are there; they come out of the water at the night, and sit upon the banks to dry themselves. An Isanusi[1] told it me."

Mashune was, I think, one of the bravest men I ever knew in the daytime, but he had a more than civilized dread of the supernatural.

"Must I go myself, thou fool?" I said, sternly.

"Nay, Macumazahn, if thy heart yearns for strange things like a sick woman, I go, even if the ghosts devour me."

And accordingly he went, and soon returned with a large bundle of watercresses, of which I ate greedily.

"Art thou not hungry?" I asked the great Zulu presently, as he sat eyeing me eating.

"Never was I hungrier, my father."

"Then eat," and I pointed to the watercresses.

"Nay, Macumazahn, I cannot eat those herbs."

"If thou dost not eat thou wilt starve: eat, Mashune."

He stared at the watercresses doubtfully for a while, and at last seized a handful and crammed them into his mouth, crying out as he did so, "Oh, why was I born that I should live to feed on green weeds like an ox? Surely if my mother could have known it she would have killed me when I was born!" and so he went on lamenting between each fistful of watercresses till all were finished, when he declared that he was full indeed of stuff, but it lay very cold on his stomach, "like snow upon a mountain". At any other time I should have laughed, for it must be admitted he had a ludicrous way of putting things. Zulus do not like green food.

Just after Mashune had finished his watercress, we heard the loud "woof! woof!" of a lion, who was evidently promenading much nearer to our little skerm than was pleasant. Indeed, on looking into the darkness and listening intently, I could hear his snoring breath, and catch the light of his great yellow eyes. We shouted loudly, and Mashune threw some sticks on the fire to frighten him, which apparently had the desired effect, for we saw no more of him for a while.

Just after we had had this fright from the lion, the moon rose in her fullest splendour, throwing a robe of silver light over all

1 *Isanusi.* witch-finder.

the earth. I have rarely seen a more beautiful moonrise. I remember that sitting in the skerm I could with ease read faint pencil notes in my pocketbook. As soon as the moon was up game began to trek down to the water just below us. I could, from where I sat, see all sorts of them passing along a little ridge that ran to our right, on their way to the drinking place. Indeed, one buck – a large eland – came within twenty yards of the skerm, and stood at gaze, staring at it suspiciously, his beautiful head and twisted horns standing out clearly against the sky. I had, I recollect, every mind to have a pull at him on the chance of providing ourselves with a good supply of beef; but remembering that we had but two cartridges left, and the extreme uncertainty of a shot by moonlight, I at length decided to refrain. The eland presently moved on to the water, and a minute or two afterwards there arose a great sound of splashing followed by the quick fall of galloping hoofs.

"What's that, Mashune?" I asked.

"That damn lion; buck smell him," replied the Zulu in English, of which he had a very superficial knowledge.

Scarcely were the words out of his mouth before we heard a sort of whine over the other side of the pool, which was instantly answered by a loud coughing roar close to us.

"By Jove!" I said, "there are two of them. They have lost the buck; we must look out they don't catch us." And again we made up the fire, and shouted, with the result that the lions moved off.

"Mashune," I said, "do you watch till the moon gets over that tree, when it will be the middle of the night. Then wake me. Watch well, now, or the lions will be picking those worthless bones of yours before you are three hours older. I must rest a little, or I shall die."

"Koos!" (chief), answered the Zulu. "Sleep, my father, sleep in peace; my eyes shall be open as the stars; and like the stars shall watch over you."

Although I was so weak, I could not at once follow his poetical advice. To begin with, my head ached with fever, and I was torn with anxiety as to the fate of the Hottentot Hans; and, indeed, as to our own fate, left with sore feet, empty stomachs, and two cartridges, to find our way to Bamangwato, forty miles off. Then the mere sensation of knowing that there are one or more hungry lions prowling round you somewhere in the dark is disquieting, however well one may be used to it, and, by keeping the attention on the stretch, tends to prevent one from sleeping. In addition to all these troubles, too, I was, I remember, seized with a dreadful longing for a pipe of tobacco, whereas, under the circumstances, I might as well have longed for the moon.

At last, however, I fell into an uneasy sleep as full of bad dreams as a prickly pear is of points, one of which, I recollect, was that I was setting my naked foot upon a cobra which rose upon its tail and hissed my name, "Macumazahn," into my ear. Indeed, the cobra hissed with such persistency that at last I roused myself.

"*Macumazahn, nanzia, nanzia!*" (there, there!) whispered Mashune's voice into my drowsy ears. Raising myself, I opened my eyes, and I saw Mashune kneeling by my side and pointing towards the water. Following the line of his outstretched hand, my eyes fell upon a sight that made me jump, old hunter as I was even in those days. About twenty paces from the little skerm was a large ant-heap, and on the summit of the ant-heap, her four feet rather close together, so as to find standing space, stood the massive form of a big lioness. Her head was towards the skerm, and in the bright moonlight I saw her lower it and lick her paws.

Mashune thrust the Martini rifle into my hands, whispering that it was loaded. I lifted it and covered the lioness, but found that even in that light I could not make out the foresight of the Martini. As it would be madness to fire without doing so, for the result would probably be that I should wound the lioness, if, indeed, I did not miss her altogether, I lowered the rifle; and, hastily tearing a fragment of paper from one of the leaves of my pocketbook, which I had been consulting just before I went to sleep, I proceeded to fix it on to the front sight. But all this took a little time, and before the paper was satisfactorily arranged, Mashune again gripped me by the arm, and pointed to a dark heap under the shade of a small mimosa tree which grew not more than ten paces from the skerm.

"Well, what is it?" I whispered; "I can see nothing."

"It is another lion," he answered.

"Nonsense! thy heart is dead with fear, thou seest double;" and I bent forward over the edge of the surrounding fence, and stared at the heap.

Even as I said the words, the dark mass rose and stalked out into the moonlight. It was a magnificent, black-maned lion, one of the largest I had ever seen. When he had gone two or three steps he caught sight of me, halted, and stood there gazing straight towards us; he was so close that I could see the firelight reflected in his wicked, greenish eyes.

"Shoot, shoot!" said Mashune. "The devil is coming – he is going to spring!"

I raised the rifle, and got the bit of paper on the foresight straight on to a little patch of white hair just where the throat is set into the chest and shoulders. As I did so, the lion glanced back over his shoulders, as, according to my experience, a lion nearly always does before he springs. Then he dropped his body a little, and I saw his big paws spread out upon the ground as he put his weight on them to gather purchase. In haste I pressed the trigger of the Martini, and not an instant too soon; for, as I did so, he was in the act of springing. The report of the rifle rang out sharp and clear on the intense silence of the night, and in another second the great brute had landed on his head within four feet of us, and rolling over and over towards us, was sending the bushes which composed our little fence flying with convulsive strokes of his great paws. We sprang out of the other side of the skerm, and he rolled on to it and into it and then right through the fire. Next he raised himself and sat upon his haunches like a great dog, and began to roar. Heavens! how he roared! I never heard anything like it before or since. He kept filling his lungs with air, and then emitting it in the most heart-shaking volumes of sound. Suddenly, in the middle of one of the loudest roars, he rolled over on to his side and lay still, and I knew that he was dead. A lion generally dies upon his side.

With a sigh of relief I looked up towards his mate upon the ant-heap. She was standing there apparently petrified with astonishment, looking over her shoulder, and lashing her tail; but to our intense joy, when the dying beast ceased roaring, she turned, and, with one enormous bound, vanished into the night.

Then we advanced cautiously towards the prostrate brute, Mashune droning an improvised Zulu song as he went, about how Macumazahn, the hunter of hunters, whose eyes are open by night as well as by day, put his hand down the lion's stomach when it came to devour him and pulled out his heart by the roots, etc., etc., by way of expressing his satisfaction, in his hyperbolical Zulu way, at the turn events had taken.

There was no need for caution; the lion was as dead as though he had already been stuffed with straw. The Martini bullet had entered within an inch of the white spot I had aimed at, and travelled right through him, passing out at the right buttock, near the root of the tail. The Martini has wonderful driving power, though the shock it gives to the system is, comparatively speaking, slight, owing to the smallness of the hole it makes. But fortunately the lion is an easy beast to kill.

I passed the rest of that night in a profound slumber, my head reposing upon the deceased lion's flank, a position that had. I thought, a beautiful touch of irony about it, though the smell of his singed hair was disagreeable. When I woke again the faint primrose lights of dawn were flushing in the eastern sky. For a moment I could not understand the chill sense of anxiety that lay like a lump of ice at my heart, till the feel and smell of the skin of the dead lion beneath my head recalled the circumstances in which we were placed. I rose, and eagerly looked round to see if I could discover any signs of Hans, who, if he had escaped accident, would surely return to us at dawn, but there were none. Then hope grew faint, and I felt that it was not well with the poor fellow. Setting Mashune to build up the fire I hastily removed the hide from the flank of the lion, which was indeed a splendid beast, and cutting off some lumps of flesh, we toasted and ate them greedily. Lions' flesh, strange as it may seem, is very good eating, and tastes more like veal than anything else.

By the time that we had finished our much-needed meal the sun was getting up, and after a drink of water and a wash at the pool, we started to try and find Hans leaving the dead lion to the tender mercies of the hyenas. Both Mashune and myself were, by constant practice, pretty good hands at tracking, and we had not much difficulty in following the Hottentot's spoor, faint as it was. We had gone on in this way for half-an-hour or so, and were, perhaps, a mile or more from the site of our camping-place, when we discovered the spoor of a solitary bull buffalo mixed up with the spoor of Hans, and were able from various indications, to make out that he had been tracking the buffalo. At length we reached a little glade in which there grew a stunted old mimosa thorn, with a peculiar and overhanging formation of root, under which a porcupine, or an ant-bear, or some such animal, had hollowed out a wide-lipped hole. About ten or fifteen paces from this thorn-tree there was a thick patch of bush.

"See, Macumazahn! see!" said Mashune, excitedly, as we drew near the thorn; "the buffalo has charged him. Look, here he stood to fire at him; see how firmly he planted his feet upon the earth; there is the mark of his crooked toe (Hans had one bent toe). Look! here the bull came like a boulder down the hill, his hoofs turning up the earth like a hoe. Hans had hit him: he bled as he came: there are the blood spots. It is all written down there, my father – there upon the earth."

"Yes," I said; "yes; but *where is Hans?*"

Even as I said it Mashune clutched my arm, and pointed to the stunted thorn just by us. Even now, gentlemen, it makes me feel sick when I think of what I saw.

For fixed in a stout fork of the tree some eight feet from the ground was Hans himself, or rather his dead body, evidently tossed there by the furious buffalo. One leg was twisted round the fork, probably in a dying convulsion. In the side, just beneath the ribs, was a great hole, from which the entrails protruded. But this was not all. The other leg hung down to within five feet of the ground. The skin and most of the flesh were gone from it. For a moment we stood aghast, and gazed at this horrifying sight. Then I understood what had happened. The buffalo, with that devilish cruelty which distinguishes the animal, after his enemy was dead, had stood underneath his body, and licked the flesh off the pendant leg with his file-like tongue. I had heard of such a thing before, but had always treated the stories as hunters' yarns; but I had no doubt about it now. Poor Hans' skeleton foot and ankle were an ample proof.

We stood aghast under the tree, and stared and stared at this awful sight, when suddenly our cogitations were interrupted in a painful manner. The thick bush about fifteen paces off burst asunder with a crashing sound, and uttering a series of ferocious pig-like grunts, the bull buffalo himself came charging out straight at us. Even as he came I saw the blood mark on his side where poor Hans' bullet had struck him, and also, as is often the case with particularly savage buffaloes, that his flanks had recently been terribly torn in an encounter with a lion.

On he came, his head well up (a buffalo does not generally lower his head till he does so to strike); those great black horns – as I look at them before me, gentlemen, I seem to see them come charging at me as I did ten years ago, silhouetted against the green bush behind; – on, on!

With a shout Mashune bolted off sideways towards the bush. I had instinctively lifted my eight-bore, which I had in my hand. It would have been useless to fire at the buffalo's head, for the dense horns must have turned the bullet; but as Mashune bolted, the bull slewed a little, with the momentary idea of following him, and as this gave me a ghost of a chance, I let drive my only cartridge at his shoulder. The bullet struck the shoulder-blade and smashed it up, and then travelled on under the skin into his flank; but it did not stop him, though for a second he staggered.

Throwing myself on to the ground with the energy of despair, I rolled under the shelter of the projecting root of the thorn, crushing myself as far into the mouth of the ant-bear hole as I could. In a single instant the buffalo was after me. Kneeling down on his uninjured knee – for one leg, that of which I had broken the shoulder, was swinging helplessly to and fro – he set to work to try and hook me out of the hole with his crooked horn. At first he struck at me furiously, and it was one of the blows against the base of the tree which splintered the tip of the horn in the way that you see. Then he grew more cunning, and pushing his head as far under the root as possible, made long semi-circular sweeps at me, grunting furiously and blowing saliva and hot steamy breath all over me. I was just out of reach of the horn, though every stroke, by widening the hole and making more room for his head, brought it closer to me, but every now and again I received heavy blows in the ribs from his muzzle. Feeling that I was being knocked silly, I made an effort and seizing his rough tongue, which was hanging from his jaws, I twisted it with all my force. The great brute bellowed with pain and fury, and jerked himself backwards so strongly, that he dragged me some inches further from the mouth of the hole, and again made a sweep at me, catching me this time round the shoulder-joint in the hook of his horn.

I felt that it was all up now, and began to holloa.

"He has got me!" I shouted in mortal terror. *"Gwasa, Mashune, gwasa!"* ("Stab, Mashune, stab!")

One hoist of the great head, and out of the hole I came like a periwinkle out of his shell. But even as I did so, I caught sight of Mashune's stalwart form advancing with his "bangwan," or broad stabbing assegai, raised above his head. In another quarter of a second I had fallen from the horn, and heard the blow of the spear, followed by the indescribable sound of steel shearing its way through flesh. I had fallen on my back, and, looking up. I saw that the gallant Mashune had driven the assegai a foot or more into the carcass of the buffalo, and was turning to fly.

Alas! it was too late. Bellowing madly, and spouting blood from mouth and nostrils, the devilish brute was on him, and had thrown him high like a feather, and then gored him twice as he lay. I struggled up with some wild idea of affording help, but before I had gone a step the buffalo gave one long sighing bellow, and rolled over dead by the side of his victim.

Mashune was still living, but a single glance at him told me that his hour had come. The buffalo's horn had driven a great hole in his right lung, and inflicted other injuries.

I knelt down beside him in the uttermost distress, and took his hand.

"Is he dead, Macumazahn?" he whispered. "My eyes are blind; I cannot see."

"Yes, he is dead."

"Did the black devil hurt thee, Macumazahn?"

"No, my poor fellow, I am not much hurt."

"Ow! I am glad."

Then came a long silence, broken only by the sound of the air whistling through the hole in his lung as he breathed.

"Macumazah, art thou there? I cannot feel thee."

"I am here, Mashune."

"I die, Macumazahn – the world flies round and round. I go – I go out into the dark! Surely, my father, at times in days to come – thou wilt think of Mashune, who stood by thy side – when thou killest elephants, as we used – as we used –"

They were his last words, his brave spirit passed with them. I dragged his body to the hole under the tree, and pushed it in, placing his broad assegai by him, according to the custom of his people, that he might not go defenceless on his long journey; and then, ladies – I am not ashamed to confess – I stood alone there before it, and wept like a woman.

First published in 1885 in *Good Cause*, 1885.

TWELVE BOOKS TO READ
BEFORE THE AGE OF TWELVE

Richard Adams, *Watership Down*, 1972.
Fiver and Hazel lead a band of rabbits to the sanctuary of Watership Down.

John Buchan, *The Thirty Nine Steps*, 1915.
On the eve of the First World War reluctant spy Richard Hannay saves Britain's military secrets from a German plot.

Susan Cooper, *The Dark is Rising*, 1973.
Supernatural thriller in which teenager Will Stanton is caught in eternal struggle between good and evil.

Stephen Crane, *The Red Badge of Courage*, 1895.
A young soldier fights through the horrors of the US Civil War.

H. Rider Haggard, *King Solomon's Mines*, 1895.
Allan Quatermain leads the search for a lost man in darkest Africa.

Willard Price, *Underwater Adventure*, 1954.
Teenagers Hal and Roger Hunt go down into the dangerous deep.

Arthur Ransom, *Swallows and Amazons*, 1930.
The Walker and Blackett children in wholesome sailing adventures in England's Lake District.

J.K. Rowling, *Harry Potter and the Deathly Hallows*, 2007.
The boy wizard takes on arch enemy Lord Voldermort in a dark and final round.

John Steinbeck, *Of Mice and Men*, 1937.
Two drifter friends in California during the Great Depression hope to earn enough for a plot of land of their own but the dream goes tragically wrong. A challenging, emotional read which is required reading in many schools worldwide.

J.R.R. Tolkien, *The Hobbit*, 1937.
Hobbit Bilbo Baggins quests for a share of the Dragon's treasure hoard.

Mark Twain, *The Adventures of Tom Sawyer*, 1876.
Orphan Tom Sawyer gets up to mischief on the Mississippi river.

T.H. White, *The Sword in the Stone*, 1938.
A boy befriends the magician Merlin and finds his destiny as King of the Britons.

UP TO SPEED

The German car designer Dr Frederick Porsche (it's properly pronounced 'poor-sher') created the ultimate humble family saloon, the VW Beetle – and his son, Ferry, conceived the ultimate sports car, the **Porsche 911 Carrera 2.7RS**. Most car buffs agree that this, built for just one year, 1972–3, is the most perfect of Porsches, with a lightweight shell and stiffer than usual suspension, plus a distinctive ducktail spoiler. *Top speed: 150 mph*

The world's fastest accelerating production car – it can get to 60 mph in 2.4 seconds – the **Bugatti Veyron 16.4** has a 7993cc W16 engine which produces so much heat that it needs no less than 10 radiators. The price is a cool £810,000 (US$1.2 million). And even if your dad can afford that he might erupt at the gas bill: it does a mere 5.82 miles to the gallon in the city. But wherever you're going you'll get there quickly: on the Ehra-Lessien test track the Veyron has reached 253.81 mph. *Top speed: 253.81 mph*

When the **Ford Mustang** was launched in 1964 it earned itself a niche in the record books as one of the fastest selling cars of all time: 418,000 were sold in the first year alone. The most muscular of these muscle cars were the finely tuned fastbacks built by Carroll Shelby, particularly the GT350 from 1965/6, which had up to 390bhp. *Top speed: 130 mph*

The **Aston Martin DB5** was driven by the coolest Bond (Sean Connery) in *Goldfinger* (1964). It was based on the Touring-styled 3.7 litre Aston DB4 and was hand built at Newport Pagnall, Britain. The Volante was the convertible version of the DB5. *Top speed: 140 mph*

When is a Ferrari not a Ferrari? When it's a **Ferrari Dino**

246 GTS. Named for Enzo Ferrari's son Dino, it was never badged by Ferrari with the prancing horse and is strictly speaking a marque of its own. But it's a Ferrari really. Styled by Pinanfarina, the great Italian coachbuilder, the Dino is beautiful to look at, while its 2418cc V-six engine produced 195bhp. It first hit the road in 1972. *Top speed: 148 mph*

The ultimate gentleman's motor from the 1950s, the **Bentley Continental R** managed to combine effortless speed with drawing room luxury: it was a four seater which could top 120 mph. The sweeping, elegant body was built by HJ Mulliner in London after a design based on research in an aircraft wind tunnel. A number of clever tricks, such as aluminium (instead of steel) bumpers, kept the bodyweight down. *Top speed: 128 mph*

Ford's answer to the Chevrolet Corvette, the **Thunderbird** was the automobile icon of the rock 'n' roll 50s. The 'T-bird' was a two-seater with rear-fins and a 4.8 Mercury V8 engine. The cost was a modest US$3000. Handling was appalling, but luckily US highways tend to be long and straight. After 1957 T-birds became flabbier and flabbier. By the 1970s they looked like any old saloon. *Top speed: 115 mph*

The **Koenigsegg CCX** is a super light carbon fibre/Kevlar supercar aimed at the US market, where it retails from US$540,000. The environmentally-friendly R version, which runs its supercharged V8 engine on biofuel, is reported to have reached a record-breaking speed of 261mph, and produced over 1000bhp. *Top speed: 261 mph (unofficial)*

Launched in 1955, the **French Citroen DS23** had a hy-draulic suspension system which allowed the ride height to be adjusted. The front wheel drive system gave exemplary hand-ling and the styling was so futuristic that people were reminded of flying saucers. Alas, it was cursed with a series of inadequate engines, including one based on a 1934 Traction-Avant. The best of the bad lot was the last-of-the-line fuel-injection 2.3 litre engine. *Top speed: 117 mph*

So admired for its long-bonnet design and curvy shaping that it has been exhibited in the Museum of Modern Art, the British **Jaguar E-Type 3.8** from the Swinging Sixties had power as well as good looks: it could reach 150 mph. Based on a Le Mans D-type racer, the Jag cost only £2000, considerably less than rivals such as the Aston Martin DB4. *Top Speed: 150 mph*

HOW TO MAKE A SIMPLE CANVAS CANOE

Boys who love boats will delight in making this serviceable canoe, for use on sheltered waters. It is 12 ft 6 in long, 2 ft 9 in wide, and has a depth of 12 in from gunwale to keel.

This canoe will safely carry one adult, or a total load of about 14 stone on a draught of water of about 6 in; it can be used safely on any smooth water, but will not do for ocean voyages.

Provided these instructions are carefully followed, any intelligent lad able to use ordinary tools can be certain of making a success of the job and building a very attractive and useful boat, light enough to be handled with ease and, if necessary, it could be carried on the car to the seaside or to a riverside camp.

To build this boat you will need a light and a heavy hammer, a keyhole saw, a small chisel, screwdriver, bradawl, pliers, small plane, carpenter's square, 2-ft rule, and a paint brush. Other tools could be used if you have a preference for them, but those mentioned are essential, although you probably already have them and know how to use them.

You must not forget that a space about 14 ft long and 6 ft or more in width will be needed for building the boat, but this could be an upstairs room if there is space enough to carry the boat downstairs when it is finished – otherwise use a room on the ground floor, and then take care to see that you could get the boat out of it either through the door or a window.

An ideal place for the job is in a small garage – but failing this the boat will have to be built out-of-doors under a temporary covering. Do not attempt to build in the open, because if it rains and soaks the wood you will not be able to carry on with the work until it has dried very thoroughly.

Almost any good wood can be used for the hull, but in the following list, the best woods for the purpose are mentioned. If you economise on the wood, do not attempt to do so with the canvas, the best is known as Egyptian Duck and can be had from a good linen draper's; alternatives are "twill" and "sail cloth" or awning canvas. You must remember that you are relying on the canvas to keep the water out of the boat, so it is most advisable to use a good quality material.

TIMBER

Keel. – Oak. 1 piece, 1 in thick, 2 in wide, 11 ft 6 in long.

Midship Frame. – Plywood. 1 piece, ⅝ in thick, 2 ft 9 ins wide, 15 in deep.

After Frame. – Plywood. 1 piece, ⅝ in thick, 2 ft 4 in wide, 15 in deep.

Stem and Stern. – Pine or Spruce, 1 in thick. 1 piece, 7 in wide, 32 in long.

Gunwales. – Pine or Spruce. 2 pieces, 1¼ in by ¼ in, 13 ft long.

Carlines. – Pine or Spruce, 1 in square. 1 piece, 6 ft 3 in long; 1 piece, 3 ft 9 in long.

Coamings. – Mahogany or Pine. 2 pieces each 2 ft 3 in long, 4 in deep, ⅜ in thick.

Fillets. – Deal. 2 pieces, 1½ in deep, ¾ in thick, 2 ft 9 ins long.

Planking. – Cedar or Pine. 18 pieces, 2 in wide, ⅛ in thick, 13 ft long. 1 piece, 6 in wide, ⅛ in thick, 12 ft 6 in long.

Deck Beams. – Pine. 3 pieces, 1 in. wide, ⅛ in thick. 2 ft 6 in long.

Ribs. – Ash or Oak, 1 in wide, ⅛ in thick. 6 pieces, 3 ft 7 in long; 5 pieces, 3 ft 2 in long.

Rubbing Strips. – Deal, 1 in wide "half round" section. 2 pieces, 13 ft long, 1 piece 16 ft long – or 2 pieces 8 ft long.

Floor Boards. – Deal. 2 pieces, 5 in wide, ½ in. thick, 4 ft long; 2 pieces, 2 in wide, ½ in thick, 2 ft long.

Seat Back. – Deal. 2 pieces, 5 in wide, ½ in thick, 12 in long.

Batten. – Deal. 1 piece, 1 in wide ½ in thick, 3 ft long.

Paddle Blades. – Pine. 2 pieces each ½ in thick, 8 in wide, 1 ft 3 in long.

Paddle Shaft. – Pine. 1 piece, 1½ in by 1¼ in, 6 ft long.

CANVAS. – 1 piece Egyptian Duck, 48 to 52 in wide, 4½ yards long for hull; 1 piece, 36 to 42 in wide, 4½ yards long, for deck.

COPPER NAILS. – 2 oz copper nails No. 16 gauge, ½ in long.

SCREWS. – 1 gross brass countersunk screws. Size, ½ in long, No. 4 gauge; 2 doz. assorted, 1 in to 3 in long.

TACKS. – 2 oz copper tacks, ⅜ in to ½ in long.

FINISHING. – 1 quart boiled linseed oil; 1 lb tin Red lead priming paint; 2 lb "outdoor" quality White paint – or other colour to choice.

You need not buy all the timber at once, but you make a start with the keel, stem and stern, the two plywood frames and the carlines, then when you have finished these pieces you can get the material for the ribs and planks, leaving the canvas, paddle and paint until the last.

First of all read through this article and study the working drawings, Fig. 1, and the other illustrations, to get a clear idea of what has to be done and just how the boat is built. This is much better than making a start without being clear about the whereabouts and purpose of all the other pieces.

This canoe has been specially designed so that any one without any knowledge of boat-building can make a good job of it, but although it may not be apparent, a great many important matters have been taken into account.

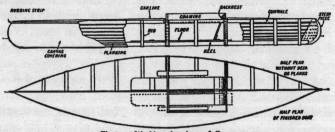

Fig. 1. —*Working drawings of Canoe.*

For example, when you have finished the boat you will want it to float level on the water, but it can only do this if the keel is perfectly straight and both sides of the boat are the same size and shape. To make sure your boat will be a good shape, what are called sawn ribs are used; another thing that has been done in this design is to use a "straight sheer" – that is, the top edge of the hull is level and does not curve upwards at the ends.

This arrangement makes it easier to keep the decks dry, because a simple timber – called a carline – which is fixed along the centre line of the deck, raises the canvas and gives it a slight "whale-back" effect which helps to keep it free of water.

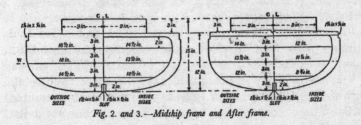

Fig. 2. and 3.—Midship frame and After frame.

Ordinary canvas canoes are generally made with a few "stringers," or thin strips fixed from end to end, and the canvas is simply stretched over them, but in this boat the hull is covered by planks which fit fairly closely, consequently the canvas is well supported and the boat will stand up to hard wear.

From this you will see that there is more in the design than meets the eye – and although a professional boat-builder would use other methods and special appliances, you can be sure of every satisfaction if you go ahead and make this canoe.

First take the large piece of plywood and draw on it in pencil all the lines shown on the diagram, Fig. 2, beginning by drawing the "waterline" W; then the vertical centre line C L, and afterwards put in all the other lines. Take great care to get them accurate and square with one another, then mark off the distances shown in inches on the diagram (Fig. 2), from each side of the centre line, then draw the curves as there shown, making them pass through the dimensioned points you have already marked off. Note that the left-hand half of the design gives the sizes for the outside curve, the right-hand half gives the sizes and shape of the part to be cut out.

Next, very carefully saw the outside to shape with a keyhole saw, and make the edge square and true with the plane and sandpaper. Then cut the notch at the bottom for the keel, and take the greatest care to keep the sides of the slot parallel with

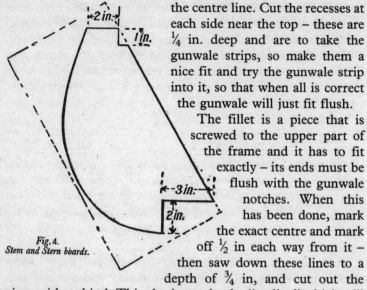

Fig. 4.
Stem and Stern boards.

the centre line. Cut the recesses at each side near the top – these are ¼ in. deep and are to take the gunwale strips, so make them a nice fit and try the gunwale strip into it, so that when all is correct the gunwale will just fit flush.

The fillet is a piece that is screwed to the upper part of the frame and it has to fit exactly – its ends must be flush with the gunwale notches. When this has been done, mark the exact centre and mark off ½ in each way from it – then saw down these lines to a depth of ¾ in, and cut out the piece with a chisel. This slot is to take the "carline" which will be fitted later on, but the slot must be cut now.

Next mark off a distance of ¾ in from the top – that is the slotted edge – and slope off this edge from the side of the slot to the outer ends at each side, then screw the fillet to the frame. Next bore holes about ¾ in diameter through the frame on the inner or waste side of the inside line on the frame, a hole at each top corner and one at the middle of the lower curve will be enough. Pass the saw-blade through one of the holes and cut with the keyhole saw from hole to hole, thus removing the middle part and leaving a nicely shaped frame. Round off the sawn edges on the inner part with a chisel or sandpaper.

Make the stern frame in the same way and also fix a fillet to it, but in this case use the dimensions given in Fig. 4; which drawing also shows the fillet fixed in place.

These pieces should be marked out on the 1 in. thick pieces of wood in a similar manner to the frame; the correct sizes and shapes are shown in Fig. 4 and both pieces should be exactly the same. When marked out, saw the two pieces to shape, then make all edges square and true with the sides, which you can do with the chisel. Test the edges for accuracy with the carpenter's

square and do your best
to make a very good job
of this part, because it is
most important.

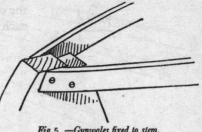

Fig. 5. —*Gunwales fixed to stem.*

The next stage is the
laying of the keel, that is
to say, the piece of wood,
for the keel must be cut
to exact length – 11 ft. 6
ins. – and the ends made
quite square. Then take the stem piece and screw in to the keel
with long thin brass screws. Screw the stern piece on to the
other end of the keel, and then inspect them to see that both are
in line and that the whole will lie perfectly flat on a level floor. If
they do not, then you must unscrew one of them and true up the
joint surfaces.

This may all seem rather elaborate and troublesome, but in
reality it is quite a simple piece of work.

Put the midship frame on the keel – set it at a distance of 6 ft
from the end of the notch in the stem piece, test it with the
square to see that it is level, then cut a little notch ½ in. deep in
the top of the keel so that the frame can drop into it and come
flush at the bottom. Place the side with the fillet on it facing the
stem, then screw the frame to the keel with a single screw.

Set the stern frame at a distance of 2 ft 3 in behind the
midship frame – with the fillet side facing towards the stern.
Then notch the keel and screw the frame in place.

Fig. 6. —*Frames, gunwales, keel and coamings in place.*

Take the two pieces of wood for the gunwales and taper one
end of each so that it will fit nicely against the stem (as shown in
Fig. 5), but do not fasten them with a screw, simply tie the two
pieces together with thick string, then while they are held in
place at the stem bend them around and push them into the
notches in the two frames. Tie them in with strong string
wrapped around both pieces so that they are held in their

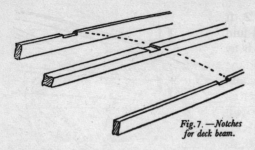

Fig. 7. —Notches
for deck beam.

notches, then bend the free ends inwards until they touch the stern piece. Tie them there and then mark on the gunwales the shape for the bevelling, remove the gunwales – bevel the ends as marked – then replace as before and screw the gunwales firmly to the stem, frames, and stern. Now you will be able to see the general shape of your boat and practically speaking the worst part of the job is over.

The coamings are simply the side pieces of the cockpit – or space in which you sit – and have only to be notched at the ends and screwed to the upright portions of the frames. The work will then appear as shown in Fig. 6, which you should study carefully to get a good idea of the position of the various parts. Now check the accuracy of this framework by looking along it from one end, when if all is as it should be, the keel will be straight, the stem and stern pieces will be upright, the two frames will bulge out equally on each side, and the two gunwale strips will each have the same curvature.

The carlines are straight pieces of 1 in. square wood, and are cut to fit exactly into the notches in the stem and stern pieces and the slots in the fillets. The under sides of the carlines should be notched if necessary, so that the top surface comes flush at each end.

Next, cut shallow recesses – $\frac{1}{8}$ in deep in the carlines and gunwales – for the deck beams; one is shown in Fig. 8, but there

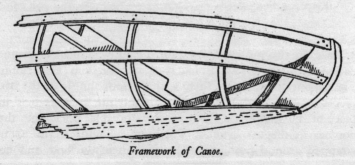

Framework of Canoe.

are two – spaced 2 ft apart – at the front, and one at the back, midway between the frame and the stern, making three in all.

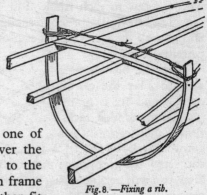

Fig. 8.—Fixing a rib.

All the ribs are fitted in the same way – first you soften them in hot or boiling water, then you take one of them, place it centrally over the keel and pull the ends up to the gunwale. Fit one over each frame first, and screw it in place, then fit one level with each deck beam. Take care to have each side the same shape, and screw them firmly to the keel and to the gunwale, as in Fig. 8; you will find it quite easy if you tie the ends together to prevent them springing apart. Bore holes through the ribs for the screws and see that they "bite" well.

Next take a plank 2 in wide and set it about 6 ins. down from the gunwale at the middle. Screw it to the frames, then curve the ends around, cut them on a bevel to fit against the stem and stern about $\frac{1}{2}$ in from the edge – and screw them firmly to the stem and stern pieces. Fit a similar plank on the opposite side.

Next you nail the plank to the ribs, clenching the nail on the inside (as in Fig. 9), after which you bend and fix the remainder of the ribs, bringing them *outside* the gunwales and keel but *inside* the planks. Nail all the ribs to these planks.

Then screw the 6 in plank to the keel so that it overlaps equally on each side, then taper the edges of these planks so that they come flush with the sides of the stem and stern pieces, then fix all the other planks by nailing or screwing to the ribs, and taper the edges by chiselling a little at each end so that they fit nicely.

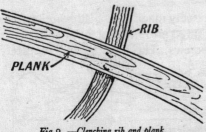

Fig 9.—Clenching rib and plank.

Make up the floorboards as in Fig. 10, and the back rest as in Fig. 11, then put the floorboards in the bottom of the boat and fix

with a screw to each frame. Rub down the
outside of the hull with rough sandpaper,
and give all the woodwork a coat of
priming paint.

Turn the boat bottom
upwards, lay the canvas
over it and fix it to the
hull with copper tacks,
draw the canvas into

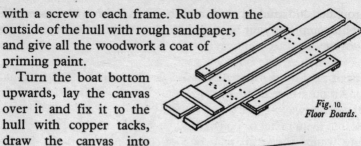

Fig. 10.
Floor Boards.

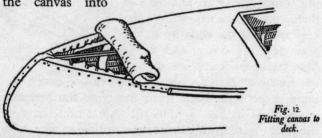

Fig. 12.
*Fitting canvas to
deck.*

place and tack it to the gunwale and all around the stem and
stern. Pull the canvas forcibly into place, but do not have

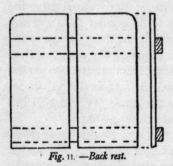

Fig. 11. —*Back rest.*

any puckers or creases. Cut off
any waste edges, then cover the
deck (as in Fig. 12), not forgetting
to fit a piece of batten each side of
the coaming to take the nails.

Then cover the joints along
the gunwale with the half round
wood; fix a piece to the keel with
screws, then bind up the ends
and screw them to the stem
and stern. Give all the canvas a
coat of linseed oil and later on when it is quite dry give several
coats of paint.

The paddles, Fig. 13, are easily made. The blades are sawn to
shape, taped at all edges, an fitted into slots cut in the ends of the
shaft, and are fixed with screws. The shaft should be nicely

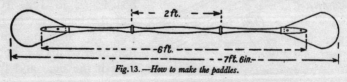

Fig. 13.—*How to make the paddles.*

rounded and sandpapered smooth. Then finish with linseed oil. This completes your boat, and it only remains to wish you "bon voyage."

Reprinted from *Modern Wonders for Boys*, circa 1938. Original instructions by E.W. Hobbs.

SOCCER WORLD CUP WINNERS

In 1930, the Federation Internationale de Football Association (FIFA, pronounced "fee-fah") held soccer's first World Cup tournament in Montevideo, Uruguay The need for an International event for the main football nations of the world was due largely to the Olympic games' restrictions against professional athletes. Since 1930 the World Cup has been held every four years, excepting the period of the Second World War.

Year	Host Country	Winner	Score
1930	Uruguay	Uruguay	Uruguay 4–2 Argentina
1934	Italy	Italy	Italy 2–1 Czechoslovakia
1938	France	Italy	Italy 4–2 Hungary
1942	not held		
1946	not held		
1950	Brazil	Uruguay	Uruguay 2–1 Brazil
1954	Switzerland	West Germany	West Germany 3–2 Hungary
1958	Sweden	Brazil	Brazil 5–2 Sweden
1962	Chile	Brazil	Brazil 3–1 Czechoslovakia
1966	England	England	England 4–2 West Germany
1970	Mexico	Brazil	Brazil 4–1 Italy
1974	West Germany	West Germany	West Germany 2–1 Holland
1978	Argentina	Argentina	Argentina 3–1 Holland
1982	Spain	Italy	Italy 3–1 West Germany
1986	Mexico	Argentina	Argentina 3–2 West Germany
1990	Italy	Germany	Germany 1–0 Argentina

1994	US	Brazil	Brazil 3–2 Italy
1998	France	France	France 3–0 Brazil
2002	Japan/S. Korea	Brazil	Brazil 2–0 Germany
2006	Germany	Italy	Italy 1–1 (5–3) France

2010 S. Af.

Brazil - 5x's
Italy - 4 xs
Argentina - 2x's

GREAT SPEECHES III

"I Have a Dream"
by Martin Luther King Jnr

Here is an excerpt from the famous speech made by the Reverend Martin Luther King delivered from the steps of the Lincoln Memorial, Washington DC, on 28 August 1963. The speech helped to galvanize the American conscience and bring an end to legal racial discrimination. Reverend King was later awarded the Nobel Peace Prize.

I am not unmindful that some of you have come here out of great trials and tribulations. Some of you have come fresh from narrow jail cells. Some of you have come from areas where your quest for freedom left you battered by the storms of persecution and staggered by the winds of police brutality. You have been the veterans of creative suffering. Continue to work with the faith that unearned suffering is redemptive.

Go back to Mississippi, go back to Alabama, go back to South Carolina, go back to Georgia, go back to Louisiana, go back to the slums and ghettos of our modern cities, knowing that somehow this situation can and will be changed. Let us not wallow in the valley of despair.

I say to you today, my friends, that in spite of the difficulties and frustrations of the moment I still have a dream. It is a dream deeply rooted in the American dream.

I have a dream that one day this nation will rise up and live out the true meaning of its creed: "We hold these truths to be self-evident; that all men are created equal."

I have a dream that one day on the red hills of Georgia the sons of former slaves and the sons of former slaveowners will be able to sit down together at the table of brotherhood.

I have a dream that one day even the state of Mississippi, a desert state sweltering with the heat of injustice and oppression, will be transformed into an oasis of freedom and justice.

I have a dream that my four little children will one day live in a nation where they will not be judged by the colour of their skin but by the content of their character.

I have a dream today.

I have a dream that one day the state of Alabama, whose governor's lips are presently dripping with the words of interposition and nullification, will be transformed into a situation where little black boys and black girls will be able to join hand with little white boys and white girls and walk together as sisters and brothers.

I have a dream today.

I have a dream that one day every valley shall be exalted, every hill and mountain shall be made low, the rough places will be made plains, and the crooked places will be made straight, and the glory of the Lord shall be revealed, and all flesh shall see it together.

This is our hope. This is the faith with which I return to the South. With this faith we will be able to hew out of the mountain of despair a stone of hope. With this faith we will be able to transform the jangling discords of our nation into a beautiful symphony of brotherhood. With this faith we will be able to work together, to pray together, to struggle together, to go to jail together, to stand up for freedom together, knowing that we will be free one day.

This will be the day when all of God's children will be able to sing with new meaning "My country 'tis of thee, sweet land of liberty, of thee I sing. Land where my fathers died, land of the pilgrim's pride, from every mountainside, let freedom ring."

And if America is to be a great nation this must become true. So let freedom ring from the prodigious hilltops of New Hampshire. Let freedom ring from the mighty mountains of New York. Let freedom ring from the heightening Alleghenies of Pennsylvania!

Let freedom ring from the snowcapped Rockies of Colorado!

Let freedom ring from the curvaceous peaks of California!

But not only that; let freedom ring from Stone Mountain of Georgia!

Let freedom ring from Lookout Mountain of Tennessee!

Let freedom ring from every hill and mole hill of Mississippi. From every mountainside, let freedom ring.

When we let freedom ring, when we let it ring from every village and every hamlet, from every state and every city, we will be able to speed up that day when all of God's children, black men and white men, Jews and Gentiles, Protestants and Catholics, will be able to join hands and sing in the words of the old Negro spiritual, "Free at last! free at last! thank God almighty, we are free at last!"

TIMELINE OF WORLD HISTORY

KEY DATES	HISTORY, POLITICS, WAR	RELIGION, SCIENCE, CULTURE	SOCIAL LIFE
9000 BC			Forming begins in Near East.
c. 3500 BC	Sumerian city-states founded.	Invention of writing, Sumer.	
c. 3000	Canaanites settle Syria. Minoans establish civilisation in Crete.	Bronze produced in Sumer.	
2780	Old Kingdom founded in Egypt.	Building of the Step Pyramid at Saqqara.	
2300			Wheeled carts in use in Europe.
2000	Aryans from Caucasian steppes conquer Indus Valley.	*Epic of Gilgamesh* written down.	Oil lamps in Middle East.
1792	Babylonian empire of Hammurabi (until 1750).		Code of Hammurabi provides first legal system.
1700		Use of iron by Hittites, Turkey. Minoan palaces built.	

KEY DATES	HISTORY, POLITICS, WAR	RELIGION, SCIENCE, CULTURE	SOCIAL LIFE
1600	Shang Dynasty founded in China.		
1560	New Kingdom founded in Egypt.		
1500		Building of Stonehenge, England.	
1360		Monotheistic worship of Aton, Egypt.	
1347		Tutankhamun reintroduces Egyptian polytheism.	
1194–1184	Trojan War		
1116	Tiglath-pileser, founder of Assyrian empire, born (d. 1077).		
1000	Accession of David to throne of Judah and Israel. Beginnings of Kush civilization in E. Africa.		
800		*Iliad* and *Odyssey* written by Homer. First recorded music, Sumer.	Iron utensils in use.
776			First recorded Olympic Games.
753	Rome founded.		
701	Sennacherib of Assyria besieges Jerusalem.		Iron weapons in Central Europe.
600		Nebuchadnezzar II builds "Hanging Gardens" of Babylon.	
551		Confucius born.	
546	Persian empire founded by Cyrus.		

KEY DATES	HISTORY, POLITICS, WAR	RELIGION, SCIENCE, CULTURE	SOCIAL LIFE
534		Buddha begins teaching.	
500	Olmecs establish civilization in Mexico. Hinduism consolidated in N. India by Aryans.	Theseum erected, Athens.	
449	Greeks defeat Persions at Salamis.		Celts settle Britain. Population of Greece reaches 3 million (inc 1 million slaves).
432	Peloponnesian War (until 404); Sparta defeats Athens.	Zenith of Greek culture, led by the democratic Athens of Pericles.	
430			Plague in Athens.
399		Socrates executed, Athens.	
336	Reign of Alexander the Great (until 323).		First Roman coins.
323		Euclid's *Elements*.	
264	First Punic War between Rome and Carthage (until 241).		
215			Great Wall of China.
206			Han dynasty in China institutes civil service examinations.
202	Scipio Africanus defeats Hannibal at Zuma, ending Second Punic War (begun 219).		
149–146	Third Punic War ends with destruction of Carthage. Greece annexed by Rome.		

KEY DATES	HISTORY, POLITICS, WAR	RELIGION, SCIENCE, CULTURE	SOCIAL LIFE
71	Slave revolts of Spartacus ended by Pompey.		
58	Julius Caesar conquers Gaul.		
48	Caesar defeats Pompey to become dictator of Rome.		
44	Julius Caesar assassinated.		
43	Roman colonization of Britain.		
30	Egypt annexed by Rome.		
4 BC	Jesus Christ thought to have been born.		
0			
AD 30		Christ executed in Judaea.	
64	Fire of Rome.	First persecution of Christians.	
70	Temple of Jerusalem destroyed by Romans.		
74			Silk Road opened between China and Rome.
79	Eruption of Vesuvius; Pompeii buried.		
c. 100	Roman Empire (under Tragan) reaches greatest extent.		
220	Han dynasty collapses in China.		
380		Christianity becomes state religion of Rome.	

KEY DATES	HISTORY, POLITICS, WAR	RELIGION, SCIENCE, CULTURE	SOCIAL LIFE
c. 400	Mexican civilization in golden age.		
410	Visigoths sack Rome.		
419	Saxons, Angles, Jutes colonize Britain.		
431		St Patrick begins mission to Ireland.	
452			Venice founded.
476	End of Western Roman Empire.		
529		Benedict of Nuria draws up rules for monastic life.	
553	Narses annexes Rome for Byzantine.		
570		Muhammad born.	
600	Sasanid (Persian) Empire of height.	Books printed in China by Buddhist monks.	
601		St Augustine becomes first Archbishop of Canterbury.	
604		Shotoko Taishi Code requires veneration of Buddha in Japan.	
637	Jerusalem captured by Muhammadans.		
650	Bosnia occupied by Croats and Serbs.		
664	Synod of Whitby; England adopts Roman Catholicism.		Easter eggs used by Christians.
	Kingdom of Ghana founded, Africa.		

KEY DATES	HISTORY, POLITICS, WAR	RELIGION, SCIENCE, CULTURE	SOCIAL LIFE
732	Franks halt Arab invasion of Europe at Tours.		Beginning of feudalism in Europe. Beds become fashionable in parts of W. Europe.
771	Charlemagne becomes sole ruler of Frankish kingdom.		
787	First Viking raid on Britain.		
814		Doge's palace, Venice, begun.	
845			Paper money in China causes inflation.
878	Alfred defeats Danes at Eddington.		
885	Vikings besiege Paris.		
c. 900	Viking raids destroy golden age of Irish Celtic civilization.		
982	Eric the Red establishes Viking colonies in Greenland.		Cane sugar arrives in W. Europe.
1066	Normans invade Britain.		Chinese under Sung dynasty establish iron and steel manufactories in esp. Kaifeng. Use of gunpowder wide-spread in China.
1085	Alfonso VI takes Toledo from Arabs.		
c. 1090			Water-powered clock invented, China.
1093	Malcolm of Scotland killed invading England.		

KEY DATES	HISTORY, POLITICS, WAR	RELIGION, SCIENCE, CULTURE	SOCIAL LIFE
1096	First Christian Crusade to Holy Land.		
1128	Khmers of Cambodia expand into Vietnam.		
1135	Stephen of Boulogne becomes King of England; civil war follows with supporters of Matilda, daughter of Henry I.		
1163		Notre Dame built, Paris.	
1167		Oxford University founded.	
1170	Thomas à Becket, Archbishop of Canterbury murdered.	Chrétien de Troyes' courtly love romance, *Lancelot*.	Glass windows in English houses.
1187	Mohammed of Ghor conquers Punjab. Saladin takes Jerusalem.		
1189	Massacre of Jews at coronation of King Richard I, England.		
1194		Gothic Cathedral at Chartres.	
1215	King John seals Magna Carta.		"St George's Day" becomes national holiday, England. Crusaders bring leprosy to Europe.
1237	Mongols conquer Russia.		
1248		Alhambra palace, Spain.	
1271	Marco Polo travels to China.		Glass mirror invented.

KEY DATES	HISTORY, POLITICS, WAR	RELIGION, SCIENCE, CULTURE	SOCIAL LIFE
1272	Kublai Khan conquers Sung of China.		
1290	Osman founds Ottoman Turkish Empire.		
1306	Philip IV expels Jews from France.		
1314	Scots under Robert Bruce defeat English at Bannockbum.		
1321		Dante writes *Divine Comedy*.	
1328	Ivan I makes Moscow capital.		
1337	Beginning of Hundred Years War between England and France.		
1346	Battle of Crécy; French defeated by English longbow.		
1347			Black Death pandemic in Europe; fifth of population dies.
1364		Aztecs build Tenochtitlan.	
1365	Charles V crowned King of Burgundy.		
1368	Ming dynasty expels Mongols, China.		
1381	Peasants Revolt, England.		
1399	Tamerlane's Mongols sack Delhi.		

KEY DATES	HISTORY, POLITICS, WAR	RELIGION, SCIENCE, CULTURE	SOCIAL LIFE
c. 1400	All Europe Christian. In N. Italy Renaissance begins. Tea-drinking introduced in Japan.		
1414	Medici become bankers to papacy.		
1415	Henry V defeats French at Agincourt.		
1429	Jean of Arc raises siege of Orleans.		
1453	Fall of Constantinople to Turks; end of East Roman (Byzantine) Empire.		
1456		Paolo Uccello paints *Battle of San Romano* – introduction of scientific perspective.	
1467			Scots prohibit golf and "fute-ball".
1474		William Caxton prints first book in English.	
1479	Castile and Aragon united under Ferdinand and Isabella.		
1484		Botticelli paints *Birth of Venus*.	
1487		Aztecs dedicate temple of sun god, Tenochtitlan, with sacrifice of 24,000 captives.	

KEY DATES	HISTORY, POLITICS, WAR	RELIGION, SCIENCE, CULTURE	SOCIAL LIFE
1492	Columbus lands on Watling Island, Bahamas. Spanish conquer Granada, last Moorish state in Spain.		
1497	Cabot lands in Canada.		
1500			First recorded Caesarean operation, Switzerland.
1505	Ivan the Great of Russia dies, having ended Mongol "Golden Horde" influence in Muscovy (Moscow).		
1508		Michelangelo begins painting ceiling of Sistine Chapel, Rome (until 1512).	
1512		Copernicus' *Commentariolus* declares that Earth moves around Sun.	
1514	Peasant's Revolt, Hungary.		
1517	Magellan embarks on first circumnavigation of globe (one ship successful, returning 1522).	Martin Luther posts 95 Theses on door of Wittenberg Church: Protestantism founded.	
1519	Hernando Cortés enters Mexico	Leonardo da Vinci dies.	Hops introduced into England.
1527	Sack of Rome by imperial troops of Charles V.		

KEY DATES	HISTORY, POLITICS, WAR	RELIGION, SCIENCE, CULTURE	SOCIAL LIFE
1529	Turks reach gates of Vienna.		
1531	Henry VIII becomes Supreme Head of Church in England: Reformation begins in England.		
1534	John of Leiden founds commutarian state of Anabaptists in Westphalia.	Jesuit Order begun by Ignatius Loyola.	
1542	Portuguese become first Westerners to reach Japan.		
1543	Spanish Inquisition burns first Protestants.		First records of cricket.
1558	Elizabeth I accedes to throne of England.		
1562	John Hawkins begins slave trade between Africa and West Indies.		
1565	Spanish colonize Florida.		Tobacco introduced into England.
1569			First public lottery in England.
1571	Christian alliance breaks Turkish sea-power at Lepanto.		
1582	English establish colony in Newfoundland.		Forks appear at French court.
1586	Spanish Armada leaves for England; defeated in Channel, scattered by storms.		
1587	Mary, Queen of Scots executed.		

KEY DATES	HISTORY, POLITICS, WAR	RELIGION, SCIENCE, CULTURE	SOCIAL LIFE
1598		Invention of first knitting machine.	
1590		Shakespeare's *Henry VI*, parts 2 and 3 completed.	Water closets installed at Queen's Palace, Richmond.
1596	English sack Cadiz.		
1603	Elizabeth I dies; succeeded by James VI of Scotland as James I of England and Ireland.		
1605	Catholic Gunpowder Plot to blow up Parliament and James I.		
1611		Authorized Version of Bible ("King James Bible").	
1618	Beginning of religious Thirty Years War in Central Europe.		
1620	Pilgrim Fathers reach New England.		
1627	Dutch Republic pre-eminent mercantile nation of world.	Rembrandt paints *The Money-Changer*.	
1637		Descartes, *Discourse on Method*.	
1642	English Civil War (until 1649); ends in execution of Charles I and establishment of republic under Cromwell.		

KEY DATES	HISTORY, POLITICS, WAR	RELIGION, SCIENCE, CULTURE	SOCIAL LIFE
1643	Louis XIV succeeds to throne of France. Reigns until 1715, the last of the great Renaissance despots.		
1660	Restoration of monarchy in England.		
1661			Famine in India.
1665		Newton discovers gravity.	Great Plague in London.
1666			Great Fire of London.
1682	French court moves to Versailles.		
1683	Turks besiege Vienna.		
1694	Bank of England founded.		
1701	Captain Kidd, pirate, executed.		
1707	Aurangzib, last great Mughal emperor of India dies; anarchy ensues.		
1739	Persians sack Delhi.		
1755			Lisbon earthquake kills 30,000.
1756	British soldiers murdered by Nawab in the "Black Hole of Calcutta".		
1770	James Cook discovers Botany Bay, Australia.		
1775	American Revolution (until 1783).	James Watt perfects steam engine.	

KEY DATES	HISTORY, POLITICS, WAR	RELIGION, SCIENCE, CULTURE	SOCIAL LIFE
1776	Thomas Jefferson drafts Declaration of Independence, America.	Adam Smith, *An Inquiry into the Nature and Causes of the Wealth of Nations.*	
1779			First outbreaks of "machine-wrecking" in England.
1783	Britain recognizes independence of USA. Slave trade to New World at peak.	Montgolfier brothers make first balloon flight, France.	
1786		Mozart writes opera *Marriage of Figaro*	Internal gas lighting in England.
1789–1791	French Revolution.	First steam-powered cotton-mill, Manchester.	
1793	Napoleonic Wars between France and England (until 1815).		France introduces compulsory schooling from age 6.
1794	Paris Commune abolished.		
1798	French capture Rome, Naples and Egypt.		
1799	George Washington dies.		
1800	US capital established at Washington DC.	Alessandro Volta constructs first electrical battery.	Population of New York reaches 65,000.
1803	"Louisiana" (most of the American West) bought by US from France.		
1805	Nelson defeats combined French and Spanish fleet at Trafalgar. Napoleon victorious over Austro-Russian army at Austerlitz.		

KEY DATES	HISTORY, POLITICS, WAR	RELIGION, SCIENCE, CULTURE	SOCIAL LIFE
1812	Napoleon enters Moscow but forced to retreat (only 10,000 troops of initial 500,000 survive campaign). US declares war on Britain.		"Luddism" at peak. Waltz popular.
1813	Mexico declares independence from Spain. Bolivar becomes dictator of Venezuela.	Jane Austen writes *Pride and Prejudice*.	
1814	Peace between US and Britain.	George Stephenson constructs first locomotive.	
1815	Wellington defeats Napoleon at Waterloo.		
1818		First steamship crossing of Atlantic.	
1819	Army attacks reform marchers at "Peterloo", Manchester.		
1829	Greece freed from Turkish rule; Ottoman Empire in decline.		
1831			Cholera pandemic sweeps much of Europe. Horse-drawn buses, already established in Europe, appear in New York.
1836	Dutch Boers make "Great Trek" to found Orange Free State and others. Battle of the Alamo; in aftermath Texas wins independence from Mexico.		Chartism, the first working-class political organization in Britain, seeks universal suffrage.
1838	Coronation of Queen Victoria.		

KEY DATES	HISTORY, POLITICS, WAR	RELIGION, SCIENCE, CULTURE	SOCIAL LIFE
1839			Baseball invented by Abner Doubleday.
1845		Engels, *The Condition of the Working Class in England.*	Irish potato famine.
1847	First California gold rush.		
1848	Worker uprisings throughout Europe.	Marx and Engels, *The Communist Manifesto.*	
1856	Dr Livingstone becomes first white to see Victoria Falls, Africa.		
1857–1858	Indian Mutiny.		
1859	Construction of Suez Canal begins.	Darwin, *Origin of Species.*	
1860	Garibaldi liberates Sicily from Bourbons.		
1861	Serfs emancipated, Russia. American Civil War begins as proslavery Southern states fight to secede from Union.		
1864	Massacre of Cheyenne at Sand Creek. In American Civil War, Sherman marches through Georgia and defeats Confederates at Atlanta.		
1865	Confederates surrender at Appomattox. President Lincoln assassinated.		Ku Klux Klan established.
1867		Zola, *Thérèse Raquin.*	
1870	Franco-Prussian War (until 1871).		
1871	Paris Commune is suppressed after 2 months. Italy unified.		FA Cup founded.

KEY DATES	HISTORY, POLITICS, WAR	RELIGION, SCIENCE, CULTURE	SOCIAL LIFE
1876	Custer and 7th Cavalry defeated by Sioux at Little Big Horn.	Alexander Graham Bell invents telephone.	
1879	Zulus massacre British at Isandhlwana.		
1881	Billy the Kid, outlaw, assassinated.		Height of cattle-ranching on Great Plains.
1882	Britain occupies Egypt.		
1885		Van Gogh paints *The Potato Eaters.*	
1890	Massacre at Wounded Knee ends Indian Wars in US. First General Election in Japan.		Global influenza endemic.
1892	Keir Hardie becames first Labour MP, Britain.		
1893		Karl Benz builds his first motor car. Advent of art nouveau.	
1896	Italy defeated by Abyssinians (Ethiopians) at Adowa; almost uniquely, Abyssinia survives the "scramble for Africa" which has seen the rest of the continent colonized by European powers.	Puccini's opera *La Bohème.*	
1898	Spanish-American War; Spain cedes Cuba and Philippines.	Marie and Pierre Curie discover radium.	Métro opens in Paris.
1899	Boer War between Britain and Boers (until 1901).	Rutherford discovers alpha and beta rays.	
1900	Nationalist Boxer Rebellion in China.	Freud, *The Interpretation of Dreams.*	

KEY DATES	HISTORY, POLITICS, WAR	RELIGION, SCIENCE, CULTURE	SOCIAL LIFE
1901	Death of Queen Victoria.	Marconi sends radio signal across Atlantic.	
1903		First powered air flight, Kitty Hawk, USA.	Henry Ford founds Ford Motor Co.
1904	Russo-Japanese War (until 1905).		
1905	"Bloody Sunday", St Petersburg: peaceful democratic protest attacked by Czarist troops. Sinn Fein founded, Ireland.	Einstein proposes Special Theory of Relativity.	
1906		Upton Sinclair, *The Jungle*.	San Francisco earthquake.
1909	Commander Peary reaches North Pole.	Blériot flies the Channel. Bakelite invented.	
1910	Coal miners riot in Tonypandy, Wales. Mexican Revolution (until 1912). Japan annexes Korea.	Post-Impressionist Exhibition, London.	Labour Exchanges open, Britain.
1911	Amundsen reaches South Pole. China becomes a republic under Sun Yat-sen.		
1913	Suffragette demonstrations in London. War in the Balkans.	Première of Stravinsky's *Rite of Spring*.	
1914	Assassination of Archduke Franz Ferdinand, Sarajevo. World War I begins. Germany invades Low Countries and France.	Gershwin, *Rhapsody in Blue*.	

KEY DATES	HISTORY, POLITICS, WAR	RELIGION, SCIENCE, CULTURE	SOCIAL LIFE
1915	WWI: Gallipoli campaign; *Lusitania* torpedoed; Zeppelins raid London.	Einstein expounds General Theory of Relativity. D.W. Griffith movie, *Birth of a Nation*.	
1916	WWI: Battles of Verdun and Somme on Western Front; tanks introduced by British; Battle of Jutland in North Sea.	Jazz gains popularity in USA.	Daylight Saving in Britain.
	Sinn Fein launches Easter Rising in Dublin.	Dadaism invented by Tristan Tzatra.	
1917	WWI: opening of battle of Passchendaele; tank battle at Cambrai: US declares war on Germany. Russian Revolution: Bolsheviks under Lenin seize power; civil war with "Whites" continues until 1920.		
1918	WWI: Germany tries last gamble on Western Front; Armistice on 11 November – WWI ends, with Allies victorious. Tsar Nicholas and family shot. Worker uprisings in Berlin. Suffrage for women over 30 introduced in Britain.		
1919	Treaty of Versailles: Germany disarmed, stripped of colonies and forced to pay reparations. Spartacist Revolution in Berlin; counter-revolutionaries murder Karl Liebknecht and Rosa Luxemburg.		
	Mussolini founds Fascist movement, Italy.		

KEY DATES	HISTORY, POLITICS, WAR	RELIGION, SCIENCE, CULTURE	SOCIAL LIFE
1920	League of Nations formed. 19th Amendment in US gives women vote. Unemployment insurance in Britain.		Prohibition in USA.
1921		Schoenberg, "Piano Suite Op 25".	
1922	Fascists take power, Italy. Irish Free State proclaimed.	James Joyce, *Ulysses*.	
1923	Turkey becomes a republic. Hyperinflation in Germany.		
1926	General Strike, Britain.		
1927			Babe Ruth hits 60 home runs for NY Yankees.
1928		D.H. Lawrence, *Lady Chatterley's Lover*.	
1929	Wall Street Crash.		"Talkies" end silent movie era.
1930	In India Gandhi leads 200-mile civil disobedience march.		
1931	Hunger March in Washington. All German banks close.	Jehovah's Witnesses founded.	First woman senator, USA.
1933	Hitler appointed Chancellor of Germany; uses pretext of the Reichstag fire to introduce Nazi dictatorship.		

KEY DATES	HISTORY, POLITICS, WAR	RELIGION, SCIENCE, CULTURE	SOCIAL LIFE
1934	Civil Works Emergency Relief in USA.		
1935	Show trials in USSR. Italy invades Abyssinia.	First TV broadcast by BBC; Metro opens in Moscow.	
1936	Spanish Civil War (until 1939).	Black athlete Jesse Owens wins four gold medals in Berlin Olympics.	
	Trotsky exiled from USSR. Chang Kai-shek declares war on Japan.		
1937		Whittle builds first jet engine.	Airship *Hindenburg* crashes, NY.
1938	Austria annexed by Germany.	Laslo Biro invents ballpoint pen.	
1939	World War II begins: Britain and France declare war on Germany. Germany invades Poland. USSR occupies eastern Poland.		Nylon stockings become fashionable.
1940	WWII: Germany occupies Norway, Denmark, Low Countries and France. Churchill becomes British PM. Luftwaffe launches "Blitz" on London. Trotsky assassinated by Stalinist agent.		
1941	WWII: German offensive in North Africa led by Rommel, attacks Tobruk; Germans invade Russia, reach outskirts of Moscow; Japan bombs Pearl Harbor; USA enters war.	Orson Welles' film, *Citizen Kane*.	Clothes rationing in Britain.

KEY DATES	HISTORY, POLITICS, WAR	RELIGION, SCIENCE, CULTURE	SOCIAL LIFE
1942	WWII: Japanese capture Singapore, lose battles of Coral Sea and Midway; in North Africa, Rommel loses battle of El Alamein. Nazis begin mass extermination of Jews in gas chambers.	Albert Camus, *The Outsider*.	
1943	WWII: German Sixth Army surrenders at Stalingrad; Germans lose campaign in North Africa; Allies invade Italy; Italy surrenders; Japanese forced from Guadalcanal.		
1944	WWII: Allied "D-Day" landings in Normandy; France liberated; Allied troops cross German border; Warsaw uprising; US troops land in Philippines; Russians occupy Hungary; V-2 rockets land on England.	Aaron Copland, *Appalachian Spring*.	
1945	WWII: Russian offensive in east reaches Berlin; Hitler commits suicide; Germany surrenders on May 7; US drops atomic bombs on Hiroshima and Nagasaki; Japan surrenders – end of WWII. Landslide Labour government in Britain.	George Orwell, *Animal Farm*.	

KEY DATES	HISTORY, POLITICS, WAR	RELIGION, SCIENCE, CULTURE	SOCIAL LIFE
1947	India granted independence from Britain.		
1948	Israel declares independence.		Bread rationing ends in Britain.
1949	Communist People's Republic proclaimed, China; Britain recognizes independence of Eire; Democratic Republic established in East Germany.		
1950	Korean War (until 1953).		
1951	McCarthyite anti-Communist witch hunts in full spate, USA.		Colour TV introduced in USA.
1953	Stalin dies.	Hillary and Tenzing Norgay climb Everest; Arthur Miller, *The Crucible*.	
1956	Anti-Stalinist revolution, Hungary; Egypt nationalizes Suez canal – Britain stages abortive invasion; Castro sails to Cuba with small rebel force.	The birth of rock 'n' roll.	
1957	Desegregation protests at Little Rock, Arkansas.	Jack Kerouac, *On the Road*. USSR launches Sputnik I.	
1959	Castro's rebels oust Batista from power, Cuba.		First motorway opens in Britain.

KEY DATES	HISTORY, POLITICS, WAR	RELIGION, SCIENCE, CULTURE	SOCIAL LIFE
1960	Massacre of black demonstrators against apartheid, Sharpeville; John F. Kennedy elected President of US.		
1961	Building of the Berlin Wall; CIA sponsors abortive Bay of Pigs invasion, Cuba.		
1962	Cuban Missile Crisis.	Bob Dylan records "Blowin' in the Wind".	
1963	Great Train Robbery, England; Freedom March on Washington; President John F. Kennedy assassinated, Dallas.		
1964	USA becomes embroiled in conflict in Vietnam; *de facto* start of Vietnam War (until 1975).	The Beatles film, *Hard Day's Night*.	Cassius Clay wins world heavyweight boxing title.
1965	Winston Churchill dies (aged 91).		
1966			England win World Cup.
1967	Six Day War between Israel and Arab states.		
1968	Student riots in Paris spark virtual revolution in France.		"Summer of love" – Hippie youth movement at peak.
1969	British troops sent to Northern Ireland.	Neil Armstrong and Buzz Aldrin land on Moon.	Woodstock rock festival.

KEY DATES	HISTORY, POLITICS, WAR	RELIGION, SCIENCE, CULTURE	SOCIAL LIFE
1972	British troops massacre 13 civil rights protesters, N. Ireland; national miners' strike, Britain.		
1973	Elected Marxist government overthrown by military, Chile.		Worldwide petroleum crisis caused by Arab embargo.
1974	US President Richard Nixon resigns over Watergate scandal; floods kill 2,500 in Bangladesh.		Muhammad Ali beats George Foreman in Zaïre to regain world heavyweight title.
1975	North Vietnamese Communists occupy South Vietnam; US evacuates troops – end of Vietnam War.		
1976		Sex Pistols record, "Anarchy in the UK" – the birth of punk rock.	Bjorn Borg wins men's singles tennis title, Wimbledon.
1979	Islamic fundamentalists overthrow Shah of Iran; Conservative government, led by Margaret Thatcher, elected, Britain.		
1980	SAS troops relieve siege at Iranian Embassy, London; Lech Walesa leads *Solidarnosc* protests in Poland.		
1982	Falklands/Malvinas War.		
1984	Miners' Strike, Britain (until 1985).		
1986	Army lead overthrow of President Marcos, Philippines.		
1987			AIDS endemic in Africa.

KEY DATES	HISTORY, POLITICS, WAR	RELIGION, SCIENCE, CULTURE	SOCIAL LIFE
1989	Pro-democracy students shot, Tiananmen Square, China; Fall of the Berlin Wall; Stalinist regimes of Romania, Bulgaria, East Germany overthrown. Yugoslavia fragments into civil war.		
1991	Persian Gulf War.		
1992	Los Angeles riot.		
1994	End of apartheid in South Africa.	Invention of Internet	
1997	British cede Hong Kong to China; Diana, Princess of Wales, and lover, Dodi Fayed, die in car crash, Paris; Labour government elected in UK.		
1998	Office of the Independent Counsel reports to US Congress ("The Starr Report") on alleged impeachable offences committed by President Clinton in Monica Lewinsky scandal.	Successful cloning of human embryo.	France wins soccer World Cup.

KEY DATES	HISTORY, POLITICS, WAR	RELIGION, SCIENCE, CULTURE	SOCIAL LIFE
1999	US Senate acquits President Clinton of perjury and obstruction of justice in Lewinsky affair; NATO airstrikes and threat of land war cause Serbs to withdraw from Kosovo; independence vote in East Timor unleashes reprisals by Indonesian militia; civilian government overthrown in Pakistan.		Total eclipse of the sun, Cape Cod to Indian Ocean. Earthquake in Turkey kills 10,000.
2000	Republican George W. Bush wins US presidential election.		Olympic games, Sydney.
2001	al-Qaeda terror attacks on NY Twin Towers and Washington; US invades Afghanistan.		
2002	Yugoslavia dissolved.		Brazil wins soccer World Cup.
2003	US and UK invade Iraq and topple Saddam Hussein; SARS alert Hong Kong.	Human genetic code deciphered.	England win Rugby World Cup.
2004	European Union expands to 25 members; Beslan school siege, Caucausus.		Indian Ocean tsunami.
2005	Islamic terrorist attack on London transport system, "7/7 bombings".		Hurricane Katrina devastates New Orleans; England wins Cricket "Ashes".
2006	Saddam Hussein hanged.		Italy wins World Cup.
2007			Worst floods in UK for 60 years.

COOKERY FOR CLOTS

Cookery is not girls' work. Every boy must be able to cook for himself. And it's great fun to have friends over to eat your culinary adventures. (Tip for Big Boys: girls are quietly impressed by boys who can cook. It shows that they are considerate and modern.) Although these four recipes are easy peazy you may want an adult to help you with them since they involve boiling water, hot oil and sharp knives! At the very least, check the basic rules of kitchen safety and hygiene with your parents first.

Garlic Mushroom Pasta

This recipe serves four people and takes about 10 minutes.

Ingredients

400g of dried fusilli pasta (the twirly wirly one)
450g mushrooms
1 clove garlic
salt
black ground pepper
200g crème fraiche (sour cream)
A tablespoon of extra-virgin olive oil
75g of butter

Equipment

A very large saucepan

A sharp knife
A wooden or plastic chopping board
Weighing scales
A small saucepan or frying pan
A garlic crusher
A wooden spoon

Step 1
Wipe the mushrooms clean with a damp paper towel, and then slice thinly. Put to one side.

Step 2
Fill saucepan with water until three-quarters full, place on hob, turn on heat and bring to boil. To avoid accidents ensure handle of saucepan does not stick out towards you. When the water is boiling add the tablespoon of olive oil – this is to stop the pasta spirals sticking together.

Step 3
Weigh your pasta and add it to the pan. Stir the pasta spirals to make sure they are separated. The pasta should be cooked for the amount of time indicated on side of packet. Time from now.

Step 4
Place the butter in a saucepan, turn the heat on low. While the butter is *gently* melting peel and crush the garlic clove. Then add the garlic, the sliced mushrooms, a pinch of salt and a twist of black pepper to the pan containing the melted butter. Cook the mixture for around five minutes. You'll need to sir it occasionally

Step 5
When the pasta has cooked for the right length of time, hold a colander/sieve over a sink and pour the pasta into it. You may need help to do this as the pan is heavy and you don't want the hot water to spill. Now tip the pasta back into the empty heavy saucepan and place back on the hob – but with the heat turned off.

Step 6
Now tip the mushroom mixture into the pasta. Add the crème fraiche and stir until it melts. Serve immediately.

Home-made Chicken Burgers

This recipe takes between 15–30 minutes and serves 4. You need:

Ingredients

450g of ground (minced) chicken
1 heaped tablespoon of tomato ketchup
1 teaspoon garlic pepper
Salt
Black pepper
Four wholemeal buns
4 leaves lettuce
Olive oil
mayonnaise

Equipment

Non-stick frying pan or skillet
Large bowl for mixing
Small bowl for water to wet hands
Wooden spatula
China plate or baking tray
1 sharp knife
1 chopping board

Step 1
Take the 4 lettuce leaves and slice into ribbons on chopping board. Place in fridge to keep cool.

Step 2
Tip the ground chicken into a large bowl, add the large dollop of tomato ketchup and season with one teaspoon of garlic pepper, plus good pinch of salt. Mix together well.

Step 3
Wet hands in small bowl of water, then divide the mixture into four and shape with your hands into round burgers (patties). Rewet your hands to stop the mixture sticking to them.

Step 4

Place burgers on a plate and drizzle lightly with olive oil. Rub the oil in with your fingers. Then flip burgers over and oil the other side.

Step 5

Put one tablespoon on olive oil in the frying pan and heat for a minute or two on medium heat, then place burgers in the pan and fry. The burgers will take 3–7 minutes to cook, depending on how thick they are. Add a little oil if they seem to be sticking.

Step 6

Serve in the buns with the lettuce ribbons, plus a dollop of mayonnaise on top.

Shipwreck Stew

In truth, you can use just about any vegetable and raw meat in a stew – you just have to remember that vegetables cook at different rates to each other and that meat has to be properly cooked through, so that no bloody juices run from it. Here's a basic recipe for a meat and vegetable stew using ingredients you'll find in most homes at most times. But check with your parents before you raid the larder. They'll not thank you for using the ingredients for tonight's at home supper with Dad's Boss.

The recipe serves 4–6 and takes about 40 minutes:

Ingredients

100g of uncooked rice
1 small onion
2 carrots
2 medium potatoes
400g red kidney beans
400g of ground (minced) beef
4 tablespoons vegetable/olive oil
2 cloves of garlic
400g tin of chopped tomatoes

1 teaspoon vegetable bouillon or 1 meat stock cube
600ml water
1 teaspoon Worcestershire sauce
1 teaspoon curry paste

Equipment

Frying pan/skillet
Crock pot or large casserole dish
Sharp knife
Garlic crush
Chopping board

Step 1
Preheat the oven to 350°F.

Step 2
Cut the potatoes, carrots into cubes.

Step 3
Put 2 tablespoons of oil into skillet and brown the ground beef over a medium heat. Stir occasionally to ensure it doesn't stick.

Step 4
Layer ground beef mixture, rice, potatoes and beans in large casserole/crock pot.

Step 5
Put 600ml water in bowl and mix in a tsp of bouillon or stock cube

Step 6
Crush garlic and add to bouillon, along with remainder of olive oil, Worcestershire sauce, curry paste and chopped tomatoes. Pour into casserole.

Step 7
Put in oven and bake covered at 350°F for 1½ hours. Then take out with oven mitts.

Cheesy Baked Potato

Arguably the nicest easiest meal on planet Earth. Serves 4 and takes approximately 1 hour.

Ingredients

Four large baking potatoes
4 knobs of butter
200g of mature cheese
1 teaspoon chopped parsley
4 small sprigs of parsley
Salt
Pepper

Equipment

Cheese grater
1 sharp knife
1 spoon
Chopping board
1 large bowl

Step 1
Turn the oven to max and put in the potatoes near the top. At around 350°F they should cook in an hour or so.

Step 2
Grate the cheese – carefully: it's an activity famous for injuring the end of fingers.

Step 3
Chop the parsley and put in fridge to keep cool

Step 4
When the potatoes are baked through, remove with mitts and put on a clean kitchen surface or plate.

Step 5
Cut the potatoes lengthways and scoop the insides into a bowl. Put the skins to one side.

Step 6
Add the cheese, parsley, pinch of salt and pinch of paper to the potatoes. Mix well.

Step 7
Pack the cheesy potato mixture back into the skins and serve each one with a sprig of parsley on top.

If the mixture has cooled you can pop the packed potatoes into the oven for a couple of minutes before serving with the parsley garnish.

SAS SURVIVAL SKILLS IV: FINDING AND PURIFYING WATER

Water is a basic human need. There is no adequate substitute, and without it you cannot live more than a few days. Within the human body water acts as a stabilizer; it helps to maintain warmth in cold environments, and is vital for staying cool in hot environments. It is also part of the body's mechanism for distributing food and removing waste. As soon as you are cut off from a source of fresh water, you begin to dehydrate.

The rate at which you dehydrate depends on a number of factors: the amount of water your body already contains, the clothing you are wearing, the local temperature, how hard you are working, whether you are in shade, or sunlight, whether you are smoking and whether you are calm or nervous.

If you allow dehydration to continue, there will come a point when you can no longer search for water. Your first priority is to minimize further dehydration and, having done this, you must find water. (If you are stranded in a desert with little chance of finding water, stay still to prevent further dehydration, and make efforts to signal for rescue.)

Points for Survival

1 Avoid eating until you have secured a source of safe water.
2 Do not ration your water; drink as much as you can when you can.
3 Urine is a good indicator of dehydration. The darker its colour, the more dehydrated you are.

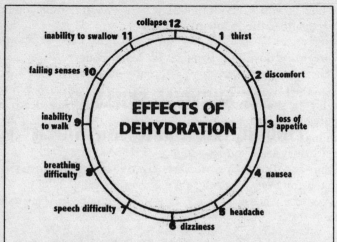

You will collapse after losing 12 per cent of your body weight; the diagram shows the progressive symptoms. Heat exhaustion is still a killer on exercises in the UK as well as abroad. You must be able to recognize the signs in your mates; it doesn't have to be a hot day to kill them. If all the danger signs are ignored, sweating will eventually stop and the victim will collapse.

4 Bacteria multiply faster in warm water, so water gathered early in the morning, at its coolest, is safer.
5 To reduce dehydration:
  • Find shade
  • Move slowly and do not smoke
  • Cover exposed skin to prevent evaporation of sweat
  • Suck a pebble (helps prevent exhalation of moisture through the mouth).

Finding Water

You do not have to be in a desert to have difficulty finding water. Forests often offer such poor visibility that, although surrounded by water-loving trees, you cannot spot readily available surface water. (In combat conditions, however, you may have to deliberately avoid obvious sources of water, for fear of ambush.)

So how do you go about finding water? The first thing you do is to remember the following points:

1 Water runs downhill, so make for lower country.
2 Where there is water, there is usually an abundance of lush vegetation. If possible, learn to recognize the moisture-loving plants in the area. If this vegetation is wilted or dead, it probably indicates chemical pollution.
3 Animals need water too. Observe the habits of the local wild-life; it may lead you to a source of water.
4 Grain-and seed-eating birds need water, so observe them too.
5 Listen for frogs croaking: they live in water.
6 Cliffs often have seepages of water at their base, so look carefully.

Sources of water (assuming no equipment)

Familiarize yourself with the various sources of water and their relative merits.

Dew
Dew is one of the most reliable sources of water for the survivor. It can be collected soon after it has started to form until it evaporates in the morning sunlight. Improvise a mop from an absorbent article of clothing. Drag this through long grass or use it to wipe the condensed moisture from shrubs and rocks. If you do not have a convenient mop, finely teased, non-poisonous inner barks or grasses can be used. When the mop is saturated, wring out the water into a container. Although labour-intensive, this is a very effective way to collect water.

Dew itself is a pure source of water, but when you wipe it off vegetation and rocks you also wipe off bacteria and perhaps parasites. It is therefore best to boil this water before consumption.

Rain and snow
Rain water is usually the safest source of water in the wilderness. If it rains, make sure you gather as much as you can. But remember the water is only as pure as your method of collection: if you are in doubt, boil it before consumption. Snow, if it is clean, is probably pure. The major problem with snow is

melting it: a time-consuming and labour-intensive process, as you require eight to ten containers of snow to produce one container of water.

Ice

Ice is not pure and should always be boiled before consumption, but is far more economical as a source of water than snow. Icicles are often found hanging from trees and rocks, so may provide you with a ready source of water. Those hanging from trees may be slightly stained brown by the tannin in the bark, but unless they are very heavily stained they will be safe to drink after boiling.

Puddles and hidden water

Rain water is often trapped in depressions in rocks, called kettles, and in puddles. While it may smell foul and be stagnant, it only needs filtering and boiling to make it drinkable.

Rain water can also be found trapped in hollows in trees. Unfortunately, this is often so badly polluted with tannin that it is undrinkable. However, if you expect rain you can bale these hollows out and let them fill with fresh rain water; as long as you use the water before it too becomes tannin-stained, you have a handy water tank. Always boil this water before drinking it, and only use water found in non-poisonous trees.

Drinkable saps

For short-term relief of thirst, you may be able to tap the sap of certain trees. The sap of maple, birch and sycamore can be tapped during the early spring (sycamore will produce sap from spring to autumn, depending on local conditions). Sap is thirst-quenching but it contains sugar, which if taken in sufficient quantity will hasten dehydration; in fact, the woodland Native Americans still boil maple and birch sap to produce sugar.

Only mature trees should be tapped, and the sap drunk while fresh, as it will ferment if stored. Some plants can also be used to provide water.

Springs and seepages

Springs are often regarded as fool-proof sources of drinking water, but unfortunately this is not true: spring water should

---

INDIAN WELL

The Indian Well is an easily prepared and efficient method of collecting reasonably good water. Selection of the ground is all-important and the water produced requires filtering and boiling. Also, it takes some time to produce clear water, and quality is dependent on soil type. In practice, watch out for sources of contamination, boil very carefully, and add Steritabs.

1. Dig a hole about half a metre deep and half a metre wide. Water will begin to seep into the hole.
2. You can push a stick into the sides of the well to increase seepage of water into the well.
3. Bale out this water carefully so that you do not stir up the sediment at the bottom of the hole. Repeat this process until the seeping water is fairly clear.
4. After some time, the water at the top of the well will be clear enough to collect. Be careful not to disturb the muddy layer that usually lurks at the bottom.

---

always be boiled before drinking. Very often, springs are covered with soil and appear as patches of saturated ground supporting lush plant growth. To obtain water from these areas, dig an Indian Well.

Ponds

These are principally a feature of farmland, and are therefore a potential source of water for the evading soldier. Such water should always be considered suspect, as at the very least there will be fluke infestation. Keep contact with this water to a minimum, and if used as a source of drinking water, filter and thoroughly boil it before drinking.

Streams, rivers and lakes

Streams are often a tempting source of water, but care should be taken as they are very often polluted by decaying carcasses of animals that have drowned or become caught in boggy ground. In alpine regions, the clear ice-cold glacial meltwaters carry an invisible hazard: sediment – rock powder scoured from living rock by the awesome power of the glacier. If this is not filtered out, you may get digestive problems.

The further water travels from its source, the more pollutants it picks up. In an age where chemicals are an integral part of farming and land management, rivers and lakes should be avoided as sources of water.

Purifying Water

Now you've found a source of water. Is it safe to drink? The answer seems obvious – assume the water is dirty and purify it – but dehydration is causing you to be uncharacteristically impatient and irritable. You are tired, hungry, lonely and somewhat frightened. Your hands and shins are covered in the scratches you sustained searching what seemed like every patch of vegetation in the last 100 miles. And but for the incessant biting of the mosquitoes you would fall asleep.

You are faced with water that will need filtering and boiling before it is safe to drink, but you have no container and no fire. Surely one little sip won't hurt?

Without the support of modern medicine to fall back on, wilderness survival is all about maintaining good health. The human body is an amazing machine, but it is finely tuned: it only takes one drop of contaminated water to make you ill.

Of the many waterborne problems you may develop, the most common is diarrhoea. In a survival situation, diarrhoea may prove fatal. It causes dehydration and makes hygiene very difficult, increasing the risk of further unpleasant infections, and destroys the will to live.

To make your water safe, you will need three things:

1 Fire
2 A container
3 A filter.

As a fire will also warm you, drive away the mosquitoes and boost your morale, it is usually best to start this first. Hopefully you will have practised your firelighting skill, as this is a bad time to learn!

Improvised water containers

Improvised water containers fall into three categories:

1 *Kettles*: containers that can be used directly over flames
2 *Cauldrons*: cannot be used directly over flames, but can be used for rock boiling
3 *Storage*: containers that should be solely used for carrying or storing safe water.

Kettles

Kettles can be made from flammable materials because the water contained within them prevents their burning. The secret is not to allow the flames to reach beyond the water level.

Bamboo
In some tropical regions, bamboo can be found with stems large enough to be turned into kettles. Many other containers can also be improvised from bamboo, and sometimes fresh drinking water can be found trapped in the stems.

Birch or cherry bark
The woodland Native Americans routinely made kettles from birch bark while on their travels. Only the outer bark is used. It

Cherry or birch bark container

should be carefully removed from an unblemished section of the trunk, and can be made pliable by either soaking or gentle warming by the fire. The brown inside of the bark is the most durable side, and is used to form the outside of containers, which are simply made by folding.

Cauldrons

Cauldrons are made from materials that will hold water but are not suitable for direct heating; put heated rocks into the water to boil it.

If your local soil is clay or clay-like enough to contain muddy water, a ground cauldron can be made. Dig a bowl-shaped depression in the ground and smooth the inside. Form a raised rim at the top, to help prevent humus falling into the cauldron.

Make the cauldron one third larger than the amount of water you intend to boil. This will allow for the water displaced by the heated rocks. To prevent sediment muddying your water, you will need to line the pit. For this you can use either some material (for example, a T-shirt) or large non-poisonous leaves such as dock or burdock. Take great care to ensure that the lining fits snugly.

The water purified in this type of cauldron will always be a little muddy, but if you leave it to settle you can skim clear water off the top.

Rocks and trees

Water can often be found in depressions in rocks, and the hollows in trees, and these can be turned into ready-made cauldrons. Again, allow for the displacement of the heated rocks by choosing a depression large enough. If possible, it is best to scrape any slime out of these depressions prior to their use. This is especially important when using tree hollows. Remember, never rock boil in a poisonous tree.

Skin

If you are able to catch an animal of the size of a rabbit upwards, you will have secured meat as well as two containers good enough to stew it in: if you are careful with the skinning and gutting, both the skin and the stomach can be used as cauldrons.

To use the skin you can leave the fur on or take it off, as you please. To use the stomach it is best turned inside out. You have a choice when making your skin cauldron. You can line a pit with it, securing it around the rim by stakes, or you can suspend it from a tripod.

Wooden bowls

Bowls and containers can be carved out of wood. While not as quickly constructed as the previous methods, wooden bowls are well within the capabilities of a survivor. If carefully made, they are portable and very durable.

The best method of producing a wooden bowl is to "burn and scrape". To achieve this, make a small depression in the centre of your bowl-to-be and place a couple of glowing coals in this depression. Then by blowing on the coals, ideally through a reed straw, you can use them to char the surrounding wood.

When you have charred a patch of wood, scrape it away using a sharp stone, and begin the process again. It does not take long to form a reasonable sized bowl.

Storage containers

The manufacture of storage containers is a long-term prospect. They can be made from the materials discussed above, and also from clay pottery and tightly-woven basketry.

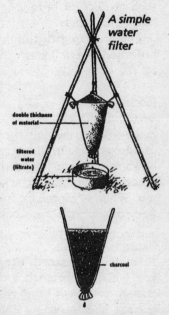

A simple water filter

double thickness of material

filtered water (filtrate)

charcoal

Filtering

Having secured a container in which to boil your water, you now need a filter to remove the particles of dirt suspended in the water.

The simplest filter that can be improvised uses a pair of ordinary trousers. Simply turn them inside out, placing one leg inside the other, and tie the leg off at the bottom. Soak the material before use: this helps tighten the weave, making the filter more efficient. Suspend the filter so that you can easily fill it, with the container positioned underneath to collect the clean water that drips out. Such filters can be improved by filling them with charcoal.

Rock boiling

Rock boiling is an easy and effective way to purify water. The rocks must be of a manageable size and weight, and thoroughly dry. (Rocks from stream beds and damp places contain moisture which, when heated, expands, causing the rock to explode. Also glass-like rocks such as flint and obsidian should be avoided.)

Heat the rocks in your fire, and when hot transfer them to your container with some improvised tongs. Tap off any ash before dropping them in the water.

Do not wait to use these skills until you have to. Practice is essential to success.

NB: When practising, only gather bark from dead trees.

POULTRY KEEPING

Chickens are not going to offer you companionship. There's no kindness in the eye of a hen as there is in the eye of a dog. But there is real pleasure to be had from possessing and caring for a good selection of well-bred fowls. Chickens are a continual source of interest. You also get something tangible back from your outlay of money and time: eggs, chicks and meat. You might even make a small profit.

Housing the Birds

Before buying a single bird you must think of where you intend to keep your fowl. In some cultures, chickens are kept in cages, barely able to turn around. This is simply cruel. Chickens need to be free to do what comes naturally: strut about, peck at things, scratch at the surface of the earth and breathe in fresh air.

Consequently, poultry-keeping is a hobby which will require a backyard or garden at a minimum. Chickens, however, do not need vast amounts of room. A moveable ark is sufficient. This is a house with a wire run attached. Arks come in various designs (see Figure 1 for example) and can be knocked up by any boy with some tools, some spare timber and a roll of chicken wire. Since the ark can be moved on a daily basis it prevents the birds from scratching up too much of your lawn. Moving the ark also stops a build-up of dung, which is detrimental to the chickens' health.

A covered run also offers maximum protection from dogs, cats, mink, foxes and every other animal which likes to eat chicken.

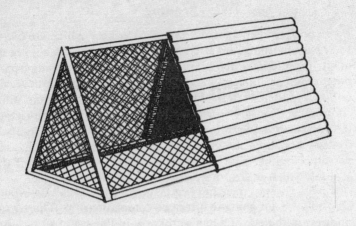

Figure 1

Inside the hut there needs to be room for the birds to perch and lay their eggs. If you have more than one perch the perches must be at the same height and you should allow 20cm (8 in) of perch per bird. Perches should be at least 5 cm (2 in wide) for large fowl and with the uppermost corners rounded off. As a guide, each chicken needs about 60 × 60 cm (2 ft × 2 ft) of space inside the house. The bottom of the house should be covered with litter to absorb night dung. Sawdust makes for the best litter since wood is naturally antiseptic. You might obtain sawdust free from a mill. Straw is perfectly acceptable as litter, but hay (dried grass) is not since it can contain mould which is injurious to the chickens' respiratory system. And yours when you clean your hens out.

Finally, the back of the ark needs to contain nest boxes for the hens to lay their eggs. These can be simple divisions just 10 cm (4 in) high, and 30 cm (11 in) square, but generally the more enclosed and cosy the space the more hens prefer it.

Your chickens will naturally wish to sleep in the shelter and safety of the house at night. Although arks are enclosed, the house should still be shut up at night, for this is when the birds are most likely to be visited by foxes and other predators.

Feeding

Some poultry keepers make special "mashes" which are fed to their hens morning and afternoon. This requires the boiling up of kitchen scraps, which are then subjected to a pounding from a potato masher. This might be economical (excepting the strain on your parents' electricity bill) but it is fiddly and time consuming. You are much better advised to buy proprietary feeding pellets and put them in a metal or plastic purpose-made feeder ("hopper") obtainable from any agricultural merchant in person or online. The feeder can be hung some inches off the ground, which makes the system less attractive to mice.

The proprietary feedstuff will contain just about everything your hens need to flourish, but even so you should give them some raw greenstuff each day. Trimmed bits from the dinner's vegetables are fine. Chickens like variety.

Chickens must also have grit, to lodge in their gizzards to help them break up their feed. Again grit is obtainable commercially, but many poultry owners simply hit seashells and stones to bits with a hammer (if you do this put a cloth over the top of the stones to prevent bits flying up into your eyes. Or wear safety glasses). Your hens also need calcium to form the shells of their eggs. You can give them their own eggshells back, after these have been dried on medium heat in the oven to prevent the recycling of infection.

Fresh clean water needs to be in constant supply. A bowl with a large stone in the bottom (to stop the chickens turning it up) will do but a commercial drinker is less likely to be fouled. Again these are available in metal or plastic, the latter being inexpensive but less durable. In the drinker crush a clove of garlic (one clove to 5 litres (10 pints) of water is the right proportion). This acts as a mild insecticide.

Choosing your birds

What sort of birds you choose depends entirely on what you want from poultry-keeping. If you want eggs, you go for an egg-laying strain which will produce 130–160 reasonably sized eggs in a year. Recommended breeds are Rhode Island Reds, Light Sussex, Wyandotte, Plymouth Rock and Marans. Some highly commercial "battery" strains such as ISA Browns or Hi-Lux may lay over 200 eggs a year; these can be very cheap to buy since commercial farmers offload them at the end of their first year at around 50p/US$1 each. In the backyard these chickens will out-lay traditional breeds for at least another year. They are, however, desperately uninteresting fowl, mere egg-laying machines on legs. One bird well worth considering is the Araucana from South America; it lays naturally green-blue eggs which you can find a ready market for. With the exception of the battery birds, all the above chickens will make a tasty meal at one year old.

The alternative to buying egg/meat fowl is to become a chicken buff and go for one of the rare or show birds, such as the Frizzle, the Poland, the Pekin, the Sebright. Buy all your chickens in one go. If you mix birds from different sources you run an increased risk of bringing in disease. You can buy day-old chicks, which are very cheap (cheep!). However, half will turn out to be cocks; the chicks die easily unless kept at the right temperature and if they do survive they will take twenty weeks to give you your first egg.

A better idea is to buy point-of-lay pullets. These will be about eighteen weeks old, all the hard work has been done by someone else and you'll have an egg (hopefully) in a fortnight.

Broody hens

If you plump for a traditional breed you will find that the hens occasionally go "broody" and sit on a nest all day without moving. After three weeks or so she will stop being broody. You will, however, have to lift her out of the house for about twenty minutes every day so she can eat, drink and defecate.

Any eggs on which a broody hen has been sitting will be infertile, unless you have been running a cockerel with your hens. In this case, you might have chicks. After the eggs have hatched, the chicks and mother should be moved to a separate "broody coop", which is a mini-ark. The floor should be covered with sawdust, and the chicks should be provided with a shallow dish of water (if it's too deep they risk drowning) and a saucer of chick crumbs.

THE LAWS OF SOCCER

Law 1: The Field of Play

The field of play must be rectangular. The minimum length is 90 m (100 yds) and the maximum length is 120 m (130 yds). The minimum width is 45 m (50 yds) and the maximum width is 90 m (100 yds)

International matches are an exception to the above. Here the minimum length of the field of play is 100 m (110 yds) and the maximum 110 m (120 yds). The minimum width is 64 m (70 yds) and the maximum 75 m (80 yds).

Law 2: The Ball

The ball must be spherical, made of leather or another suitable material. The circumference must not more than 70 cm (28 ins) and not less than 68 cm (27 ins). At the start of a match the ball must be at least 410 g (14 oz) but not more than 450 g (16 oz) in weight. The pressure must be equal to 0.6–1.1 atmosphere.

If a ball becomes defective during a match play is stopped and the ball replaced. Play is restarted by dropping the replacement ball at the place where the first ball became defective. A ball can only be replaced on the orders of the referee.

Law 3: The Number of Players

A match is played by two teams, each consisting of not more than eleven players. A match may not start if either team has fewer than seven players.

Substitutes

In any competition played under the auspices of FIFA (pronounced "fee-fah"), the confederations or the national soccer associations, the maximum number of substitutes is three.

To replace a player with a substitute the referee must first be informed. The substitute only enters the field of play after the player to be replaced has left it and upon a signal from the referee. The substitute enters the field of play at the halfway mark and during a stoppage in play. If the substitute enters the field without the referee's permission he is cautioned and shown a yellow card. Play is restarted with a ball dropped at the place it was stopped. A replaced player takes no more part in the game.

Any player may change places with the goalkeeper provided that the referee is informed before the change. Failure to observe this rule results in the players concerned being cautioned and shown a yellow card.

A named substitute who has been sent off may not be replaced.

Law 4: Equipment

The compulsory equipment consists of:
- a shirt
- stockings (socks)
- shin guards (these should be covered by stockings)
- footwear.

The goalkeeper must wear colours which distinguish him from the other players and the officials.

A player must not use or wear anything (including jewellery) which is dangerous to himself or others.

Law 5: The Referee

Each match is controlled by a referee in cooperation with the assistant referees (and where applicable the fourth official). The referee has full authority to enforce the Laws of the Game. The decisions of the referee regarding facts connected with play are final. The referee may only change a decision upon realizing that it is incorrect or, at his discretion, on the advice of another official provided he has not restarted play.

Law 6: The Assistant Referees

Two assistant referees are appointed whose duties are to indicate:

- which side is entitled to a corner kick, goal kick or throw-in
- when the whole of the ball has passed out of play
- when a player may be penalized for being in an offside position
- when a substitution is requested
- when misconduct or any other incident has occurred out of the view of the referee
- at penalty kicks whether the goalkeeper has moved forward before the ball has been kicked and if the ball has crossed the line.

The assistant referees also assist the referee to control the match in accordance with the Laws of the Game.

Law 7: The Duration of the Match

The match lasts two equal periods of forty-five minutes, unless otherwise mutually agreed between the referee and the participating teams before the start of play.

Players are entitled to an interval at half-time which must not exceed fifteen minutes.

Allowance is made in either period for all time lost through:

- substitution(s)
- the assessment, treatment or removal of injured players
- wasting time
- any other cause.

The allowance for time lost is at the discretion of the referee.

If a penalty kick has to be taken or retaken, the duration of either half is extended until the penalty kick is completed.

Competition rules provide for two further equal periods of extra time to be played should a match so designated be drawn at full time. The conditions of Law 8 will apply.

An abandoned match is replayed unless the competition rules provide otherwise.

Law 8: The Start and Restart of Play

Preliminaries

A coin is tossed and the team which wins the toss decides which goal it will attack in the first half of the match. The other team takes the kick-off to start the match.

In the second half the teams switch ends. The team which won the toss take the kick-off to start the second half.

Kick-off

A kick-off is a way of starting or restarting play:
- at the start of the match
- at the start of the second half of the match
- after a goal has been scored
- at the start of each period of extra time (if applicable).

The Procedure for a Kick-off

- all players are in their own half of the field
- the ball is stationary on the centre mark
- the referee gives a signal (usually a blow on the whistle) to commence kick-off
- the opponents of the team taking the kick-off are at least 9.15 m (10 yds) from the ball
- the ball is in play when it is kicked and moves forward
- the kicker cannot touch the ball a second time until it has touched another player; if he does an indirect free kick is awarded to the opposing team on the site of the infringement.
- After a team scores a goal, the kick-off is taken by the opposing team.

A goal may be scored directly from the kick-off.

Dropped Ball

A dropped ball is a way of restarting the match after a temporary stoppage which becomes necessary, while the ball is in play, for any reason not mentioned elsewhere in the Laws of the

Game. The referee drops the ball at the place where it was located when play was stopped. The ball is in play as soon as it touches the ground. Infringements (such as a player touching the ball before it makes contact with the ground) require the ball to be dropped again.

Play restarts when the ball touches the ground.

A dropped ball to restart the match after play has been temporarily stopped inside the goal area takes place on the goal area line parallel to the goal line at the point nearest to where the ball was located when play was stopped.

Special Circumstances

An indirect free kick awarded to the attacking team in its opponents' goal area is taken from the goal area line parallel to the goal line at the point nearest to site of the infringement.

A free kick awarded to the defending team inside its own goal area is taken from any point within the goal area.

Law 9: The Ball In and Out of Play

The ball is out of play when:
- it has wholly crossed the touch line or goal line whether on the ground or in the air
- play has been stopped by the referee.

The ball is in play at all other times.

Law 10: The Method of Scoring

A goal is scored when the whole of the ball passes over the goal line, between the goalposts and under the crossbar, provided that no infringement of the Laws of the Game has been committed by the team in the scoring of the goal.

The winning team is the team scoring the greatest number of goals by the end of the match. If both teams score an equal number of goals, or if no goals are scored, the match is drawn.

For matches ending in a draw, competition rules may state provisions involving extra time, or other procedures approved by the International FA Board to determine the winner.

Law 11: Offside

A player is in an offside position if:
- he is nearer to his opponents' goal line than both the ball and the second-last opponent.

A player is **not** in an offside position if:
- he is in his own half of the field of play or
- he is level with the second last opponent or
- he is level with the last two opponents.

A player in an offside position is only penalized if, at the moment the ball is touched by one of his team, he is, in the opinion of the referee, involved in active play by:
- gaining an advantage by being in that position
- interfering with an opponent or interfering with play.

There is no offside offence if a player receives the ball directly from:
- a throw-in or
- a corner kick
- a goal kick.

For any offside offence, the referee awards an indirect free kick to the opposing team to be taken from the place where the infringement occurred.

Law 12: Fouls and Misconduct

Fouls and misconduct are penalized as follows:

Direct Free Kick

A direct free kick is awarded to the opposing team if a player commits any of the following six offences in a manner considered by the referee to be careless, reckless or using excessive force:
- charges an opponent
- strikes or attempts to strike an opponent
- pushes an opponent

- kicks or attempts to kick an opponent
- trips or attempts to trip an opponent
- jumps at an opponent.

A direct free kick is also awarded to the opposing team if a player commits any of the following four offences:
- in tackling an opponent to gain possession of the ball he makes contact with the opponent before touching the ball
- holds an opponent
- spits at an opponent
- handles the ball deliberately (except for the goalkeeper within his own penalty area).

A direct free kick is taken from where the offence occurred.

Penalty Kick

A penalty kick is awarded if any of the above ten offences is committed by a player inside his own penalty area provided that the ball is in play.

Indirect Free Kick

An indirect free kick is awarded to the opposing team if a goalkeeper, inside his own penalty area, commits any of the following offences:
- takes more than six seconds while controlling the ball with his hands, before releasing it from his possession
- touches the ball again with his hands after it has been released from his possession (and has not touched any other player)
- touches the ball with his hands after it has been deliberately kicked to him by a team-mate
- touches the ball with his hands after he has received it directly from a throw-in taken by a team-mate.

An indirect free kick is also awarded to the opposing team if a player commits any of the following offences:
- plays in a dangerous manner
- impedes the progress of an opponent

- prevents the goalkeeper from releasing the ball from his hands
- commits any other offence, not previously mentioned in Law 12, for which play is stopped to caution or dismiss a player.

The indirect free kick is taken from where the offence occurred.

Cautionable Offences

A player is cautioned and shown the yellow card if he commits any of the following seven offences:
- unsporting behaviour
- shows dissent by word or action
- persistently infringes the Laws of the Game
- delays the restart of play
- fails to respect the required distance when play is restarted with a corner kick or free kick
- enters or re-enters the field of play without the referee's permission
- deliberately leaves the field of play without the referee's permission.

Sending-Off Offences

A player is shown the red card and sent off if he commits any of the following seven offences:
- is guilty of serious foul play
- is guilty of violent conduct
- spits at an opponent or any other person
- denies an opponent a goal or an obvious goal-scoring opportunity by deliberately handling the ball (this does not apply to a goalkeeper within his own penalty area)
- denies an obvious goal-scoring opportunity to an opponent moving towards the player's goal by an offence punishable by a free kick or a penalty kick
- uses offensive, insulting or abusive language
- receives a second caution in the same match.

A player who has been sent off must leave the field of play and the technical area beside it.

Law 13: Free Kicks

Free kicks are either direct or indirect.

For both direct and indirect free kicks, the ball must be stationary when the kick is taken. The kicker must not touch the ball for a second time until it has touched another player.

The Direct Free Kick

- if a direct free kick is kicked directly into the opponents' goal, a goal is awarded
- if a direct free kick is kicked directly into the team's own goal, a corner kick is awarded to the opposing team.

The Indirect Free Kick

The referee indicates an indirect free kick by raising his arm above his head. He maintains his arm in that position until the kick has been taken and the ball has touched another player or goes out of play.

A goal can be scored only if the ball subsequently touches another player before it enters the goal.

- if an indirect free kick is kicked directly into the opponents' goal, a goal kick is awarded
- if an indirect free kick is kicked directly into the team's own goal, a corner kick is awarded to the opposing team.

Free Kick Inside the Penalty Area

Direct or indirect free kick to the defending team:

- all opponents must be at least 9.15 m (10 yds) from the ball
- all opponents remain outside the penalty area until the ball is in play
- the ball is in play when it is kicked directly beyond the penalty area
- a free kick awarded in the goal area is taken from any point inside that area.

Indirect free kick to the attacking team:
- all opponents are at least 9.15 m (10 yds) from the ball until it is in play, unless they are on their own goal line between the goalposts
- the ball is in play when it is kicked and moves
- an indirect free kick awarded inside the goal area is taken from that part of the goal area line which runs parallel to the goal line, at the point nearest to where the infringement occurred.

Free Kick Outside the Penalty Area

- all opponents are at least 9.15 m (10 yds) from the ball until it is in play
- the ball is in play when it is kicked and moves
- the free kick is taken from the place where the infringement occurred.

Infringements and Sanctions

If, when a free kick is taken, an opponent is closer to the ball than the required distance:
- the kick is retaken.

If, when a free kick is taken by the defending team from inside its own penalty area, the ball is not kicked directly into play:
- the kick is retaken.

Free kick taken by a player other than the goalkeeper: if, after the ball is in play, the kicker touches the ball a second time (except with his hands) before it has touched another player:
- an indirect free kick is awarded to the opposing team, the kick to be taken from the place where the infringement occurred.

If, after the ball is in play, the kicker deliberately handles the ball before it has touched another player:
- a direct free kick is awarded to the opposing team, the kick to be taken from the place where the infringement occurred
- a penalty kick is awarded if the infringement occurred inside the kicker's penalty area.

If, after the ball is in play, the goalkeeper touches the ball a second time (except with his hands), before it has touched another player:

- an indirect free kick is awarded to the opposing team, the kick to be taken from the place where the infringement occurred.

For free kicks taken by the goalkeeper: if, after the ball is in play, the goalkeeper deliberately handles the ball before it has touched another player:

- a direct free kick is awarded to the opposing team if the infringement occurred outside the goalkeeper's penalty area, the kick to be taken from the place where the infringement occurred
- an indirect free kick is awarded to the opposing team if the infringement occurred inside the goalkeeper's penalty area, the kick to be taken from the place where the infringement occurred.

Law 14: The Penalty Kick

A penalty kick is awarded against a team which commits one of the ten offences for which a direct free kick is awarded, inside its own penalty area while the ball is in play.

A goal may be scored directly from a penalty kick.

Additional time is allowed for a penalty kick to be taken at the end of each half or extra time.

The ball is placed on the penalty mark.

The defending goalkeeper must stay on his goal line, facing the kicker, between the goalposts until the ball has been kicked.

The players other than the kicker are located outside the penalty area:

- behind the penalty mark
- at least 9.15 m (10 yds) from the penalty mark.

The procedure for the penalty kick is that the referee signals that the kick be taken. The player taking the penalty then kicks the ball forward. He cannot play the ball a second time until it has touched another player.

A goal is awarded if, after the penalty kick is taken, the ball passes between the goalpost and under the crossbar. The goal stands if the ball touches either or both of the goalposts and/or the crossbar, and/or the goalkeeper.

Infringements and Sanctions

If the referee gives the signal for a penalty kick to be taken and, before the ball is in play, one of the following situations occurs: The player taking the penalty kick infringes the Laws of the Game:

- the referee allows the kick to proceed
- if the ball enters the goal, the kick is retaken
- if the ball does not enter the goal, the kick is not retaken.

The goalkeeper infringes the Laws of the Game:

- if the ball does not enter the goal, the kick is retaken
- if the ball enters the goal, a goal is awarded
- the referee allows the kick to proceed.

A team-mate of the player taking the kick enters the penalty area or moves in front of or within 9.5 m (10 yds) of the penalty mark:

- the referee allows the kick to proceed
- if the ball enters the goal, the kick is retaken
- if the ball does not enter the goal, the kick is not retaken.

A team-mate of the goalkeeper enters the penalty area or moves in front of or within 9.15 m (10 yds) of the penalty mark:

- the referee allows the kick to proceed
- if the ball enters the goal, a goal is awarded
- if the ball does not enter the goal, the kick is retaken.

A player of both the defending team and the attacking team infringe the Laws of the Game:

- the kick is retaken.

If, after the penalty kick has been taken: The kicker touches the ball for a second time (except with his hands) before it has touched another player:

- an indirect free kick is awarded to the opposing team, the kick to be taken from the place where the infringement occurred.

The kicker deliberately handles the ball before it has touched another player:
• a direct free kick is awarded to the opposing team, the kick to be taken from the place where the infringement occurred.

The ball is touched by an outside agent as it moves forward:
• the kick is retaken.

The ball rebounds into the field of play from the goalkeeper, the crossbar or the goalposts, and is then touched by an outside agent:
• the referee stops play
• play is restarted with a dropped ball at the place where it touched the outside agent.

Law 15: The Throw-In

A throw-in is a method of restarting play. A goal cannot be scored directly from a throw-in.
   A throw-in is awarded:
• when the whole of the ball passes over the touch line, either on the ground or in the air
• from the point where the ball crossed the touch line
• to the opponents of the player who last touched the ball.

At the moment of delivering the ball, the thrower must face the field of play with his feet on or behind the touch line. In throwing the ball, he must use both hands and deliver the ball from behind and over his head. The thrower may not touch the ball again until it has touched another player. If he does so an indirect free kick is awarded to the opposing team from the place where the infringement occurred.
   The ball is in play immediately it enters the field of play.
   If an opponent unfairly distracts or impedes the thrower he is cautioned for unsporting behaviour and shown the yellow card.
   For any other infringement of this Law the throw-in is taken by a player of the opposing team.

Law 16: The Goal Kick

A goal kick is a method of restarting play. A goal kick is awarded when the whole of the ball, having last touched a player of the attacking team, passes over the goal line, either on the ground or in the air, and a goal is not scored in accordance with Law 10. A goal may be scored directly from a goal kick, but only against the opposing team. The procedure for the goal-kick is that: the ball is kicked from any point within the goal area by a player of the defending team. Opponents remain outside the penalty area until the ball is in play. The kicker must not play the ball a second time until it has touched another player.

Infringements and Sanctions

If the ball is not kicked directly into play beyond the penalty area the kick is retaken.

For a goal kick taken by a player other than the goalkeeper: if, after the ball is in play, the kicker touches the ball a second time (except with his hands) before it has touched another player:
- an indirect free kick is awarded to the opposing team, the kick to be taken from the place where the infringement occurred.

If, after the ball is in play, the kicker deliberately handles the ball before it has touched another player:
- a direct free kick is awarded to the opposing team, the kick to be taken from the place where the infringement occurred
- a penalty kick is awarded if the infringement occurred inside the kicker's penalty area.

For a goal kick taken by the goalkeeper: if, after the ball is in play, the goalkeeper touches the ball a second time (except with his hands) before it has touched another player:
- an indirect free kick is awarded to the opposing team, with the kick to be taken from the place where the infringement occurred.

If, after the ball is in play, the goalkeeper deliberately handles the ball before it has touched another player:
- a direct free kick is awarded to the opposing team if the infringement occurred outside the goalkeeper's penalty area,

with the kick to be taken from the place where the infringement occurred

- an indirect free kick is awarded to the opposing team if the infringement occurred inside the goalkeeper's penalty area, the kick to be taken from the place where the infringement occurred.

For any other infringement of this Law the kick is retaken.

A goal may be scored directly from a free kick.

Law 17: The Corner Kick

A corner kick is a method of restarting play.

A goal may be scored directly from a corner kick, but only against the opposing team.

A corner kick is awarded when the whole of the ball, having last touched a player of the defending team, passes over the goal line, either on the ground or in the air, and a goal is not scored in accordance with Law 10.

The procedure:

- the ball is placed inside the corner arc at the nearest corner flag post (which must not be removed)
- opponents remain at least 9.15 m (10 yds) from the ball until it is in play
- the ball is kicked by a player of the attacking team
- the ball is in play when it is kicked
- the kicker does not play the ball a second time until it has touched another player.

Infringements and Sanctions

For a corner kick taken by a player other than the goalkeeper: If, after the ball is in play, the kicker touches the ball a second time (except with his hands), before it has touched another player an indirect free kick is awarded to the opposing team. The kick to be taken from the place where the infringement occurred.

If, after the ball is in play, the kicker deliberately handles the ball before it has touched another player a direct free kick is awarded to the opposing team, the kick to be taken from the place where the infringement occurred. A penalty kick is awarded if the infringement occurred inside the kicker's penalty area.

For a corner kick taken by the goalkeeper: If, after the ball is in play, the goalkeeper touches the ball a second time (except with his hands) before it has touched another player an indirect free kick is awarded to the opposing team. The kick is to be taken from the place where the infringement occurred.

If, after the ball is in play, the goalkeeper deliberately handles the ball before it has touched another player a direct free kick is awarded to the opposing team if the infringement occurred outside the goalkeeper's penalty area, with the kick to be taken from the place where the infringement occurred. If the infringement occurred inside the goalkeeper's penalty area, an indirect free kick is awarded to the opposing team, the kick to be taken from the place where the infringement occurred.

For any other infringement the kick is retaken.

Procedures to Determine the Winner of a Match

The Golden Goal and taking kicks from the penalty mark are methods of determining the winning team where competition rules require there to be a winning team after a match has been drawn.

The Golden Goal

- During the period of extra time played at the end of normal playing time, the team which scores the first goal is declared the winner.
- If no goals are scored the match is decided by kicks from the penalty mark.

Kicks from the Penalty Mark

- The referee chooses the goal at which the kicks will be taken.
- The referee tosses a coin and the team whose captain wins the toss takes the first kick.
- Both teams take five kicks.
- The kicks are taken alternately by the teams.
- Each kick is taken by a different player and all eligible players must take a kick before any player can take a second kick.

- If, before both teams have taken five kicks, one team has scored more goals than the other could score, even if it were to complete its five kicks, no more kicks are taken.
- If, after both teams have taken five kicks, both have scored the same number of goals, or have not scored any goals, kicks continue to be taken in the same order until one team has scored a goal more than the other team from the same number of kicks.
- A goalkeeper who is injured while kicks are being taken from the penalty mark and is unable to continue as goalkeeper may be replaced by a named substitute provided his team has not used the maximum number of substitutes permitted under the competition rules.
- With the exception of the case above, only players who are on the field of play at the end of the match (including extra time,) where appropriate) are allowed to take kicks from the penalty mark An eligible player may change places with the goalkeeper at any time when kicks from the penalty mark are being taken.
- All players, except the player taking the kick and the two goalkeepers, must remain within the centre circle.
- Before the start of kicks from the penalty mark the referee shall ensure that only an equal number of players from each team remain within the centre circle and they shall take the kicks. The goalkeeper who is the team-mate of the kicker must remain on the field of play, outside the penalty area in which the kicks are being taken, on the goal line where it meets the penalty area boundary line.
- When a team finishes the match with a greater number of players than their opponents, they shall reduce their numbers to equal that of their opponents and inform the referee of the name and number of each player excluded.

A HOMEMADE CLINOMETER

A clinometer is a useful little gadget for measuring the height of buildings and trees.

You need:
A plastic protractor
A piece of card
A piece of string
A small weight (a metal nut is ideal)
A nail
Drawing pins
A narrow piece of wood 8–10 inches long
Tangents tables or a calculator with a tan function

Take the length of wood and tap a nail into the top of one end. And then the other end. You are making sights like those on a gun. Glue, if you want, a handle to the underside of one end.

Now glue the plastic protractor to the wood so that the straight side of the protractor is "flush" (level with) the top

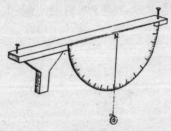

Figure 1

side of the wood as in Figure 1. Tie the weight to a 6-inch piece of string. Attach the string and a weight by a third drawing pin to the mid point at the top of the protractor. You now have a clinometer.

To use it, stand a measured distance (say 30 metres) from the tree you wish to determine the height of. Hold the clinometer out at arms length and sight along it until your eye and your arm make a straight line to the top of the tree. Get a friend to read the angle the string shows on the protractor.

You now need to use a branch of mathematics called trigonometry to work out the height of the tree.

The height of the tree = **h**[distance from ground to eye level of observer] + **B**[baseline] × tan(**A**, the angle on protractor).

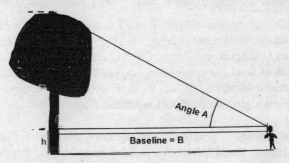

Figure 2

GREAT SPEECHES IV

John F. Kennedy's Inaugural Address, 1961

The 35th President of the United States, John F. Kennedy delivered his Inaugural Address on 20 January 1961. The speech vividly expresses Kennedy's "New Frontier" politics, based on the conquest of social and economic injustice. Kennedy himself was assassinated in 1963 but his "New Frontier" vision continues to influence the politics of the Democratic Party of the US.

Vice President Johnson, Mr Speaker, Mr Chief Justice, President Eisenhower, Vice President Nixon, President Truman, Reverend Clergy, fellow citizens:

We observe today not a victory of party but a celebration of freedom – symbolizing an end as well as a beginning – signifying renewal as well as change. For I have sworn before you and Almighty God the same solemn oath our forebears prescribed nearly a century and three-quarters ago.

The world is very different now. For man holds in his mortal hands the power to abolish all forms of human poverty and all forms of human life. And yet the same revolutionary beliefs for which our forebears fought are still at issue around the globe – the belief that the rights of man come not from the generosity of the state but from the hand of God.

We dare not forget today that we are the heirs of that first revolution. Let the word go forth from this time and place, to friend and foe alike, that the torch has been passed to a new generation of Americans – born in this century, tempered by war, disciplined by a hard and bitter peace, proud of our ancient heritage – and unwilling to witness or permit the slow undoing of those human rights to which this nation has always been committed, and to which we are committed today at home and around the world.

Let every nation know, whether it wishes us well or ill, that we shall pay any price, bear any burden, meet any hardship, support any friend, oppose any foe to assure the survival and the success of liberty.

This much we pledge – and more.

To those old allies whose cultural and spiritual origins we share, we pledge the loyalty of faithful friends. United, there is little we cannot do in a host of new cooperative ventures. Divided, there is little we can do – for we dare not meet a powerful challenge at odds and split asunder.

To those new states whom we welcome to the ranks of the free, we pledge our word that one form of colonial control shall not have passed away merely to be replaced by a far more iron tyranny. We shall not always expect to find them supporting our view. But we shall always hope to find them strongly supporting their own freedom – and to remember that, in the past, those who foolishly sought power by riding the back of the tiger ended up inside.

To those peoples in the huts and villages of half the globe struggling to break the bonds of mass misery, we pledge our best efforts to help them help themselves, for whatever period is required – not because the Communists may be doing it, not because we seek their votes, but because it is right. If a free society cannot help the many who are poor, it cannot save the few who are rich.

To our sister republics south of our border, we offer a special pledge – to convert our good words into good deeds – in a new alliance for progress – to assist free men and free governments in casting off the chains of poverty. But this peaceful revolution of hope cannot become the prey of hostile powers. Let all our neighbours know that we shall join with them to oppose aggression or subversion anywhere in the Americas. And let every other power know that this hemisphere intends to remain the master of its own house.

To that world assembly of sovereign states, the United Nations, our last best hope in an age where the instruments of war have far outpaced the instruments of peace, we renew our pledge of support – to prevent it from becoming merely a forum for invective – to strengthen its shield of the new and the weak – and to enlarge the area in which its writ may run.

Finally, to those nations who would make themselves our adversary, we offer not a pledge but a request: that both sides begin anew the quest for peace, before the dark powers of destruction unleashed by science engulf all humanity in planned or accidental self-destruction.

We dare not tempt them with weakness. For only when our arms are sufficient beyond doubt can we be certain beyond doubt that they will never be employed.

But neither can two great and powerful groups of nations take comfort from our present course – both sides overburdened by the cost of modern weapons, both rightly alarmed by the steady spread of the deadly atom, yet both racing to alter that uncertain balance of terror that stays the hand of mankind's final war.

So let us begin anew – remembering on both sides that civility is not a sign of weakness, and sincerity is always subject to proof. Let us never negotiate out of fear. But let us never fear to negotiate.

Let both sides explore what problems unite us instead of belabouring those problems which divide us.

Let both sides, for the first time, formulate serious and precise proposals for the inspection and control of arms – and bring the absolute power to destroy other nations under the absolute control of all nations.

Let both sides seek to invoke the wonders of science instead of its terrors. Together let us explore the stars, conquer the deserts, eradicate disease, tap the ocean depths and encourage the arts and commerce.

Let both sides unite to heed in all corners of the earth the command of Isaiah – to "undo the heavy burdens . . . [and] let the oppressed go free."

And if a beachhead of cooperation may push back the jungles of suspicion, let both sides join in creating a new endeavour – not a new balance of power, but a new world of law, where the strong are just and the weak secure and the peace preserved.

All this will not be finished in the first 100 days. Nor will it be finished in the first 1,000 days, nor in the life of this Administration, nor even perhaps in our lifetime on this planet. But let us begin.

In your hands, my fellow citizens, more than mine, will rest the final success or failure of our course. Since this country was founded, each generation of Americans has been summoned to give testimony to its national loyalty. The graves of young Americans who answered the call to service surround the globe.

Now the trumpet summons us again – not as a call to bear arms, though arms we need – not as a call to battle, though embattled we are – but a call to bear the burden of a long twilight struggle year in and year out, "rejoicing in hope, patient in tribulation" – a struggle against the common enemies of man: tyranny, poverty, disease and war itself.

Can we forge against these enemies a grand and global alliance, north and south, east and west, that can assure a more fruitful life for all mankind? Will you join in that historic effort?

In the long history of the world, only a few generations have been granted the role of defending freedom in its hour of maximum danger. I do not shrink from this responsibility – I welcome it. I do not believe that any of us would exchange places with any other people or any other generation. The energy, the faith, the devotion which we bring to this endeavour will light our country and all who serve it – and the glow from that fire can truly light the world.

And so, my fellow Americans: ask not what your country can do for you – ask what you can do for your country.

My fellow citizens of the world: ask not what America will do for you, but what together we can do for the freedom of man.

Finally, whether you are citizens of America or citizens of the world, ask of us here the same high standards of strength and sacrifice which we ask of you. With a good conscience our only sure reward, with history the final judge of our deeds, let us go forth to lead the land we love, asking His blessing and His help, but knowing that here on earth God's work must truly be our own.

NATIONAL ANTHEMS

While there is no international law that requires countries to have anthems, every nation currently in existence has one. An anthem is the musical expression of the country's identity and a means of uniting its people.

The first countries to adopt national anthems were the monarchies of Europe, beginning with Britain in the late eighteenth century. Few of these early national anthems were formally adopted as such, but through custom and practice became the *de facto* (in effect) national songs of their respective countries. The tradition of anthems spread across the globe during the late nineteenth century, largely because the European imperial powers introduced their ways into conquered territories. In the twenty-first century one country did briefly lack a national anthem: this was Afghanistan during the rule of the Taliban, 1999–2002, when music was banned.

The United States of America: "The Star Spangled Banner"

During the war of 1812, poet Francis Scott Key wrote a verse entitled "Defense of Fort McHenry" after being inspired by seeing the American flag flying amidst the battle. Key never meant for it to become a song, but his brother-in-law Judge Joseph H. Nicholson noticed the poem could fit the well-known tune "To Anacraeon in Heaven" by John Stafford Smith. Soon afterwards a Baltimore music store owner printed the lyrics and music under the title "The Star Spangled Banner". So titled the song gained popularity and in 1889 was made the official tune to accompany naval flag raisings. In 1916 it was ordered to be played at military and other occasions and, after a large public relations effort, it was officially adopted by Congress as the first official national anthem of the United States in 1931.

Oh, say can you see by the dawn's early light
What so proudly we hailed at the twilight's last gleaming?
Whose broad stripes and bright stars thru the perilous fight,
O'er the ramparts we watched were so gallantly streaming?
And the rocket's red glare, the bombs bursting in air,
Gave proof thru the night that our flag was still there.
Oh, say does that star-spangled banner yet wave
O'er the land of the free and the home of the brave?

On the shore, dimly seen through the mists of the deep,
Where the foe's haughty host in dread silence reposes,
What is that which the breeze, o'er the towering steep,
As it fitfully blows, half conceals, half discloses?
Now it catches the gleam of the morning's first beam,
In full glory reflected now shines in the stream:
'Tis the star-spangled banner!
Oh long may it wave
O'er the land of the free and the home of the brave.

And where is that band who so vauntingly swore
That the havoc of war and the battle's confusion,
A home and a country should leave us no more!
Their blood has washed out of their foul footsteps' pollution.
No refuge could save the hireling and slave'
From the terror of flight and the gloom of the grave:
And the star-spangled banner in triumph doth wave
O'er the land of the free and the home of the brave.
Oh! thus be it ever, when freemen shall stand
Between their loved home and the war's desolation!

Blest with victory and peace, may the heav'n rescued land
Praise the Power that hath made and preserved us a nation.
Then conquer we must, when our cause it is just,
And this be our motto:

"In God is our trust."
And the star-spangled banner in triumph shall wave
O'er the land of the free and the home of the brave.

Great Britain: "God Save the Queen"

"God Save the Queen" (or "God Save the King", if the monarch is male) was a patriotic song first publicly performed in London in 1745, although versions of words can be dated back to 1545. Authorship of the melody has been claimed by many, including John Bull, Henry Carey, Henry Purcell and Joseph Haydn. "God Save the Queen" has never been officially adopted or declared as the national anthem of the country and its status as such is a matter of tradition. One of the most recognizable tunes in the world, it has been utilized by over a hundred composers in their compositions. "God Save the Queen" also serves as the royal anthem for most Commonwealth countries.

God save our gracious Queen,
Long live our noble Queen,
God save the Queen.
Send her victorious,
Happy and glorious,
Long to reign over us:
God save the Queen.

O Lord our God, arise,
Scatter our enemies,
And make them fall;
Confound their politics,
Frustrate their knavish tricks;
On thee our hopes we fix:
God save us all.

Thy choicest gifts in store
On her be pleased to pour,
Long may she reign.
May she defend our laws,
And ever give us cause
To sing with heart and voice,
God save the Queen.

Not in this land alone,
But be God's mercies known,
From shore to shore!
Lord make the nations see,
That men should brothers be,
And form one family,
The wide world over.

From every latent foe,
From the assassins blow,
God save the Queen!
O'er her thine arm extend,
For Britain's sake defend,
Our mother, prince, and friend,
God save the Queen!

New Zealand: "God Defend New Zealand" & "God Save the Queen"

Along with Denmark, New Zealand is the only country in the world to have two national anthems of equal standing: "God Defend New Zealand" and "God Save The Queen" (see National Anthem: Great Britain). "God Defend New Zealand" was written by Irish-born New Zealand citizen Thomas Bracken in 1870, and the music composed by John Joseph Woods for a newspaper contest in 1876. It was adopted as New Zealand's national song in 1940 (New Zealand's centennial year), although "God Save the Queen" remained the sole national anthem. A petition in 1976 prompted the government to seek royal assent to make "God Defend New Zealand" as a national anthem on equal status with "God Save the Queen" and this was granted. In the New Zealand version of "God Save the Queen" the militaristic third verse is replaced with a "Commonwealth verse". "God Defend New Zealand" is the more commonly used of the two anthems.

ENGLISH LYRICS
God of Nations at Thy feet,
In the bonds of love we meet,
Hear our voices, we entreat,
God defend our free land.

Guard Pacific's triple star
From the shafts of strife and war,
Make her praises heard afar,
God defend New Zealand.

Men of every creed and race,
Gather here before Thy face,
Asking Thee to bless this place,
God defend our free land.
From dissension, envy, hate,
And corruption guard our State,
Make our country good and great,
God defend New Zealand.

Peace, not war, shall be our boast,
But, should foes assail our coast,
Make us then a mighty host,
God defend our free land.
Lord of battles in Thy might,
Put our enemies to flight,
Let our cause be just and right,
God defend New Zealand.

Let our love for Thee increase,
May Thy blessings never cease,
Give us plenty, give us peace,
God defend our free land.
From dishonour and from shame,
Guard our country's spotless name,
Crown her with immortal fame,
God defend New Zealand.

May our mountains ever be
Freedom's ramparts on the sea,
Make us faithful unto Thee,
God defend our free land.
Guide her in the nations' van,
Preaching love and truth to man,
Working out Thy glorious plan,
God defend New Zealand.

MAORI LYRICS

E Ihowä Atua,
O ngä iwi mätou rä
Äta whakarongona;
Me aroha noa
Kia hua ko te pai;
Kia tau tö atawhai;
Manaakitia mai
Aotearoa

Öna mano tängata
Kiri whero, kiri mä,
Iwi Mäori Päkehä,
Repeke katoa,
Nei ka tono ko ngä hë
Mäu e whakaahu kë,
Kia ora märire
Aotearoa

Töna mana kia tü!
Töna kaha kia ü;
Töna rongo hei pakü
Ki te ao katoa
Aua rawa ngä whawhai
Ngä tutü a tata mai;
Kia tupu nui ai
Aotearoa

Waiho tona takiwä
Ko te ao märama;
Kia whiti töna rä
Taiäwhio noa.
Ko te hae me te ngangau
Meinga kia kore kau;
Waiho i te rongo mau
Aotearoa

Töna pai me toitü
Tika rawa, ponu pü;
Töna noho, tana tü;

Iwi nö Ihowä.
Kaua möna whakamä;
Kia hau te ingoa;
Kia tü hei tauira;
Aotearoa

Australia: "Advance Australia Fair"

The official anthem of Australia since 1984 (before then it was "God Save the Queen") is "Advance Australia Fair". With lyrics and music both written by Peter Dodds McCormick, "Advance Australia Fair" topped both a 1974 national opinion poll and a 1977 plebiscite seeking an official national song.

Australians all let us rejoice,
For we are young and free;
We've golden soil and wealth for toil,
Our home is girt by sea;
Our land abounds in Nature's gifts
Of beauty rich and rare;
In history's page, let every stage
Advance Australia fair!
In joyful strains then let us sing,
"Advance Australia fair!"

Beneath our radiant southern Cross,
We'll toil with hearts and hands;
To make this Commonwealth of ours
Renowned of all the lands;
For those who've come across the seas
We've boundless plains to share;
With courage let us all combine
To advance Australia fair.
In joyful strains then let us sing
"Advance Australia fair!"

Canada: "O Canada"

Until 1980 the national anthem of Canada, a Commonwealth country, was "God Save the Queen"; in that year a new anthem, "O Canada", was adopted. "O Canada" was not a new tune and had been in circulation for a century. Composed by Calixa Lavallee in 1880, the French words (by Adolphe-Basile Routhier) to "O Canada" have remained constant but the English lyrics have undergone frequent rewrites; in its current usage the English lyrics of "O Canada" are substantially the work of Montreal lawyer Robert Stanley Weir.

ENGLISH LYRICS

O Canada! Our home and native land!
True patriot love in all thy sons command.
With glowing hearts we see thee rise,
The True North strong and free!
From far and wide,
O Canada, we stand on guard for thee.
God keep our land glorious and free!
O Canada, we stand on guard for thee.
O Canada, we stand on guard for thee.

O Canada! where pines and maples grow.
Great prairies spread and lordly rivers flow.
How dear to us thy broad domain,
From East to Western Sea,
Thou land of hope for all who toil!
Thou True North, strong and free!
God keep our land glorious and free!
O Canada, we stand on guard for thee.
O Canada, we stand on guard for thee.

O Canada! Beneath thy shining skies
May stalwart sons and gentle maidens rise,
To keep thee steadfast through the years
From East to Western Sea,
Our own beloved native land!
Our True North, strong and free!
God keep our land glorious and free!
O Canada, we stand on guard for thee.
O Canada, we stand on guard for thee.

Ruler supreme, who hearest humble prayer,
Hold our dominion within thy loving care;
Help us to find, O God, in thee
A lasting, rich reward,
As waiting for the Better Day,
We ever stand on guard.
God keep our land glorious and free!
O Canada, we stand on guard for thee.
O Canada, we stand on guard for thee.

FRENCH LYRICS

O Canada! Terre de nos aïeux,
Ton front est ceint de fleurons glorieux!
Car ton bras sait porter l'épée,
Il sait porter la croix!
Ton histoire est une épopée
Des plus brillants exploits.
Et ta valeur, de foi trempée,
Protégera nos foyers et nos droits.
Protégera nos foyers et nos droits.

Sous l'oeil de Dieu, près du fleuve géant,
Le Canadien grandit en espérant,
Il est né d'une race fière,
Béni fut son berceau;
Le ciel a marqué sa carrière
Dans ce monde nouveau.
Toujours guidé par Sa lumière,
Il gardera l'honneur de son drapeau,
Il gardera l'honneur de son drapeau.

De son patron, précurseur du vrai Dieu,
Il porte au front l'auréole de feu;
Ennemi de la tyrannie,
Mais plein de loyauté,
Il veut garder dans l'harmonie
Sa fière liberté.
Et par l'effort de son génie,
Sur notre Sol asseoir la vérité,
Sur notre Sol asseoir la vérité!

Amour sacré du trône et de l'autel
Remplis nos coeurs de ton souffle immortel.
Parmi les races étrangères
Notre guide est la foi;
Sachons être un peuple de frères,
Sous le joug de la loi;
Et répétons comme nos pères
Le cri vainqueur: "Pour le christ et le Roi"
Le cri vainqueur: "Pour le christ et le Roi".

AUTHORS: A CARD GAME

Players

This is a card game for 3–7 players up to the age of 14.

Dealing

A full pack of 52 cards is used. Starting with the player on his left, the dealer deals all the cards out. Unless there are four players, some will have received more cards than others. It doesn't matter.

The Game

The player on the dealer's left names another player in the game. The choice is entirely free. He then asks that player for a specific card. The card must be of a rank that he already holds. So for instance, if player one, James, says "Celia, give me the four of diamonds" he must have a four of some suit in his hand already. Players cannot ask for cards they hold themselves.

If the player of whom a card is requested has the card he/she must give it up. So if Celia has the four of diamonds she must pass it to James. If a player is successful in requesting a card he has another turn. He can ask the same player for another card or a new player for a card. A player can keep on asking for cards until he is unsuccessful. When he fails to successfully request a card, play passes to the player on his left.

When a player obtains all four cards in a rank he must show them and then lay them down on the table in front of him. A collection of four cards of the same rank is called a "book".

If a player runs out of cards he sits in until the end of the game. The winner is the player with the most "books".

STORY: "IN THE ABYSS" BY H.G. WELLS

The lieutenant stood in front of the steel sphere and gnawed a piece of pine splinter. "What do you think of it, Steevens?" he asked.

"It's an idea," said Steevens, in the tone of one who keeps an open mind.

"I believe it will smash – flat," said the lieutenant.

"He seems to have calculated it all out pretty well," said Steevens, still impartial.

"But think of the pressure," said the lieutenant. "At the surface of the water it's fourteen pounds to the inch, thirty feet down it's double that; sixty, treble; ninety, four times; nine hundred, forty times; five thousand, three hundred – that's a mile – it's two hundred and forty times fourteen pounds; that's – let's see – thirty hundredweight – a ton and a half, Steevens; *a ton and a half* to the square inch. And the ocean where he's going is five miles deep. That's seven and a half –"

"Sounds a lot," said Steevens, "but it's jolly thick steel."

The lieutenant made no answer, but resumed his pine splinter. The object of their conversation was a huge ball of steel, having an exterior diameter of perhaps nine feet. It looked like the shot for some Titanic piece of artillery. It was elaborately nested in a monstrous scaffolding built into the framework of the vessel, and the gigantic spars that were presently to sling it overboard gave the stern of the ship an appearance that had raised the curiosity of every decent sailor who had sighted it, from the Pool of London to the Tropic of Capricorn. In two places, one above the other, the steel gave place to a couple of circular windows of enormously thick glass, and one of these, set in a steel frame of great solidity, was now partially unscrewed. Both the men had seen the interior of this globe for the first time that morning. It was elaborately padded with air cushions, with little studs sunk between bulging pillows to work the simple mechanism of the affair. Everything was elaborately padded, even the Myers apparatus which was to absorb carbonic acid and replace the oxygen inspired by its tenant, when he had crept in by the glass manhole, and had been screwed in. It was so elaborately padded that a man might have been fired from a gun in it with perfect safety. And it had need to be, for presently a man was to crawl in through that glass manhole, to be screwed up tightly, and to be flung overboard, and to sink down – down – down, for five miles, even as the lieutenant said. It had taken the strongest hold of his imagination; it made him a bore at mess; and he found Steevens, the new arrival aboard, a godsend to talk to about it, over and over again.

"It's my opinion," said the lieutenant, "that that glass will simply bend in and bulge and smash, under a pressure of that sort. Daubree has made rocks run like water under big pressures – and, you mark my words –"

"If the glass did break in," said Steevens, "what then?"

"The water would shoot in like a jet of iron. Have you ever felt a straight jet of high pressure water? It would hit as hard as a bullet. It would simply smash him and flatten him. It would tear down his throat, and into his lungs; it would blow in his eyes –"

"What a detailed imagination you have!" protested Steevens, who saw things vividly.

"It's a simple statement of the inevitable," said the lieutenant.

"And the globe?"

"Would just give out a few little bubbles, and it would settle down comfortably against the day of judgment, among the oozes and the bottom clay – with poor Elstead apread over his own smashed cushions like butter over bread."

He repeated this sentence as though he liked it very much. "Like butter over bread," he said.

"Having a look at the jigger?" said a voice, and Elstead stood behind them, spick and span in white, with a cigarette between his teeth, and his eyes smiling out of the shadow of his ample hat-brim. "What's that about bread and butter, Weybridge? Grumbling as usual about the insufficient pay of naval officers? It won't be more than a day now before I start. We are to get the slings ready today. This clean sky and gentle swell is just the kind of thing for swinging off a dozen tons of lead and iron, isn't it?"

"It won't affect you much," said Weybridge.

"No. Seventy or eighty feet down, and I shall be there in a dozen seconds, there's not a particle moving, though the wind shriek itself hoarse up above, and the water lifts halfway to the clouds. No. Down there –" He moved to the side of the ship and the other two followed him. All three leant forward on their elbows and stared down into the yellow-green water.

"*Peace*," said Elstead, finishing his thought aloud.

"Are you dead certain that clockwork will act?" asked Weybridge presently.

"It has worked thirty-five times," said Elstead. "It's bound to work."

"But if it doesn't."

"Why shouldn't it?"

"I wouldn't go down in that confounding thing," said Weybridge, "for twenty thousand pounds."

"Cheerful chap you are," said Elstead, and spat sociably at a bubble below.

"I don't understand yet how you mean to work the thing," said Steevens.

"In the first place, I'm screwed into the sphere," said Elstead, "and when I've turned the electric light off and on three times to show I'm cheerful, I'm swung out over the stern by that crane, with all those big lead sinkers slung below me. The top lead weight has a roller carrying a hundred fathoms of strong cord rolled up, and that's all that joins the sinkers to the sphere, except the slings that will be cut when the affair is dropped. We use cord rather than wire rope because it's easier to cut and more buoyant – necessary points, as you will see.

"Through each of these lead weights you notice there is a hole, and an iron rod will be run through that and will project six feet on the lower side. If that rod is rammed up from below, it knocks up a lever and sets the clockwork in motion at the side of the cylinder on which the cord winds.

"Very well. The whole affair is lowered gently into the water, and the slings are cut. The sphere floats – with the air in it, it's lighter than water – but the lead weights go down straight and the cord runs out. When the cord is all paid out, the sphere will go down too, pulled down by the cord."

"But why the cord?" asked Steevens. "Why not fasten the weights directly to the sphere?"

"Because of the smash down below. The whole affair will go rushing down, mile after mile, at a headlong pace at last. It would be knocked to pieces on the bottom if it wasn't for that cord. But the weights will hit the bottom, and directly they do, the buoyancy of the sphere will come into play. It will go on sinking slower and slower; come to a stop at last, and then begin to float upward again.

"That's where the clockwork comes in. Directly the weights smash against the sea bottom, the rod will be knocked through and will kick up the clockwork, and the cord will be rewound on the reel. I shall be lugged down to the sea bottom. There I shall stay for half an hour, with the electric light on, looking about me. Then the clockwork will release a spring knife, the cord will be cut, and up I shall rush again, like a soda-water bubble. The cord itself will help the flotation."

"And if you should chance to hit a ship?" said Weybridge.

"I should come up at such a pace, I should go clean through it," said Elstead, "like a cannon ball. You needn't worry about that."

"And suppose some nimble crustacean should wriggle into your clockwork –"

"It would be a pressing sort of invitation for me to stop," said Elstead, turning his back on the water and staring at the sphere.

They had swung Elstead overboard by eleven o'clock. The day was serenely bright and calm, with the horizon lost in haze. The electric glare in the little upper compartment beamed cheerfully three times. Then they let him down slowly to the surface of the water, and a sailor in the stern chains hung ready to cut the tackle that held the lead weights and the sphere together. The globe, which had looked so large in deck, looked the smallest thing conceivable under the stern of the ship. It rolled a little, and its two dark windows, which floated upper-most, seemed like eyes turned up in round wonderment at the people who crowded the rail. A voice wondered how Elstead liked the rolling. "Are you ready?" sang out the commander. "Ay, ay, sir!" "Then let her go!"

The rope of the tackle tightened against the blade and was cut, and an eddy rolled over the globe in a grotesquely helpless fashion. Someone waved a handkerchief, someone else tried an ineffectual cheer, a middy was counting slowly, "Eight, nine, ten!" Another roll, then with a jerk and a splash the thing righted itself.

It seemed to be stationary for a moment, to grow rapidly smaller, and then the water closed over it, and it became visible, enlarged by refraction and dimmer, below the surface. Before one could count three it had disappeared. There was a flicker of white light far down in the water, that diminished to a speck and vanished. Then there was nothing but a depth of water going down into blackness, through which a shark was swimming.

Then suddenly the screw of the cruiser began to rotate, the water was crickled, the shark disappeared in a wrinkled confusion, and a torrent of foam rushed across the crystalline clearness that had swallowed up Elstead. "What's the idea?" said one A.B. to another.

"We're going to lay off about a couple of miles, 'fear he should hit us when he comes up," said his mate.

The ship steamed slowly to her new position. Aboard her almost everyone who was unoccupied remained watching the breathing swell into which the sphere had sunk. For the next half-hour it is doubtful if a word was spoken that did not bear directly or indirectly on Elstead. The December sun was now high in the sky, and the heat very considerable.

"He'll be cold enough down there," said Weybridge. "They say that below a certain depth sea-water's always just about freezing."

"Where'll he come up?" asked Steevens. "I've lost my bearings."

"That's the spot," said the commander, who prided himself on his omniscience. He extended a precise finger southeastward. "And this, I reckon, is pretty nearly the moment," he said. "He's been thirty-five minutes."

"How long does it take to reach the bottom of the ocean?" asked Steevens.

"For a depth of five miles, and reckoning – as we did – an acceleration of two feet per second, both ways, is just about three-quarters of a minute."

"Then he's overdue," said Weybridge.

"Pretty nearly," said the commander. "I suppose it takes a few minutes for that cord of his to wind in."

"I forgot that," said Weybridge, evidently relieved.

And then began the suspense. A minute slowly dragged itself out, and no sphere shot out of the water. Another followed, and nothing broke the low oily swell. The sailors explained to one another that little point about the winding-in of the cord. The rigging was dotted with expectant faces. "Come up, Elstead!" called one hairy-chested salt impatiently, and the others caught it up, and shouted as though they were waiting for the curtain of a theatre to rise.

The commander glanced irritably at them.

"Of course, if the acceleration is less than two," he said, "he'll be all the longer. We aren't absolutely certain that was the proper figure. I'm no slavish believer in calculations."

Steevens agreed concisely. No one on the quarterdeck spoke for a couple of minutes. Then Steevens' watchcase clicked.

When, twenty-one minutes after, the sun reached the zenith, they were still waiting for the globe to reappear, and not a man aboard had dared to whisper that hope was dead. It was Weybridge who first gave expression to that realisation. He spoke while the sound of eight bells still hung in the air. "I always distrusted that window," he said quite suddenly to Steevens.

"Good God!" said Steevens; "you don't think –?"

"Well!" said Weybridge, and left the rest to his imagination.

"I'm no great believer in calculations myself," said the commander dubiously, "so that I'm not altogether hopeless yet." And at midnight the gunboat was steaming slowly in a spiral round the spot where the globe had sunk, and the white beam of the electric light fled and halted and swept discontentedly onward again over the waste of phosphorescent waters under the little stars.

"If his window hasn't burst and smashed him," said Weybridge, "then it's a cursed sight worse, for his clockwork has gone wrong, and he's alive now, five miles under our feet, down there in the cold and dark, anchored in that little bubble of his, where never a ray of light has shone or a human being lived, since the waters were gathered together. He's there without food, feeling hungry and thirsty and scared, wondering whether he'll starve or stifle. Which will it be? The Myers apparatus is running out, I suppose. How long do they last?"

"Good heavens!" he exclaimed; "what little things we are! What daring little devils! Down there, miles and miles of water – all water, and all this empty water about us and this sky. Gulfs!" He threw his hands out, and as he did so, a little white streak swept noiselessly up the sky, travelled more slowly, stopped, became a motionless dot, as though a new star had fallen up into the sky. Then it went sliding back again and lost itself amidst the reflections of the stars and the white haze of the sea's phosphorescence.

At the sight he stopped, arm extended and mouth open. He shut his mouth, opened it again, and waved his arms with an impatient gesture. Then he turned, shouted "El-stead ahoy!" to the first watch, and went at a run to Lindley and the searchlight. "I saw him," he said. "Starboard there! His light's on, and he's just shot out of the water. Bring the light round. We ought to see him drifting, when he lifts on the swell."

But they never picked up the explorer until dawn. Then they almost ran him down. The crane was swung out and a boat's crew hooked the chain to the sphere. When they had shipped the sphere, they unscrewed the manhole and peered into the darkness of the interior (for the electric light chamber was intended to illuminate the water about the sphere, and was shut off entirely from its general cavity).

The air was very hot within the cavity, and the india-rubber at the lip of the manhole was soft. There was no answer to their eager questions and no sound of movement within. Elstead seemed to be lying motionless, crumpled up in the bottom of the globe. The ship's doctor crawled in and lifted him out to the men outside. For a moment or so they did not know whether Elstead was alive or dead. His face, in the yellow light of the ship's lamps, glistened with perspiration. They carried him down to his own cabin.

He was not dead, they found, but in a state of absolute nervous collapse, and besides cruelly bruised. For some days he had to lie perfectly still. It was a week before he could tell his experiences.

Almost his first words were that he was going down again. The sphere would have to be altered, he said, in order to allow him to throw off the cord if need be, and that was all. He had had the most marvellous experience. "You thought I should find nothing but ooze," he said. "You laughed at my explorations, and I've discovered a new world!" He told his story in disconnected fragments, and chiefly from the wrong end, so that it is impossible to re-tell it in his words. But what follows is the narrative of his experience.

It began atrociously, he said. Before the cord ran out the thing kept rolling over. He felt like a frog in a football. He could see nothing but the crane and the sky overhead, with an occasional glimpse of the people on the ship's rail. He couldn't tell a bit which way the thing would roll next. Suddenly he would find his feet going up, and try to step, and over he went rolling, head over heels, and just anyhow, on the padding. Any other shape would have been more comfortable, but no other shape was to be relied upon under the huge pressure of the nethermost abyss.

Suddenly the swaying ceased; the globe righted, and when he had picked himself up, he saw the water all about him greeny-blue, with an attenuated light filtering down from above, and a shoal of little floating things went rushing up past him, as it seemed to him, towards the light. And even as he looked, it grew darker and darker, until the water above was as dark as the midnight sky, albeit of a greener shade, and the water below black. And little transparent things in the water developed a faint tint of luminosity, and shot past him in faint greenish streaks.

And the feeling of falling! It was just like the start of a lift, he said, only it kept on. One has to imagine what that means, that keeping on. It was then of all times that Elstead repented his adventure. He saw the chances against him in an altogether new light. He thought of the big cuttle-fish people knew to exist in the middle waters, the kind of things they find half digested in whales at times, or floating dead and rotten and half eaten by fish. Suppose one caught hold and wouldn't let go. And had the clockwork really been sufficiently tested? But whether he wanted to go on or to go back mattered not the slightest now.

In fifty seconds everything was as black as night outside, except where the beam from his light struck through the waters, and picked out every now and then some fish or scrap of sinking matter. They flashed by too fast for him to see what they were. Once he thinks he passed a shark. And then the sphere began to get hot by friction against the water. They had under-estimated this, it seems.

The first thing he noticed was that he was perspiring, and then he heard a hissing growing louder under his feet, and saw a lot of little bubbles – very little bubbles they were – rushing upward like a fan through the water outside. Steam! He felt the window and it was hot. He turned on the minute glow-lamp that lit his own cavity, looked at the padded watch by the studs, and saw he had been travelling now for two minutes. It came into his head that the window would crack through the conflict of temperatures, for he knew the bottom water is very near freezing.

Then suddenly the floor of the sphere seemed to press against his feet, the rush of bubbles outside grew slower and slower, and the hissing diminished. The sphere rolled a little. The window had not cracked, nothing had given, and he knew that the dangers of sinking, at any rate, were over.

In another minute or so he would be on the floor of the abyss. He thought, he said, of Steevens and Weybridge and the rest of them five miles overhead, higher to him than the very highest clouds that ever floated over land are to us, steaming slowly and staring down and wondering what had happened to him.

He peered out of the window. There were no more bubbles now, and the hissing had stopped. Outside there was a heavy blackness – as black as black velvet – except where the electric light pierced the empty water and showed the colour of it – a yellow-green. Then three things like shapes of fire swam into sight, following each other through the water. Whether they were little and near or big and far off he could not tell.

Each was outlined in a bluish light almost as bright as the lights of a fishing smack, a light which seemed to be smoking greatly, and all along the sides of them were specks of this, like the lighter portholes of a ship. Their phosphorescence seemed to go out as they came within the radiance of his lamp, and he saw then that they were little fish of some strange sort, with huge heads, vast eyes, and dwindling bodies and tails. Their eyes were turned towards him, and he judged they were following him down. He supposed they were attracted by his glare.

Presently others of the same sort joined them. As he went on down, he noticed that the water became of a pallid colour, and that little specks twinkled in his ray like motes in a sunbeam. This was probably due to the clouds of ooze and mud that the impact of his leaden sinkers had disturbed.

By the time he was drawn down to the lead weights he was in a dense fog of white that his electric light failed altogether to pierce for more than a few yards, and many minutes elapsed before the hanging sheets of sediment subsided to any extent. Then, lit by his light and by the transient phosphorescence of a distant shoal of fishes, he was able to see under the huge blackness of the superincumbent water an undulating expanse of greyish-white ooze, broken here and there by tangled thickets of a growth of sea lilies, waving hungry tentacles in the air.

Farther away were the graceful, translucent outlines of a group of gigantic sponges. About this floor there were scattered a number of bristling flattish tufts of rich purple and black, which he decided must be some sort of sea-urchin, and small, large-eyed or blind things having a curious resemblance, some to wood-lice, and others to lobsters, crawled sluggishly across the track of the light and vanished into the obscurity again, leaving furrowed trails behind them.

Then suddenly the hovering swarm of little fishes veered about and came towards him as a flight of starlings might do. They passed over him like a phosphorescent snow, and then he saw behind them some larger creature advancing towards the sphere.

At first he could see it only dimly, a faintly moving figure remotely suggestive of a walking man, and then it came into the spray of light that the lamp shot out. As the glare struck it, it shut its eyes, dazzled. He stared in rigid astonishment.

It was a strange vertebrated animal. Its dark purple head was dimly suggestive of a chameleon, but it had such a high forehead and such a braincase as no reptile ever displayed before; the vertical pitch of its face gave it a most extraordinary resemblance to a human being.

Two large and protruding eyes projected from sockets in chameleon fashion, and it had a broad reptilian mouth with horny lips beneath its little nostrils. In the position of the ears were two huge gill-covers, and out of these floated a branching tree of coralline filaments, almost like the tree-like gills that very young rays and sharks possess.

But the humanity of the face was not the most extraordinary thing about the creature. It was a biped; its almost globular body was poised on a tripod of two frog-like legs and a long thick tail, and its fore limbs, which grotesquely caricatured the human hand, much as a frog's do, carried a long shaft of bone, tipped with copper. The colour of the creature was variegated; its head, hands, and legs were purple; but its skin, which hung loosely upon it, even as clothes might do, was a phosphorescent grey. And it stood there blinded by the light.

At last this unknown creature of the abyss blinked its eyes open, and, shading them with its disengaged hand, opened its mouth and gave vent to a shouting noise, articulate almost as speech might be, that penetrated even the steel case and padded jacket of the sphere. How a shouting may be accomplished without lungs Elstead does not profess to explain. It then moved sideways out of the glare into the mystery of shadow that bordered it on either side, and Elstead felt rather than saw it was coming towards him. Fancying the light had attracted it, he turned the switch that cut off the current. In another moment something soft dabbed upon the steel, and the globe swayed.

Then the shouting was repeated, and it seemed to him that a distant echo answered it. The dabbing recurred, and the globe swayed and ground against the spindle over which the wire was rolled. He stood in the blackness and peered out into the everlasting night of the abyss. And presently he saw, very faint and remote, other phosphorescent quasi-human forms hurrying towards him.

Hardly knowing what he did, he felt about in his swaying prison for the stud of the exterior electric light, and came by accident against his own small glow-lamp in its padded recess. The sphere twisted, and then threw him down; he heard shouts like shouts of surprise, and when he rose to his feet, he saw two pairs of stalked eyes peering into the lower window and reflecting his light.

In another moment hands were dabbing vigorously at his steel casing, and there was a sound, horrible enough in his position, of the metal protection of the clockwork being vigorously hammered. That, indeed, sent his heart into his mouth, for if these strange creatures succeeded in stopping that, his release would never occur. Scarcely had he thought as much when he felt the sphere sway violently, and the floor of it press had against his feet. He turned off the small glow-lamp that lit the interior, and sent the ray of the large light in the separate compartment out into the water. The sea-floor and the man-like creatures had disappeared, and a couple of fish chasing each other dropped suddenly by the window.

He thought at once that these strange denizens of the deep sea had broken the rope, and that he had escaped. He drove up faster and faster, and then stopped with a jerk that sent him flying against the padded roof of his prison. For half a minute, perhaps he was too astonished to think.

Then he felt that the sphere was spinning slowly, and rocking, and it seemed to him that it was also being drawn through the water. By crouching close to the window, he managed to make his weight effective and roll that part of the sphere downward, but he could see nothing save the pale ray of his light striking down ineffectively into the darkness. It occurred to him that he would see more if he turned the lamp off, and allowed his eyes to grow accustomed to the profound obscurity.

In this he was wise. After some minutes the velvety blackness became a translucent blackness, and then, far away, and as faint as the zodiacal light of an English summer evening, he saw shapes moving below. He judged these creatures had detached his cable, and were towing him along the sea bottom.

And then he saw something faint and remote across the undulations of the submarine plain, a broad horizon of pale luminosity that extended this way and that way as far as the range of his little window permitted him to see. To this he was being towed, as a balloon might be towed by men out of the open country into a town. He approached it very slowly, and very slowly the dim irradiation was gathered together into more definite shapes.

It was nearly five o'clock before he came over this luminous area, and by that time he could make out an arrangement suggestive of streets and houses grouped about a vast roofless erection that was grotesquely suggestive of a ruined abbey. It was spread out like a map below him. The houses were all roofless enclosures of walls, and their substance being, as he afterwards saw, of phosphorescent bones, gave the place an appearance as if it were built of drowned moonshine.

Among the inner caves of the place waving trees of crinoid stretched their tentacles, and tall, slender, glassy sponges shot like shining minarets and lilies of filmy light out of the general glow of the city. In the open spaces of the place he could see a stirring movement as of crowds of people, but he was too many fathoms above them to distinguish the individuals in those crowds.

Then slowly they pulled him down, and as they did so, the details of the place crept slowly upon his apprehension. He saw that the courses of the cloudy buildings were marked out with beaded lines of round objects, and then he perceived that at several points below him, in broad open spaces, were forms like the encrusted shapes of ships.

Slowly and surely he was drawn down, and the forms below him became brighter, clearer, more distinct. He was being pulled down, he perceived, towards the large building in the centre of the town, and he could catch a glimpse ever and again of the multitudinous forms that were lugging at his cord. He was astonished to see that the rigging of one of the ships, which formed such a prominent feature of the place, was crowded with a host of gesticulating figures regarding him, and then the walls of the great building rose about him silently, and hid the city from his eyes.

And such walls they were, of water-logged wood, and twisted wire-rope, and iron spars, and copper, and the bones and skulls of dead men. The skulls ran in zigzag lines and spirals and fantastic curves over the building; and in and out of their eye-sockets, and over the whole surface of the place, lurked and played a multitude of silvery little fishes.

Suddenly his ears were filled with a low shouting and a noise like the violent blowing of horns, and this gave place to a fantastic chant. Down the sphere sank, past the huge pointed windows, through which he saw vaguely a great number of these strange, ghostlike people regarding him, and at last he came to rest, as it seemed, on a kind of altar that stood in the centre of the place.

And now he was at such a level that he could see these strange people of the abyss plainly once more. To his astonishment, he perceived that they were prostrating themselves before him, all save one, dressed as it seemed in a robe of placoid scales, and crowned with a luminous diadem, who stood with his reptilian mouth opening and shutting, as though he led the chanting of the worshippers.

A curious impulse made Elstead turn on his small globe-lamp again, so that he became visible to these creatures of the abyss, albeit the glare made them disappear forthwith into night. At this sudden sight of him, the chanting gave place to a tumult of exultant shouts; and Elstead, being anxious to watch them, turned his light off again, and vanished from before their eyes. But for a time he was too blind to make out what they were doing, and when at last he could distinguish them, they were kneeling again. And thus they continued worshipping him, without rest or intermission, for a space of three hours.

Most circumstantial was Elstead's account of this astounding city and its people, these people of perpetual night, who have never seen sun or moon or stars, green vegetation, nor any living, air-breathing creatures who know nothing of fire, nor any light but the phosphorescent light of living things.

Startling as is his story, it is yet more startling to find that scientific men, of such eminence as Adams and Jenkins, find nothing incredible in it. They tell me they see no reason why intelligent, water-breathing, vertebrated creatures, inured to a low temperature and enormous pressure, and of such a heavy structure, that neither alive nor dead would they float, might not live upon the bottom of the deep sea, and quite unsuspected by us, descendants like ourselves of the great Theriomorpha of the New Red Sandstone age.

We should be known to them, however, as strange meteoric creatures, wont to fall catastrophically dead out of the mysterious blackness of their watery sky. And not only we ourselves, but our ships, our metals, our appliances, would come raining down out of the night. Sometimes sinking things would smite down and crush them, as if it were the judgment of some unseen power above, and sometimes would come things of the utmost rarity or utility, or shapes of inspiring suggestion. One can understand, perhaps, something of their behaviour at the descent of a living man, if one thinks what a barbaric people might do, to whom an enhaloed, shining creature came suddenly out of the sky.

At one time or another Elstead probably told the officers of the *Ptarmigan* every detail of his strange twelve hours in the abyss. That he also intended to write them down is certain, but he never did, and so we have to piece together the discrepant fragments of his story from the reminiscences of Commander Simmons, Weybridge, Steevens, Lindley and the others.

We see the thing darkly in fragmentary glimpses – the huge ghostly building, the bowing, chanting people, with their dark chameleon-like heads and faintly luminous clothing, and Elstead, with his light turned on again, vainly trying to convey to their minds that the cord by which the sphere was held was to be severed. Minute after minute slipped away, and Elstead looking at his watch, was horrified to find that he had oxygen only for four hours more. But the chant in his honour kept on as remorselessly as if it was the marching song of his approaching death.

The manner of his release he does not understand, but to judge by the end of cord that hung from the sphere, it had been cut through by rubbing against the edge of the altar. Abruptly the sphere rolled over, and he swept up, out of their world, as an ethereal creature clothed in a vacuum would sweep through our own atmosphere back to its native ether again. He must have torn out of their sight as a hydrogen bubble hastens upward from our air. A strange ascension it must have seemed to them.

The sphere rushed up with even greater velocity than, when weighted with the lead sinkers, it had rushed down. It became exceedingly hot. It drove up with the windows uppermost, and he remembers the torrent of bubbles frothing against the glass. Every moment he expected this to fly. Then suddenly something like a huge wheel seemed to be released in his head, the padded compartment began spinning about him, and he fainted. His next recollection was of his cabin, and of the doctor's voice.

But that is the substance of the extraordinary story that Elstead related in fragments to the officers of the *Ptarmigan*. He promised to write it all down at a later date. His mind was chiefly occupied with the improvement of his apparatus, which was effected at Rio.

It remains only to tell that on February 2, 1896, he made his second descent into the ocean abyss, with the improvements his first experience suggested. What happened we shall probably never know. He never returned. The *Ptarmigan* beat about over the point of his submersion, seeking him in vain for thirteen days. Then she returned to Rio, and the news was telegraphed to his friends. So the matter remains for the present. But it is hardly probable that no further attempt will be made to verify his strange story of these hitherto unsuspected cities of the deep sea.

GROW A GARDEN IN A BOTTLE
BY A.A. REEVE

If you were to plant a flower, a miniature tree or shrub in a bottle and seal it up, how long do you think it would be before the plant died?

Two days? A week perhaps? No, it would live, and thrive, for anything up to *four years*, using the same air and water over and over again! Not only that but it would look better than the usual house plant. Its colours would be brighter and it would be a stronger and sturdier plant.

This is because plants breath through their leaves and there is always *some* dust in a house, floating in the air, which clogs the pores and dulls the colours. Then, if gas is used for cooking or heating, this will poison the plants. Finally there is the biggest danger of all to house plants – draughts. All these things are eliminated if the plant is safe in a bottle.

These bottle gardens make wonderful ornaments and just need care in the preparation to last a very long time with practically no attention.

They are very useful as Christmas and birthday presents.

The first thing to find is a suitable bottle and the most obvious thing about this is that it must be a clear glass, preferably without any names or trade marks embossed on it. Then the neck of the bottle is important; the length as well as the diameter. If the neck is very long the tools will only be able to work in the *centre* of the bottle. A wide, short neck is best.

Types of bottle which are suitable are Chianti bottles (Chianti is an Italian wine), which can often be bought from a wine merchant (these have a rounded base and need some support. They can be hung on a wall when planted and look very well), or, perhaps best of all, a cider flagon. These are well-shaped bottles holding about 6 pints of farmhouse cider; they have a neat little glass handle on the side, which is very useful.

Look around at your next neighbourhood Jumble Sale. You will often find quite curious jars and bottles which people have given. I have even seen a goldfish bowl with a butter dish lid used as a garden. Empty aquariums with a glass sheet over the top make excellent containers. And then there are the giant carboys, standing about 2 feet high, in which complete gardens can be planted.

The next important thing is the tools because ordinary implements are no use for this kind of gardening. Fortunately all the tools can be made quite quickly and cheaply, mainly from oddments round the house. The most important of these is the all-purpose tool shown in the diagram.

For this you need a piece of bamboo, or even a stick, about ½ inch in diameter and 18 inches long. Bamboo is best because it splits easily. First cut a piece off the thicker end about ½ inch long and save this piece because you will need it later. Then split the cane carefully down the centre. Sandpaper the inside and edges of these pieces really hard because a bamboo splinter can be very nasty.

Now take the ½-inch piece and split that down the centre also. Glue the flat inside of one small piece to the inside of one of the longer pieces, exactly in the centre. Now you need two small pads to be glued to the inner sides of the long pieces, at the thin ends. Foam plastic is the best to use, two pieces about ½-inch

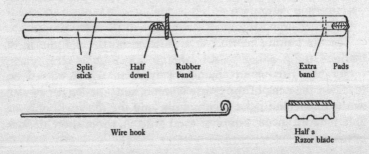

Split stick   Half dowel   Rubber band   Extra band   Pads

Wire hook   Half a Razor blade

square are just right. You can sometimes find this in the tops of pill boxes. Some draught excluders are foam plastic and two pieces off the end of this is just right. Small pieces of sponge or even lint from the First Aid box will also do.

Now place the two padded ends of the tool together, so that the small piece of bamboo acts as a rocker, and slip a small rubber band over the two sticks. Move it up until it is just in front of the rocker. There you have a pair of over-sized tweezers which can handle delicate plants or other tools. And the other tools you will need are a plastic spoon and half a razor blade. Just grip them between the pads, but first add two or three more rubber bands near the pads.

Two more simple and useful tools are a funnel and a wire hook. The funnel is made by cutting a liquid detergent plastic bottle in half and pulling out the plastic plug from the neck. This is useful for pouring the soil into the bottle. The wire hook is made from a piece of stiff wire about 18 inches long. Bend the last ½ inch up like a shepherd's crook and then bend the whole hook up sideways.

The soil is next and this must be prepared carefully. Although just plain earth from the garden *can* be used the plants will never really thrive. The soil needs to be sterilized so that no weeds can take advantage of the excellent growing conditions in the bottle. Sterilization is not difficult. All you need is an old saucepan or other container which can be used to boil up a mixture of earth and water. (Make sure it *is* an old pot or your mother won't be very pleased.)

Get a few cupsful of earth from your garden, the best you can find; leaf mould if possible. Sieve it if you can; if not go through it with your fingers and take out any stones, pieces of wood and other rubbish and break up any lumps. Have about an inch of water in your saucepan and get it boiling then pour in the earth and keep it simmering for 15 minutes. Turn it out onto a plate or piece of board or even paper. When dry mix in a cupful of sand.

Now you need some charcoal, small pieces, just enough to cover the bottom of the bottle, and some small pebbles. Mix the two together and pour them gently into the bottle. The final thing you will need is some peat. A big bag, enough for about a dozen small bottle gardens, can be bought from any garden centre. Pour a layer of this about an inch thick over the pebbles and then add some sterilized soil and you are all ready to plant.

Now, what to plant? Well, the first thing to remember is that you cannot have anything that will grow too large. Secondly, anything that flowers or sheds its leaves in winter will need special attention during that time. When flowers die off the bottle is opened, the half razor blade is held in the tweezers and the dead blooms sawn off gently. Then the tweezers are used to pick the blooms out of the bottle. Deal with dead leaves in the same way.

From florists and garden centres you can buy miniature roses which grow to only about six inches high and have perfect little blooms only $\frac{1}{4}$-inch across. From the same store you can get miniature cypress trees about the same height. These trees may tend to grow taller after a couple of years and can then be planted elsewhere.

Ferns are particularly good to grow in a bottle and these can be collected on Pack nature rambles. Dig them up, don't pull them, and choose small, sturdy specimens. Mosses, too, can be collected and these make a good carpet over the bottom of the garden. As for the rest of the plants to use, the answer is to experiment. If you can make two or three bottle gardens and keep one just for experimenting it can be really interesting.

Before planting be sure that the plant itself is as clean as you can get it; rinse it in warm water to be sure. Now slip the plastic spoon into the tweezers and add two or three rubber bands round the jaws. Insert the tool into the bottle and carefully dig out a hollow for the plant. When the hole is large enough, take out the tool, remove the spoon and also the extra bands. Now pick up the first plant very gently in the tweezers and put it into the hole you have dug.

Slip the wire hook in and support the stem of the plant with the hook, releasing the plant from the tweezers. Cover in the roots of the plant very gently. You may need to use the spoon again if the plant is large. When the roots are well covered tamp the soil down with the tip of the tweezers. Add any more plants in the same way but do not overcrowd the bottle.

When planting is complete the soil must be moistened. The best way is to *spray* water into the bottle but if this is not possible just add water slowly. Do not saturate the soil. Trial and error is about the only way to find out how much water is needed. Close the top of the bottle and if after a few hours a film of moisture appears on the glass, open up the top for about half an hour.

Don't let your bottle garden stand in direct sunlight for long; it gets very warm inside. As long as you have chosen good plants and the soil is clean and moist your bottle garden should last a long time as an attractive ornament and an interesting hobby.

Adapted from *The Wolf Cub Jubilee Book*, 1965. Copyright © 1965 Arthur Pearson Ltd.

FIFTEEN BOOKS TO READ BEFORE FIFTEEN

Douglas Adams, *The Hitchhiker's Guide to the Galaxy*, 1979
Arthur Dent and Ford Prefect on nonsensical journey into space; they know the answer (42) but what *is* the question which reveals the truth about life and everything?

Raymond Chandler, *The Big Sleep*, 1939
The first case for Philip Marlowe, the definitive hardboiled, wise-cracking private detective. For 14+.

Erskine Childers, *The Riddle of the Sands*, 1903
Spy and sailing adventure set off the coast of Germany.

Ian Fleming, *Casino Royale*, 1953
007's first and most violent outing, complete with the best of all Bond girls (Vesper Lynd) and a worthy villainous enemy in gambler Le Chiffre. For 14+.

C.S. Forester, *Mr Midshipman Hornblower*, 1950
Atmospheric and accurate novel of the boy Hornblower's introduction to life in the navy of Nelson.

Anne Frank, *The Diary of Anne Frank*, 1947
Records two years in the life of Frank, a Jewish girl in hiding in the Netherlands during the Nazi occupation.

Geoffrey Household, *Rogue Male*, 1939
Thriller in which a hunter who has his sights on a European dictator becomes the hunted.

Harper Lee, *To Kill a Mockingbird*, 1960
Prize-winning story of Atticus Finch's noble struggle against racism in a small town in US South. Cited in America as the most influential book on morality excepting only the Bible.

George Orwell, *Animal Farm*, 1945
At one level a simple tale of farmyard animals, at another a deep satirical insight into the failure of left-wing political ideals, namely the 1917 Russian Revolution.

Terry Pratchett, *Moving Pictures*, 2002
Cut Me Own Throat Dibber seeks to become a film mogul. In other words, Discworld goes to Holy Wood.

F. Scott Fitzgerald, *The Great Gatsby*, 1925
Slim, near perfect story of the mysterious Gatsby, pursuer of the American Dream during the Jazz Age.

William Shakespeare, *Macbeth*, circa 1606
The most accessible of Shakespeare's plays, the dark story of a man led astray by his ambition. Evil dissected.

John Steinbeck, *The Grapes of Wrath*, 1939
The "Okie" Joad family migrate to California in search of a better life during the Great Depression. Helped Steinbeck win the Nobel Prize for Literature.

J.R.R. Tolkien, *Lord of the Rings*, 1954–5
The three volume epic story of Frodo and "The One Ring".

H.G. Wells, *The Invisible Man*, 1897
Sci-fi classic about a scientist who renders himself invisible – and almost mad.

"EVEREST WITHOUT OXYGEN"
BY PETER HABELER

Peter Habeler, together with his climbing partner Reinhold Messner, was the first mountaineer to summit Everest without using bottled oxygen to overcome the "thin air" of the higher reaches. Habeler and Messner's summit push came on 28 May 1978.

I sat in front of the small tent which was half covered by snow, while inside Reinhold tried desperately to get a cooker going to brew up tea. I snuggled up to the side of the tent in order to rest in the lee side, and stared out into the fog. Occasionally the wall of fog would lift for a moment, and I could see deep below me the Valley of Silence. I could see Lhotse, and again and again I looked up to the South Summit where an enormous trail of snow signified that up there a far more violent storm was raging than down here in Camp V. The weather would undoubtedly worsen. The fine weather period was over.

Perhaps our attempt on the summit was finally over too, our Everest expedition wrecked once and for all. Of one thing I was convinced: I would never come up here a second time. Already the desire to turn back was almost overpowering. To bivouac here in Camp V, and perhaps to wait for the weather to improve, was also completely out of the question. We would probably never have got out of the tent at all again, and in no event would we have had the physical or mental strength to climb any further. Our energy would have lasted at the most for the descent and no more. Yet climbing on was, under these circumstances, also a "way of no return".

In 1956, two Japanese had mastered the route from the South Col to the summit in one go. This had taken them a whole day, and having therefore reached the main summit late in the afternoon, they were forced to bivouac on the way back. Consequently, in spite of carrying oxygen, they had suffered terrible injuries through frost-bite. But neither Reinhold nor I had time to think of these dangers. The will to push on blotted out everything else, even the wish to turn back or at least to sleep. We wanted in any case to go on up, even if we could only reach the South Summit which is 8,760 metres high. After all, to conquer even the South Summit without oxygen would have been a tremendous success. It would have proved that one day it would be possible to reach the main summit by human strength alone.

It took exactly half an hour for Reinhold to prepare the tea. My deliberations were also shared by him; we exchanged them wordlessly. We were completely united in our determination to continue the assault on the summit.

Once again we set off. The tracks of our predecessors, which could still be seen in the snow, served as an excellent orientation guide. The clouds were moving over from the south-west, from the bad weather corner of the Himalayas. We had to push ourselves even more because that promised bad news. We found ourselves in the lower area of the jet stream, those raging winds of speeds up to 200 kilometres per hour, upon which the enormous passenger planes are carried from continent to continent. We had traversed the troposphere and were approaching the frontier of the stratosphere. Here cosmic radiation was already noticeable and the intensity of the ultra-violet radiation had multiplied. Only a few minutes without our snow-goggles sufficed, even in the fog, to diminish our powers of vision. In a very short space of time direct insolation would lead to snow-blindness and painful conjunctivitis.

Reinhold and I photographed and filmed as often as we had the opportunity. To do this, we had to take off our snow-goggles and we also had to remove our overgloves.

Each time it became more difficult for us to put the gloves back on again. But losing them would have led to the very rapid paralysis and frost-bite of our hands.

Since it was no longer possible to go on in this deep snow, we had made a detour towards the South-East Ridge. Here the wall dropped 2,000 metres down to the south-west. One false step and we would have plunged down into the Valley of Silence. The exposed and airy climb on brittle rock without any rope demanded extreme concentration. Reinhold was right behind me. I took the lead to the South Summit. Completely without warning, we suddenly found we had passed through the clouds and now stood on the last stage before our goal.

At this point the storm attacked us with all its might. However, in spite of the storm and the fatigue, my fear of the mountain had dissipated with the clouds. I was quite sure of myself. Over there lay the main summit, almost near enough to touch, and at this precise moment I was sure we were going to do it. Reinhold, too, told me later: "This was the moment in which I was convinced of the success of our adventure."

A sort of joyful intoxication overcame the two of us. We looked at each other – and shrank back. From Reinhold's appearance I could only conclude that my own was very similar. His face was contorted in a grimace, his mouth wide open while he gasped panting for air. Icicles hung in his beard. His face was almost without human traits. Our physical reserves were exhausted. We were so utterly spent that we scarcely had the strength to go ten paces in one go. Again and again we had to stop, but nothing in the world could have held us back now.

We had roped ourselves together because the Summit Ridge, as Hillary has already described it, was densely covered in cornices. It is true, however, that in an emergency a rope would not have helped us.

We crawled forwards at a snail's pace, trusting to instinct alone. The sun glistened on the snow, and the sky above the summit was of such an intense blue that it seemed almost black. We were very close to the sky, and it was with our own strength alone that we had arrived up here at the seat of the gods. Reinhold signified to me with a movement of his hand that he wanted to go on ahead. He wanted to film me climbing up over the ridge, with the bubbling sea of clouds below.

To do this he had to take off his snow-goggles in order to focus the camera better. It occurred to me that his eyes looked inflamed, but I thought nothing more of it, no more than he did. Our altitude was now 8,700 metres, and we had obviously reached a point in which normal brain functions had broken down, or at least were severely limited. Our attentiveness and concentration declined; our instinct no longer reacted as reliably as before; the capacity for clear logical thinking had also apparently been lost. I only thought in sensations and loose associations, and slowly I was overcome by the feeling that this threatening fearful mountain could be a friend.

Today I am certain that it is in these positive and friendly sensations that the real danger on Everest lies. When one approaches the summit, one no longer perceives the hostile, the absolutely deadly atmosphere. I have probably never been so close to death as I was during that last hour before reaching the summit. The urgent compulsion to descend again, to give in to fatigue, which had overcome me already in Camp V, had disappeared. I was now feeling the complete opposite. I had been seized by a sense of euphoria. I felt somehow light and relaxed, and believed that nothing could happen to me. At this altitude the boundaries between life and death are fluid. I wandered along this narrow ridge and perhaps for a few seconds I had gone beyond the frontier which divides life from death. By a piece of good fortune I was allowed to return. I would not risk it a second time, my reason forbids me to gamble with my life in such a way again.

In spite of all my euphoria, I was physically completely finished. I was no longer walking of my own free will, but mechanically, like an automaton. I seemed to step outside myself, and had the illusion that another person was walking in my place. This other person arrived at the Hillary Step, that perilous 25-metre-high ridge gradient, and then climbed and pulled himself up in the footsteps of his predecessors. He had one foot in Tibet and the other in Nepal. On the left side there was a 2,000 metre descent to Nepal; on the right the wall dropped 4,000 metres down towards China. We were alone, this other person and myself. Although he was connected to me by the short piece of rope, Reinhold no longer existed.

This feeling of being outside myself was interrupted for only a few moments. Cramp in my right hand bent my fingers together, and tore me violently back to reality. I was attacked by a suffocating fear of death. "Now I've had it." This thought went through my head, "Now the lack of oxygen is beginning its deadly work." I massaged my right forearm and bent my fingers back, and then the cramp eased.

From then on I prayed, "Lord God, let me go up right to the top. Give me the power to remain alive, don't let me die up here." I crawled on my elbows and knees and prayed more fervently than I have ever done in my life before. It was like a dialogue with a higher being. Again I saw myself crawling up, below me, beside me, higher and higher. I was being pushed up to the heights, and then suddenly I was up again on my own two feet: I was standing on the summit. It was 1.15 on the afternoon of 8 May 1978.

And then suddenly Reinhold was with me too, still carrying his camera and the three-legged Chinese surveying instrument. We had arrived. We embraced each other. We sobbed and stammered and could not keep calm. The tears poured from under my goggles into my beard, frozen on my cheeks. We embraced each other again and again. We pressed each other close. We stepped back at arm's length and again fell round each other's necks, laughing and crying at the same time. We were redeemed and liberated, freed at last from the inhuman compulsion to climb on.

After the crying and the sense of redemption, came the emptiness and sadness, the disappointment. Something had been taken from me; something that had been very important to me. Something which had suffused my whole being had evaporated, and I now felt exhausted and hollow. There was no feeling of triumph or victory. I saw the surrounding summits, Lhotse, Cho Oyu. The view towards

Tibet was obscured by clouds. I knew that I was standing now on the highest point in the whole world. But, somehow, it was all a matter of indifference to me. I just wanted to get home now, back to that world from which I had come, and as fast as possible.

Habeler made the descent to the South Col in a record one hour.

Reprinted from *Impossible Victory* by Peter Habeler, 1979. Copyright © 1979 Peter Habeler.

CLIMBING EVEREST:
FACTS AND STATISTICS

The First Ascent:
29 May 1953, by Sir Edmund Hillary, NZ, and Tenzing Norgay, Nepal, via South Col.

The First Ascent Without Oxygen:
8 May 1978, Reinhold Messner, Italy, and Peter Habeler, Austria, via South-East Ridge.

The First Solo Ascent:
29 August 1980, Reinhold Messner, Italy, via North Col.

The First Ascent by a Woman:
16 May 1975, Junko Tabei, Japan, via South Col.

The First Winter Ascent:
17 February 1980, Leszek Cichy and Krzysztof Wielickï, Poland, via South Col.

The First Ascent of the North Ridge:
25 May 1960, Wang Fu-zhou and Chu Yin-hua, China.

The First Ascent of the West Ridge:
22 May 1963, Willi Unsoeld and Tom Hornbein, USA.

The First Ascent of the South-West Face:
24 September 1975, Dougal Haston and Doug Scott, UK.

The First Ascent of the East Face:
8 September 1983, Lou Reichardt, Carlos Buhler and Kim Momb, USA.

The Fastest Ascent:
24 May 1996, Hans Kammerlander, Italy, 16 hours and 45 mins from base camp via North Col.

The Oldest Summiteer:
25 May 2001, Sherman Bull May, USA, aged 64 years.

The Youngest Summiteer:
22 May 2001, Temba Tsheri, Nepal, aged 15 years.

Most Ascents:
24 May 2000, Apa (Sherpa), Nepal, summited for the eleventh time.

Fastest Descent:
26 September 1988, Jean-Marc Boivin, France, in 11 minutes, paragliding.

First Person to climb all four sides of Everest:
28 May 1999, Kusang Dorje (Sherpa), India.

Deaths on Everest:
186 (to 2004)

The most dangerous area on the mountain is the Khumbu Ice Fall with 19 deaths. The worst year for fatalities was 1996, with 15 deaths. More than 4 per cent of summiteers have died during the descent.

THE ORIGIN OF THE NAMES
OF THE MONTHS

January From Janus, a Roman god.

February From Februs, a Roman god.

March From Mars, the Roman god of war.

April From the Latin *Aprilis*.

May From Maia, a Roman goddess.

June From Juno, the Roman mother of the gods.

July Named for Julius Caesar.

August Named for Augustus Caesar, the first Roman emperor.

September From the Latin for "seven", it being the seventh month in the Roman calendar.

October From the Latin for "eight", it being the eighth month in the Roman calendar.

November From the Latin for nine, it being the ninth month in the Roman calendar.

December From the Latin for ten, it being the tenth month in the Roman calendar.

THE DESPERATE BOY'S GUIDE TO PUNCTUATION

Punctuation matters. It's an essential way of helping people understand the sense of what you write. Here's a famous example, taken from the title of a guide to punctuation [*Eats, Shoots and Leaves* by Lynne Truss], on the difference punctuation makes:

> Eats shoots and leaves.
> Eats, shoots and leaves.

The first sentence means that someone consumes plant shoots and plant leaves. The second means that someone eats a meal, shoots (with a gun) and then departs. Punctuation is an enormous subject, but following a few basic rules will take you far.

Stops

There are three main ways to mark where a sentence ends.
a) A full stop (.). The most used method.
b) An exclamation mark (!). This is for use when you really want to draw attention to something, as though you were speaking in a loud voice. Get it!
c) A question mark (?), used when a sentence asks a question. Do you understand?

The Comma

Trickier, but essentially a comma (,) is used to make a pause in your sentence, to mentally (and even physically) draw breath. Or the comma is used to break up items in a list. First we did stops, then commas, next it's the semi-colon.

The Semi-Colon

Again used to make a break in a sentence, but not where you want something quite as definite as a full stop or something as brief as a comma. It's important that the two halves of the sentence broken by the semi-colon (;) are also joined in meaning – that the second half is connected with the sense of the first half.

Here's an example: *His golf lesson was cancelled this morning; the course was covered in snow.*

Colon

The colon (:) is the break used before a list. Or before a quotation. Here are two examples:

Ceasar said: "Friends, Romans, countrymen . . ."
The rider checked her equipment: saddle, bridle, stirrups, boots and hat.

The Apostrophe

The apostrophe (') is the one that people get wrong most. Even government departments are not immune to its misuse. But basically the apostrophe does just two things:

a) It shows possession: Freda's pony, Dad's watch, Mum's car, Tristram's kayak. That is to say, the apostrophe shows that Freda owns the pony, Dad owns the watch and so on.

b) The apostrophe can only show where letters are missing in a word because its has been shortened to make it easier to say or write. For example: It's (it is), don't, and can't (cannot). As the last example shows the apostrophe can mark the absence of more than one letter.

The big mistake people make with the apostrophe is to put it in plurals. For instance a local taxi sign says "Taxi's". This actually means that the taxi owns something. What the local council meant was "Taxis" (i.e. a lot of them, find them here.) If you want to sell your surplus DVDs at a rummage sale, they are DVDs not DVD's.

Quotation Marks and Inverted Commas

These are the same thing and can be used like (' ') or (" "). Inverted commas are used to mark out the actual words said by somebody. Their speech, in other words.

I was writing this book, when my son came in and said, "Can you come and play rugby?"

It matters not a jot whether you use single (') or double (") quotation marks, except in the case where someone speaking quotes someone else. A quotation inside a quotation. You'll understand what I mean from this example:

Jasper came home from school and said, "Miss Smitt, the English teacher, likes this line from Shakespeare best of all: 'To be, or not to be' ".

The inner quote is marked out by the single quotation marks.

Brackets

Brackets () are another way of marking things off in a sentence, but this time in a quiet way. You want to give the information, but almost as an aside.

Private Johnny Clarkson was standing inside the trench (which was now filled with mud), holding his gun at the ready, awaiting the order to go over the top towards the German lines.

The main sentence is about Clarkson waiting to attack the Germans. The state of his trench is secondary, but adds something to the picture made with words.

You can use a dash (–) to much the same effect as brackets. The above sentence would work in the same way if you put dashes instead of the brackets.

Hyphen

The hyphen (-) is used to pull two words together. Double-barrelled surnames are one example: *Mr Hetherington-Smythe of Yale was most exceeding angry*.

Hyphens can be very important, since they are used to bring together two things which, if separate, would have a very different meaning.

A *Nazi-hunter* is someone who pursues Nazis in order to bring them to justice.

A *Nazi hunter* is a Nazi who hunts duck (or whatever).

BUILD YOUR OWN STOMP ROCKET

This is about as much fun as you'll ever get from a pop/soda bottle. First you get to drink the contents, then you get to launch your very own rocket into the stratosphere.

If you are in brain mode the rocket also happens to perfectly illustrate Newton's Law of Gravity, aerodynamics and the effects of air resistance.

You need:
A 2-litre/4-pint soda/pop bottle
1 metre/yard of clear, bendy, vinyl tubing (or any equivalent plastic or rubber tubing, such as garden hose) with 12 mm/½ in diameter and 15 mm/⅝ in outer diameter
60 cm/23 in of PVC pipe with half-inch diameter
30 cm/11 in of PVC pipe or any tube with half-inch diameter
Duct tape
Clear sticky tape
Sheets of A4 paper
Some sheets of thick card
Scissors
A pencil
Ruler

The operation comes in two parts: building the launcher; building the rockets.

The Launcher

Step 1: Remove cap from pop bottle, empty contents into something useful. Like your stomach.

Step 2: Insert about an inch of the flexible tubing into the bottle opening and fix in place with duct tape. Make sure that the connection is air tight.

Step 3: Using duct tape fix the 60 cm/23 in length of PVC to the other end of the flexible tubing. Again make sure that the connection is airtight. You should now have something which looks like Figure 1.

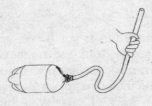

Figure 1

The Rocket

Step 1: Take the 30 cm/11 in length of PVC pipe (or similar) and roll a sheet of A4 paper around it into a hollow tube shape. It is important that the paper tube is not too tightly wound around the tube; it should be able to slide up and down it easily. Tape the paper tube so it remains rolled up. Slide the paper tube off the PVC pipe.

Step 2: Cut the top of the paper tube into an arrow shape and, using the sticky tape, seal the point so that it is airtight. This is the cone of the rocket.

Step 3: Time to make the rocket fins. Cut three triangular fins from the card. The fins have to be the same size and shape, but otherwise they can be pretty much any design you choose. Experiment for the best effect. Tape the fins to the sides of the rocket

Blast Off!

To launch the rocket, slide the open end over the PVC pipe and hold the pipe up (but not towards your face!) Then stomp on the pop bottle . . . and watch the rocket go.